THE HOUSE OF WAR

OSPREY
PUBLISHING

DEDICATION

This book is dedicated to my tutor, mentor and friend, Maurice Keen.

SIMON MAYALL

THE HOUSE OF WAR

THE STRUGGLE BETWEEN CHRISTENDOM AND THE CALIPHATE

OSPREY PUBLISHING
Bloomsbury Publishing Plc
Kemp House, Chawley Park, Cumnor Hill, Oxford OX2 9PH, UK
29 Earlsfort Terrace, Dublin 2, Ireland
1385 Broadway, 5th Floor, New York, NY 10018, USA
E-mail: info@ospreypublishing.com
www.ospreypublishing.com

OSPREY is a trademark of Osprey Publishing Ltd

First published in Great Britain in 2024

A catalogue record for this book is available from the British Library.

ISBN: HB 9781472864338; PB 9781472864369; eBook 9781472864352; ePDF 9781472864345;
XML 9781472864314; Audio 9781472864321

24 25 26 27 28   10 9 8 7 6 5 4 3 2 1

Plate section image credits and captions are given in full in the List of Illustrations and Maps (pp. 9–13).
Maps by www.bounford.com
Index by Zoe Ross

Typeset by Deanta Global Publishing Services, Chennai, India
Printed and bound in Great Britain by CPI (Group) UK Ltd, Croydon, CR0 4YY

MIX
Paper | Supporting
responsible forestry
FSC® C171272

Contents

Author's Note and Acknowledgements

From an early age, I loved stories and storytelling. This enthusiasm soon translated into a love of history, that study of past events, particularly as they relate to human affairs. In this embrace of storytelling and history I was wholeheartedly encouraged by my parents, and then by a succession of exceptional history teachers and historians.

From St George's College, I owe a debt to Fr Peter Murtough, Dudley Woodget and Fr Walter Munton, while at Balliol College I was spoilt by being tutored by Maurice Keen, Colin Lucas and Christopher Hill, while also being able to listen to lectures by Hugh Trevor Roper and AJP Taylor. This good fortune continued in my early days at Sandhurst, and during my many years in the British Army. The British military put a high premium upon the study of military history, and in its capacity to offer instruction, inspiration and warning. As such, battles and campaigns, from across the ages, are examined for relevance, and for the eternal verities of conflict, while the record and conduct of leaders are studied for important lessons in the exercise of command. In such studies many of us were privileged to have read, listened to, or conversed with the likes of John Keegan, David Chandler, Gary Sheffield, Richard Holmes, Max Hastings, James Holland, Anthony Beevor, Andrew Roberts and many others. In addition, those successful senior officers with whom I worked closely in my career were also invariably keen students of military history, and always generous with their guidance in recommending additional writers and further areas of useful and absorbing study.

These distinguished historians, teachers and mentors all believed in the importance of readable, accessible, objective, evidence-based, narrative history, which would inspire or educate, and which never neglected the human stories that lay at the centre of great events. Many others, like Steven Runciman, Roger Crowley and Barnaby Rogerson, whose books I have used as reference works for *The House of War*, are listed in the bibliography of this book.

In recent times, a thematic approach to the study of history has often replaced the more traditional chronological approach. In doing so, I believe it has undermined confidence in the knowledge and understanding of the sequence of significant events, and of how great actions, and the characters at the heart of them, relate to each other. Therefore, the writings of our many distinguished historians serve a hugely important public service in bringing good historical storytelling to a wide audience. In doing so, they give people the confidence to challenge some of the ahistorical, politicized and highly selective narratives that are in circulation, which ignore context, and which apply totally inappropriate modern sensitivities to historical events, and to the motivations and perceptions of historical characters and classes. I hope that *The House of War*, in relating the story of several of the most epic and consequential military encounters in history, is also true to the context of the times in which they were fought.

As with my last book, *Soldier in the Sand*, I found that the only way to concentrate on writing was to take myself away from the distractions of my own 'home base'. I am therefore grateful to Dominic and Louise, David and Sarah, Rupert and Pammy, and Sarah for offering me 'writer's retreats' in their own homes. I would also like to thank those many friends who offered me encouragement and support over the last year, not least my brothers, Mark and Justin, and my darling mother, Alexis Mayall. I am only sorry that my beloved father, Paul Mayall, did not live long enough to see either of my books in print.

Last, and by no means least, I want to thank Osprey for having the confidence to publish *The House of War*, and particularly Marcus Cowper and Gemma Gardner for their editorial guidance and support, and their tactful patience.

List of Illustrations and Maps

Matthew of Clermont, Marshal of the Knights Hospitaller, defending the walls of Acre against the Mamluks in 1291. The fall of Acre to the Mamluk Sultan, al-Ashraf Khalil, led to the final destruction of 200 of crusader presence in Syria and the Holy Land. (Photo by Fine Art Images/Heritage Images/Getty Images)

Assault by the forces of Sultan Mehmet II on the Theodosian Walls of Constantinople in May 1453. The conquest of the city marked the final episode in the fall of the Byzantine Empire. (Ian Dagnall / Alamy Stock Photo)

Hagia Sophia, the Church of Holy Wisdom, was built by Emperor Justinian and completed in 537. The centre of the Christian Orthodox religion for nearly 1,000 years, it was converted into a mosque by Sultan Mehmet II in 1453. Mehmet II added a single minaret after the fall of Constantinople, but the existing minarets were added by the great Ottoman architect Sinan in the 16th century. It was converted into a museum in 1935 by Mustapha Kemal Ataturk, after the abolition of the caliphate in 1924, and became a mosque again in 2020. (tunart/Getty Images)

Sultan Mehmet II enters Constantinople. After the taking of the city, Mehmet took the title *Al-Fatih*, 'The Conqueror'. He moved the Ottoman capital from Edirne to Constantinople, where it remained until 1923. (Photo by Pictures From History/Universal Images Group via Getty Images)

Suleiman the Magnificent, also known as 'the Lawgiver', ruled the Ottoman Empire from 1520 to 1566. He inherited an empire that had doubled in size under his father, Sultan Selim the Grim, and with it the title of Caliph. He fought the Knights of St John in Rhodes and Malta, and took the Ottoman Empire to the gates of Vienna. (Photo by Fine Art Images/Heritage Images/Getty Images)

In 1522, Sultan Suleiman besieged Rhodes in an attempt to stamp out the last crusader presence in the eastern Mediterranean. After a siege that lasted over six months, Suleiman offered the Knights of St John generous surrender terms. (Danvis Collection / Alamy Stock Photo)

The d'Amboise Gate was part of Grand Master d'Aubusson's ambitious plans to strengthen the defences of Rhodes after the failed Ottoman siege of 1480. It formed an integral part of the defence of the city in 1522. Behind the vast double towers can be seen the Grand Master's Palace. (Tuul & Bruno Morandi/Getty Images)

Map of Malta in 1565, showing the fortified peninsulas of Senglea (left) and Birgu (right). Mount Sciberras and the Fort of St Elmo are at the top of the picture. This image also shows Fort St Angelo at the tip of Birgu, and the protective chain and pontoon bridge that joined the peninsulas. (Niday Picture Library / Alamy Stock Photo)

The Ottomans finally overwhelmed the defences at St Elmo on 23 June 1565. Dragut's severing of the fragile logistic link between St Angelo (top right) and St Elmo had eventually doomed the defenders. (The Picture Art Collection / Alamy Stock Photo)

In September 1565, after an heroic defence of three and a half months, the Knights of St John and their Maltese allies were relieved by the Spanish forces of Don García de Toledo, who broke the Ottoman siege of the island. (ARTGEN / Alamy Stock Photo)

Jean Parisot de la Valette was 70 years old when he led the defence of Malta, and his personal example was vital in defeating the Ottoman assault. The new capital city of Malta was named after him, and he is buried in St John's Co-Cathedral. (Sparrow (2019), CC BY-SA 4.0, https://creativecommons.org/licenses/by-sa/4.0/)

Dragut, the great Barbary corsair, was 80 at the time of the siege of Malta. He had been the scourge of the Mediterranean for nearly six decades, and his late arrival, and untimely death, were pivotal in the outcome of the siege. (Photo by Culture Club/Bridgeman via Getty Images)

These views of Lepanto give a useful depiction of the order of battle of the opposing fleets of the Holy League and the Ottomans. However, they cannot capture the sheer violence, bloodshed and chaos of this massive sea battle, which saw perhaps 200 galleys sunk, and 40,000 soldiers, sailors and galley oarsman, freemen and slaves, killed in the space of four hours. (Top: Zoom Historical / Alamy Stock Photo; bottom: brandstaetter images/Getty Images)

For commanders, soldiers, sailors and oarsmen, Lepanto was a visceral, large-scale, close-quarter fight, often, when several galleys were locked together, resembling a land battle fought across a large wooden platform. Many galleys were burnt to the waterline, and little quarter was asked, or given. (Album / Alamy Stock Photo)

The heroes of Lepanto. Don Juan of Austria (left) commanded the fleet of the Holy League at the battle of Lepanto. Among his key subordinate commanders were Marcantonio Colonna (centre),

commanding the naval contingent of the Papal States, and the
irascible Sebastian Veniero (right) commanding the Venetian
forces. (Photo by Fine Art Images/Heritage Images via Getty
Images)

Kara 'Black' Mustapha was an Albanian Christian orphan, adopted by
the great Koprulu family, who rose to be Grand Vizier for Sultan
Mehmet IV. His ambition to take Vienna in 1683 was bold but
realistic; however, his arrogance and complacency cost him the
siege, and this defeat marked the start of the long Ottoman decline
from imperial greatness. (Rijksmuseum, RP-P-1894-A-18289,
http://hdl.handle.net/10934/RM0001.COLLECT.117606)

The Holy Roman Emperor, Leopold I, with the distinctive Habsburg
lower jaw, was a cold, unimaginative, and ungracious figure, but
he did just enough in 1683 to pull together a coalition that would
defeat an Ottoman army on the verge of taking the city of Vienna.
(Niday Picture Library / Alamy Stock Photo)

King John III Sobieski of Poland was originally in the pro-French camp,
but shifted his allegiance to the Habsburgs as the Ottoman threat to
Central Europe became more insistent. A very seasoned warrior, he
made a major contribution to victory at Vienna in 1683. (Photo by
Fine Art Images/Heritage Images/Getty Images)

Duke Charles of Lorraine. A Frenchman who transferred his loyalty to
the Habsburgs, Duke Charles was a much-admired professional
soldier, and a gifted diplomat. His subtle handling of Emperor
Leopold I, and of the other senior commanders of the Christian
coalition force, was key to success at Vienna in 1683. (Photo by
Sepia Times/Universal Images Group via Getty Images)

The battle for the Burg Bastion. During the siege of Vienna almost
all of Kara Mustapha's energies were poured into breaching the
defences of Vienna between the Burg and Löbl bastions. This
picture gives some idea of the intensity of the fighting on the city's
walls. (Photo By DEA PICTURE LIBRARY/De Agostini
via Getty Images)

This scene shows the Ottoman siege of Vienna in 1683 continuing (note
the siege trench network), while the Christian forces of King John
III Sobieski and Duke Charles of Lorraine pour down the slopes of
the Wienerwald to overwhelm Kara Mustapha's hastily positioned
defences. (Photo by Imagno/Getty Images)

When King John and his cavalry, including the famous 'winged hussars', poured onto the battlefield from the Wienerwald, the Ottoman forces on the west flank were overwhelmed and destroyed. (Photo by VCG Wilson/Corbis via Getty Images)

Kaiser Wilhelm II, the aggressive King of Prussia, and Emperor of the new German Empire, sought closer relations with the Ottoman Empire. In 1898, as part of this policy, he visited Jerusalem, where the Jaffa Gate had to be partly demolished to facilitate his entry. (Photo by ullstein bild via Getty Images)

General Edmund Allenby entered Jerusalem on foot on 11 December 1917, in deliberate contrast to the Kaiser's flamboyant entry in 1898. Ottoman defeat in World War I signalled another period of Christian dominance in the Holy Land and Near East that lasted until World War II. (Library of Congress, LC-USZ62-93094)

Sultan Mehmet VI was the last Ottoman sultan. When the new Turkish Republic of Mustapha Kemal Ataturk abolished the sultanate on 1 November 1922, Mehmet was declared *persona non grata* and sought refuge with the British. On 17 November 1922 he was taken by HMS *Malaya* from Constantinople to Malta. He died in 1926. His cousin, Abdul Mecid, had succeeded him as Caliph, but the 1300-year-old caliphate was abolished shortly afterwards, in March 1924. (Everett Collection Historical / Alamy Stock Photo)

MAPS

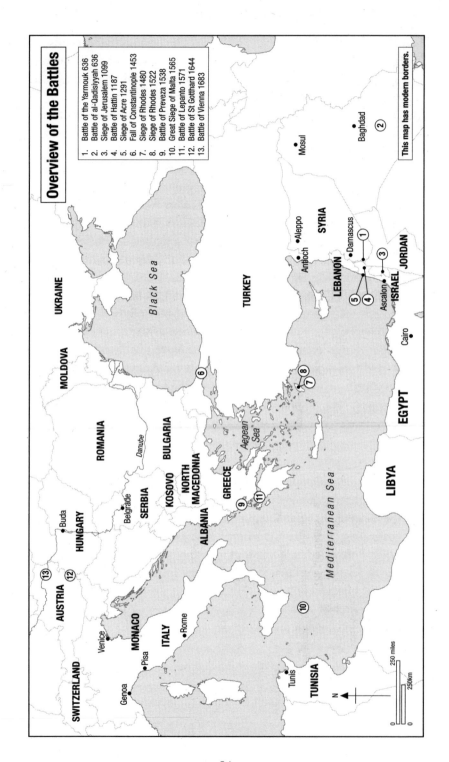

Overview of the Battles

1. Battle of the Yarmouk 636
2. Battle of al-Qadisiyyah 636
3. Siege of Jerusalem 1099
4. Battle of Hattin 1187
5. Siege of Acre 1291
6. Fall of Constantinople 1453
7. Siege of Rhodes 1480
8. Siege of Rhodes 1522
9. Battle of Preveza 1538
10. Great Siege of Malta 1565
11. Battle of Lepanto 1571
12. Battle of St Gotthard 1644
13. Battle of Vienna 1683

This map has modern borders.

14

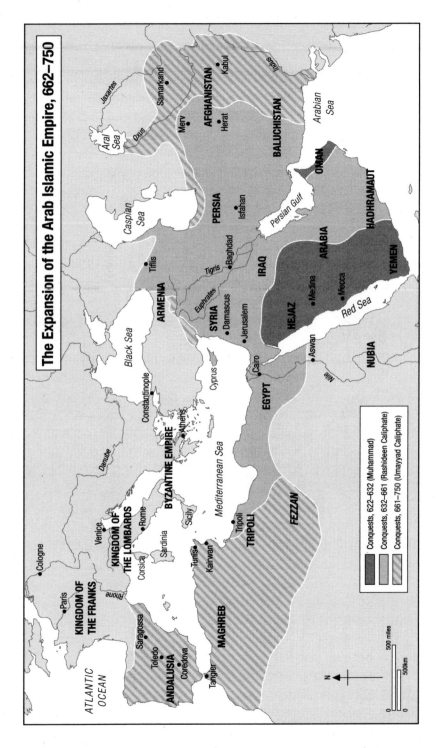

The Expansion of the Arab Islamic Empire, 662–750

Legend:
Conquests, 622–632 (Muhammad)
Conquests, 632–661 (Rashideen Caliphate)
Conquests, 661–750 (Umayyad Caliphate)

Samarkand
AFGHANISTAN
Kabul
Merv
Herat
BALUCHISTAN
Arabian Sea
Javaxtes
Oxus
Aral Sea
OMAN
HADHRAMAUT
PERSIA
Isfahan
Persian Gulf
Caspian Sea
ARABIA
YEMEN
Tiflis
Tigris
Baghdad
IRAQ
Medina
Mecca
Red Sea
ARMENIA
Euphrates
Damascus
SYRIA
Jerusalem
HEJAZ
Black Sea
Cyprus
Aswan
NUBIA
Constantinople
Cairo
EGYPT
Nile
Athens
BYZANTINE EMPIRE
Danube
Mediterranean Sea
Venice
Rome
KINGDOM OF THE LOMBARDS
Sicily
Tripoli
TRIPOLI
FEZZAN
Cologne
Corsica
Sardinia
Tunis
Kairwan
Rhone
Paris
KINGDOM OF THE FRANKS
MAGHREB
Saragossa
Toledo
Cordova
ANDALUSIA
Tangier
ATLANTIC OCEAN

N

500 miles
500km

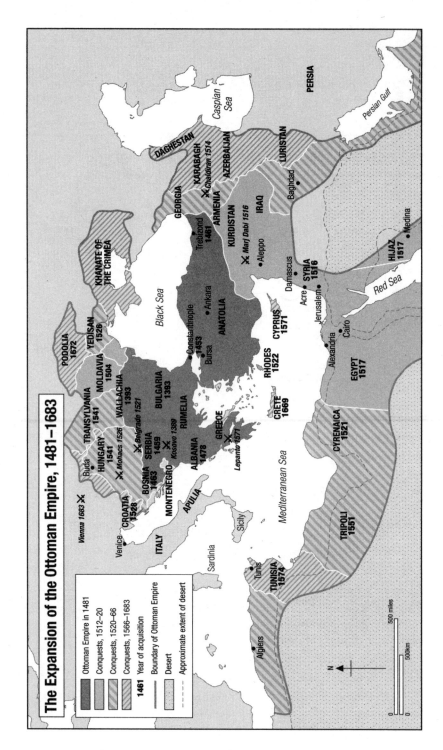

The Expansion of the Ottoman Empire, 1481–1683

Legend:
- Ottoman Empire in 1481
- Conquests, 1512–20
- Conquests, 1520–66
- Conquests, 1566–1683
- 1461 Year of acquisition
- Boundary of Ottoman Empire
- Desert
- Approximate extent of desert

PERSIA

Caspian Sea

Persian Gulf

DAGHESTAN

KARABAGH
✗ Chaldiran 1514

AZERBAIJAN

LURISTAN

GEORGIA

ARMENIA
✗ Trebizond 1461

KURDISTAN

IRAQ
• Baghdad

✗ Marj Dabi 1516
• Aleppo

HIJAZ
1517
• Medina

Red Sea

KHANATE OF
THE CRIMEA

YEDISAN
1526

Black Sea

• Ankara

ANATOLIA

Damascus •
Acre •
Jerusalem •

SYRIA
1516

PODOLIA
1672

MOLDAVIA
1504

Constantinople
1453
• Bursa

CYPRUS
1571

• Cairo

TRANSYLVANIA
1541

WALLACHIA
1393

BULGARIA
1393

RHODES
1522

Alexandria •

EGYPT
1517

HUNGARY
1541
Buda •

✗ Belgrade 1521

RUMELIA

CRETE
1669

CYRENAICA
1521

✗ Mohacs 1526

SERBIA
1459
✗ Kosovo 1389

GREECE

Venice •

BOSNIA
1463

ALBANIA
1478

✗
Lepanto 1571

CROATIA
1528

MONTENEGRO

APULIA

Mediterranean Sea

TRIPOLI
1551

Vienna 1683 ✗

ITALY

Sicily

Sardinia

Tunis •
TUNISIA
1574

Algiers •

N

500 miles

500km

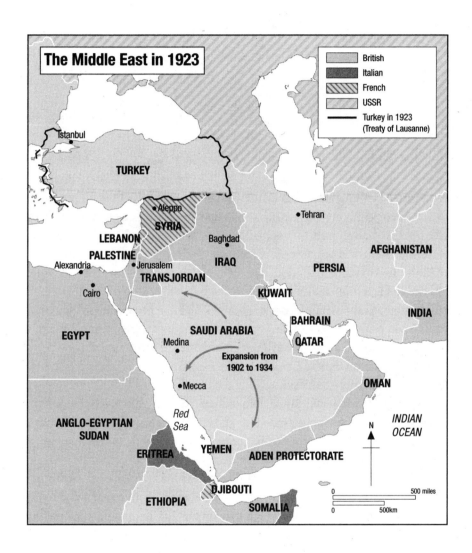

The Middle East in 1923

British
Italian
French
USSR
Turkey in 1923
(Treaty of Lausanne)

Istanbul

TURKEY

Aleppo
SYRIA
LEBANON
PALESTINE
Alexandria
Jerusalem
TRANSJORDAN
Cairo

Baghdad
IRAQ

Tehran

AFGHANISTAN

PERSIA

KUWAIT
BAHRAIN
QATAR

INDIA

EGYPT

SAUDI ARABIA
Medina

Expansion from
1902 to 1934

Mecca

OMAN

ANGLO-EGYPTIAN
SUDAN

Red
Sea

YEMEN

ERITREA

ADEN PROTECTORATE

INDIAN
OCEAN

N

DJIBOUTI

ETHIOPIA

SOMALIA

0   500 miles

0   500km

Introduction

In 1996 and 1998, in the wake of the Gulf War, Osama bin Laden issued two fatwas.[1] One was entitled, 'Declaration of War against the Americans Occupying the Land of the Two Holy Places', and the other, 'World Front for Combat against Jews and Crusaders'. While Osama bin Laden had no authority to issue fatwas, these two lengthy statements carried considerable influence among Muslim listeners and readers. In them, Bin Laden had mined Muslim history and Islamic law in order to launch an attack on what he perceived and claimed to be an unholy alliance between the 'Zionists', 'crusaders' and the House of Saud. Every date, battle, triumph, failure and grievance that would strike a chord with a global Muslim audience was evoked, in support of an agenda that sought a return to the former days of Islamic unity and greatness.

President George W. Bush had added fuel to this narrative when, after 9/11, he unwisely issued a statement using the words, 'This crusade, this war on terrorism is going to take a while. It is time for us to win the war of the 21st century decisively, so that our children and our grandchildren can live peacefully into the 21st century.' Although President Bush was using the word 'crusade' as a synonym for a righteous cause,[2] he did not necessarily mean to imply a religious element to any military action. However, his use of this language threatened to put the campaign against Al-Qaeda into the context of an historical conflict between Christianity and Islam[3] that was assumed to have finished in the early 20th century. In response, Osama bin Laden wrote, 'In a war of civilizations, our goal is for our nation to unite in the face of the Christian Crusade. This is a recurring war. The original crusade brought

Richard the Lionheart from Britain, Louis from France and Barbarossa from Germany. Today the crusading countries rushed as soon as Bush raised the cross. They accepted the rule of the cross.' Bin Laden's appeal to historical entitlement, inspiration and grievance was clear to all who knew the story of the long competition between the followers of Jesus Christ, and those of the Prophet Muhammad.

In 1992, as the communist ideology had crumbled, the Soviet Union had collapsed, and the international world order had been upheld on the battlefields of Iraq and Kuwait, Francis Fukuyama had published his seminal book *The End of History and the Last Man*. In this he contended that history, as a battle of key political, social and economic ideas, was now effectively 'over'. Samuel Huntington, in his own book, *The Clash of Civilizations*, was less sanguine. Defining a civilization as 'the highest cultural grouping and the broadest cultural identity people have, short of that which distinguishes humans from other species', he argued against assuming the west's recent triumphs represented a global acceptance of President George H. W. Bush's 'new world order'. He contended that modern western civilization, with its increasing emphasis on globalism, individualism, secularism and liberalism, and its rejection of history and religion, was becoming a much less cohesive concept than during the long period when Europe and the west was broadly synonymous with Christianity. During this period, which probably lasted nearly a thousand years from Emperor Charlemagne to Emperor Napoleon Bonaparte, there had been a broad construct known as 'Christendom', where Christendom meant, literally, the dominion or sovereignty of the Christian religion. That had now gone and, with it, the cohesion and the confidence to meet the challenges that Huntington still perceived would continue to come from the Orthodox (Russian), Sino (Chinese), and Islamic 'civilizations'.

Huntington believed that the Islamic 'civilization', for better or worse, retained a much greater acknowledgement of, and attachment to, its historical and religious roots and origins. Central to this, certainly to the likes of Osama bin Laden, was the concept of the 'caliphate', which had provided an organizing principle for much of the Islamic world for nearly 1,300 years, until its arbitrary abolition by the new Turkish Republic in 1924. The caliphate had expressed a similar notion to that of 'Christendom', in this case the sovereignty of the Islamic faith. However, it represented a much closer and more formal alignment between the temporal and religious powers, embodied in the person of the Sultan-Caliph, than that between the Christian emperors and kings of Europe, and the Pope. This was because the caliph, from the outset, had been assumed to be the 'righteous successor' to Muhammad, who had been prophet, military leader and civil administrator. As dynastic power in the Islamic Middle East shifted over the centuries from the Arab leadership of the Rashideen, the Umayyad and the Abbasid caliphates, to the caliphate of the Egyptian Mamluks and, finally, to that of the Turkic Ottomans, the spiritual capital of Islam had migrated from Mecca to Damascus, then to Baghdad, to Cairo and, at last, to Constantinople.

However, with the collapse of the Ottoman Empire at the end of World War I, the dissolution of the caliphate, and the dominance of the Christian European powers, increasingly evident since the failure of the Ottomans to take Vienna in 1683, seemed to be confirmed. At a stroke, the organizing principle of the Muslim world vanished, and in its place were a bewildering range of new political entities, with new borders, all forced to conform to the western idea of statehood. For Muslims in their successive empires, there had always been twin loyalties: to the Islamic religion, personified by the Sultan-Caliph, and to their own tribe and family. Where now did the nation-state fit in? Did Muslims identify themselves by religion, ethnicity, nationality or tribe? It was this sense of confusion, lost greatness and humiliation that Osama bin Laden had felt so strongly, and which he was addressing in the fatwas.

———

Because of geography, Christianity and Islam, Christendom and the caliphate, had found themselves in violent confrontation from their first engagements in the early seventh century. This confrontation shaped the modern world, and indeed the clash also shaped the Christian and the Islamic worlds themselves, as these two great religions generated their own divisions – Catholic, Orthodox and Protestant, Sunni and Shia – each battling for power within their own spheres of influence, and competing for the hearts, souls and loyalties of their own followers.

From the taking of Jerusalem in 637 by Caliph Umar, a mere five years after the death of Muhammad, to the collapse of the Ottoman Empire in 1918, Christian popes, emperors and kings, and Muslim caliphs, sultans and emirs were locked in a 1,300-year battle for political, military, economic and religious dominance. This struggle was fought out in France and in the Iberian Peninsula, across North Africa, in the Levant, the Holy Land and Mesopotamia, and in the Balkans and central Europe. It was also fought throughout the Mediterranean Sea and, in time, in the Indian Ocean, the Red Sea and the Persian Gulf. Echoes of it even reverberated in the impetus behind the discovery and conquest of the Americas, when Christian powers sought to outflank Muslim domination of the trade routes to the east and, by doing so, usurp the wealth that underwrote Muslim military power.

This was an era when issues of heaven and hell, the nature of God, salvation and damnation, were of supreme concern to individuals and societies alike, and it is important to acknowledge this context. The infidel, the heretic and the apostate were seen as genuine, existential threats to life and to spiritual well-being. Jerusalem was the Heavenly City to both Christians and Muslims, as it was, of course, to the Jews. Popes and caliphs were deemed to have been chosen and appointed by God, as were emperors and kings. Their word was law, and for much of this period rebellion was either seen as an affront to God, or it was justified because a ruler had betrayed his earthly responsibilities to the Almighty.

The realities of life and death in medieval Europe, or in the Arab and Ottoman empires, are sometimes difficult for us to comprehend, and the attitudes of contemporaries, Christian and Muslim alike, to authority, hierarchy, class, race, sex, gender, time and distance can also be difficult to grasp. Violent and sudden death, in conflict, or by disease and famine, was an ever-present danger, as was the fear, or the hope, of what lay beyond the grave. The recurrent waves of the Black Death, which haunted Europe and the Middle East from the mid-1300s until the early 1500s, killed between a third and a half of the population of the time, while maybe 40,000 people died within four hours at the battle of Lepanto. Individuals, communities and societies were often in an extended period of trauma, but humans are resilient, and these periods of history were also times of great economic, technological and cultural advances. In contrast to modern life, the realities of the battlefield and those of day-to-day living were far closer than today and, for many, in terms of exertion, hardship and risk, the transition from peasant to foot soldier was less dramatic, and more familiar, than it would become in later centuries. Indeed, for the chivalric Christian knights, and for the *ghazi* warriors of Islam, war and combat were their raison d'être, and battlefield glory or an heroic death their ambition. The longbow, the musket and artillery may have blunted these sentiments, but even in the Napoleonic Wars, General LaSalle is famously quoted as saying, 'no respectable hussar should live beyond 30'!

Some anthropologists believe that nothing we observe about ancient societies, particularly those of a different religion and culture, can be accurate, and that however empathetic we seek to be, our interpretations are inevitably 'modern'. Others counter that the essence of the human mind has changed very little in thousands of years, and that basic desires and instincts remain broadly the same. Both may be valid, but individual behaviour is importantly shaped by the cultural assumptions of the time. The great Greek historian Thucydides, writing in the fifth century BC, claimed that the reasons for war were invariably based on fear, honour and interest. These motivations sound reassuringly modern, but he was writing at a time when personal and individual fears, sense of honour and perception of interest, particularly among rulers and the ruling classes, were inextricably bound up with those of a kingdom, a city or a state, as they would be for a further millennium. In addition, while the clash between Christendom and caliphate was not always about religion, and often about personalities, power and territory, the wars were always fought between people for whom religion was a key element of their identity.

Given the stakes, earthly and heavenly, military friction proved to be the dominant leitmotif of the relationship between Islam and Christendom. Indeed, Muslims referred to those lands where Muslims did not dominate as the House of War, the *dar al-Harb*, while those regions that were under Muslim domination, even where Muslims were not a majority, were known as the House of Peace, the *dar al-Islam*. Christians shared a similar worldview, and prejudices on both sides hardened over time. This was a global 'Cold War' for much of medieval and modern history, periodically erupting into large-scale violence, while the physical and ideological borders between Muslim and Christian states were the 'Iron Curtain' of their day. Armies manned the land frontiers, and rival navies, privateers, corsairs and pirates prowled the sea routes from the Atlantic, through the Mediterranean, to the Indian Ocean. The lines of battle, in a state of perpetual friction, moved to and fro, sometimes significantly when a great clash-of-arms had been settled. However, they could also stay static for years, as the balance of power stabilized, or permanent and temporary 'truces' were in force between the popes and caliphs, and between the kings and sultans.

For large periods of this history, both blocs were often distracted from war with each other, by also having to confront challenges from within their own religions. Sunni Muslims were always conscious of the ideological threat from the Shia, while the Arabs and the Turks were always in competition with each other, and both were opposed to the Persians. Catholic and Orthodox Christians disdained each other, and Protestantism posed an existential threat to the moral authority of the papacy and contributed to disrupting the balance of power in 16th- and 17th-century Christian Europe. It is little surprise that so many heraldic crests of the time boasted double-headed eagles, reflecting the requirement to face in two directions, sometimes more, at the same time.

The Habsburgs, on the front line with Islam for several centuries, were always forced to look over their shoulders at their French Valois and Bourbon rivals who, from 1525, would have a 250-year alliance with the Ottomans. The Ottomans themselves, when not pursuing civil wars of succession, routinely embarked on long, bloody and expensive campaigns against the Shia Safavid dynasty of Persia, to the profound relief of all Christendom. The Italian merchant cities of Genoa, Pisa and, particularly, the Republic of Venice played an important, but cynical, disruptive and duplicitous role from the early formation of the crusader kingdoms in the Holy Land, until they were swept away by the forces unleashed in the French Revolution. Meanwhile, across and around these battle lines, the merchants, scholars and diplomats of the day manoeuvred, sensitive to the capricious nature of the times, exchanging the riches, spices, textiles, technology, news and scholarship of both civilizations.

———

At the heart of this centuries-long confrontation were some of the most significant military encounters in human history, upon whose outcome depended the very existence of empires, kingdoms, city-states, rulers and peoples. *The House of War* focuses on a selection of these key, pivotal battles and sieges, and on the protagonists who determined their conduct, conclusions and consequences. They are all epic stories, each of them historically significant, while some of them are historically decisive: the first clashes between the armies of the new religion of Islam, and those of the great empires of Christian Byzantium and Zoroastrian Persia; the taking and the retaking of Jerusalem; the expulsion of the crusaders from Acre and the Holy Land; the fall of Constantinople, and the final demise of the Byzantine Empire; the great sieges of Rhodes and Malta, and the struggle for domination of the Mediterranean Sea; the titanic sea battle of Lepanto; the siege of Vienna, and the 'high-water mark' of the Ottoman advance into Europe; the collapse of the Ottoman Empire, and the dissolution of the caliphate.

The first and last of these military engagements are separated by over a thousand years, a period in which societies and cultures changed dramatically, as did the way in which armies were raised, paid for, logistically supplied, organized, trained, led, and equipped. The armies who fought at Hattin in 1187 were markedly different from those who contested the walls of Vienna in 1683, let alone those who manoeuvred around Jerusalem in 1917. However, the study of battle is one in which the nature of conflict remains enduring, although its character is dynamic. In other words, while policy, culture, society and technology may change, combat always remains a violent, chaotic, human clash of wills, conducted for a political purpose. *The House of War* therefore seeks to make these individual military engagements between the forces of Christendom and the caliphate explicable and accessible to the general reader, but also to place them in a continuous narrative that provides the critical context within which to examine them.

Each chapter opens 'on the battlefield' in order to set the scene, and to introduce key personalities. It then attempts to track the course of events, in both the Christian and Islamic worlds, that had led to this specific clash-of-arms, at this time and in this place. In doing so, the narrative sometimes has to go back in time some considerable way in order to provide an appropriate degree of historical context. Each chapter then takes up the action again, in order to describe the events and the outcomes of the battle, in a manner that tries to bring to life for the reader what was at stake, be it personal survival and sacrifice, individual glory and honour, defeat and disgrace, or imperial collapse and dynastic destruction.

The written word can only do so much to capture what conflict actually feels like, in any age. Among the technicalities of fortification, weapons, siege engines, armour, and logistics, and the descriptions of terrain and weather, there is also the noise, smell and squalor, and the anticipation, apprehension, exertion, fatigue and boredom familiar to any soldier down the ages. The passage of time is also difficult to convey, where an exciting episode on one small sector of a battlefield can absorb a whole chapter, while the passage of several months of a protracted siege can be dismissed in a paragraph. And, for almost all the period covered in the book, this was, in William Manchester's telling phrase, 'a world lit only by fire'.

We must also bear in mind the vast variety and range of human stories, emotions and motivations that lie at the heart of these momentous events. It is inevitable that the reader, and writer, often finds it easier to identify with the knightly paladin, exultant in victory, or dying gloriously, rather than with the anonymous, wounded, defeated foot soldier facing a painful, lingering death, imprisonment, or a life shackled to the oars of a galley. So, it is important to recognize and acknowledge that across the battlefield, on the ramparts and in the trenches, within besieged cities and ravaged countryside, the *dramatis personae* might contain: royalty, nobility, the warrior-class, and the priesthood; civilians and non-combatants; women and children; military commanders and professional soldiers; mercenaries, volunteers, conscripts and new recruits; the wounded and the dying; looters, prisoners, the enslaved and those marked for execution. Each would have had a very different perspective on the events in which they were compelled to play a role.

In his book *The Face of Battle*, the military historian John Keegan reminds us that the study of conflict is most certainly one of plans, equipment and numbers, engagements and outcomes, but it is also always a study of violence, fear and courage; of leadership, obedience, compulsion and sometimes insubordination; of anxiety, doubt and uncertainty; of faith, honour, bravery and stoicism; of panic and cowardice, shame and exaltation, cruelty, self-sacrifice and compassion; of loneliness and comradeship, group solidarity and group disintegration. On all of these individual and collective emotions hang the outcome of military engagements, and they demand the empathy, and the sympathy, of the student and the reader of history.

As Osama bin Laden's words demonstrate, history remains a key component of modern politics, and he aimed to utilize history in support of his messianic vision to re-establish the lost glories of the caliphate, however selective his choice of inspiration and grievance may have been. Many people in the west may believe that society has moved beyond the stifling shackles of history and religion, and that the modern world no longer needs to be beholden to the past. However, as the philosopher George Santayana so wisely wrote, 'Those who cannot remember the past are condemned to repeat it.' In 2010, Al-Qaeda in the Arabian Peninsula (AQAP) sent a parcel bomb to New York. It was addressed to Reginald of Chatillon. The addressee had died at the hands of Saladin in 1187, in the aftermath of the battle of the Horns of Hattin. Among other misdemeanours, his 12th-century crime had been an attempt to attack the Holy City of Mecca. Truly, history is not dead.

PART ONE

The Battle Lines are Drawn

Rise of the Caliphate

Yarmouk and al-Qadisiyyah 636

Eighteenth-century historian Edward Gibbon famously quipped that the Byzantine Empire was in perpetual decline for 1,100 years. If so, then the series of immense volcanic eruptions that took place somewhere in the Pacific Ocean in the mid-500s certainly played their part in that process. Opinions vary as to the scale of the consequences on the climate, but there is no doubt that some form of sustained atmospheric pollution led to significant, if uneven, global cooling. The Roman statesman Cassiodorus wrote of the sun's rays being weak and of a 'bluish colour', of the lack of shadows at noon, feeble heat, prolonged frost and eerie skies, and of the requirement to empty the food stores to stave off hunger. Similar reports exist from English chroniclers of the same period, one of them even referring to the great mortality in the islands at the time of Camlann, the battle in which the legendary figures of King Arthur and Mordred supposedly fell. All severe weather conditions can affect day-to-day living, but the sustained cold and damp of the mid-sixth century AD appear to have put such pressures on many of the subsistence societies of the day that they could not handle them without economic collapse and social disorder, which in turn would drive political change of historical proportions.

Hard on the heels of this disastrous climatic period came the so-called 'plague of Justinian', named for the Byzantine emperor of the time. It was the first recorded major outbreak of plague pandemic, generated by the bacterium *Yersinia pestis*, closely akin to the bacterium responsible for the better-known Black Death some 800 years later, and displaying many of the same grisly symptoms. It was estimated to have killed between 15 and 100 million people in the Mediterranean area and that of the Near East, including about a quarter of the population of Constantinople. With death and sickness came depopulation, and with depopulation came falling crop yields, famine and reduced economic activity and taxes. With this economic collapse came the inability to pay for the armies that defended the Byzantine Empire's borders, at exactly the same time as similar economic pressures were galvanizing the belligerent, aggressive nomadic tribes of the Eurasian steppes once again to push west.

In 540, at the moment of this heightened economic and social pressure, the Persian Sasanians broke the much-heralded 'Perpetual Peace' that had been agreed with the Byzantine Empire only eight years earlier, and its breach initiated a century of new conflict. At the end of this period, the Sasanians would have suffered total defeat and capitulation, while the Byzantines would be left frantically defending the walls of their capital city, Constantinople. Having exhausted each other, their shared nemesis would be the Arab, Rashideen caliphate of the new challenger religion, Islam.

Having largely secured their positions on the Rhine and the Danube, the frontiers of the late Roman Republic and the early Roman Empire had been progressively extended to the east as Rome's legions came into contact with the decaying Seleucid Empire[1] in Anatolia, in Armenia and in Syria. This came at the same time as the Seleucids were under attack from a new band of central Asian raiders – the Parthians. Pompey the Great extinguished the weakened Seleucid dynasty in 63 BC, but the new Parthian power bloc inflicted a monumental defeat on the Roman general Crassus at Carrhae in 54 BC. This defeat, and Rome's determination to avenge the blow to its reputation, became the catalyst for nearly seven centuries of bitter confrontation and conflict in the Near East. In the course of this extended period, a period as long as that between the battles of the Hundred Years War and the present day, the contesting powers developed and changed, often dramatically.

Rome went from republic to empire under Augustus Caesar, while the Persian Sasanians overthrew the Parthians in the early third century AD and took up their predecessor's competition and conflict with Rome. In view of the persistent and significant challenge in the east, the Roman Empire itself was divided in two under Emperor Diocletian. Such a dramatic move was a recognition of the impossibility of a single man running the whole Roman imperial project, given the perennial barbarian threats from the north and the west, and the increasing, and unceasing, demands of war in the east. In the early fourth century AD, Emperor Constantine adopted Christianity as the official religion of the empire and moved the primary imperial capital from Rome to the eponymously named Constantinople. In the fifth century AD, while the Western Roman Empire collapsed under the pressures of internal decay and external assault, the Eastern Empire, despite manifold threats, endured. Such bald historical statements disguise the human misery of sustained tension and conflict on the frontiers of empire.

Towns, cities, fortifications, whole provinces, were continually sacked, captured, destroyed and traded. Populations were massacred, deported, sold into slavery or impoverished. Armies marched, triumphed or died, maintained lonely vigils, conducted sieges, built forts, destroyed cities. Military commanders returned in imperial triumph, died in battle or of thirst and wounds, were killed by their own troops or, famously, in Crassus's case, had their skulls turned into gold drinking bowls. The fate of emperors – Roman, Byzantine, Parthian and Sasanian – was no less capricious, often killed on campaign by the enemy, royal rivals, disgruntled generals or hired assassins. Indeed, civil wars often proved more dangerous to an empire's stability than foreign invasion, and military defeat could lead to sustained periods of uncertainty, unrest and imperial reputational damage. The Roman Emperor Valerian had been defeated by Shah Shapur I[2] at Edessa in 260, and he was used as a 'mounting block' by the Sasanian Emperor in order to get on his horse. He was subsequently killed by having molten gold poured down his throat, and then flayed and his skin stuffed and paraded around the Persian Empire. The effect on Roman morale can be imagined.

Over the centuries, the treasuries of the rival empires were poured into sustaining the conflict, and the nature of imperial structures was changed irrevocably as the demands of war, on every border and boundary, demanded taxes and soldiers. For Rome, collapse had come in the west, but in the east, although the competing imperial frontiers buckled and stretched, neither side had the logistical strength or manpower, despite the extensive use of allies, vassals, mercenaries and proxies, to maintain large and lengthy campaigns far from their own heartlands. Of these auxiliary forces, it was the Arab tribes of the Ghassanids[3] and Lakhmids,[4] the first allied to the Byzantines, the latter to the Sasanians, who would make their own mark in history. Both empires did achieve occasional conquests beyond the frontier territories, and the Romans reached as far as the Sasanian capital of Ctesiphon, on the River Tigris, on several occasions. However, it had been Emperor Trajan[5] who had recognized and acknowledged the dangers of imperial overstretch, the realities of terrain, distance, climate and lack of water, and the short- and long-term limitations of imperial resources. Even before the formal division of the Roman Empire, he had looked to stabilize the frontier with Persia on the River Euphrates.

In their turn, both the Parthians and Sasanians had periodically seized cities and lands in Syria and Anatolia, and occasionally further. However, in time the balance of power was almost always restored, and military vainglory was traded away for money, a truce, peoples or land. In the late fifth century AD, pressure from large and predatory nomadic tribes, both on the Danube and in central Asia, forced the empires to turn away from their confrontation in the Levant and Near East in order to focus on more pressing and existential threats. The result had been almost a century of uneasy peace or truce.

———

The growth of Christian influence in the Roman Empire was slow, gradual and not without its failures and setbacks. However, in historical terms, the conversion of this small, persecuted, Judaic sect into the state religion of the Roman Empire was sudden, and the consequences were seismic and transformative. Jesus had been crucified on Golgotha, 'the place of skulls', outside the walls of Jerusalem in Palestine, in 33, his messianic mission an apparent failure, and his rejection by the Jewish religious elite seemingly complete. However, his resurrection inspired his small band of loyal supporters to keep the faith, and to continue to bear witness to his teachings and his example. Instead of Christianity withering, doomed to be yet another transitory Jewish sect, with another failed messiah, the apostle Paul[6] had managed to hurdle its potential doctrinal, ethnic and geographical constraints. He had declared that Jesus Christ's life and death were a gift from God for all the peoples of the world, the circumcised and the uncircumcised, the Jew and the gentile, the rich man and the pauper. Indeed, he asserted that Jesus Christ was both man and god, both Son of God and God himself. It was a revolutionary message, and Paul and the other disciples took advantage of the unity and extent of the Roman Empire to spread their message throughout the Near East, the Balkans and Europe, gathering converts along the way, and generating martyrs in times of persecution. The promise of reward in the 'kingdom of heaven' struck a chord, not just with the poor and oppressed, but also, in time, among the Roman elites and in the ranks of the military.

In the year 312, Constantine,[7] a co-emperor under the provisions of the tetrarchy[8] set up by Diocletian, was nearing Rome during the culmination of his campaign against his imperial rival, Emperor Maxentius, nominal head of the Western Roman Empire. Constantine's army was drawn from all parts of the empire, and its soldiers reflected the range of religious beliefs that infused the vast empire at the time: sceptics and agnostics; adherents of imperial-cult polytheism; worshippers of Mithras and the sun god, Sol Invictus; and Christians. While as effective as any other soldiers, the doctrinal inflexibility and religious certainty of the Christians made them uncomfortable bedfellows and, while no one could deny their sincerity and commitment, they had become a divisive influence in the army. Constantine, whose mother, Helena, had been a Christian, had consistently attempted to bridge the religious differences that had often set legion against legion, even as they were marching to war against the armies of an imperial rival. As they approached the Milvian Bridge, an important crossing over the River Tiber, legend has it that Constantine and his soldiers had a vision sent by the Christian God. In the most popular version of the story, Constantine looked up to the sun and saw a cross of light above it and, with it in Greek, the words, 'Through this sign, you shall conquer.' The following night Constantine had a dream in which God promised him victory if the sign of the *Chi Rho*, the first two letters of Christ's name in Greek, was painted on the soldiers' shields. They did so, although some claimed that the daubs on the shields could as easily have been the mark of Sol Invictus as that of the *Chi Rho*. In this sign Constantine did indeed conquer, and his victory gave him total control of the Western Roman Empire, thereby paving the way for Christianity to become the dominant religion for the Roman Empire, and ultimately for all of Europe. The following year, 313, Constantine issued the Edict of Milan which, despite its minority status, made Christianity an officially recognized and tolerated religion across the Roman Empire. In the course of the next ten years, Constantine defeated all the other members of the tetrarchy, emerging as sole ruler. Although Constantine's eulogists claimed his success as a victory of Christianity over paganism, it remains uncertain just how deep and genuine was his attachment to the religion at this stage.

Constantine had already served in the east, against the Sasanians and, while he acknowledged the continuing threats from across the Rhine, he recognized the military strategic importance of protecting the Danube from barbarian incursions, and Syria and the Levant from a hostile Persia. The east became his priority. In due course, he settled on the Greek city of Byzantium as his new capital, which was dedicated as Constantinople[9] in 330. Despite scepticism about his own religious sincerity, Constantine's importance for the spread of Christianity cannot be questioned. He convoked the First Council of Nicaea in 325, which produced the statement of Christian belief known as the Nicene Creed, and he went on to build the Church of the Holy Sepulchre in Jerusalem, deemed to be the holiest place in all of Christendom, and also the first Basilica of St Peter's in Rome. In due course the Catholic Church would expand, establishing a structure and a hierarchy to mirror that of the temporal power of the emperors, setting themselves up for centuries of cooperation, compromise, competition and even conflict, between the religious and secular arms of Christianity.

Alongside his religious conversion, and his theological and ecclesiastical measures, Constantine instituted a range of major administrative reforms, introducing a currency that lasted a thousand years, and stabilizing the frontiers through a succession of successful campaigns. Constantine had inherited a war in the east that had already lasted for over 400 years. Religion now added a new dimension and, in a letter written to Shah Shapur II, Constantine had asserted his patronage over the Christian subjects of the Sasanian leader, and he urged him to treat them well. In 336, after a Persian invasion of Armenia, a newly Christian kingdom for only 40 years, Constantine resolved on war, and he treated the war as a Christian campaign, calling for bishops to accompany the army, and commissioning a tent in the shape of a church to follow him everywhere. He planned to be baptized in the River Jordan before crossing into Persian lands, but he had fallen ill after having only advanced into Anatolia. He was recovered as far as the city of Nicomedia,[10] and he had requested to be formally baptized there and then. He was buried in his Church of the Holy Apostles in Constantinople. Thus, the titanic imperial struggle in the east now began to take on the characteristics of a religious conflict – Christian against pagan – in addition to its long-standing political, ethnic and economic dimensions.

The expansion and embedding of Christianity in the Roman Empire could not be reversed. Theodosius I succeeded Emperor Valens, who had died at Adrianople[11] fighting the Goths, who had finally breached the Roman imperial frontier of the Danube. In 380, Theodosius endorsed the Council of Nicene orthodoxy and decreed that only Christians who believed in the consubstantiality of God the Father, Son and Holy Ghost could style themselves as 'Catholic'. In 395, he confirmed Constantine's work by endorsing Christianity as the official religion of the empire, although Christians at that time probably only constituted around 20 per cent of the population. In this manner the extensive Roman Empire began to become synonymous with an early idea of 'Christendom', a religio-political system by which governments upheld and promoted Christianity.[12] It was on Theodosius's death that the Roman Empire was finally and formally divided into east and west, and with it the church, into its recognizably Catholic and Orthodox branches. This double division would have long-term consequences for the future development of Christianity, for the continued prosecution of the wars against the Persians and, in time, for the confrontation with the shock troops of the new religion of Islam.

Theodosius's son Honorius, who succeeded him in the west, suffered the sack of Rome by Alaric and the Visigoths in 410, and the Western Empire itself would collapse in 476, shattering into its constituent parts, although all of them would, in due course, eventually subscribe to some form of Christianity. In the east matters had been markedly different. After Theodosius I had divided Armenia with Shah Shapur III in 384, a largely peaceful century had ensued, with only two brief periods of conflict. Indeed, the infant Emperor Theodosius II, in whose reign the great Theodosian Walls of Constantinople were built, had the Sasanian King Yazdegerd, a Zoroastrian, appointed as his guardian. Large-scale war in the east did not break out again until the early 500s when Emperor Justinian, and his remarkably talented military commander, Belisarius, attempted to recover significant elements of the Western Empire, and also chose to renew the confrontation with the Sasanians in the east. This new Roman–Persian war saw both sides mobilize their vassals, including the Ghassanid and Lakhmid Arabs, and embark again on a ruinously expensive set of campaigns, whose drain on resources would be compounded and exacerbated by the cold, famine and plague of the mid-sixth century.

In around 570, as inconclusive war ebbed and flowed across Mesopotamia, a thousand miles to the south, in the desert trading town of Mecca, a young man was born into the Al-Hashem[13] family of the Al-Quraysh[14] tribe. Named Muhammad, and orphaned while very young, he was destined to be the inspiration and leader of the third great monotheistic religion, that of Islam, with its doctrine of submission to God's will, and of his followers, Muslims, 'those who submit'. Like Jesus, nearly 600 years earlier, Muhammad would have a long, largely unremarkable apprenticeship, until his message and his example catalysed a transformation of the 'known world'. However, whereas Christians had waited nearly 400 years for their religion to become the defining ideology of a previously pagan, idolatrous empire, Muslims would turn the 'known world' on its head within six years of the Prophet's death. In a short century, they would have overthrown the great Persian Empire of the Sasanians and presented an existential challenge to both the western and eastern divisions of the Roman Empire. In this historically remarkable process, the Muslims converted to Islam much of Spain, all of North Africa, the Holy Land, Mesopotamia, and all the lands out to the frontiers of India, or at least put them under Muslim domination.

It would be an extraordinary achievement, and for Europe and the Middle East the next millennium would be defined by the confrontation between these competing religions and between the loyalties, identities and commitment that both ideologies inspired.

That was in the future. In 602, a new round of conflict broke out between the eastern Romans and the Persians, but this time the Persians also found themselves at war with their long-term Arab vassals, the Lakhmids. In this phase of their struggle with Constantinople, the Persians were highly successful, completing the conquest of the Caucasus, Mesopotamia and Syria by 611, and removing the 'True Cross' of Christ's crucifixion from the Church of the Holy Sepulchre in Jerusalem and bringing it to Ctesiphon. However, against the Lakhmids they were surprisingly outmanoeuvred and defeated at the battle of Dhi Qib, near modern-day Najaf in Iraq. While it was not a major battle, it was significant in dealing a blow to Persian pride and reputation, and this defeat left the southern borders of the Sasanian Empire not just undefended, but now occupied by a newly hostile state.

It was around 610, while the Persian and Roman empires were wrestling with these convulsions, that the Archangel Gabriel[15] is first recorded as having appeared to Muhammad. From his unpromising beginnings, Muhammad had followed a merchant's life, accompanying his uncle to Syria where, according to Islamic tradition, a Christian monk or hermit had predicted his later life as a prophet of God. Back in Mecca, Muhammad had routinely prayed to a deity, often for weeks at a time, in the Cave of Hira on the Mountain of Light, just over one mile outside the city. Tradition holds that it was during one of these visits that Gabriel first appeared to him, on behalf of the 'true God', and commanded him to recite the verses that would, in time, and over many years, be pulled together to constitute the Koran, 'the recitation'. For several years after this visitation Muhammad struggled with the implications of these first revelations, until he could convince himself that he was both able and worthy to be a messenger for God. The Koran is different from the Christian Bible, since it is believed to be the direct word of God, merely 'recited' by Muhammad, and it is therefore considered to be a divine text. The New Testament of the Bible is seen to be 'divinely inspired', but is also accepted as a potentially fallible human record of Christ's words and actions, and therefore open to challenge.[16] The Koran also goes beyond the biblical remit of merely the moral and ethical, by setting out a set of laws, akin to the Jewish Torah, which govern most aspects of life, including the contentious issues of political authority. While Christ instructed his followers to 'render unto Caesar what is Caesar's, and to God what is God's', implying a capacity to adapt in the face of political, social and cultural change, the Koran is deemed, by its most committed adherents, not to be liable to subsequent human interpretation.

Muhammad increasingly attracted enemies in Mecca as the divine revelations led him to preach against the prevailing polytheism of the local tribes. In 620, according to tradition, he travelled with the Angel Gabriel, on the winged steed Buraq,[17] to Jerusalem and the site of what would become the 'furthest mosque', the Masjid al-Aqsa.[18] From here he was transported to heaven, leaving his footprint on a stone. In 622, fearing for their lives, Muhammad and other early Muslims migrated to seek the protection of Medina, a city that better understood monotheism through its long engagement with Judaism. This was the fabled *hijra*, from which the Islamic calendar is dated. From here, Muhammad proclaimed a greater religious community, the *umma*, in which he intended to include all 'peoples of the book': the Torah, the Bible, and now the Koran.

However, the concept of the *umma* increasingly applied only to those who adopted Islam, and in time it came to imply the universal community of all in the Islamic faith. In the crucial last decade of his life, 622–632, as Muhammad moved between the cities of Mecca and Medina, the five basic pillars of Islam were established. These are: the *shahada* or 'creed', the most basic foundation of Islam which opens with the statement, 'I testify that there is no God but God, and Muhammad is the messenger of God'; *salat*, 'daily prayers', normally said five times a day; *zakat*, 'almsgiving', traditionally supposed to equate to 5 per cent of a person's wealth; Ramadan, 'fasting' during the ninth month of the Islamic calendar; and *hajj*, the pilgrimage to Mecca, to be undertaken at least once in a Muslim's lifetime.

In this time Muhammad spoke and acted like a traditional religious prophet. However, he was also a political leader, an administrator and a military commander. These multiple responsibilities meant that he encompassed within himself both spiritual and temporal leadership, something which was to have long-lasting implications for his successors, the caliphs. Within Christendom, the spiritual and temporal domains may overlap – indeed religion would infuse every aspect of life – but the Roman Emperor, and his successors, and the Pope jealously guarded their respective authorities. Muhammad also drew attention to the Islamic requirement to conduct *jihad* ('struggle'), although drawing a fine distinction between the 'greater *jihad*' (the inner struggle to lead a good Muslim life), and the 'lesser *jihad*' (the martial defence of the religion against infidels, heretics and apostates).

Muslims accepted Jesus's importance as a prophet but rejected his status as 'the son of God'. Muhammad was deemed by Muslims to be the last and the greatest of the prophets, and Islam was the 'last word' of God. When the Muslims seized Jerusalem in 637 and completed the construction of the Dome of the Rock Mosque in 692,[19] they would add Koranic verses to denounce Christian error: 'Praise be God, who begets no son, and has no partner' and, 'He is God, one, eternal. He does not beget, He is not begotten, and He has no peer.'

In this period of Muhammad's revelations, including his fabled flight to Jerusalem, Emperor Heraclius strove to recover from the Persian defeats of a decade earlier, rebuilding his army, slashing non-military expenditure, devaluing the currency and, with the support of his patriarch, melting down church silver, all to raise the necessary funds in order to continue the war. In 622, as Muhammad was fleeing to Medina, Heraclius left Constantinople and launched a new offensive, which took on the character of a papally endorsed holy war. His military victories were important, but not decisive, and in 626 a Persian coalition had even, unsuccessfully, besieged Constantinople itself. However, 627 was a much more successful year, leading to a massive Persian defeat, the death of the Sasanian Shah in a palace coup, and the return of the True Cross to a reconquered Jerusalem, which was marked by a magnificent ceremony.

The devastating impact of this latest war, added to the cumulative effects of a century of almost continuous conflict, had effectively left both empires crippled. Although they did not know it, neither empire would get the chance to recover, as their mutually destructive wars had now left the way open for the astonishing early triumphs of Islam (see map on p.15). If the imperial intelligence networks of Constantinople and Ctesiphon knew what was happening in the deserts of Arabia, they showed little evidence of understanding its significance, or of the threat it posed. Muhammad had by now welded his Muslim followers into a formidable and highly motivated force. Military success against enemies and rivals in and around Mecca, notably at the battle of Badr, had cemented his military reputation, and that of his creed. In 627, while Heraclius was celebrating the recovery of the True Cross, Muhammad had sealed his primacy by marching into Mecca at the head of a 10,000-man Muslim army. In 629, he sent an army to confront the Byzantines over the death of one of his envoys. Although defeated at the battle of Mu'tah, it was the opening salvo in the new confrontation between Islam and Christendom, and in May 632, Muhammad ordered a large expedition to be prepared in order to avenge the 'martyrs of Mu'tah'. However, by the next month the Prophet had died in Medina, and his followers were faced with an internal issue as to whom to nominate as his successor. A power struggle soon developed across the Arabian Peninsula, as rivals and enemies sought to take advantage of this initial Muslim disarray.

The issue of who had the moral and spiritual authority to be the Caliph, or to give the full title, '*Al caliph al rasool al Allah*', the 'righteous successor of the messenger of God', was to prove deeply divisive within Islam from the outset. It would have seismic consequences for the religion itself, and for Islam's interface and interaction with competing religions, and centres of power. Islam had taken root in the desert culture and traditions of seventh-century Arabia, and this profoundly affected the Koranic and *hadith* guidance on a whole range of attitudes and strictures regarding diet, dress and relations between the sexes, let alone politics and war. This body of legal instruction was cumulatively aggregated into *sharia*, those issues subject to the immutable, divine word of God, and *fiqh*, issues of legal consensus determined by Islamic jurists. In terms of succession, tradition – the *sunna*, from which the designation of the majority Muslim grouping, Sunni, derives – determined that the successor should be chosen from those best qualified to lead. However, given the pre-eminence of Muhammad as the last, and therefore the greatest, of God's prophets, others felt that the succession should hereafter come through a bloodline descendant. Having no surviving sons from his several marriages, Muhammad's closest male relative was Ali ibn Abu Talib, a first cousin, and also Muhammad's son-in-law by marriage to his daughter, Fatima.

Ali ibn Abu Talib was clearly a remarkable boy, and man. He was with Muhammad when the Prophet began to receive the divine words that would form the Koran. Ali had been the first to accept God's message from God's Prophet and, at 12, was the first young male to embrace Islam and become a Muslim. With Fatima he had four children, including two significant sons, Hassan and Hussein, and, right up until Muhammad's death in 632, Ali was a trusted confidant and lieutenant. By then many assumed that Muhammad had chosen Ali as his successor. However, even while Ali and others were preparing Muhammad's body for burial, another significant group of his followers chose Abu Bakr – the father of Muhammad's youngest wife, Aisha – to be the first Caliph, in what came to be known as the Caliphate of the Rashideen, the 'Righteous Successors'. Despite the outrage of his own supporters, Ali accepted the judgement, for the sake of Muslim unity, but this issue of succession would haunt the history of Islam, and the region, to the current day.

On his first day as Caliph, Abu Bakr gave orders to relaunch the campaign against Byzantium, but a succession of desert uprisings diverted his attention, and he and his primary commander, Khalid al-Walid – later given the soubriquet *Saif al-Allah*, the Sword of God – spent the next year fighting the Campaign of Apostasy, or the Ridda Wars, against rebel tribes and self-proclaimed prophets across Arabia, including in Bahrain, Oman and Yemen. By early 633 Arabia had been reluctantly united under the central authority of Abu Bakr, ruling from his capital in Medina, who was by now intent on expanding his new caliphate, by first bringing the word of God to his fellow Arabs in the Ghassanid and Lakhmid tribes, many of the former of whom were Christians. To achieve this would mean confronting the great, albeit weakened, Roman and Persian empires.

In mid-633 AD, Khalid al-Walid marched out of Arabia and headed for the western banks of the River Euphrates, in modern-day Iraq, defeating several significant Sasanian garrisons as he went. In due course, despite this success in Iraq, he was ordered to reinforce Muslim forces who were on a similar raiding mission in Syria, and he crossed the desert wastes in a march that went down in Arab and Muslim folklore. In some versions of this tale, al-Walid watered his camels, then sewed up their mouths to stop them eating. Killing the animals as they went, his followers were then able to drink the unpolluted liquid from their stomachs. These followers of the Prophet united in Syria in July 634, and the first major clash in history between Muslim and Christian armies took place in the same month, as Khalid pressed on towards Damascus and into Palestine, and Emperor Heraclius's forces were pushed back. Abu Bakr died in Medina in August, the only one of the four Rashideen caliphs to die in his bed, and it was his successor, Umar, who subsequently oversaw the capture of the great city of Damascus in September 635, and who would go on to be the decisive leader of the early history of Islam.

By now both the Byzantines and the Sasanians were fully alert to the threat posed by these new Islamic 'warriors of God'. The Muslims displayed all the motivation and fervour of the religiously inspired, and their leaders were proving to be worryingly agile, adept and imaginative. In the spring of 636, Khalid al-Walid withdrew from Damascus to the old capital of the Ghassanids at Jabiyah, as news reached him of the approach of a major Byzantine army. As the Romans set up camp to his west, Khalid withdrew further, to take up a position north of the River Yarmouk. This area spanned high hilltops, water sources, some critical routes connecting Damascus to Galilee, and the historic pasture grazing lands of the Ghassanids. There they stayed, negotiating and occasionally skirmishing, for nearly three months. The Byzantine army was formidable, and probably outnumbered the Muslims, but it was beset with the usual problems of a coalition army which, in this case, contained Slavs, Franks, Armenians, Christian Arabs, Lombards, Avars and Khazars.[20] The chain of command was cumbersome, logistics were a challenge, and the loyalties, motivations and steadfastness of this heterogenous force were mixed. In a sign of how seriously the threat from Islam was now being taken, Heraclius had secured both a truce and a military alliance with the new Persian king, the eight-year-old Yazdegerd III, which included the marriage of the Christian Emperor's daughter to the Zoroastrian Shah in order to seal the deal. Under the terms of the agreement, Yazdegerd's generals were to launch an offensive in Iraq, while Heraclius was advancing against the Muslims in the Levant. In the event, Yazdegerd was unable to execute his vital part of the plan. Despite this, Heraclius's generals, who had been told to avoid getting decisively engaged in Syria, assessed that their logistical position was becoming tenuous, while dissension was growing in their ranks. They now felt compelled to confront the Muslim army.

At last, in the heat of the Syrian summer of 636, the Byzantine and Rashideen armies opened hostilities with a traditional set of personal duels between opposing commanders and champions. The main armies then fell upon each other. For five days arrows flew, swords rose, flashed and sliced, shield walls clashed, infantry advanced and withdrew through the sanguinary horrors of close combat, and cavalry charged, wheeled and retired. On the fifth day, Byzantine resolve cracked, and retreat became a rout, and then a massacre, as the Romans and their allies found their withdrawal routes over the River Yarmouk were already held by Khalid al-Walid's forces. When news of this major defeat reached Heraclius in Antioch, he took a ship, that night, to Constantinople, ordering the evacuation of all Syria and the Holy Land, and the strengthening of the border fortresses of Anatolia.

In the wake of this stunning victory, the Muslims now held uncontested power in the Levant and in the Holy Land, and a Christian army would not march through these lands for another 450 years. Yarmouk is rightly celebrated throughout the Muslim world as opening the door to the extraordinary expansion of Islam that swiftly followed, but it is hardly known in the west although, if Heraclius's forces had prevailed, the whole history of the world would have been decisively altered. Despite his contribution to this victory, the new Caliph, Umar, removed Khalid al-Walid from command, announcing that he had done so to show the people that it was God alone who had given them this victory. Khalid complained at his treatment but resisted the encouragement to rebel against Umar, and he went to his grave in 642, his reputation as one of Islam's greatest generals intact.

Meanwhile, Yazdegerd's generals resolved to carry out their delayed part in Heraclius's grand strategy, by attempting to retake the lands in Iraq. In the face of this new offensive, albeit by a largely new and untested Persian army, Umar had ordered a southerly retreat to the

THE HOUSE OF WAR

borders of Arabia and the land of the Lakhmids. Therefore, by the time of the battle of Yarmouk, both sides had forces in the vicinity of al-Qadisiyyah, near the River Ateeq, a branch of the Euphrates, negotiating while nervously awaiting the news from Syria. Despite Persian dismay when they learnt of the Byzantine defeat and withdrawal, they resolved to fight, while Caliph Umar called up more volunteers, including those from the apostate tribes defeated in the Ridda Wars,[21] and welcomed into his ranks a significant force of battle-hardened veterans of the battle of Yarmouk, who had marched, at speed, to his assistance. In negotiation, the Persians appealed to the Arabs as neighbours and former allies, offering inducements of money, clothing and animals if they would retire back to their desert fastness. In response, the Muslim ambassadors insisted that the Sasanians had to choose between converting to Islam or paying *jizya*, a new per-capita yearly taxation imposed on the non-Muslim subjects of an Islamic state. The demands were both sincere and arrogant, reflecting the ideological certainty of the Muslim leadership, and a confidence reinforced by their recent triumphs in Syria.

To Yazdegerd and his satraps, guardians of a 400-year-old dynasty and a 1,000-year-old civilization, their demands sounded astonishing. To deal as equals with these Arab interlopers, propounding a new, challenger religion of hardly a decade's standing, was humiliating and scarcely to be contemplated. To humiliate the Arab emissaries, Yazdegerd ordered his servants to place baskets full of earth on their heads. One optimistic Muslim ambassador exclaimed, 'Congratulations, you have voluntarily surrendered your land to us!' In mid-November, and in this spirit of civilizational superiority, the Sasanian forces, including a 40-strong force of Indian elephants, embarked on battle. In the course of another five-day encounter, during which fortunes favoured both sides, the Sasanian commander was killed, the war elephants neutralized, and the Persians retreated in disorder across the Ateeq. Umar, knowing that Sasanian defeat could not be assured until the capture of their capital at Ctesiphon, ordered his commanders to continue the pursuit, and the great imperial city was finally taken by siege in March 637.

As the battle of al-Qadisiyyah was unfolding, Umar's remaining forces in Syria had taken advantage of Heraclius's withdrawal to lay siege to the formidable walled city of Jerusalem, which had been heavily refortified after Heraclius had retaken it from the Persians only a decade earlier. The Patriarch, Sophronius, had already collected all the holy relics, including the True Cross, and had had them secretly sent to the coast to be taken to Constantinople. The Arabs, in recognition of the place the city already had in Muslim iconography, opted to encircle rather than assault its well-fortified walls. After six months, the Patriarch, by now aware of the Sasanian defeat at al-Qadisiyyah, and conscious that no Christian relief army was in prospect, agreed to surrender the city, but only to the Caliph himself. Thus, in late 637 Umar travelled to Jerusalem and received its surrender, in person. In return for civil and religious liberty, the Christians agreed to pay the *jizya*, while the Jews, after 500 years of oppressive Roman rule, were allowed to live in the city again. Patriarch Sophronius graciously invited Umar to pray in Constantine's Church of the Holy Sepulchre, but the Caliph declined, fearing that the invitation, and his presence, might endanger the church's status as a place of Christian worship, and that, as a result, future Muslims might break the spirit of the treaty and convert the church into a mosque. Instead, Umar built a small mosque, opposite the church, which is still there. He also ordered that the Temple Mount – all that was left of the great Temple of Herod – be cleared of refuse and debris, where he constructed a new, large, albeit makeshift mosque on the site. More than half a century later, the Umayyad Caliph, Abd al-Malik, would commission the construction of the magnificent Dome of the Rock, seeking to compete in grandeur with the city's Christian churches.

In 639, Umar was persuaded to invade Egypt, the breadbasket of the Roman Empire. A small Muslim army advanced slowly, but decisively, as far as Tripoli in modern Libya, before the Caliph ordered them to halt, and he again turned eastwards, in order to complete the destruction of the Sasanian Empire. In the period since the Muslim victory at al-Qadisiyyah, the Zagros Mountains, a natural barrier, had marked the border between the Rashideen Caliphate and the Sasanians. Indeed, Umar had stated, 'I wish between the Suwad [Mesopotamia] and the Persian hills there were walls that would prevent them from getting to us and prevent us from getting to them. The fertile Suwad is sufficient for us; and we prefer the safety of the Muslim lands to the spoils of war.' Alas, there were no walls, and the Rashideen were already being threatened with a resurgent and vengeful Sasanian Empire. In 642, Umar ordered a full and final invasion of Persia, and at the battle of Nahavand he decisively defeated the Persians, marking the final dissolution of the Sasanian imperial army. Yazdegerd III, King of Kings and now 27 years old, was killed in 651 as he travelled ever eastwards, trying to gather forces to make a last-ditch stand. His son, Peroz III, ultimately died in China in 679, and with him died the last whispers of a thousand years of Iranian Zoroastrian greatness. A senior Muslim historian[22] wrote:

> If you ask me what the most important event in the history of Islam is, I shall say without hesitation 'the Conquest of Persia'. The battle of Nahavand gave the Arabs not only a beautiful country, but also an ancient civilization... But for the conquest of Persia, the civilization of Islam would have been one-sided. The conquest of Persia gave us what the conquest of Greece gave Rome.

By 644, Umar had also taken a third of the Eastern Roman Empire. For nearly 300 years the shoreline of all the Mediterranean, north and south, had been Christian. It would never be so again. At his death in that year, only 12 years after that of the Prophet, and the result of a bizarre and banal assassination over the payment of taxes, Caliph Umar's rule had extended throughout the Arabian Peninsula; from present-day Libya in the west, to the River Indus in the east; and to Anatolia and the River Oxus in the north, encompassing all of the Holy Land, the Levant and Mesopotamia. He had been an extraordinary individual and leader, and his time as Caliph had seen one of the most astonishing military expansions in history. For the early Muslims, the only explanation for this success could be the justice of their cause, and the divine inspiration and assistance of Allah. That spirit was to propel continued Islamic expansion for a further 1,000 years, despite many defeats, setbacks and challenges. Many of these setbacks would emanate from the divisions within Islam itself as a religion, and from the ethnic tensions between diverse groups within this expanding physical and spiritual 'empire'.

The mantle of Caliph now fell upon the shoulders of Uthman bin Affan of the important Umayyad clan, another companion of the Prophet and, once again – and as it would be for over 900 years – from the dominant Al-Quraysh tribe of Mecca. Under his caliphate, the Muslim armies pushed further west along the North African coast, continuing to convert the local populace to Islam, including the populous Berber tribes. In 651 they defeated a large Byzantine army in modern-day Tunisia, and some elements of his army are believed to have traversed the rest of North Africa, and even to have crossed briefly into Spain. Muslims now also contested the Byzantine dominance of the eastern Mediterranean, winning a notable naval victory at the battle of the Masts in 655. However, in 656, amid widespread accusations of tribal favouritism, nepotism and corruption, Uthman was besieged in his house in Medina and assassinated.

This was Ali's moment, and he became the fourth Caliph at the age of 56. He moved his capital to Kufa[23] in Iraq. Despite the Prophet Muhammad's exhortations about Muslim unity, Ali was immediately confronted by members of the strong Umayyad clan, who militarily contested his right to be Caliph. The Umayyads had their power base in Damascus, while Ali's support was largely centred on Kufa, and both inherited old tribal animosities and, significantly, the deeply rooted historical, political and cultural differences between Syria and Iraq, formed through centuries of contrasting styles of earlier rule by the Romans and Persians.

Division soon escalated into conflict, and after a violent but inconclusive clash in 657, at the battle of Siffan, on the banks of the Euphrates, Ali sought to sustain the unity of the *umma* by offering a 'ceasefire' and a chance for arbitration. The lengthy, inconclusive and unsatisfactory nature of this arbitration weakened Ali's position, even among his own supporters. Under the slogan 'arbitration belongs to God', a vociferous minority broke away who came to be known as the Kharijites, 'those who leave', claiming that only God could determine the legitimate Caliph through battle, not man-made negotiation. They demonstrated their opposition to almost everyone in a series of violent attacks on their former allies in Ali's forces, and on those other Muslims they deemed to have compromised with Koranic direction, declaring them to be *kafir* (unbelievers, heretics and infidels). Inspired by their example, this *takfiri*[24] ideology grew within Islam, nurturing a violent hatred of perceived heresy in all its forms. In the successive cycles of historical expansion, decline and renewal in the Muslim world, Al-Qaeda and Islamic State would be merely among the most virulent and violent modern manifestations of this tendency to demonize non-conformists.

It was around this time of heightened religious and political tension that Ali's supporters chose to designate themselves as Shia'at al-Ali, the 'followers of Ali', more recognizable today as the Shia. Given the geographical power centres of the competing factions, Shi'ism became most deeply entrenched in the areas east of the River Tigris, in eastern Iraq and, crucially, in Persia. There were, however, also strong Shia opponents of the Sunni Umayyads in what are now the coastal areas of Syria and south Lebanon. These developed, in time, into the Alawite branch of Shi'ism, the modern power base of the Syrian Assad family, and more recently they would form the core adherents of Hezbollah, the Lebanese Shia 'Party of God'.

In 661, Ali was attacked in the Grand Mosque of Kufa, by a Kharijite wielding a poison-coated sword, and he died a few days later. Ali's death ended the 30-year period of the Rashideen, which had contained within it the consolidation of the Prophet's teachings and the springboard for the extraordinary success and early expansion of Islam. Although Ali's son, Hassan, was acclaimed as the fifth Caliph, the Umayyad leader Muawiyah gradually eroded his support through bribery and intimidation. At last, Hassan offered to yield the Islamic leadership to him, on the single condition that Muawiyah would not name a successor during his caliphate, and that he would allow the *umma* to choose a successor on his, Muawiyah's, death. Hassan died in 669 – possibly poisoned by his own wife on the instigation of Muawiyah – and his younger brother, Hussein, was acclaimed by his followers as the sixth Caliph. However, in 680 Muawiyah, breaking his understanding with Hassan, named his own son Yazid as a competing caliph, and so began the Umayyad dynasty, with its capital in Damascus, which would last until 750. Hussein, by now living in Medina, refused to give allegiance to Yazid, and he moved to Mecca. Here letters reached him from Kufa, the first Shia 'capital', appealing to him for help against the orthodox Sunni supporters of the Umayyads. Hussein marched north but, near the city of Karbala on the Euphrates, he and his small band of followers were ambushed by Yazid's soldiers. The story of his final death struggle, his killing and beheading, are the core elements of Shia mythology and iconography. The anniversary of his death is marked every year by Shias with very public displays of grief, on the Day of Ashura, and the anniversary remains a key event in the Shia calendar. The murder of Caliph Ali, and the subsequent 'martyrdom' of his sons Hassan and Hussein, institutionalized the confessional division within Islam and brought with it lasting confrontation and conflict. The formal adoption of Shi'ism, by the Persian Safavid dynasty in the early 16th century, would turn a bitter confessional division into an ethnic contest, and a titanic imperial power struggle, whose ramifications would last to the present day.[25]

This grievous split between the Sunni and Shia branches of Islam would be accompanied by an almost equally virulent conflict within the Sunni world itself, as the struggle for leadership over the centuries moved between rival interpretations, competing families and ethnic groups. This would be compounded by the violent opposition of the *takfiri* ideologues of the Sunni Kharijites, who rejected all the imperial pretensions and the trappings of power of successive Sunni caliphs. In classical Islamic thought, with its emphasis on the integrity of the universal *umma*, the existence of competing Muslim states, let alone conflicts between them, should have been a theological impossibility. It should have made the application of the concept of *jihad* to competition between Muslims equally impossible. However, from the death of Muhammad, Muslims almost immediately entered a period of internecine warfare that not only split Islam between Sunni and Shia but would provide a body of precedent and theological interpretation to justify war against a range of enemies. In this Islam was akin to Christianity which, already split between the Catholic and Orthodox branches, was routinely riven by charges and accusations of 'heresy', culminating in the inexorable rise of reformist Protestantism in the 15th, 16th and 17th centuries. The enemies of Islam were not just the obvious Christian 'infidel' but, increasingly over time, the Muslim 'heretics', whose beliefs were at variance with Islamic orthodoxy; the 'apostate', who might explicitly renounce Islam; the 'blasphemer', who made impious remarks about Islam; and the 'compromiser', who was corrupted by 'false' political models and seduced by alien cultural mores. All could, indeed must, be confronted in a generalized 'defence of Islam'.

Until Islam triumphed universally, Muslim theology theoretically divided the world in two: the *dar al-Islam*, the House of Peace, where Muslims ruled but other 'peoples of the book' were permitted to exist on payment of the *jizya*; and the *dar al-Harb*, the House of War, the rest of the world. A truce was, however, possible for those Muslims unfortunate enough to live in 'infidel' lands, for as long as their Islamic worship and customs were protected by law. Thus, over an extended period, the centuries of conflict between a pagan Rome and a Zoroastrian Persia were eventually superseded by a new competition between a Christian Byzantine Empire and a new Muslim Arab caliphate. However, while the conflict between Rome and Persia had been long and bloody, it had largely been confined to the Levant, Mesopotamia and the Caucasus. The battle lines of this new Christian–Muslim confrontation would rapidly stretch from the Pyrenees and the Iberian Peninsula, through North Africa, across the Mediterranean Sea, and eventually into the Balkans and the heartlands of central Europe. Fought intensely, both by land and by sea, the shape of the confrontation between Christendom and Islam, and the outcomes of their military clashes, would also be determined by splits and divisions within each religious bloc, where power politics, dynastic survival, and the personalities of rulers would often trump confessional identities.

Despite the weakness and division following the deaths of Ali, Hassan and Hussein, the Umayyad caliphs had ruthlessly continued the Islamic expansion (see map on p.15), and also the conversion programme of their Rashideen predecessors. Having already been prominent in defending Syria against the Byzantines, the Umayyads transferred the capital of the caliphate to Damascus, rapidly absorbing many of the former Arab allies of the Byzantines into their own army, while embarking on almost annual land and sea offensives against their Christian opponents. Their capture of Carthage in 698 signalled the final, irretrievable end of Roman power in Africa, and they founded the port town of Tunis with the aim of establishing a powerful naval base from which to challenge for dominance in the Mediterranean. In 711, having finally defeated the last of the Berber kingdoms of North Africa, including that of the legendary warrior queen Al-Kahina,[26] they crossed into the Visigothic Kingdom of Hispania, near Gibraltar, named for the Umayyad general, Tariq ibn Zayed.[27] In the east, they gained the surrender of the great Silk Road towns of Bokhara and Samarkand, pushing into the Ferghana Valley of modern Uzbekistan, and on into the province of Sind. In doing so, they also demolished the great, millennia-old Zoroastrian fire temples, in the name of Islamic religious purity.

There were setbacks and defeats, and although the Umayyads reached the suburbs of Constantinople, they were defeated by the great Theodosian land walls, and by the Byzantine navy. By the early eighth century, the eastern frontier between the two empires had stabilized along the line of the Taurus and Anti-Taurus Mountains in Anatolia, where it stayed, punctuated by periodic raids and incursions, for most of the next two centuries. Meanwhile, in Spain, the Umayyad forces pushed as far north as the Pyrenees, and their armies moved through and over them into France. Although opinion remains divided as to the significance of the encounter between the Muslim armies and those of Charles Martel, at the battle of Tours in 732, defeat there marked a clear end to Islamic expansion in the west. Edward Gibbon supposedly opined that he was in no doubt about the importance of the battle's outcome and that, but for the victory of Tours, 'Europe might have been contemplating the "dreaming minarets of Oxford", rather than its spires'.

———

The Muslim expansion under the Umayyads (see map on p.15), described variously as a 'jihad state' and a 'booty economy', contributed to their own downfall. Mass conversions, forced and voluntary, brought Persians, Berbers, Copts and Aramaics into the Islamic faith, and these new 'clients' were often better educated and more civilized than their Arab overlords, while the long-lasting feud between Syria and Iraq offered competing sources of power, wealth and influence to those people whose cultural and religious identities were often fluid and conflicted. In 747, capitalizing on Umayyad military defeats in Europe and, more recently, in central Asia, and taking advantage of the crumbling of the Umayyad's moral authority as caliphs, Abu Muslim of the Abbasid family, another senior and influential branch of the Prophet's Al-Quraysh tribe, was successful in initiating an open revolt in Khorasan, against Damascus, under the sign of the black flag.

In January 750, at the battle of Zab in northern Iraq, the Umayyad army was defeated, and the last Umayyad Caliph, Marwan, was hunted down and killed in Egypt, while the Syrian tombs of his Umayyad predecessors were desecrated. When the Abbasids declared an amnesty for all remaining members of the Umayyad family, 80 of them gathered to receive pardons, and all were massacred. One grandson of a former caliph survived, and he escaped across North Africa pursued, for many years, by Abbasid assassins.[28] He crossed to Al-Andalus, as Spain was known to the Arabs, and established an emirate. In a claim unrecognized outside his own emirate he maintained that the Umayyad caliphate, the true, authentic caliphate, remained more legitimate than that of the Abbasids, and was continued through him in Cordoba. It was to survive, in one form or another, for centuries, until the Catholic monarchs of Spain, Ferdinand of Aragon and Isabel of Castile, finally evicted the last Muslims from Iberia in 1492.

The Abbasids swiftly moved the capital of the caliphate east, to the newly founded city of Baghdad,[29] on the River Tigris and some 20 miles north of the old Persian capital of Ctesiphon. Although Baghdad would become a fabled centre of science, culture, invention and innovation, ushering in what became known as 'the Golden Age of Islam', particularly in the areas of jurisprudence, astronomy, medicine, literature and architecture, the Abbasids would preside over a slow decline in Arab leadership of the extensive Sunni Muslim world. Despite the early glory days of caliphs such as al-Mansur and Harun al-Rashid, the latter best known in the west for the tales of Scheherazade and the *One Thousand and One Nights*, the Abbasids were incrementally forced to cede control over Al-Andalus, Morocco, Algeria and Sicily, and of large areas of central Asia and Persia. In 969, they importantly lost control of wealthy Egypt to the rival Shia caliphate of the Fatimids, named for the daughter of the Prophet. With that, they also lost control of the Holy Cities of Mecca, Medina and Jerusalem.

The political power of the caliphs themselves was also increasingly constrained during this period through a combination of individual weakness, financial extravagance, military defeat, and a progressive reliance on mercenaries. In 1055, the Turkic dynasty of the Seljuks, having converted to Islam, seized all temporal power from the Abbasids and, with it, the title of Sultan. The model of the Sultan-Caliph, one man holding both religious and secular authority, ushered in under the Rashideen and Umayyads, was for now destroyed. The Abbasid caliphs remained the titular head of the Sunni Islamic community and retained a degree of moral and religious authority as descendants of the Prophet but, for now, the glory days of Arab pre-eminence were gone. There would be a brief Abbasid renaissance in the 12th and 13th centuries, until the relentless and bloody Mongol invasions led to the sacking of Baghdad. Only with the Ottoman rise to regional dominance in the 16th century would the idea of a sultan-caliph once again be given full expression.

———

In 1071, the Seljuk Sultan Alp Arslan fought and defeated a large Byzantine army at Manzikert, near Lake Van, taking the Emperor,

Romanos IV Diogenes, prisoner. This army had included a force of around 500 mounted warriors from France and Normandy.[30] Alp Arslan had originally wanted to confront the 'heretic' caliphate of the Fatimids in Syria and Egypt, but his unexpected victory at Manzikert, which had swiftly provoked a destabilizing Byzantine civil war, now opened Anatolia to his armies, and they surged westwards inspired both by Islamic religious fervour and by the *ghazi* predatory, military raiding culture of the Turkic tribes. Constantinople itself would not eventually fall for another 400 years, but historians would pinpoint the battle of Manzikert as a further turning point in the empire's long and gradual decline. Alp Arslan had refused to believe that the bloody and tattered man brought before him was the mighty Emperor of the Romans. Although he was subsequently to treat Romanos with great consideration and generosity, on being convinced of his identity he put his foot on his neck and forced him to kiss the ground. There could be no greater demonstration of how the wheel of fortune had turned in the Near East. In 1073, the Seljuks captured the city of Jerusalem from the Fatimids, holding it until 1098. On the back of Byzantine turmoil, the Seljuks now advanced their capital to Nicaea in 1077, deep into Anatolia, and almost on the Sea of Marmara. In due course Nicaea would become an early capital city of the nascent Ottoman Empire. Meanwhile, a new Emperor, Alexius I Comnenus, had managed to stabilize Byzantine decline and, like Heraclius before him, initiated a slow financial, economic, military and territorial imperial recovery. Although the split in Christendom between the Catholic and Orthodox churches remained real and profound, and although he was being challenged in the Mediterranean and western Balkans by the Normans of south Italy, Alexius would still feel constrained to look to the religious and secular leaders of western Europe for help in confronting the Seljuk threat.

———

Within Christendom, as the empire adopted Christianity, so the church had adopted the same organizational boundaries as the empire, and the dioceses corresponded to the territorial divisions of the imperial government, with five pre-eminent 'sees': Rome, Constantinople, Jerusalem, Alexandria and Antioch, with Rome as *primus inter pares* ('first among equals'). In 476, when Rome had fallen, and the last

Emperor of the Western Roman Empire had been deposed, the Senate, in a last act of historical bathos, had sent the imperial insignia to Constantinople. From this time on, the Apostolic See of Constantinople became dominant throughout the Byzantine Empire, although the fractured western lands continued to look to Rome.

Although Rome, for a long time, continued to profess a nominal allegiance to the Emperor in Constantinople, the realities of power forced the papacy to negotiate new arrangements with newly converted barbarian rulers. One of the most significant of these was Clovis,[31] who succeeded in uniting several large tribes under his leadership. He underwent conversion to Christianity in 496, leading to further widespread conversion among many other tribes and, with that process, the religious unification of much of northern Europe. It was under his Merovingian dynasty that Charles Martel had won the decisive battle against the Umayyads at Tours in 732. Under the successor dynasty, the Carolingians, the great Christian warrior Charlemagne succeeded in uniting the majority of western and central Europe, taking Christianity to regions that had never been under either Roman or Frankish rule, and in time he became the first recognized emperor to rule in western Europe since the fall of Rome three centuries earlier. In 800, he was crowned Emperor by the Pope in Rome, both of them claiming that, as a result of this elevation, Charlemagne was now head of a Roman Empire that was, once again, 'one and indivisible'. For centuries the succeeding emperors of both west and east would make competing claims of sovereignty over the whole of Christendom. Indeed, Charlemagne exchanged emissaries with the noted Abbasid Caliph Harun al-Rashid as part of a joint strategy to extinguish the Umayyad caliphate in Umayyad Spain, and to put pressure on the Byzantines. An important part of this campaign was the opening of the *Reconquista*, the reconquest, in Spain, where the Pope was being encouraged to offer papal sanction and blessing for those Christian knights and soldiers who would undertake military service against the Muslims.

Saint James, a favourite of Jesus, had been beheaded and martyred by King Herod, and his body had found its way to Galicia, where he had been adopted as the patron saint of Spain and had already been given the soubriquet *Matamoros*, 'killer of the Moors'. The idea of harnessing the martial fervour of western Europe's warrior class in support of a religious cause was beginning to become a socially accepted focus of soldiering. As such, it helped square the circle between the Christian teaching of 'loving your neighbour' and 'turning the other cheek', and St Augustine's doctrine of 'just war' in pursuit of a 'just cause'.

On his deathbed, Charlemagne had divided his empire between his three sons, beginning the slow process of defining the internal borders of Europe, and the succeeding centuries saw the slow, gradual consolidation of western Europe and of the Catholic Church and the papacy, and the further spread and triumph of the Christian conversion mission. In 1054, just as the Seljuk Turks were about to make their move to usurp the powers of the Abbasid caliphs, Christendom became 'formally' split between the Catholic and Orthodox branches of the Christian religion. Although Constantine's Council of Nicaea in 325 had established a Christian doctrinal orthodoxy, the intervening centuries, including both the collapse and the recovery of the Western Roman Empire, had led to significant divergences in liturgical, linguistic and organizational practices between the eastern and western branches of Christianity. Among these were important doctrinal assumptions about the significance, and the relative importance of, the Father, the Son and the Holy Ghost. Did the Holy Ghost 'proceed' from the Father, God, or from both the Father and the Son, Jesus Christ, God made flesh? This Great Schism[32] came at a time when the See of Rome was, once again, attempting to establish its pre-eminence. Anathematizing each other was a poor way for the two churches to try to establish a common front against the new common foe of the Seljuk Turks, and the proof of that pudding had been amply exposed in the Christian defeat at the battle of Manzikert.

Therefore, by the second half of the 11th century, events, motivations and attitudes, both within Christendom and Islam, and between these politico-religious blocs, were coalescing to provide the political, military and religious environment within which that extraordinary historical phenomenon, the First Crusade, would be launched.

In March 1095, Pope Urban II received ambassadors from Emperor Alexius I Comnenus, seeking new military and financial assistance in his fight against the Seljuk Turks. Both Emperor Alexius and Pope Urban had already faced multiple internal and external challenges, and Alexius had even been excommunicated by Urban's predecessor. However, despite a long record of political, personal and doctrinal frictions, there were important shared threats and shared interests. Perhaps

Alexius's military problems now offered an opportunity to help heal the Great Schism, and perhaps it would herald a more unified Christian response to the Islamic threat. Urban had already called for a church council in Clermont in November 1095. The agenda was ostensibly to address administrative and organizational matters, and to censure the French king for a very public adulterous affair, but Urban now began to think far more ambitiously than that. On 27 November 1095, Urban addressed a packed council. He bemoaned the state of affairs in western Europe, and the prevalence of violence among Christians; he referred to the great work being done by Christian knights in Spain; he set out, in graphic detail, the fate of the Holy Land, the Holy Sites, and the treatment of pilgrims; and the Pope spoke of the threat to the Byzantine Empire, and to the Orthodox Church of the east. Warming to his theme, he called upon kings and knights to put aside their feuding, and to focus their military prowess and ardour on the defence of Christendom, the destruction of the infidels, and the recovery of the Holy City of Jerusalem. Defining this papally sanctioned 'military pilgrimage' as both a defensive 'just war', in line with St Augustine's teachings, and also a religious 'holy war', he then promised immediate absolution to all who died on the way to the Holy Land, or in battle against the infidels. The response was immediate and deafening: *Deus lo vult!* 'God wills it!'

PART TWO

The Contest for the Holy Land

2

Victory in the East

Jerusalem 1099

On 12 July 1099, Count Raymond St Gilles of Toulouse, Godfrey of Bouillon, Duke Robert of Normandy, and Count Robert of Flanders met on the Mount of Olives to discuss launching a final assault on Jerusalem the following day. They had arrived outside the Holy City on 7 June. It was over three and a half years since the Council of Clermont,[1] almost a year since the capture of the great city of Antioch, and nearly six months since a mutiny by their followers had forced the great leaders of the crusade[2] to cease their bickering and resume the march on Jerusalem. Having followed the coast road from Tripoli to Jaffa, past the great city-ports of Beirut, Sidon, Tyre and Acre, they had approached the city by way of Ramleh. As they had passed through the village of Emmaus, where Christ had first revealed himself to his disciples after his crucifixion, envoys from the town of Bethlehem had come to meet them, begging to be delivered from the Muslim yoke. The crusaders' arrival had been greeted with an ecstatic reception and a procession of every Christian relic the town possessed.

Their early, hasty assaults on the city had failed. Some had argued that the attempt to assault the walls of Jerusalem should be delayed until the cool of autumn, but many had no time for further procrastination when the City of God was so near; others, more practically, had pointed out the strong likelihood of a Muslim counter-attack. A month earlier, on 12 June, the crusader leaders had made a pilgrimage to the Mount of Olives, where an aged hermit had addressed them, urging them to attack the walls the next day. The princes had protested that they lacked siege machines and, along with that, the numbers or siege ladders for a successful assault, but the hermit was having none of it. With enough faith, he said, God would guarantee success. Emboldened by his words, the princes had ordered a general attack for the next day but either the hermit was mistaken, or crusader faith was not strong enough, and the assault, as anticipated, had failed.

The city of Jerusalem was one of the great fortresses of the medieval world. The 11th-century walls beneath which the crusaders found themselves followed the same lines as the walls that would be built nearly five centuries later by the Ottoman Sultan, Suleiman the Magnificent.[3] They had been laid out by Emperor Hadrian in around 132, when he had rebuilt the city after its complete destruction by Titus in 70, and had been added to, and improved, by the Byzantines, the Umayyads and, most recently, the Seljuks and the Fatimids. On the east, from where the crusader commanders were once again surveying their prize, the walls were protected by the steep slopes of the ravine of Kedron. To the south-east, the ground fell to the Vale of Gehenna. A third valley, which was only slightly less steep, skirted the western wall. It was only on the south-west, where the wall cut across Mount Sion, and along the length of the northern wall, that the terrain favoured an attack on the fortifications.

The walls themselves were nearly 2½ miles long, and in good condition, with seven major gates. Within the walls were four distinct districts: in the north-west, the Christian Quarter, with the Church of the Holy Sepulchre and the New Gate, which the Fatimid commander assessed as the most likely focus for the main crusader assault; in the north-east quadrant, the Muslim Quarter, including Herod's Gate, with the road running north to Damascus; in the south-east, the Jewish Quarter, encompassing the remains of the great Temple of Herod with the Wailing Wall, the Dome of the Rock and the Al-Aqsa Mosque; and in the south-west, the Armenian Quarter, with the city's citadel, the Tower of David, commanding the road that slanted up the hillside to the Jaffa Gate. Though there were no springs in the city, its ample cisterns assured the defenders a secure water supply.

The defence of the city had been entrusted to the Egyptian Fatimid governor of Palestine, Iftikhar ad-Daula. The Fatimids, as a Shia caliphate, were almost more virulently opposed to the Sunni Abbasid caliphs and their Seljuk Turk sultans than they were to the Orthodox Byzantines and Catholic crusaders. Indeed, the Fatimids had even sent envoys to the crusaders to congratulate them on their taking of Antioch in 1098. However, the opportunity for an accord between the crusaders and the Fatimids had clearly passed, and Iftikhar had now put Jerusalem into a state of defence, while relying on the Fatimid navy to control the coastline and the ports, and summoning a relief force from Egypt, and from the Fatimid garrison of the city of Ascalon. Iftikhar had taken the precaution of blocking or poisoning all the wells outside the city, and of driving the local flocks and herds to places of safety. He had then expelled the whole Christian community. Despite the prohibition on them bearing arms, they represented both an internal threat and a drain on limited resources. The Jews were permitted to remain, as they were as alarmed as the Muslims by the prospect of a crusader victory. They had every right to be so.

Iftikhar had time, and the local conditions, on his side. He also had his personal bodyguard of 400 Nubian[1] cavalrymen with him, in order to reinforce the regular Fatimid garrison. An energetic commander, he had concentrated on bolstering the defences around the New Gate in the north wall, and the citadel of King David. He had had large bales of hay and cotton hung over the walls in order to absorb the strikes of any crusader siege engines and, given the topography of the city, his forces had regularly sallied out to ambush the crusaders' camp and their foraging parties.

Even had the lie of the land permitted it, the crusaders had insufficient forces to invest the whole city. By this stage their army numbered around 1,200 knights, and maybe 10,000 foot soldiers, accompanied by an unknown number of civilian pilgrims. These were the remnants of an overall movement of possibly 100,000 that had set out from various points in Europe in 1096, inspired by Pope Urban II's exhortation to embark on a 'military pilgrimage' to retake Jerusalem. 'On the road' for nearly three years, they had covered over 2,000 miles, mostly on foot. They were driven on by the prospect of reaching the Holy City and returning it to the Christian world. In doing so they had been assured that they would be absolved of all their sins and spared purgatory or, if dying in the attempt, going straight to heaven. Their numbers, both pilgrim and soldier, had dwindled dramatically in the face of death, wounds, disease, hunger and thirst, faint-hearts, and diversions and desertions. Several leaders and their feudal followers had departed when the crusade seemed destined to fail, when they had been trapped between the walls of Antioch and the forces of the Seljuk commander of Mosul, Emir Kerbogha. Indeed, their defeatist message had persuaded Emperor Alexius I Comnenus to abandon his intention to join forces with the crusaders at Antioch, and this decision had further reinforced the distrust between the empire and the western knights. One of Godfrey of Bouillon's brothers, Eustace of Boulogne, was with him at Jerusalem, but their younger sibling, Baldwin of Boulogne, had already established himself in the Armenian fortress town of Edessa, taking with him his own contingent of troops. Baldwin had always planned to take his chances in the east, and the death of his wife and two children on the journey had left him free to make an advantageous marriage to a local Armenian heiress. The County of Edessa was to be the first of the four new Christian states of Syria and Palestine.[5]

Meanwhile, the commander of the Norman forces from Sicily and south Italy, Bohemond of Taranto, now the self-styled Prince of Antioch, had remained in that city after its fall, along with many of his Norman contingent. His landless nephew, Tancred of Hauteville, had continued on to Jerusalem, hopeful of carving out a separate domain for himself in the Holy Land. This latest plan for an assault on Jerusalem was to be the final throw of the dice by the crusaders. This 'divinely inspired', 'papally sanctioned' military pilgrimage would now end either in glory, eternal triumph, and an inspiration for all the ages, or in defeat and ignominy, death, captivity and enslavement.

Conscious of their numbers, the crusaders had had to concentrate their strength, by contingents, on those sectors in the north and south where they could come close to the walls. Duke Robert of Normandy had taken up position along the northern wall opposite Herod's Gate, with Robert of Flanders on his right, opposite the Damascus Gate, where Iftikhar felt the main blow would fall. Godfrey of Bouillon had initially covered the north-west corner of the wall, down to the Jaffa Gate, where he had been joined by Tancred, along with a huge flock of sheep that he had gathered up on his journey from Bethlehem, and which had escaped Iftikhar's scorched earth policy. Count Raymond of Toulouse was, at first, to his right but, after a day or two, he realized that he could not get close enough to the walls to engage the Tower of David, and he had moved to Mount Sion in the south. The eastern and south-eastern sectors were left unguarded, although under observation.

As they stood on the Mount of Olives, the leaders of the crusade were well aware of the stakes. They were an ill-matched group, leading contingents of Normans, Lothringians and Lorrainers,[6] French and Provençals, but they were all members of the professional military classes, from a society where leadership was vested in those whose *raison d'être* was armed conflict. Despite being Christian members of the western European aristocracy, and having shared so many trials and so much success on their long journey to the Holy Land, they were not a 'band of brothers'. Individualism marked out the knightly classes, particularly on the battlefield. These men were jealous of their position in society, quick to anger and quick to take offence. There were no professional armies in western Europe, unlike in the former Roman Empire, or now in the Byzantine Empire. The warrior classes of the west were bound together by the bonds of emergent feudalism, with its understood set of duties, loyalties and obligations, and its collective sense of shame and honour, which elevated the hero and damned the coward. Leadership was personal and visceral. It required kings, princes, counts, dukes and knights to take their place in the 'shield wall', on the battlements of great castles or lonely outposts, in the cavalry charge, or on the scaling ladders alongside those they commanded. Better armed, armoured and trained they may be, but they took an equal share in the shock of battle and combat, and in the chances of wounding or death. The peasants tilled the fields, the merchants moved and traded goods, and the clerics read, wrote and preached, but the warrior class devoted their time to the profession of arms.

Much of this had been inherited from the warrior ethos of the barbarian tribes that had progressively dismantled the Western Roman Empire, but it had then been tempered by their incremental adoption of Christianity. The concept of Christian 'holy war' had gradually been developing over the course of several centuries. It had been driven by a wider ecclesiastical and societal desire to limit violence within Christendom by harnessing and channelling the martial skill and fervour of the warrior classes. In doing so it sought to counter the increasing threats to western society and Christendom from an aggressive and expansionist competing religion – Islam. At the Council of Clermont, Pope Urban II had brought all the building blocks of holy war together in his exhortation to embark on a 'military pilgrimage' to recover the Holy Land, and the City of God.

Count Raymond St Gilles was, by wealth, rank and age, one of the primary leaders of the First Crusade. He had been a close confidant of Pope Urban II, and his early adoption of the cross after Clermont suggests that he already knew what Urban had in mind. Raymond had also been close to the Papal Legate, Bishop Adhemar of Puy,[7] who, despite the fact that he was a cleric, had been nominated by the Pope to be the 'leader' of the expedition, and whose untimely death at Antioch had undermined crusader cohesion. Raymond was already 54 years old at the time of Clermont, and nearly 60 by the time he stood surveying the walls of Jerusalem. This was a considerable age for anyone at this time, and particularly for someone who had already undertaken a succession of military campaigns in Spain, and had undertaken the rigours of the long journey to the Holy Land, including combat, thirst, hunger and disease. He was a profoundly religious man, and one with a deep sense of feudal obligation. Assuming success, he appears to have intended to stay and to end his days in the Holy Land, and he had therefore embarked on this enterprise accompanied by his wife, Elvira of Castile, and their infant son, who had died on the journey.

Raymond had fought in the battle of Dorylaeum[8] and in the early stages of the siege of Antioch, but he had been incapacitated by disease for the confrontation with Kerbogha. Rich, with high feudal status, and accompanied by a large Provençal contingent, he would have hoped to have been de facto temporal leader of the crusade, but he was aloof, his manner was condescending, and his relationship with the other commanders was strained. At one stage in his fractious relationship with Bohemond of Taranto, he had attempted to bribe the other leaders to support his own cause, which had further muddied the waters of their collective effort.

Duke Robert of Normandy was the eldest son of William the Conqueror, known by the slightly disparaging nickname Curthose, or 'short stockings'. Born in 1051, he was in his mid-40s when he took up his post opposite the Damascus Gate of Jerusalem. He had had a combative relationship with his father – once unhorsing him in a skirmish – and with his two younger brothers, William Rufus and Henry, who both inherited the crown of England. His grandfather, Duke Robert the Magnificent, had made an earlier pilgrimage to Jerusalem in 1035, dying on his return journey. Impetuous and easy to anger, and with questionable political judgement, he was, nevertheless, a man of proven courage and military skill. To participate in the crusade, he had mortgaged his duchy to his brother William Rufus for 10,000 marks. He had set off for Italy with his brother-in-law, Stephen of Blois, a reluctant crusader, who was married to Robert's sister, the diminutive but fiery Adela, with whom he had had 11 children. Going via the Norman holdings in southern Italy, Duke Robert had fallen in love with Sybil of Conversano. A bachelor, he was as committed to the cause as any other crusader and had more than proved his worth in the field, but he had no intention of making Palestine his home. Stephen of Blois, by contrast, had been one of those who had given up hope before the walls of Antioch, and had departed back to Normandy. Their fellow commander, Count Robert of Flanders, had been only 30 years old when he had departed for the Holy Land, leaving his lands in the hands of his wife, Clementia of Burgundy. He was an altogether more formidable personality than the Duke. He had supported Bohemond at Antioch, and then had transferred his support to Godfrey when they marched on Jerusalem.

The last of the great leaders of the First Crusade, and the best known to history, was Godfrey of Bouillon. Disappointed by his domestic circumstances, he had responded enthusiastically to Urban's call to go east, and had meticulously prepared for his departure, raising money, and with it a large contingent of Lothringians and Lorrainers, by blackmailing the local Jewish community, selling estates, and pledging his castle to the Bishop of Liège. Another bachelor, Godfrey was in his mid-30s, and he was described as tall, well built and fair, with a yellow beard and hair, and 'pleasant manners'. Courageous as a warrior, he was an indifferent military commander, and he demonstrated a 'thin skin' that coloured his judgement when criticized. It was in Jerusalem that the legend of Godfrey of Bouillon was born, but the crusaders still had to get over the walls.

Via word of mouth, via the bonds of feudalism that bound society, and through the pulpits of the church, the news of the Pope's call to arms at Clermont had spread widely and rapidly, and people of the highest and the meanest social stature had surged forward to take the cross. Motivations varied, but modern attitudes should not let us lightly dismiss the sincerity of those who embarked on this extraordinary endeavour, or of their courage. By the time the great secular lords – now standing outside the walls of Jerusalem, or ensconced in Edessa and Antioch – had set their affairs in order, marshalled their vassals and made provision for a major military expedition to the east, a vast mass of common folk and peasants had already departed. They were led by a rabble-rousing cleric known as Peter the Hermit. Attacking Jewish communities along the route, and pillaging as they went, they had passed through the Kingdom of Hungary, across the River Danube, and into the western lands of the Byzantine Empire, unwanted and unappreciated. Arriving outside the massive gates of Constantinople, this vast, spontaneous manifestation of religious fervour, poorly led, quarrelsome, predatory, and wholly without military utility, was the last thing Emperor Alexius had wanted. With great tact and generosity, he had them shipped across the Bosporus to the Asiatic side, advising them to wait for the arrival of their great lords. Convinced of the righteousness of their cause, confident of divine protection, and also motivated by a less worthy appetite for booty and plunder, the pilgrims had ignored his advice, advanced into Anatolia, and had been duly massacred by the Seljuks. Peter the Hermit returned to Constantinople, a sadder, but not a much wiser, figure.

Around the end of 1096, Count Raymond, Duke and Count Robert, Bohemond, Tancred and Godfrey had all arrived at the court of the Emperor, while their truculent contingents camped outside the walls. Once again, with great tact accompanied by great generosity, the Emperor elicited reluctant oaths of allegiance from the Frank, Flemish, Norman and Provençal barons, whereby all former Byzantine lands and fortresses would be returned to the empire, in return for imperial support. Rapidly, the crusader forces had crossed into Anatolia, marched past the rotting remains of the Pilgrims' Crusade, besieged and taken the city of Nicaea, and roundly defeated the Seljuks of Kilij Arslan after the close-run battle of Dorylaeum.

In October 1097, the crusader forces had stood before the great city of Antioch, lost by the Byzantines to the Seljuks a decade earlier. Baldwin of Boulogne had already departed to seek his fortune at Edessa, and tension and competition between the other crusader lords was only kept in check by the tact and impressive sagacity of Bishop Adhemar. The crusaders were poorly equipped for a deliberate siege, and painfully conscious that their progress must soon provoke some form of counter-response from the Saracens. However, in the late 11th century that potential Muslim response was fractured and incoherent. Although they had been dismissed, the Shia Fatimids of Cairo had actually sent emissaries to the crusader camp to discuss a potential division of spoils in Syria and Palestine. The Seljuks themselves were confronted by threats from several directions, and their reputation had already been badly damaged by crusader successes in Anatolia. Meanwhile, the rich and powerful cities of Damascus, Aleppo and Mosul viewed each other with as much suspicion as they did the crusader army. However, disciplinary problems, fragile morale, enemy action, disease, desertion and food shortages had all threatened to conspire against Christian success. In their despondency, the crusaders accepted Bohemond's proposal that whoever secured the city of Antioch would keep it, unaware that the wily Norman had already been in correspondence with a disillusioned Armenian Christian within the walls, who was prepared to betray his Seljuk masters. Just the day before Bohemond pulled off his coup de main, convinced the crusading enterprise was doomed, Stephen of Blois, and several others, had given up hope and ridden away. It was to everyone's misfortune that his path home crossed that of Emperor Alexius, marching south to fulfil his own commitment to the joint crusading endeavour. Insecure in his own realm,

Stephen's premature tale of defeat and failure convinced Alexius to cut his losses and retreat. In due course this would be interpreted by the Franks as a betrayal that absolved them of their own obligations to the empire. Mistrust and antagonism between Frank and Greek, and Catholic and Orthodox, would consistently undermine a united Christian front against the armies of Islam. Across the years, worse was to follow.

The taking and sack of Antioch and its citadel had raised crusader morale, as had the defeat of two major Muslim relief armies, the second only after a Peter Bartholomew had 'miraculously discovered' the lance that had pierced Christ's side at the crucifixion. However, this falling-out with the Byzantine Empire, and the untimely death of Bishop Adhémar from typhus not long after these successes, had long-term implications for both the foundation and the longevity of the crusader states.

Although Antioch had been secured by the defeat of Kerbogha's relief force in June 1098, the crusader army had not moved against Jerusalem until January 1099, and only under compulsion from those soldiers and pilgrims who threatened to continue to the Holy City without their leaders, if those leaders could not contain their mutual antagonisms and jealousies. Thus it was that, after delays, diversions, skirmishes and squabbles, the crusader army had appeared before the walls of Jerusalem in early June, and had settled down to besiege the city.

As a result of the failed assault on 12 June, the crusader leaders had determined that they would not launch another attempt on the walls until they had assembled sufficient siege machines and ladders. By chance, on 17 June, a small flotilla of Genoese and English ships had docked in a deserted Jaffa harbour. They were carrying food supplies and armaments, including the ropes, nails and bolts required for making those vital engines of war. The contingent, sent to escort these valuable assets across the 40 miles to Jerusalem, was itself ambushed and only just survived the encounter. Meanwhile, Fatimid warships now blockaded Jaffa, and the decision was taken to dismantle the ships for their timbers, while other timber was brought in from Samaria. Dozens of scaling ladders were made, and a battering ram, while both Raymond and Godfrey constructed siege towers to be used against the north and the south walls. Gaston of Béarn coordinated the construction work. Despite the parlous situation regarding water and food, lack of wood, and the mind-numbing, energy-sapping effect of several days of the *sirocco* wind, this new sense of purpose restored unity to the leadership. This was helpful, as the barons were already threatening to fall out over issues of land rights, the status of Jerusalem and Bethlehem, and the governance of any future kingdom. It also inspired new confidence in the soldiers and in the pilgrims, despite many having deserted in the weeks since their arrival at the city.

The siege engines were being assembled well away from the sight of the Fatimid garrison on the walls of Jerusalem, and they were protected by a screen of sentries to ensure the security of the work. Large, and cumbersome to manoeuvre, these towers were several stories high, designed to top the walls of the city and to allow soldiers to make the hazardous crossing onto the ramparts. Once there, they had to hope that they could take and hold a precarious position long enough for their compatriots to add their weight and numbers to their efforts. At that stage, they would use their armour and greater strength to gradually push the defenders back to the towers, until they could descend into the city and force open the gates. They had breached the walls of Antioch by deception, and the fighting in the city had still been intense and bloody. Here they would have to fight for the walls. The Fatimids were expecting their assault, and both sides knew what the brutal consequences of failure would be.

On 6 July, Father Peter Desiderius, who had been a close follower of Bishop Adhemar, and who had claimed to have seen him after his death in Antioch, came to Adhemar's brother, William Hugh of Monteil, and told him that the bishop had appeared to him again. In this dream, Adhemar had once again urged the crusader leadership to stop their selfish squabbling, and their pursuit of personal agendas, and he had directed the rank and file to live lives appropriate to Christians and pilgrims. He had ordered the army to fast, and to walk, barefoot, in penance around the walls of Jerusalem. If they did so, with repentant hearts, within nine days they would take the city. The vision was at once accepted as genuine by the whole army, and Adhemar's reported instructions were eagerly obeyed. Despite their own poor state of health, and the crushing weather conditions, a fast was ordered and steadfastly observed for three days. Prostitutes and sundry hangers-on were cleared from the camp, and a startling climate of silence, calm and piety descended on the crusader host. On Friday 8 July, a solemn procession wound around the path that circled Jerusalem. The bishops and priests of the crusade went first, bearing crosses and holy relics. The princes and knights followed, then the men-at-arms, foot soldiers and pilgrims. All were barefoot. The garrison troops were both intrigued and mocking, but the procession walked on, making for the Mount of Olives. Here the spiritual leaders of Urban's great military pilgrimage preached to the army and exhorted them to fulfil their crusader vows by taking the Heavenly City for the glory of God. The response was universally positive.

This enthusiasm was sustained over the next days as they worked to complete the siege towers, including putting catapults on the top decks, in order to help try to clear the ramparts. In this work the non-combatants did their part in sewing ox hide and camel skins onto the vulnerable sections of the woodwork, as protection against fire. On 10 July the siege engines had at last been exposed, one in the south opposite St Sion, and the other to the north in front of the New Gate in the north-west corner. This came as a shock to Iftikhar and his garrison, who had been expecting the arrival of the Fatimid relief force imminently. They needed no educating about what a threat these engines of war posed to the defenders. They immediately started to bombard them with their own catapults in order to try to destroy them, or at least to keep them away from the walls. Given it now seemed obvious where the crusaders would attack, Iftikhar moved to strengthen further the defences in those sectors, and to manage a growing sense of panic in the city. The rules of war at this time were too well known for anyone to have illusions about what fate awaited the inhabitants of a city that had dismissed the opportunity to surrender, and who had then failed to keep the besieging force out.

In this last council of war, up on the Mount of Olives, the crusader leaders now determined that the decisive assault would begin on the night of 13 July, and that, in an attempt to stretch the defence, it would be launched simultaneously by Count Raymond from St Sion, and by Godfrey, Robert of Normandy and Robert of Flanders on the northern wall. This would involve both assault parties filling in the defensive ditches, while under intense fire, and then moving the siege towers to the walls while attempting to stop them being shattered by catapult fire or set alight. If all this could be achieved, brave individuals would then have to face a hail of arrows, swords, axes and stones in order to cross a narrow wooden bridge to engage in hand-to-hand fighting on the ramparts. They would be trusting their fellow soldiers to be piling-in behind them. Godfrey now also intended to add to the defenders' confusion by shifting his siege tower to the east. It was currently facing the New Gate, where Iftikhar expected an assault, and Godfrey would now roll it, as soon as night fell, to face the Fatimid defenders of Herod's Gate.

With gaunt, determined faces, the commanders shook hands and received a blessing from the assembled priests. They then called in the security screen, sent out to ensure against ambush or assassination, and, gathering up their closest followers and the squires who stood close by holding their helmets and swords, they made their way back to their contingents.

At last, late in the night of 13 July, on a prearranged signal, the crusaders and all able-bodied men closed in on the walls to try to fill in the ditches. Hails of arrows flew upwards to help clear the ramparts of defenders, while mangonels and catapults bucked and reared, attempting to smash down walls and gates, while sowing panic within the city itself. For their part, the Fatimids replied with a similar hail of arrows and missiles, aiming to disrupt the crusader attacks. Both sides were conscious that the next 24 hours would be critical. All night, and for all of the following day, the battle hung in the balance. By the evening of the 14th, Raymond's men had succeeded in wheeling their tower over the ditch and up to the walls. However, the defence here was fierce, and it seems that it was here that Iftikhar had chosen to command during the fight.

By nightfall on 14 July, both attackers and defenders were exhausted. The crusaders had so far failed to breach the walls, but the defenders had failed to destroy the siege towers, despite their very best efforts. At one stage the attackers' own battering ram had got between Godfrey's siege tower and the wall. The crusaders had then found themselves in the unusual position of trying to burn their own siege machine, while the Fatimid garrison poured water on it to try to maintain it as an obstacle. In due course the crusaders succeeded, and the smoking ashes were still there when, on the morning of the 15th, Godfrey's tower closed in on the north wall, again near Herod's Gate. He had ordered it pulled back during the night, when it was clear the assault was faltering, in order to ensure its safety. Now his soldiers and followers prepared to drive it forward again, against the fortifications. Godfrey and his brother Eustace, both armed with crossbows, scaled the tower, in order to command the assault from the top storey. Their Lorrainers filed in behind them, filling the tower from top to bottom, and the Normans of Robert and Tancred closed up behind the structure, in order to add their strength to pushing the tower, and to be able to rush up the ladders and reinforce any success on the walls. Robert of Flanders held his own troops in reserve. If the ramparts could be taken, and a gate in the great walls of Jerusalem opened, then the crusaders would need numbers on the ground, inside the city, rapidly.

The waves of arrows and rocks rose again as the crusaders closed the distance to the walls. The morning sun was already hot. Faces were grim, as tense eyes looked past the nose-guards of helmets, and perspiration fell from nervous brows. Sweaty hands grasped swords, shields and axes. There was little light inside the tower, and the atmosphere was close and fetid. The soldiers could hear the commands of Godfrey and Eustace, filtering down from above, and they could feel the impact of stones and arrows on the wood and hide of the tower. They were all veterans of Dorylaeum, Antioch and the other battles and skirmishes on the long road to Jerusalem, but combat in the open was one thing; being caught in a burning wooden structure would be quite another.

Raymond, meanwhile, was keeping up pressure on the southern wall, and the proximity of his threat stopped Iftikhar shifting anyone to the northern wall. At last, at around midday, Godfrey's tower got close enough to the walls for a plank to be thrust out and rested on Jerusalem's battlements. In an instant, Litold and Gilbert of Tournai, two Flemish brothers and knights, advanced across the narrow gap, as archers strove to clear the walls on either side, and they leapt down onto the shallow ramparts. Standing back to back, legs braced, shields held close, they pushed the Muslims back. The Lorrainers surged forward behind them. Suddenly there was room on the ladders, and knights and men-at-arms, confined in suffocating heat for hours, moved swiftly up the tower, as the Normans charged in behind them. No one, attacker or defender, could be unaware of how critical this moment was. As the attackers pushed outwards along the wall, and towards the towers and access to the city, more and more scaling ladders were put up against the walls, and more and more crusaders clambered through the crenelations to join their comrades.

The ramparts were now slippery with blood, and the defenders found themselves crushed back on each other, unable to wield their weapons, and looking over their shoulders for a way of escape. Most were Egyptians and Nubians with little desire to die for Jerusalem, and the local garrison were poorly trained and equipped, with houses and families in the narrow streets and squares of the city. Godfrey continued to direct the battle on the northern wall from his vantage point on top of the tower, yelling encouragement and orders above the cacophony of battle. Success was looking greater on his right, and so he sent reinforcements there, with his brother and Tancred, to open the Damascus Gate in order to admit the bulk of the crusader forces who still stood anxiously outside the walls. Forming a shield wall across every road to stop the defenders cutting off the small numbers now inside the city wall, the Lorrainers and Normans cut down the gate guard and, stumbling over the corpses, removed the great timber crossbar, and pulled open the impressive double gates.

As the gates of the Damascus Tower, the oldest in Jerusalem, fell open, with a mighty cry those outside surged forward and poured into the city. The Muslims, seeing that their defences had been broken, fled before them, hoping to claim some sanctuary on the Temple Mount, and to turn the Dome of the Rock and the Al-Aqsa Mosque into some form of fortress, but they had not anticipated a crusader irruption into the city, and there was now no time to put a defence plan in place. Tancred was too close behind them and, as they crowded in and up on the roof, he was upon them. As cries, screams and wails arose from

The Siege of Jerusalem: Final Assault, 13–15 July 1099

Crusader forces
A. Godfrey of Bouillon, 13–15 July
B. Tancred, 13–15 July
C. Robert of Normandy & Robert of Flanders, 13–15 July
D. Raymond of Toulouse, 13–15 July
E. Raymond of Toulouse's siege tower
F. Godfrey of Bouillon's siege tower, 13–15 July

Fatimid forces
1. Iftikhar ad-Daula's first HQ
2. Iftikhar ad-Daula's HQ in St David's Citadel
3. Fatimid garrison & Jerusalem militia, 13–15 July
4. Fatimid mangonels

Mount of Olives

Damascus Gate

JEWISH QUARTER

CHRISTIAN QUARTER

Church of the Holy Sepulchre

Dome of the Rock

Jaffa Gate

St David's Citadel

MUSLIM QUARTER

Al-Aqsa Mosque

ARMENIAN QUARTER

Sion Gate

1. 13–15 July: The Crusaders launch their final assault on the northern wall.
2. 15 July: The Crusaders break through the northern defences and begin massacring the Jewish and Muslim population of the city.
3. 15 July: Fatimid troops defending the southern wall withdraw to St David's Citadel. Raymond of Toulouse's men break in to the city and accept Iftikhar's surrender and safe passage.
4. 15–16 July: Crusaders massacre defenders and civilians on the Temple Mount.

N

0   300yds
0   300m

all parts of the city, the Temple Mount was filled with the sound of weapons being flung to the ground, as the garrison troops surrendered to him, promising a large ransom if their lives were spared. Tancred's banner was hastily taken to the roof of the mosque and flown there in the hope that it would offer some protection.

Meanwhile, the crusaders had been driving all before them and, despite some sporadic and brave rear-guard action by the Fatimids, the population of Jerusalem was either killed on the spot or driven to the southern Jewish and Armenian quarters, where Iftikhar was still holding out against Raymond's frenzied attempts to get onto the walls, and into the city. He had been receiving regular reports throughout the last days, but during the course of the 15th he had become increasingly aware that the battle was going against him. The collective cry that went up as the Damascus Gate was breached was enough to tell him that the defences had failed. With the bulk of his Nubian bodyguard, he withdrew inside the citadel of the Tower of David, and prepared to conduct a robust defence, if required. He knew that the Fatimid relief column was on its way, and that history was littered with examples of cities and towns that had fallen but where a stoutly held citadel had been able to hold out until fortunes had changed; but his nerves were shattered by the siege, and by the fall of the city.

With Iftikhar's withdrawal, resistance in the south had collapsed and Raymond's Provençals had made it over the walls and through the St Sion Gate. Iftikhar sent out an emissary to offer to hand the citadel over to Raymond, in return for a great sum of treasure, the lives of himself and his bodyguard, and safe passage to the Fatimid fortress of Ascalon, 50 miles away on the coast. Raymond agreed, and by mid-afternoon he had occupied the citadel. With the horrendous sounds of the sack of the city rising up around them, and the acrid smell of blood and burning houses assailing every nostril, Iftikhar and his men formed up and were escorted out of the St Sion Gate, passing Raymond's battered and smoking siege tower. They were the only Muslims in Jerusalem to save their lives.

While this episode of relative discipline and dignity was taking place in the south-west corner of the city, elsewhere the crusaders, maddened by such a great victory after so much suffering, rushed through the streets and into the houses, shops and mosques, killing all they met – men, women and children. They knew there were no Christians left in Jerusalem, so everyone they encountered was treated as an enemy. All that afternoon, and well into the night, the massacre continued, and neither commanders nor clergy could control the barbarism, even had they wished to. Tancred's banner had proved no protection to those refugees in the Al-Aqsa Mosque, where systematic butchery had taken place the following morning. The Jews had fled as a body to their chief synagogue, pleading for mercy and offering a ransom to be spared, but to a virulent anti-Semitism among many of the crusaders was added an assumption that they had aided the Muslims, and the building was set on fire, killing all within.

The massacre at Jerusalem profoundly impressed the world. It is impossible to say how many victims were involved, but it emptied the city of its Muslim and Jewish inhabitants. It was not just another example of the routine barbarism of the time, which was occasionally mitigated by an appeal to Christian and chivalric values. It was of a scale and significance, particularly within the walls of the City of God, that horrified many Christians, even those who had participated in the hysteria, avarice and bloodlust. The Byzantines, whose religious squeamishness when it came to conflict, war and killing, the Franks had never understood, or empathized with, were shocked. In their opinion, like that of Bishop and Prince Talleyrand Perigord, many centuries later, it was a horrific crime, but worse than that, it was a mistake. The unlikely success of the First Crusade had largely been based on the divisions, and on the personal and confessional in-fighting of the Muslim world at that time. It is often a truism that in matters of religion the heretic is seen as more dangerous, and more of an existential challenge, than the infidel.

Despite the significance of Jerusalem, many Muslims had hitherto been prepared to accept the Franks as, up to a point, yet another factor in the tangled and complex politics of the region. Like the Byzantines, the Franks might be, indeed had been, employed in the incessant balance-of-power struggles that characterized the region. After news of the taking of Jerusalem, there slowly developed a clear determination that the Franks must be driven out, and that long-term coexistence was impossible. This bloodthirsty proof of Christian fanaticism would, in time, be used to help generate an equally bloodthirsty Islamic response. Tactical accommodation with the infidel would be a fact of life in the complexity of relations between Muslim Turks, Egyptians, Arabs, Sunni and Shia, but when later, wiser Latins in the east sought to find some basis on which Muslim and Christian could work together, the memory of the Jerusalem massacre was always in the background.

With no more Muslims or Jews to slay, the crusade leaders went through the deserted Christian Quarter to the Church of the Holy Sepulchre in order to give thanks for this great victory and this extraordinary climax to an enterprise that had begun with the words and exhortation of Urban II at Clermont in 1095. On 29 July, two weeks after the crusaders had forced the Damascus Gate, but before the news of the taking of Jerusalem had reached him, Urban II had died. On 17 July, the leaders met again to address some serious administrative issues, not least the clearance of bodies from streets and houses in the middle of summer, the quartering of soldiers and pilgrims, the distribution of plunder, and the preparations to counter the Fatimid relief column that was still expected imminently. In addition, despite the religious nature of the enterprise, the issue of a ruler for Jerusalem was now raised.

The man they would most have welcomed, Bishop Adhemar, was dead. Given his extraordinary dominance throughout the whole crusade, it seemed unbelievable that he had not been there to witness the culmination of this mighty military pilgrimage, although soldier after soldier testified that they had seen him in the forefront of the fighting. His death was a blow on many levels, given his authority, his understanding of Urban's ambitions, and his administrative genius. He would probably have envisaged an ecclesiastical state, under a patriarch, with himself as papal legate in an advisory role, and with his friend and senior leader, Raymond of Toulouse, as lay protector and commander of the army. That was not now to be, and the question of a king arose.

By all rights Raymond had the greatest claim to be considered for such a position and role. By age, piety, wealth and commitment, he was the premier candidate, but he was neither liked nor trusted by his fellow crusader leaders, and his Provençals were outnumbered by the Normans, Lorrainers and those knights from Flanders. Eustace of Boulogne had always played a shadowy role behind his brother Godfrey, and Tancred had few followers, and was seen as little more than a poor relation of his uncle, Bohemond. Duke Robert of Normandy and Count Robert of Flanders were both well regarded, but both had made it clear that their crusading vows were now complete, and that they wished to return to their lands in Europe. This left Godfrey, gallant enough, and prominent in the taking of Jerusalem, but whose statesmanship and administrative skills were unknown. When Raymond turned down a half-hearted offer for him to be king, Godfrey agreed to be 'Defender of the Holy Sepulchre', asking to be excused from accepting the title of king, for 'no man should wear a crown of gold in the city where the Son of God had worn a crown of thorns'. No one was particularly satisfied by this outcome, least of all Raymond, and Godfrey somehow fell out with the other princes. Only the reality of the Fatimid army at last approaching Ascalon convinced the crusader leaders that they were in danger of losing all they had achieved, and they hurried to bring their contingents to join Godfrey, who had already gone to Ramleh.

On 12 August, the combined crusader army surprised the Fatimid commander outside the gates of Ascalon. Like the well-drilled team that they were, Raymond took up the right flank, the two Roberts the centre, and Godfrey the left. With a minimum of discussion or orders, they advanced at speed and within minutes had the opposing army fleeing, leaving behind mountains of booty, by anybody's standards. This battle, seen as the last of the First Crusade, could have now been crowned with the success of taking the fortress of Ascalon, a vital junction point between Egypt and Palestine. The Muslim garrison knew they could not resist the combined crusader army and had no wish to suffer the fate of Jerusalem, but they knew from Iftikhar that the only survivors had been those who had surrendered to Raymond, and they therefore sent an emissary saying they would give up the city to him alone. Godfrey, suspicious of Count Raymond, and slighted by this perceived slur on his piety and chivalry, petulantly refused these terms, at which point Raymond and the two Roberts, angry and shocked by Godfrey's pettiness, withdrew from the field. Godfrey could neither get them to return, nor could he take the town on his own, and thereby Ascalon was lost to the Franks for more than a further half-century.

Godfrey would not last long as 'Defender', dying almost exactly a year after the taking of Jerusalem, and being buried in the Church of the Holy Sepulchre. This was a dangerous time for the crusaders. Godfrey had never married, so those nobles who had remained in the Holy Land after their crusading vows had been discharged turned to his brother, Baldwin of Edessa, to come to Jerusalem to be crowned King. Bohemond of Antioch wanted to contest his succession but, fatally to his cause, had been taken prisoner by the Saracens while on a raiding expedition. Baldwin proved to be a wise choice, and as King Baldwin I he was a diligent, competent and successful monarch until his own death in 1118, when he was succeeded by his cousin, Baldwin of le Bourcq, who had earlier succeeded him as ruler of the County of Edessa.[9]

Raymond, who had always intended to remain in the east, had mixed fortunes. After the failed siege of Ascalon, he had returned to Constantinople where he allied himself with Emperor Alexius against his former ally and rival, Bohemond. He took part in the doomed expeditions of 1101, where the attempts by a further wave of crusading enthusiasts to capitalize on the success of the First Crusade foundered miserably in the wastes of Anatolia. After the capture and imprisonment of Bohemond, Raymond had then returned to Antioch, to be imprisoned, in his turn, by another old fighting colleague, Tancred of Galilee. He would spend the last years of his life trying to establish the County of Tripoli, dying in early 1105. It would fall to his nephew finally to take the city of Tripoli from the Fatimids in 1109.

Robert, Duke of Normandy, travelled slowly back to his duchy, via Constantinople, where Alexius showered him with gifts and an offer of service in the imperial army, and then to Italy, where he married Sybil of Conversano. This delay ensured that he was still some way from home when his brother William Rufus was killed in mid-1100 and his other younger sibling seized the English throne as Henry I. Robert invaded England, but found little support there, and in 1106 Henry repaid the compliment and invaded Normandy. He took it for the English crown, until it was lost again in 1204 during the reign of 'Bad' King John.

Duke Robert was captured, and he was imprisoned for over 25 years. He died in Cardiff Castle in 1134. He was over 80.

His brother-in-law, Stephen of Blois, fared worse. After his desertion and betrayal at Antioch, the failure to fulfil his crusading vows, and his dismal role in breaking the imperial–crusader alliance, he returned to Normandy and to the wrath and contempt of his wife, Adela. He was shamed and pressurized into joining the abortive crusade of 1101, fighting alongside Raymond, failing to rescue Bohemond, and only reaching Jerusalem in early 1102. Christian failure had re-energized the Muslim world after the successes of the First Crusade, and had damaged the image of crusader invincibility. Now returning home, Stephen's ship was blown back onto the Palestinian coast, where King Baldwin was on hand to persuade him to take part in an expedition against a local Fatimid force. Stephen recommended caution and reconnaissance, but his reputation stood against him, and the crusaders blundered into an army far larger than they had anticipated. Baldwin, a good king and soldier but, at the best of times, with a questionable sense of honour, escaped, but Stephen fought on, was captured, and was executed in Ascalon, his honour finally redeemed.

Count Robert of Flanders also returned home via Constantinople, bringing back with him a precious relic: the arm, shoulder and ribs of St George. In 1105, in one of those sadly routine squalid aristocratic skirmishes that Pope Urban had so eloquently preached against at Clermont, he was trampled to death by his horse.

So began a Christian military occupation of Palestine and large swathes of coastal Syria, which would last, on and off, expanding and contracting, faltering and recovering, inspiring and provoking frustration and despair, for nearly two centuries. The County of Edessa, the Principality of Antioch, the County of Tripoli and the Kingdom of Jerusalem would always be in a state of precarious security. They would dominate the coastline and its ports, they would erect stunning examples of military architecture, and they would nurture the development of the 'shock troops' of the kingdom: the Knights of the Temple and the Knights of the Hospital. However, they would never have enough manpower; they would always be in a state of uneasy truce, often antagonism, with each other and with their fellow Christians of the Orthodox Byzantine Empire; and their feudal model would not provide enough unity or cohesion against the potential threat from a unified Muslim world. In 1187, at the Horns of Hattin, in the face of the armies of the great Muslim warlord, Saladin, who had by now marshalled the combined resources of Baghdad, Damascus and Cairo, these crusader weaknesses would be decisively exposed, and Jerusalem lost again.

3

Disaster at the Horns

Hattin 1187

Sepphoris lies around 15 miles from the fortress port of Acre, about the same distance from the town of Tiberias on the Sea of Galilee, and 3 miles north of the village of Nazareth. Mary, the mother of Jesus Christ, may have lived nearby, and her husband Joseph, and Jesus himself, almost certainly plied their trade as carpenters there, among the rich and ambitious citizens of this prosperous town. Sepphoris had been built astride the major trade route from Egypt to Damascus. It was already a strongly fortified city in 100 BC, and King Herod had a palace there at the time of Christ's ministry. At the time of the great Jewish Revolt of 70, the town chose to side with the Romans and was spared the destruction meted on Jerusalem and other towns in Palestine. Rising about a thousand feet above the surrounding valleys, it was the source of several significant freshwater springs. Sepphoris had been taken by the Muslims in the early years of their expansion in the sixth century, but the town had already changed hands several times during the crusader period, during which time the Franks built a fort and watchtower, and a church dedicated to St Anne, the mother of the Virgin Mary.

During the long summer days of early July 1187, when the midday temperatures hovered around 40 degrees centigrade, the army of the Kingdom of Jerusalem had moved from their temporary base outside Acre and began to assemble around the town of Sepphoris and its springs.

Totalling around 15,000 men, there were knights and men-at-arms from all the major towns, garrisons, castles and forts of the kingdom, including many from the County of Tripoli and the Principality of Antioch, who set up their tents and awaited orders.[1] There were also contingents from the great papal military orders of the Knights of the Temple and the Knights of the Hospital of St John, although not as many as there might have been before the catastrophe at the Springs of Cresson two months earlier, where a reckless charge against a much larger Saracen[2] force had decimated their ranks. The participation of the military orders had been heavily subsidized by money from King Henry II of England, raised and sent to the Holy Land as contrition for the murder of Archbishop Thomas Beckett. Also there were almost every significant military leader in the Holy Land, including King Guy of Jerusalem himself.

Guy of Lusignan[3] had succeeded his young step-son, King Baldwin V, who had died in the fortress of Acre in August of the previous year, at the age of nine. Under the provisions of the will of his uncle, the 'Leper King', Baldwin IV, if the young king died before his tenth birthday, then his guardian, and the regent of the kingdom, Count Raymond III of Tripoli, would remain as regent until a council of the Pope, the Byzantine Emperor, and the kings of France and England could determine the succession. The tragic King Baldwin IV had, rightly, little faith in the good-looking but feckless French nobleman who had married his sister, Sybilla, in 1180 and had already removed Guy once before as regent and potential successor. However, on the death of the infant king, Count Raymond and his supporters had been outmanoeuvred by their opponents in Jerusalem, and Guy had taken the throne. Now, with the great Salah ad-Din bin Yousef bin Ayyub, better known in the west as Saladin, bringing a major army into crusader lands, old rivalries had to be put aside, and old opponents come together, in the face of a serious threat to the continuing Christian presence in the Holy Land, and to Christian control of the Holy City of Jerusalem.

So, Count Raymond III of Tripoli was there. Around 45 years old, he was a highly experienced warrior. Described as tall and thin, with dark hair and dark skin, his face was apparently dominated by a large nose. He was seen as cold, self-controlled and a little ungenerous. He was a minor when his father had been murdered by the Assassins,[4] and he had spent his early years at the royal court in Jerusalem. He had taken part in campaigns against the Saracens, but he had also conducted operations against the Byzantine Emperor, Manuel I Comnenus, who had earlier refused to marry his sister, Melisande.[5] Like many crusader nobles, he had been taken captive in the aftermath of a military defeat and had spent ten years in captivity,[6] while the King of Jerusalem had administered the County of Tripoli on his behalf. In prison he had read widely, studied Islam and learnt Arabic. He had eventually been ransomed for a huge sum of money, borrowed off the Knights Hospitaller, but marriage to the widowed Eschiva of Bures had subsequently made him one of the richest nobles in Outremer. His rivalry with Guy stretched back nearly a decade, and he had not only refused to do homage to the new king, but he had an ongoing truce with Saladin, which included his wife's lands around Tiberias. Court gossip insinuated that his alliance with Saladin included an agreement to place Raymond on the throne.

Reginald of Chatillon was also at Sepphoris. He was a close ally of King Guy and, arguably, a major cause of the current crisis in the kingdom, with his routine and brazen breaches of the periodic truces the crusaders had with the Saracens. He was deeply loathed and distrusted by Count Raymond. Having lost land in France, Reginald had arrived in the Holy Land with the Second Crusade, launched in the wake of the loss of the County of Edessa in 1144. He had remained in Palestine and had become a mercenary with the royal army. To the dismay of her subjects, he then married Constance, Princess of Antioch, and proceeded to beggar the principality with his need for money. In his pursuit of funds, he had even taken captive the Patriarch of Antioch, and tortured him by covering the cleric in honey and leaving him out for the insects in the midday sun. He subsequently launched a raid of astonishing brutality on the island of Cyprus, then an imperial possession. In due course he had no option but to prostrate himself before the Byzantine Emperor and beg for mercy.[7] In 1160 he had been taken prisoner by the governor of Aleppo, and he had spent 16 years in captivity awaiting ransom, or prisoner exchange. Unlike Raymond, this experience had only served to harden his dislike of Islam and the Saracens.

By the time of his release in 1176, and in the face of the ever-growing threat from an increasingly united Muslim world, two distinctive parties were forming in Outremer.[8] One grouping was composed of most of the native-born barons, now third- or fourth-generation Franks in the Holy Land, also known as the *poulains*, and the Knights Hospitaller, who broadly had followed the leadership of Count Raymond of Tripoli in the succession rivalry. They were conscious of the fundamental military and economic weaknesses of the crusader states, and often sought an understanding and an accommodation with their foreign neighbours, be they Muslim, Armenian or Byzantine. They were increasingly reluctant to embark on risky adventures.

The other party comprised many of the 'newcomers' from the west, and the Knights Templar. This party was characterized by a more aggressive and militant Christianity, which demanded that crusaders maintain a holy war against the Saracen infidels and also against 'heretics', which included many of the minority Christian sects in the Levant. Reginald, an uncompromising and rapacious militant, had soon become a key leader of this faction. His wife, Constance of Antioch, had died while he had been held in captivity, but his position had been enhanced when he had married Stephanie of Milly, the wealthy heiress of Jordan. This marriage had given him control of the crucial southern fortress of Kerak of the Moab, putting him astride the major caravan routes between Egypt and Syria. His routine attacks on these caravans, truce or not, and his sponsorship of a marauding fleet in the Red Sea, threatening the Muslim pilgrim routes to Mecca and Medina, had made his enmity with Saladin very personal.

Gerard of Ridefort, Grand Master of the Knights Templar, was another powerful supporter of King Guy and Reginald, and an equally committed member of the 'war party'. A Flemish knight, he had arrived in Outremer in the 1170s and had taken service with Count Raymond of Tripoli. The story had it that he had been promised the hand of the first suitable heiress in the County of Tripoli, but when Cecile Dorel inherited her father's coastal fief of Botrun some months later, Raymond had ignored his claim and gave her to a rich Pisan called Plivano, who, it was reported, had ungallantly placed her on weighing scales and offered the Count her weight in gold. Gerard, angry and disappointed, had joined the Order of the Temple, and soon became one of its most influential members and, in due course its Seneschal and Marshal. He had never forgiven Raymond, and when Raymond had been outwitted over the election of Guy as king, had been overheard to say, 'That pays for Botrun.' A recklessly aggressive, fighting soldier, he had taken over as Grand Master of the Temple in 1185, but at the Springs of Cresson, it had been his impetuosity that had led to the deaths of 130 Templars and Hospitallers, including the Temple's own Marshal, and the Grand Master of the Hospitallers, Roger de Moulins. The loss of the latter knight was a severe blow to Raymond of Tripoli.

Balian of Ibelin was one of the primary leaders of the *poulains*, the descendants of those crusaders who had remained in the Holy Land after the capture of the city in 1099. Despite not being of high nobility themselves, an important factor in those chivalric times, the *poulains* had been stalwart defenders of the crusader kingdoms, demonstrating sound political and administrative judgement, and impressive battlefield competence. After the death of her first husband, William Longsword of Montferrat, the father of Baldwin V, in 1177, the young, newly widowed Sybilla, sister of King Baldwin IV, had fallen in love with Balian's brother, Baldwin. The match would have been popular in the kingdom. Unfortunately, before any betrothal could be announced, Baldwin had been captured at the battle of Marj Ayun, where a combination of King Baldwin IV's infirmity and insubordination by the Knights Templar had handed Saladin victory. Sybilla had written to Baldwin in captivity to assure him of her love; however, when he was released on parole in return for the promise of a large ransom, she then coldly informed him she could not marry a man owing so much debt. It was a reasonable but discouraging argument, and Baldwin had gone to Constantinople to beg the Byzantine Emperor for help. Emperor Manuel, who had a love of generous gestures, paid the ransom in full. Baldwin came back, triumphant, to the Holy Land in early 1180, only to find Sybilla now betrothed to another man: Guy of Lusignan. The Ibelins were no friends of the court party, and Baldwin himself had gone into self-imposed exile.

After initially meeting at Acre, the crusader leaders had agreed to move as far as Sepphoris and establish their base there. At the insistence of Count Raymond and Balian of Ibelin, they had also agreed to remain at Sepphoris until they were clearer about Saladin's intentions. However, as they advanced from Acre, news reached them that Saladin had moved fast from his mustering position on the Golan Heights and, going to the south of the Sea of Galilee, had already laid siege to the town of Tiberias, had breached the walls of the town, and was now assaulting the citadel. In the citadel was Eschiva, the wife of Raymond of Tripoli. Every chivalric bone in the crusader knights' bodies cried out that the army must advance to rescue this archetypal 'damsel in distress', but Count Raymond himself argued against it. He knew Saladin, and he knew his reputation. Even if Saladin took the citadel, he advised, his wife would be well treated, according to the laws of war and the Muslim code of military conduct. The army must stay at Sepphoris, he continued to insist.

Sepphoris was a well-defended and easily defensible position, close to the great fortress of Acre, and well supplied with both water and food. Raymond argued that Saladin must either come to them, in which case the advantage would lie with the crusaders, or his own army would begin to disintegrate as his soldiers, already in the field for several months, looked to go back to their homes to gather in the harvest. If and when Saladin withdrew, the crusaders could pursue him and savage his rear guard, while if he advanced and things did go badly for the crusaders at Sepphoris, they could fall back on Acre. His advice was that of a seasoned soldier of Outremer, who knew the local conditions well, and who understood the strengths and weaknesses of both the Franks and the Saracens. In normal times – if such times existed in the precarious lives of the crusader states – his sound military advice would have been accepted, and the wisdom of staying on the defensive would have been agreed. The Kingdom of Jerusalem could only field one army, and this was it. Every castle and fort had been emptied of its garrison of knights, men-at-arms, foot soldiers and turcopole[9] light cavalry. All the great military bastions that had sustained the kingdom for nearly 100 years had been emptied to meet the King's call. Even Jerusalem itself had only two knights to command a defence now largely based on an uncertain militia. Winning a major battle against Saladin might be militarily satisfactory, and would certainly buy the crusader states more time, in the hope of encouraging a further large-scale crusade from the west, but losing one would be catastrophic for the crusader cause.

However, these were not normal times, and a range of other personal factors influenced the attitudes and thinking of key protagonists. Twice Raymond's advice had been accepted by King Guy, and twice Reginald of Chatillon and Gerard of Ridefort had urged him to reject Raymond's 'defeatist talk'. Now, late at night, having woken the King in his tent, the older men played on Guy's weaknesses and his lack of confidence, reminding him of a similar moment in 1184 when, as regent, Guy had vacillated in the face of a similar provocation by Saladin. They argued that Count Raymond was no friend of the King's, or of Queen Sybilla, and that his relationship with Saladin – indeed his friendship with many Saracen leaders – made his advice suspect. His refusal to go to the aid of his wife was, frankly, unworthy of a nobleman. Uncertain in his kingship, and aware of the hostility of many of his own commanders, King Guy felt the pressure to act in a manner that would dispel any doubts among both crusaders and Saracens that he was a worthy king and a notable warrior. In the face of this psychological brow-beating, Guy capitulated. Emerging from the King's tent, Reginald and Gerard issued orders that the army was to prepare to advance on Tiberias at daybreak. And so, the fate of the Kingdom of Jerusalem was sealed.

The new crusading expeditions of 1101, designed to reinforce the success of the First Crusade, had all come to a disastrous finish, and these disasters affected the whole trajectory of the crusading movement. Failure further blighted the already strained relationship between Catholic crusaders and Orthodox Byzantines and, in their failure, the Seljuk Turks had been comprehensively avenged for their defeat at Dorylaeum. They were not going to be driven out of Anatolia by the combined armies of Christendom, and, despite Byzantium regaining some control in the west, the long route across Asia Minor to the Holy Land would always remain unsafe for Christian armies and for pilgrims. Military and civilian travellers could now only come to Outremer, in relative safety, by sea, and this was an extremely expensive undertaking, individually or collectively, and very dependent on the weather. Therefore, instead of the thousands of useful colonists that should have reinforced the success of the First Crusade, only a small number of quarrelsome leaders, who had already lost their armies and their reputations, arrived in a land where there were already quite enough quarrelsome leaders. The physical demands of the Near East – both the climate and the prevalence of disease, added to the reality of routine armed conflict – led to a consistently high mortality rate among the crusaders and their families. This was exacerbated by poor diet, lack of hygiene and unsuitable clothing for the conditions of the region.

It was also to be a perennial problem for the crusaders that female infants proved to be hardier in this environment than the male offspring. In addition, many of the young men who made it to the Holy Land on the First, and subsequent crusades, had no intention of staying once they had earned their proverbial spurs, visited the holy places and, possibly, been blooded in an engagement with the Saracens. A lack of manpower would constantly haunt the Frankish states, and it would materially contribute to the precarious nature of their two-century presence in Syria and Palestine.

The beneficiaries of the early crusader problems had been the competing Italian maritime states of Venice, Pisa and Genoa, and the failure to establish a secure land route across Asia Minor significantly increased their influence and their wealth. The Italians had already been crucial in the siege and capture of Jerusalem, and now their dominance in the eastern Mediterranean, against weak Muslim navies, helped ensure the survival and consolidation of the new kingdom and states. However, their cooperation came at a price, and it was secured and paid for by extensive commercial concessions in the great fortress ports, where their vicious and long-standing domestic rivalries routinely spilled over into partisan politics and even violence.

To reinforce their strong position in the coastal areas, the crusaders also embarked on a widespread programme of castle building, in order to protect their flanks with the Muslim world. In time, every pass through the Syrian highlands and down to the Egyptian border would come to be dominated by massive fortifications, such as Reginald of Chatillon's castle of Kerak in south Jordan, and the mighty Crac de Chevaliers, in the Homs Gap. Consistently short of manpower, these castles became the administrative centres for those areas the crusaders controlled or contested, and their refuge when the region periodically exploded into conflict.

This same early period of crusader occupation also saw the establishment of the great military orders of the Poor Fellow-Soldiers of Christ and of the Temple of Solomon, better known as the Knights Templar,[10] and the Order of Knights of the Hospital of St John of Jerusalem, the Knights Hospitaller. After the capture of Jerusalem, many Christians would undertake pilgrimages to visit the various sacred sites in the Holy Land. Although Jerusalem itself was relatively secure, the hinterland and the surrounding areas were not, and pilgrims were routinely harassed, robbed or slaughtered, sometimes in their hundreds. In 1119, a French knight, Hugues de Payens, had approached King Baldwin II and the Patriarch of Jerusalem, proposing the creation of a Catholic monastic religious order for the protection of pilgrims. They agreed, and in early 1120, Hugues and his companions, adopting as their emblem two knights riding on a single horse, to emphasize their poverty, took up residence on the Temple Mount, in the captured Al-Aqsa Mosque. Very soon, the Knights Templar, recognizable by their white surcoats with a red cross, became a favoured Christian charity, attracting money, and noble-born recruits, from across Europe. In contrast, the Knights Hospitaller built on an existing pilgrim charity and hospital in Jerusalem that had been established as early as the seventh century.[11] Also expanding their remit to provide pilgrims with an armed escort, they too became a significant military force, although never losing their charitable character, and their core mission. In 1243 Pope Innocent IV approved a red surcoat, emblazoned with a white cross, as the standard military dress for the order.[12] This would become an equally famous feature on the battlefield for centuries to come.

In due course both orders became formidable fighting forces, largely answerable only to the Pope. Utilizing huge resources, based on papal funding, charitable donations, and estates and trade across all Europe and the Near East, they were able to field large contingents of highly trained and motivated soldiers for service with the crusader states, alongside the more traditional feudal knights. Bound by vows of poverty and chastity, the Knights of the Temple and the Hospital became the mounted and armoured shock troops of the Kingdom of Jerusalem, forbidden from refusing or retreating in battle, unless outnumbered three to one. They built, or garrisoned, many of the great castles in the kingdom, often paid to do so by the great crusader lords, and, like the Italian maritime states, they were an often fractious, partisan and disruptive element of a complex network of regional relationships.

Aided by the divisions in the Islamic world, the crusaders were fortunate in their first kings. Following the death of Godfrey, Baldwin I and his kinsman Baldwin II were impressive warriors and good administrators, as was Fulk of Anjou, who was lured from France to the Holy Land by the prospect of the crown of Jerusalem in return for marrying Baldwin II's daughter Princess Melisande.[13] King Fulk's reign, from 1131 to 1143, was marked by tensions with the Principality of Antioch and the County of Tripoli, and by renewed assertions of Byzantine sovereignty in Syria, while the growing power of Imad ed Din Zengi[14] in Mosul and Aleppo raised the prospect of a new, and much more coherent, Muslim threat to the Christian states. Fulk's death in 1143, the result of tumbling from a horse during a hare-hunting expedition, had led to Queen Melisande competing with her own 13-year-old son, Baldwin III, for control of the kingdom, and the loyalty of the local barons, at just the time when unity was critical for the security of the crusader position in the Near East. In 1144, the County of Edessa fell to Zengi. The news of the loss of the first and earliest of the crusader states fell like a hammer blow on the Franks, on the papacy, and on the Christian kingdoms of Europe.

The early crusader kings had slowly, but surely, recognized that for the Franks to survive, given their weaknesses, they needed to be less intransigent towards the Muslims, that continuing Muslim disunity was firmly in their interest, and that they should always be ready to exploit this by reaching a tactical accommodation with the less dangerous of their foes. This had required a large degree of judgement, understanding, cynicism, realism and tolerance. Many of the next wave of newcomers from the west would be more aggressive and confrontational, less tolerant and less prepared to understand the compromises on which their position rested. Their attitudes, actions and their in-fighting would, in time, fatally compromise the crusader cause.

During the second half of the 12th century there was a dramatic Muslim revival that would reach its zenith under the leadership of Saladin, a courageous and brilliant leader who was known to contemporary Muslims as *Al-Nasir*, 'The Victorious'. From an early stage, Saladin had sought nothing less than to unite all Muslims between the Euphrates and the Nile against a common enemy, the crusader kingdoms. In the late 11th century, the Fatimid caliphate had been in decline and the Abbasid Empire and caliphate had been crumbling, with the Seljuks seizing the sultanate. It was in this period of Muslim weakness that the

First Crusade had struck through the Levant, and why Christian lords and knights had been able to impose the institutions of western Europe on the social and political structures of a conquered land. For a while there had been relative stability, largely thanks to Muslim disunity, but, less than five decades since European crusaders had arrived in the region, the Zengid dynasty had risen to prominence in northern Iraq under the competent leadership of Zengi. Their conquest of Edessa in 1144 had catalysed the Pope, Eugene III, to call for a new crusade, and his agent, Bernard of Clairvaux, did a magnificent job in drumming up support for another major military pilgrimage to the Holy Land, offering the same indulgences as those Pope Urban II had accorded the First Crusade. Although Zengi was assassinated two years later, in 1146, his son, Nur ed Din, successfully continued the fight against the crusader presence in Syria and Palestine, while he progressively attempted to unify the various Muslim power bases.

The Second Crusade, unlike the First, had royal sponsorship. A largely French army was led by King Louis VII of France, who embarked on this papally sanctioned crusade with his queen, Eleanor of Aquitaine. The German contingent was commanded by King Conrad III, King of the Romans, and the son of the Holy Roman Emperor,[15] and he took with him his nephew, the future Emperor, Frederick Barbarossa.[16] Setting out in early 1147, and impervious to good advice from the Byzantine Emperor, Manuel I, both armies were badly mauled by the Seljuk Turks as they negotiated a difficult crossing of Anatolia. Louis and Eleanor eventually reached Antioch, where there were soon rumours of an affair between Eleanor and Count Raymond of Poitiers, her uncle. Louis, now keener on a pilgrimage to Jerusalem than the recovery of Edessa, or an attack on Aleppo, moved on to Acre, with Eleanor under some form of arrest,[17] where he met up again with a chastened King Conrad, and with King Baldwin III. In July 1148, the crusaders decided to attack Damascus. The siege had swiftly turned into a fiasco and, amid accusations and recriminations, the crusader army and its leaders had retreated to Jerusalem, and subsequently to their home countries. Nothing positive had been achieved. Edessa was still held by Nur ed Din, Damascus, hitherto a usefully neutral centre of Muslim power, had been alienated, the fissure between the western powers and the Eastern Empire had widened, and the crusading ideal had been further sullied and, with it, the willingness of Christendom to commit to supporting the crusader kingdoms. Those knights who remained in the kingdom, like Reginald of Chatillon, proved to be a mixed blessing. Baldwin III, at last, took Ascalon in 1153,[18] but Nur ed Din conquered the rich city of Damascus the following year. This new success continued a process that brought much-needed stability and prosperity to the Muslim areas, put further pressure on the Franks, and would help catapult Saladin to pre-eminence across the Muslim world over the next decades.

Saladin is one of those rare and dominant figures in history. A Kurd, born in 1137 in Tikrit[19] in modern-day Iraq, Saladin had spent his formative years in Damascus. From a young age he had been educated in Greek, philosophy, semantics, poetry, astronomy and law. Above all, he became an ardent student of the Koran and Islamic theology. His upbringing was greatly helped by members of his family who had served as skilful diplomats and administrators in the Seljuk Empire, and later for Zengi and Nur ed Din. As Saladin grew up, his uncle Shirkuh,[20] a commander in the Zengid army, became his biggest influence, imbuing in him the values of piety, justice, humility, generosity, brotherhood, mercy and forgiveness, all of which would come to define Saladin's life and legacy. He had joined the military at the age of 14 and had been ably trained by Shirkuh. He had been a quick learner, and Saladin had soon impressed his mentor, and his own soldiers, while his performance in early battles enabled him to take on a leading responsibility in the military campaigns. Over these years he distinguished himself through his bravery, his military leadership, his sharp intellect and, often rare for the times, his loyalty to his leaders.

Saladin's star had truly begun to rise in the 1160s, when Nur ed Din moved to intervene in the affairs of the weakening Fatimid caliphate, aiming to forestall King Amalric's quest to expand the Kingdom of Jerusalem into Egypt,[21] in alliance with the Byzantines. Recognized as a competent, trustworthy and ambitious leader, in 1164 Saladin was sent to Egypt as part of the command structure of a Zengid army, commanded by his uncle Shirkuh. He became an integral part of several campaigns over the years, and his uncle's second-in-command. In early 1169, the army of King Amalric had finally been expelled from Egypt, and Shirkuh, albeit a Sunni, had been named Vizier of the Shia Fatimid caliphate.[22] This appointment now gave Nur ed Din de facto control of Egypt, and of all its resources. However, just one month later Shirkuh had suddenly died, after a short illness. Without his trusted subordinate, Nur ed Din's influence in Egypt was now threatened, and the Fatimid ruler had quickly appointed Saladin, without reference to Nur ed Din, thinking that a young vizier, with no political power or personal status in Egypt, would be easy to control. However, the 31-year-old Saladin proved himself to be much more ambitious and calculating than the weak Fatimid leadership had anticipated, and the young vizier took advantage of the fractured Fatimid political system to gradually instal his close family members in key government and military positions. In a very short space of time, this had enabled him to consolidate his power swiftly and effectively enough to overthrow and dissolve the Fatimid Shia caliphate just two years later, in 1171. As a result, the Sunnis now, once again, after 200 years, controlled the Holy Cities of Mecca and Medina.

Thus, Saladin founded the Ayyubid dynasty,[23] and he could now concentrate on strengthening Egypt as a renewed bastion of Sunni Muslim power, with himself as governor, all in the name of Nur ed Din. He revitalized the economy of Egypt and greatly improved the educational establishment, by building a vast number of schools all over Egypt which attracted many scholars from across Asia and Europe. In doing so, he helped re-establish Egypt as an intellectual powerhouse of the late 1100s, a position it would retain for centuries. With Nur ed Din secure in Baghdad, Aleppo, Mosul and Damascus, Saladin now transformed Egypt into a further salient against the crusaders. He created an entirely new army, loyal only to him, while he started to rebuild the neglected navy, in order to protect Egypt's coasts and ports in the Mediterranean and Red Seas, and to threaten the Christian sea lanes of the eastern Mediterranean. Importantly, Saladin had turned his attention towards tightening his grip over the deserts of the Hejaz, and over Mecca and Medina. He cut tolls for Muslim pilgrims who crossed the Red Sea, making him a 'patron' of the Holy Cities, a move which greatly enhanced his moral authority across the Muslim world. This ambitious programme of expansion inevitably began to create friction with his master in Syria. Tensions rose early on, and they may well have resulted in conflict between Saladin and Nur ed Din, if the latter had not suddenly died in 1174, probably of a heart attack, at the age of 56.

In the ensuing power vacuum, Saladin now saw before him a grand vision of uniting Egypt and Syria for a holy war against the Christian invaders. His reputation, existing power, and his control of the Holy Cities of Mecca and Medina had earned him credibility in the wider Muslim world. As a result, Saladin was now able to bring most, although not all, of the Zengid territory under his control, becoming, in the process, Sultan of both Egypt and Syria, while still owing nominal allegiance to the Abbasid Caliph in Baghdad. Meanwhile, across the border, the Kingdom of Jerusalem was in a weakened state. King Amalric had died of dysentery in the same year as Nur ed Din, and the throne had passed to his son, Baldwin IV, a boy of only 13 years, who had already been identified as suffering from the debilitating disease of leprosy.[24] The great Byzantine Emperor, Manuel I Comnenus, died not long afterwards, having suffered a catastrophic defeat at the hands of the Seljuks at the battle of Myriokephalon[25] in south-west Turkey, while the Frankish nobles, the military orders and the Italian maritime states continued to jostle for position, prestige and power in the increasingly fragile kingdom.

Although the threat of any major new Christian invasion had subsided, Saladin knew that the time was not yet right to fight the crusaders, as he needed to consolidate his own position against Nur ed Din's relatives who still posed a threat from their important and powerful bases in Aleppo and Mosul. However, as Baldwin IV matured, the kingdom chose to adopt a more aggressive foreign policy, under the influence of Reginald of Chatillon, and the Templars, and in 1177 their actions had provoked Saladin into leading a large army into Palestine. Against the odds, Baldwin, 16, sick and outnumbered, united the Christian nobles and, to his great credit, managed to catch Saladin by surprise at Montgisard, where the Sultan suffered a rare and crushing defeat, only narrowly escaping with his own life.

However, Baldwin lacked the resources to follow up on the victory and, in April 1179, Saladin struck back decisively, defeating Baldwin and his commanders in the Golan region and nearly capturing the

King himself. Both leaders were still distracted by affairs in their own domains, and in 1180 Saladin and Baldwin agreed a two-year truce, although it was fragile from the outset. Reginald of Chatillon, from his great castle of Kerak in southern Jordan, was not minded to observe this useful pause in the fighting. His fortress sat astride the key roads between Damascus and Cairo, and Damascus and Mecca, and from here, truce or no truce, this truculent baron was able to tax, raid and rob the passing camel caravans of traders and pilgrims. In the summer of 1181, he had ridden deep into Arabia and intercepted a major Muslim caravan, stripping the travellers of their possessions and taking many prisoners. Saladin had demanded compensation from Baldwin, but the limits of the King's power and influence had been made painfully apparent in his failure to force Reginald's obedience. Saladin, in his turn, imprisoned a large group of Christian pilgrims who had been unfortunate enough to have been shipwrecked on the Egyptian coast, holding them as hostages. However, Reginald still refused to free his Muslim prisoners, and the Christian pilgrims were sold into slavery. Saladin had both sympathy and regard for Baldwin, but in 1182 Reginald put further strain on the already delicate truce by sending troops into the Red Sea, declaring that he planned to destroy the Kaaba[26] in Mecca, and to exhume the Prophet's body from his tomb in Medina. In response, Saladin's brother and his governor in Egypt, Saphadin,[27] had despatched the Ayyubid fleet in pursuit of these blaspheming infidels, and most of the Christian raiders had been captured and publicly executed, either in Mecca or in Cairo.

In the meantime, the tide had turned decisively in favour of the Ayyubids when, in 1180, the mighty, and vastly rich, city of Aleppo finally surrendered to Saladin. As a result, he was now the mightiest ruler of the Muslim world, and the leader of the unified Muslim front against the Latin crusaders, exercising uncontested authority over Egypt and Syria. In this position, and in this role, he was reluctantly supported by the Sunni Abbasid Caliph in Baghdad, while being recognized as the Lord of Arabia, and the Patron of the Holy Cities. The news of Saladin's conquest of Aleppo had shocked the crusader states, as Saladin was now in a position to concentrate his vast resources into putting pressure on the Kingdom of Jerusalem, along almost its entire border. Shortly after, a devastating raid into Christian lands was followed by several probing attacks on the fortress of Kerak,[28] testing the resolve of the Franks and putting additional strain on their stretched resources. To make matters even worse for the crusaders, the tragic life of Baldwin IV had ended in Tyre. Dying of the most debilitating of diseases, his final act had been to try to secure peace by sending Count Raymond of Tripoli to negotiate a four-year truce, to which Saladin, still trying to consolidate the Muslim world, while countering threats from Mosul, had readily agreed. The weakened crusader states posed no direct threat to him, and Saladin was determined that his own actions should do nothing to provoke any new, papally endorsed crusade from the west.

In an era when leadership was very personal, the Leper King's life, reign and his passing had all created problems for the crusader states. The ensuing political turmoil, the untimely death of the infant Baldwin V, the succession crisis, and the ultimate accession as King of Jerusalem of the weak and divisive Guy of Lusignan, offered no solutions to the endemic problems and weaknesses of the kingdom. In December 1186 came troubling news from the south again. Reginald of Chatillon had once again violated a truce, overrunning another large and rich caravan from Egypt, and slaughtering or imprisoning many Muslims. Saladin once again despatched an envoy, demanding the return of the hostages and the treasure. However, Reginald, safe behind the walls of Kerak, refused even to receive the envoy. Hearing of this, Saladin finally lost his patience and publicly swore that he would take the life of Reginald with his own hand. In early 1187, Saladin gathered his generals in Damascus to draw up plans for a major invasion. Messengers galloped to all corners of the Ayyubid state urging action, vengeance and a war of liberation and annihilation. The words 'jihad' and 'Jerusalem' were now on the lips of all those Muslims who answered his call. Saladin left garrisons along the border to protect his northern flank against his Muslim opponents in Mosul, while his forces began raiding Christian lands.

In early May, taking advantage of a local truce with Count Raymond of Tripoli, Saladin had sent a strong Muslim cavalry advance guard into Palestine, where they had clashed with the Templar and Hospitaller contingents at the Springs of Cresson, ending in disaster for the Christians. This shocking military engagement had catalysed the crusader leaders to set aside their differences in order to unite in the face of this burgeoning threat and assemble the army of the kingdom. On 26 June 1187, Saladin had regrouped his army and marched towards the River Jordan. His force numbered around 30,000, large for the time, and was divided into three wings, with Emir Taki ad Din commanding the right, Emir Kukburi the left, and Saladin himself in the centre. On 27 June, the army reached the River Jordan, south of the Sea of Galilee, and made camp in a marshy area. More raiding parties were sent into Christian territory to ravage the area and set the stage for the invasion. Some 15 miles to the west, the Christian army, possibly by now some 20,000 strong, was concentrating in camps in and around Acre and Sepphoris.

On 30 June, Saladin sent a contingent north to block the town of Tiberias, and then challenged the crusaders to come to him by moving his main camp to within 10 miles of their own base. On 2 July, as King Guy and his nobles were debating their strategy in response to Saladin's incursion, the Sultan's scouts confirmed to him that the crusaders were not yet moving, and Saladin took the initiative, marching back east towards Tiberias with most of his infantry, a cavalry contingent, and his siege engineers with their equipment. By late morning they had reached the town, where Raymond's wife was residing, and had breached the walls. Eschiva had, by now, barricaded herself inside the citadel with her bodyguards, and sent messengers to her husband in Sepphoris, from where plumes of smoke from the besieged town could already be seen in the sky.

Despite the gravity of this news, but on the basis of his own instincts, Raymond of Tripoli had made a persuasive argument against marching to raise the siege, insisting that the Christian army was in a strong defensive position at Sepphoris, and should stay put. However, the Count's cautiousness had been met with accusations of cowardice and treachery, mainly from Gerard of Ridefort and Reginald of Chatillon, who had given King Guy a compelling set of political, military and psychological arguments for ignoring Raymond's advice, and Raymond's most influential ally, Roger de Moulins, Grand Master of the Hospitallers, had been killed in the fiasco of Cresson. Now, to Raymond's despair, the heralds had been sent through the camp to order the army to be ready to march to the rescue of Tiberias at dawn. Therefore, early on the still, hot, airless morning of 3 July, the whole crusader army broke camp. As the army was camped on land owned by Count Raymond, he was given the dubious honour of commanding the vanguard. King Guy led the centre division, with the Bishop of Acre carrying Christendom's greatest relic, the True Cross,[29] while Balian of Ibelin commanded the rear guard, where the Templar and Hospitaller contingents were also concentrated, as was Reginald of Chatillon. King Guy had ordered the men to march with haste, planning to reach the besieged town, and the freshwater of the Sea of Galilee, by the end of the day; however, even by mid-morning, as the sun rose across the clear, cloudless sky, it had already been apparent that the day would be extremely hot, and the pace slower than anticipated. There was no water on the route, no breeze, and no escape from the scorching heat, or the thick clouds of dust which the crusader army raised as it marched. Fatigue and thirst slowed down the column, and Saracen skirmishers continuously attacked the van and the rear guard, pouring arrows into their midst, and riding away before the armoured cavalry could mount any effective counter-attack. The divisions marched in three slow box formations, with the foot soldiers using their large shields to try to protect the knights and their horses, who rode in the middle, champing for the opportunity to charge out and disperse their Saracen tormentors. Soon the path of the army was marked by the corpses of soldiers, horses and mules, while the supply wagons were already full of the wounded.

By midday, the army had only just reached the first watering point at the village of Turan, a mere 5 miles from Sepphoris. Some miles ahead of them rose a rocky hill with two summits, the so-called 'Horns of Hattin'. These 'horns' were the last remnants of a volcanic crater. They were still only one-third of the way to their objective. There was not nearly enough water at Turan for all the men and the horses of the army, and, as they pressed on, there was no escaping the sun, the thick dust, or the arrows. It became increasingly clear to King Guy and his commanders that there was now little or no chance they would be able to reach Tiberias in a single day. As the column moved away from Turan, more and more detachments of Saladin's fast-moving horse archers appeared from nearby hills and began harassing the Christians, cutting off their line of retreat to Sepphoris. There was no option but for the crusaders to press on. The crusader infantry continued to close ranks in order to protect the cavalry against these hit-and-run attacks, but the number of casualties in men and animals inexorably rose as the day wore on, and the constant harassment and sporadic clashes slowed the crusader rear guard down to a crawl, separating Balian and the military orders from the rest of the army. The Templars sent a messenger to the King to say that they could go no further that day. Other nobles, mindful that Count Raymond's advice to hold fast at Sepphoris had been ignored, now urged Guy to fight through to Galilee and Tiberias, whatever the losses. However, King Guy, fearing the loss of the elite shock cavalry of the military orders, ordered the centre to stop to allow the rear guard to catch up, and he relayed a message to Raymond, ordering him to halt the vanguard. To the despair of the crusaders, the entire column was now gradually encircled by the ever-increasing numbers of Saladin's horse archers, and it had become horribly clear that the whole army had fallen into precisely the trap about which Raymond had warned. When the messenger reached Raymond to order him to halt, the Count rode back down the line crying, 'Ah, Lord, the war is over; we are dead men; the kingdom is finished.'

Saladin, leaving only a small garrison to block the citadel at Tiberias, brought up his main contingent to block the roads leading to the lake. He could hardly believe his luck. With nightfall fast approaching, the exhausted Christian fighters had been fatally slowed by casualties, fatigue and thirst, and were now hemmed in, across the lower southwestern slopes of the Horns of Hattin, by Muslim forces. Unable to retreat, they were unable to find their way past Saladin's fresh troops. King Guy, horribly conscious of the consequences of his decision to march, had no choice but to order his men to make camp where they were. The main Muslim contingent also camped for the night, but Saladin had no intention of allowing the crusaders to rest or regroup. The crusader column, by now stretched out along a mile or so, was not protected by any natural terrain features. Muslim horse archers continued to circle and fire arrows into the camp throughout the night, while skirmishers clashed with the crusader picquets and set tents on fire along the camp perimeter. Chroniclers' reports painted a vivid picture of prayers and songs in the Arab camp during the night. To make their suffering worse, the Saracens now set fire to the dry scrub that covered the hill, and hot smoke poured in over the crusader camp. Unable to rest, and with their water supplies dwindling, the Christian ranks were already tired, demoralized and deeply worried. Dawn broke early on 4 July, while Saladin waited for the heat to rise and to see what the Christians would do next. 'Not a cat', said a chronicler of the battle, 'could have slipped through the net.'

The crusaders, without any water and tormented by thirst, now had only one aim: to get to the village of Hattin, where there was supposedly a water source. They were fearful, but their only salvation lay in maintaining their formation, and trusting in God and in their training as professional soldiers. The Horns of Hattin were ahead and off to the left as they made their way along and across the valley, doggedly trying to keep the same formation of three large squares, with the infantry continuing to attempt to shield the cavalry, who were increasingly their last and only hope of breaking Saladin's ever-tightening hold. Saladin's troops set fire to the nearby brushwood once again, sending choking clouds of smoke on a westerly breeze towards the crusaders, and, with the July, Palestine sun beating down from a clear sky, the Christians pushed on towards Hattin, desperate to reach its water well. To prevent this, Saladin now sent Taki ad Din's wing galloping to block the valley, determined to fully encircle the enemy and not allow them to quench their thirst. He especially wanted to wear down the knights and their cavalry, aware of just how dangerous their frontal charges had proved in the past. Skirmishers and horse archers, riding ever closer to the crusaders, unleashed volley after volley onto the crusader column. Ever more exhausted, thirsty and demoralized, the crusader infantry started to break away from the mounted knights. Abandoning their wounded, who were soon despatched by the Saracens, the foot soldiers dispersed and fled, with a large group heading east towards Hattin, and another group fleeing north towards the village of Nimri. Seeing the fleeing troops, Muslim fighters opened gaps in their line in order to draw the enemy infantry out of the formations. King Guy and his officers realized they were doomed, unless they could break through and regroup, but the Muslims charged the rear of the column, and the Templars and Hospitallers became so heavily engaged that King Guy had no option but to order a halt for the second time, in order to prevent the cavalry formations from being broken up.

However, in the vanguard, Raymond of Tripoli and his household knights had already been edging away from King Guy's cavalry formation, opening up a gap between his troops and the centre and, as he advanced, the Muslim riders too began opening a gap in their own line. Under pressure, horrified at the way the battle had unfolded, and hoping to

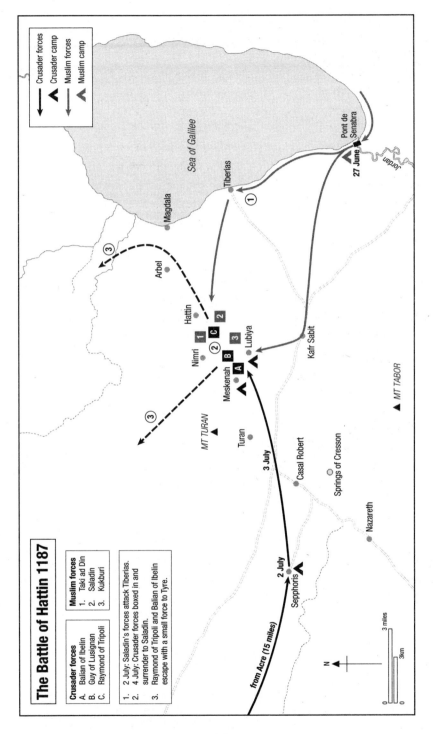

The Battle of Hattin 1187

Crusader forces
A. Balian of Ibelin
B. Guy of Lusignan
C. Raymond of Tripoli

Muslim forces
Taki ad Din
1. Saladin
2. Kukburi

1. 2 July: Saladin's forces attack Tiberias.
2. 4 July: Crusader forces boxed in and surrender to Saladin.
3. Raymond of Tripoli and Balian of Ibelin escape with a small force to Tyre.

stake all on a desperate last charge, Raymond decided not to sit and wait. He gathered his own knights and those of the other contingents in his force and charged Taki ad Din's cavalry. The surge of hope that initially inspired both the horsemen and their infantry support quickly turned to despair, as the disciplined Muslim riders pulled aside to let the galloping Christians pass through, showering Raymond and his men with arrows as they punched into thin air, wheeled north and retreated from the battlefield, hardly stopping until they reached the walls of Tyre. Only a little later, Balian of Ibelin and Reginald of Sidon mounted another charge and they, accompanied by several Knights Templar of the rear guard, also broke out, riding hard for the safety of Tyre. They were the last crusaders to escape the killing fields of Hattin.

Back in the smoke-filled valley, the Christian knights and foot soldiers were dying, and Guy ordered what was left of his cavalry to move towards the Horns of Hattin, through a gap already created by the retreating infantry. He knew that there were shallow pools of water at the top of the hill and had hoped they would not be dried out, although it is difficult to imagine what Guy now hoped to salvage from this disaster, other than survival. Meanwhile, on the hill itself, Saladin's troops had closed in and were engaging a Christian infantry that was so exhausted that they could now barely put up a fight. Having quickly overwhelmed them, the Muslims turned towards the King of Jerusalem himself. Throughout the incessant close-quarter fighting, Christian knights had continued to gather around the True Cross to protect it, as they retreated towards the hill. However, as they struggled to the top, in ones, twos and small groups, they found no water and no relief from the fighting.

King Guy may have lacked judgement, but he was no coward, and he was a courageous fighter. He rallied his knights one more time and raised his red tent on the summit of the Horns to provide a focal point for his men, but all this, by this stage, was to no avail. Saladin's young son, al-Afdal, was at his father's side, witnessing his first battle. Many years later he paid tribute to the courage of the Franks:

When the Frankish King had withdrawn to the hill-top, his knights made another gallant charge and the Muslims fell back upon my father. I watched his dismay. He changed colour and pulled at his beard, then rushed forward crying: 'Give the devil the lie.' So our men fell on the enemy, who retreated back up the hill. When I saw the Franks flying, I cried out with glee: 'We have routed them.' But they charged again and drove our men back to where my father stood. Again, he urged our men forward, and again they charged up the hill. Again, I cried out: 'We have routed them.' But my father turned to me and said: 'Be quiet. We have not beaten them so long as that tent stands.' At that moment the tent was over-turned. Then my father dismounted and bowed to the ground, giving thanks to God, with tears of joy.

The Bishop of Acre had been killed in the fighting, and the True Cross that he had borne into the battle was now again in the hands of infidels. King Guy ordered the survivors to surrender, and the few remaining mounted knights dismounted to collapse on the ground. King Guy was found sitting on the cloth of his collapsed tent, utterly exhausted, with barely enough strength left to hand over his sword. Saladin's army had won a great victory. The King of Jerusalem had now been captured, along with his brother, Amalric, and many nobles and knights, among them Reginald of Chatillon and Gerard of Ridefort. They were then led to a tent that by now had been erected on the battlefield for the Sultan, where Saladin greeted them graciously. He seated King Guy next to him and, seeing his thirst, handed him a goblet of rosewater, iced with the snows from Mount Hermon. Guy drank deeply; then, according to the chronicler Imad ad Din, having drunk, Guy handed the cup to Reginald, who was standing beside him. By the laws of Muslim hospitality, to give food or drink to a captive was to guarantee his life, so Saladin quickly said to an interpreter, 'Say to the King that it is you who give him [Reginald] to drink, but I give him neither to drink nor to eat.' The Sultan, whose hatred of Reginald was personal, then accused him of the crimes of brigandage, impiety, treachery and greed. The Lord of Kerak was not without courage, and Reginald responded insolently, at which point Saladin swung his sword and struck off his head, 'thereby', as the Arab chroniclers reported, 'fulfilling his oath to kill the truce-breaker'.

Guy, too, did not lack for courage, but he had watched in horror as his companion was decapitated in front of him, assuming that he would be next to suffer the same fate. However, Saladin reassured him, saying, 'A king does not kill a king, but that man's perfidy and insolence went too far.' He then gave orders that while all the lay barons were to be treated with courtesy and respect during their captivity, he would not spare the knights of the military orders. Apart from Gerard of Ridefort, some 400 Templar and Hospitaller prisoners were brutally butchered outside Saladin's tent, before the Sultan marched his army away, leaving the battlefield of Hattin to the crows and to the jackals.

The Christians of the east had suffered disaster and defeat before, but at Hattin the greatest army the kingdom had ever assembled had been annihilated, and the True Cross lost. The victor was not some venal warlord, or a local potentate out for petty advantage, it was Sultan Saladin, lord of the whole Arab Muslim world. With their castles emptied and their field army destroyed, it only remained for Saladin to occupy the fortresses of Palestine and Syria. On 5 July, Eschiva, Countess of Tripoli, surrendered the citadel of Tiberias. Treated with the honour she deserved, she and her household were escorted to Tripoli. Saladin then marched his army to Acre where, on 10 July, Joscelin of Courtenay cravenly handed him the keys to the city and sailed away, accompanied by many of the Christian nobles and merchants. As other towns, cities and castles capitulated, Saladin laid siege to the great fortress port of Tyre. By August, although Tyre continued to hold out, Saladin controlled most of the coastline. In September, King Guy and the Templar Grand Master,[30] in return for their freedom, urged the towns of Ascalon and Gaza to surrender, which they reluctantly did.

On the day that Saladin entered Ascalon there was an eclipse of the sun, and, in the darkness, the Sultan met a delegation from Jerusalem, summoned to discuss terms for the surrender of the Holy City. The delegates courageously said they would not hand over the city where their God had died for them, and with Saladin promising to take the city by storm, they returned proudly but fearfully to Jerusalem. In the meantime, Balian of Ibelin had obtained safe passage from Saladin to go to Jerusalem and to take his wife and family back to Tyre.[31] Saladin had granted his request on the condition that he spend only one night in the city, and did not bear arms. However, when there, Balian was approached by the Patriarch, who had been too ill to accompany the True Cross to its loss at Hattin, and other officials, and they pleaded with him to lead the defence of the city. Balian felt he could not refuse this plea, and he sent a message to Saladin to explain the violation of his oath. Saladin, always courteous to an enemy he respected, not only forgave him but sent an escort to Jerusalem in order to take Balian's family, household and possessions back to Tyre.

On 20 September 1187, Saladin began his attack on the walls of Jerusalem, and by the 26th his sappers were already mining under the fortifications, not far from the spot where Godfrey of Bouillon had broken into the city 88 years earlier. A large breach in the walls had been effected by the 29th, and, despite calls for a last desperate sally by the defenders, on 30 September Balian went to Saladin's camp to discuss terms. The assault on the walls continued, even as they spoke, and Saladin reminded him of the massacres committed by the Christians in 1099. Above the noise of battle, Saladin grabbed Balian by the arm, pointing to the Muslim battle standard being raised on the city's ramparts, just at the moment that it was hurled down again as the defenders rallied one more time. Balian once again asked for honourable terms, warning that the defenders, in their desperation, may well destroy the buildings in the Temple area sacred to the Muslims, and slaughter all their Muslim prisoners. Saladin did not want to inherit a smoking wasteland. He knew Balian and respected his sincerity. For 30,000 dinars the Christians could ransom 7,000 of Jerusalem's citizens, and the defenders could leave in peace with their weapons and their goods. On Balian's orders the garrison now laid down their weapons and, on Friday 2 October, Saladin entered the Holy City. There was little violence and minimal looting, but, although appealing to the Patriarch and to the military orders for additional funds, Balian could not raise more than the 30,000 dinars Saladin demanded. Despite using some of the remaining money donated by King Henry II of England, which had been held for safekeeping in the city, two streams of Christians were soon pouring out through the gates. One consisted of those who had paid for themselves, or had been ransomed by Balian's efforts, while the other consisted of those who could afford no ransom, and who were destined for the slave markets of Damascus and beyond. Saladin's brother, Saphadin, intervened on their behalf, securing the release of a further thousand souls, and Saladin himself gave gifts from his own treasury to the orphans and widows of Hattin. This behaviour was in striking contrast to the actions of the conquerors of the First Crusade. Saladin resisted calls from his commanders to destroy the Church of the Holy Sepulchre, although the Byzantine Emperor, Isaac II Angelus Comnenus, actually sent a message of congratulations to the Sultan, asking for the Holy Places to revert to the Orthodox Church.

Saladin's one major failure, which would tarnish his extraordinary success in this campaign as a leader and commander, was not taking the fortress port of Tyre. Here, many of the crusader leaders who had survived Hattin, defied him, led by Conrad of Montferrat. This commander had arrived in the city, quite by chance and quite unaware of the recent catastrophe, after sensing something was wrong when he had approached Acre, which was already in the hands of the Muslims. Despite Saladin threatening to execute his father in front of the walls unless he surrendered the port, Conrad held firm.[32] This foothold on the Syrian coast would buy the Christians just enough time for the assembly and launch of the Third Crusade, thereby giving the remaining crusading states a further century of precarious survival.

The Archbishop of Tyre had speedily sailed to bring the news of the catastrophe of Hattin to Rome, where, as a result and even before anyone knew of the subsequent loss of the Holy City, Pope Urban III had died of shock. King Guy, recently released by Saladin, also found himself repulsed from entry to Tyre by Conrad of Montferrat, and, in a bold move, he went south to besiege Acre where he, in his turn, was encircled by Saladin. Despite his wife, Queen Sybilla, and both their daughters dying during the siege, Guy would hold out in his siege lines long enough to be relieved by the arrival of the forces of the Third Crusade.[33] In spite of his responsibility for the disaster at Hattin, his Lusignan family background made him a vassal of King Richard of England, and Richard backed him to remain as King of Jerusalem. Eventually, in the face of extreme resistance from those who blamed Guy for the disaster of Hattin, Richard had helped him purchase the island of Cyprus from the Knights Templar. Guy died in 1194, but the Lusignan family would rule as kings of Cyprus for nearly three centuries, until 1474, when the Venetians would assume overlordship.[34]

4

Expulsion from Eden

Acre 1291

There was silence at the southern end of the siege lines around Acre, as two men appeared in the gate of the Tower of the Legate. They were Sir William of Villiers, a knight from the regiment of French soldiers committed to the defence of Acre by King Louis XI after the disastrous 1249 crusade against Egypt, and William of Caffran, a soldier from the household of the Grand Master of the Templars. They hesitated for a moment, and then picked their way through the debris and destruction of five weeks of brutal siege warfare, making their way towards the large red tent that stood some third of a mile away from the city walls, on a small rise. The walls and towers of Acre were crammed with crusaders watching this minor drama playing out. Among the watchers was the young Henry of Lusignan, King of Jerusalem, and his younger brother, and Constable of the Kingdom, Amalric, both fresh from their base in Cyprus, having arrived just days earlier with reinforcements of 100 horsemen and 2,000 foot soldiers. Close by stood William of Beaujeu, Grand Master of the Templars, and John of Villiers, Grand Master of the Knights Hospitaller, the traditional rivalry of their two great military orders put aside as they contemplated the final destruction of the Kingdom of Jerusalem. Alongside John of Villiers was his marshal, Matthew of Clermont, a veteran of many clashes with the Muslim Mamluks, whose armies encircled Acre. The warrior monks of the Temple and the Hospital were themselves manning the walls that enclosed the old gardens of Montmusart, stretching from the coast, down to that area of the defences that both the defenders and the attackers deemed the most vulnerable: the Accursed Tower, and the towers of the English, the Countess of Blois and King Hugh. These bastions were now held, under the command of Amalric, by the French Regiment, the new troops from Cyprus and the Teutonic Knights,[1] whose Grand Master, Burchard of Schwanden, had chosen to resign his office just as the imminence of an Egyptian Mamluk attack became apparent. On Amalric's right, the walls were held by Otto of Grandison, a Swiss knight and friend of King Edward I of England, along with fellow Savoyard John of Grailly[2] and a small contingent of English knights and foot soldiers. Beyond them, manning the defences to the Bay of Acre, including the Tower of the Legate, were the Venetians and the Pisans, another set of fierce rivals who had reluctantly set aside their differences in the common cause. Their steadfastness, in this instance, contrasted with that of the Genoese, who had reached a separate treaty with the Mamluks, in order to protect their own Mediterranean trade links, and had already departed the city.

With a deep breath, the two Williams stepped forward, conscious of the stare of several thousand pairs of eyes. Their chain mail, freshly polished, gleamed in the early morning sun, and their surcoats were newly washed. They were bare-headed and carried no weapons. Putting on as brave a face as they could muster, they made their way through the lines of Mamluk soldiers, who, moving aside to let them pass, regarded them with a mixture of contempt, disgust and thinly veiled hostility. First, they passed through the barriers of wood and dirt thrown up to protect the Mamluk miners, then through the network of deep trenches by which the attackers had gradually moved closer and closer to Acre's defences, until their engineers could begin to undermine the walls and towers. Beyond these were the massed troops of the Mamluks, the slave-soldiers who had overthrown their Egyptian masters, the last sultans of Saladin's Ayyubid dynasty. Further beyond lay the extensive tented city of administration and logistics, and the usual hangers-on that accompanied every great army that went to war.

The Mamluk line stretched a further mile to the north, lapping around as far as the English Tower, while the Arab army of Damascus was opposite the Hospitallers, and that of Hama rested its right-hand flank on the northern shoreline, opposite the Templar troops. In among the ranks of soldiers stood the great engines of war that had battered Acre day in, day out, and through the long nights since the start of the siege, gradually wearing down the strength, and the morale, of both the defenders and the citizens of the city. Many – the old, the women and children – had already departed, seeking a place in the boats that continued to bring supplies and reinforcements to Acre, and taking themselves to Cyprus where they fearfully awaited the outcome of the siege. However, many remained, placing their faith in God, in the massive double walls of the city, in the stout hearts of the defenders, and in the hope, fast fading, of a relief operation from Christian Europe.

Seated in front of the great red tent, its doors open towards the enemy, in traditional Muslim style, was Sultan al-Ashraf Khalil,[3] about 25 years old and the newly appointed leader of the Mamluks, surrounded by his personal bodyguard and his battle captains. The knights approached and prostrated themselves three times before him. Al-Ashraf imperiously bade them rise and asked them if they had brought with them the keys of the city. The emissaries had no such remit. Through interpreters, although William of Caffran spoke passable Arabic, they replied that Acre could not be surrendered so easily, but that they had come to ask the Sultan for some measure of mercy to be shown to the poor people of the city. At this the Sultan was recorded as saying, 'I will give you this much grace, that you cede me the bare stones of the city itself, and carry off everything else, and go forth and leave this place. I will do this for your king, who has come here and who is a youth, just as I am, but I will do nothing more for you.' William of Villiers spoke for the chivalric spirit of the defenders of Acre, and wider Christendom, when he replied that that could not happen, as 'The people overseas would hold us to be traitors.' It was a bold albeit futile gesture, but they could give no other. Al-Ashraf's response sealed Acre's fate: 'Then you should go away, for I shall offer nothing more.'

As this conversation was taking place, under the eyes of both armies, the Pisans, manning a siege catapult somewhere within Acre, loosed off, by accident or design, a large stone missile. In the silence, this missile arched over the walls of the city, and landed, by chance, and with a resounding crash, just yards from the Sultan's tent. As the dust settled, al-Ashraf leapt to his feet, theatrically half-drawing his scimitar, and screamed at the knights, 'Ah, you filthy swine, what prevents me from striking off your heads?' Villiers and Caffran were as shocked as the

Sultan himself, and all the other observers. It was a gross abuse of the rules governing a truce. Into this tense tableau Emir Sanjar al-Shujai intervened to stop any violence, saying to the Sultan, 'Sir, God forbid that you should foul the iron of your sword with the blood of these pigs. Those who fired the siege engine are traitors, but you should let these men go, for they are here with you.' Thrusting his sword back into its scabbard, al-Ashraf dismissed the envoys, and they made their lonely way back to the Tower of the Legate. As the gates closed behind them, the massed drums of the Mamluk Sultan's army sounded once again, and the defenders on the walls dispersed rapidly as the siege engines took up their wall-shattering rhythm once more.

The city of Acre occupied a strategic location at the eastern end of the Mediterranean, sitting in a natural harbour at the northern extremity of the Haifa Bay. Some 25 miles north was Tyre, south was Jaffa, and Jerusalem lay 100 miles to the south-east. As an urban trading centre, it had been occupied since around 2000 BC. The Persians had used it as a rendezvous for their military expeditions against the Pharaohs, massing their huge polyglot armies on the plains outside the city. Through this city marched the future Roman Emperor, Titus, and his legions, on their way to crush the Jewish Revolt of 67–70. Following the defeat of Heraclius's army at Yarmouk in 637, Acre was taken by the Muslims, at around the same time as Jerusalem, and the city served as a major port for the Umayyads, the Abbasids and, in due course, the Fatimids. In 1104, after a four-year siege, King Baldwin I had taken the city, and he had made it the chief port in the Kingdom of Jerusalem. The taxes and tolls from Acre provided more income for the crusader crown than the total revenues of the King of England. This revenue was vital, as the crusader kingdom needed money to meet the costs of sustaining a persistent conflict with the surrounding Muslim states, especially since the rise of Saladin, and for the prodigious cost of the upkeep of the defences of the cities, castles and fortresses.

Acre, along with Sidon and Beirut, had capitulated to Saladin after the catastrophic battle of Hattin, having been stripped of their garrisons by King Guy's disastrous call to arms. Tyre had held out, thanks to the fortuitous arrival of Conrad of Montferrat, who had kept both the Ayyubid warlord, and King Guy himself, out of the city. In an extraordinarily quixotic move, Guy had then marched on Acre and put it under siege, awaiting the arrival of the new western crusade that he knew was being preached and prepared for. In his turn, Guy and his small army were themselves besieged by Saladin, but, although this rump crusader force could not take Acre, they could be resupplied from the sea, as the Italian city-states still dominated the eastern Mediterranean. This slightly bizarre standoff had continued for nearly two years, until the arrival of the advance forces of King Philip Augustus of France, Richard the Lionheart of England, and Philip of Swabia, now deputizing for the great Emperor Frederick Barbarossa, who had died in a freak accident crossing a river in Anatolia.

In July 1191, Acre had, at last, been retaken by the crusaders. The Muslim garrison had held on as long as they could, but Saladin had proved unable to relieve them. As negotiations dragged on, regarding the status of Jerusalem, indemnities, and the return of the True Cross, lost to the Christians at Hattin, King Richard, keen to advance on the Holy City, marched his 2,700 Muslim prisoners out onto the Acre plains and, in full view of the Saracen army, executed them. It was not an altogether unusual battlefield atrocity, but, like the sack of Jerusalem a hundred years earlier, it would be remembered when the time for retribution came.

The armies of the Third Crusade had failed to retake Jerusalem, although an agreement had been reached whereby Christian pilgrims were guaranteed access to the Holy Sites. Having lost so many fortresses and bases in the aftermath of Hattin, the crusaders knew that, even if they could take Jerusalem, they lacked the strength and numbers to hold it, and Acre now became the de facto crusading capital city. It was a bitter disappointment, and Philip Augustus and Richard departed to resume the long-standing quarrel between their two kingdoms, with Richard being taken prisoner and held hostage for a huge ransom by the Germans on his journey home.

The great Saladin had died of fever in 1193, but the new crusader kingdom was a pale shadow of its former self; it was no more than 10 miles wide, stretching 90 miles from Jaffa to Tyre. Although no galaxy of princes would ever again go eastwards for holy war, Saladin's career of conquest had been checked by the Third Crusade, and, as a result, the kingdom would survive for a further 100 years. Saladin left 17 sons, and on his death in 1193 the unity of Islam began to crumble again. Family squabbles now prevented the Muslims from taking advantage of crusader weakness, but the perennial competition between Pope and Emperor, Catholic and Orthodox, Templars and Hospitallers, Acre and Tyre, Italian city-states, newcomers and *poulains* continued unabated. Worse was to follow.

A further crusade had been launched in 1201, but it became politically dominated by the Venetians, whose enormous bill for providing the maritime transport for the crusader forces could not be met. In these circumstances the Fourth Crusade found itself diverted to attack Zara, a castle on the Balkan coast loyal to the Catholic King Andrew of Hungary, and then being diverted, once again, to Constantinople as part of the power-play in a much wider Byzantine internal conflict. In 1204, the crusaders breached the sea walls of the city and, in a frenzy of destructive mania, sacked the great capital of the Eastern Roman Empire, setting up a 'bastard' replacement Latin Empire that would last – poor, weak and beleaguered – for little more than half a century.[4] Any hopes for long-term reproachment between the Catholic and Orthodox churches died in the fires, violence and destruction of Constantine's city and, with it, any chance of a united Christian front in the east against the Saracens.

In the wake of this sanguinary fiasco, western Europe had once again identified Egypt as the main source of Muslim strength, and they saw military success in that arena as the key to retaking Jerusalem. A series of misguided campaigns throughout the first half of the 13th century culminated in King Louis IX of France, St Louis, being captured amid the flooded tributaries of the Nile Delta in 1250. A deal with the Saracens to recover Jerusalem for Christendom had in fact been made in 1228, by the Holy Roman Emperor, Frederick II. However, given that Frederick was under excommunication by the Pope at the time, his diplomatic triumph was largely spurned by Christian Europe, although for a while it did tenuously reopen the pilgrim routes. In 1244 even that success had been overturned, when a powerful Turkish tribe, the Khwarezmians – swept up in a renewed inter-Muslim conflict between the forces of Cairo, Damascus and Baghdad – captured and sacked Jerusalem, ravaging the Church of the Holy Sepulchre and scattering the bones of the kings of Jerusalem. At the subsequent battle of La Forbie, an unlikely alliance of crusaders, the military orders and renegade Ayyubid emirs, was crushed by the Sultan of Egypt and his new Khwarezmian mercenaries. Nearly seven centuries would pass before a Christian army would again enter Jerusalem's gates. Meanwhile, two great and powerful military dynasties were now rising, whose combined impact would significantly shape the history of the region for the next centuries. One, in the Far East, was that of Genghis Khan and his Mongols; the other, in Egypt, was that of a group of slave-warriors, the Mamluks.

Genghis Khan was born in 1167. In 1206, having united the warlike, nomadic tribes of Mongolia, he embarked on an extraordinary campaign of expansion. His offer to his followers was of new countries, great booty and hordes of slaves; his army of cavalry, mounted on small, swift ponies, and accustomed from birth to hard living, presented a combination of speed of movement, discipline and vast numbers that had never been known before. When he died in 1227, his dominions already stretched from Korea to Persia, and from the Indian Ocean to Siberia. His armies left in their wake a trail of devastation, marked by empty and destroyed cities, and vast pyramids of skulls. Shockwaves of terror preceded his armies. At Herat the Mongols spent an entire week executing the whole population of the city. Bizarrely, his ruthless attacks on the Muslim kingdoms in central Asia fuelled the Christian myth of Prester John,[5] giving those in the crusader kingdom hope for an alliance against their own Muslim foes – a hope, based on a complete misunderstanding of the culture of the Mongols, that nevertheless lasted well into the 14th century.

Meanwhile, in the wake of the Egyptian triumphs at La Forbie in 1244, and over King Louis IX in 1250, the powerful leaders of the slave-warriors of the Sultan, the Mamluks – akin to the later Ottoman Janissaries – turned on their Ayyubid masters and massacred them, thus reigniting the conflict between Cairo and Damascus. Louis's campaign had been a disaster for the crusader cause. Not only were the manpower losses never fully recovered, but the failure of a leader with such apparent moral authority called the whole crusader ideology into question. As the Mamluks consolidated their power, and the Mongols thrust deep into Russia, central Europe and the Middle East, the crusaders once again fell to bickering among themselves, the Italian city-states renewed their perennially violent competition, and the Byzantine imperialists re-established themselves, retaking Constantinople from the Latins in 1261. Given the bloody legacy of the Fourth Crusade, the Orthodox Byzantines had next to no sympathy for the plight of the rump Catholic crusader presence in the Holy Land.

In early 1258, Genghis Khan's grandson, Hulagu, had sacked the great Abbasid capital of Baghdad. The population was massacred, and the River Tigris ran black with the ink of the tens of thousands of books that had been hurled into its currents. The Caliph was spared, until he had revealed the whereabouts of the vast Abbasid treasure, accumulated over five centuries, whereupon he was wrapped in a carpet and trampled to death by Mongol horsemen, in order that imperial blood should not be shed on the ground. The last of the Abbasid family made their way to Cairo, where the Mamluks allowed them a shadowy existence for the next 250 years, bereft of all power and influence, yet bestowing a veneer of legitimacy on the new Egyptian military regime. In turn, both the Mamluks and the 'shadow caliphs' of the Abbasids would be relegated to obscurity by the inexorable rise of the Ottomans in the following centuries.

The Mongols now took Aleppo and Damascus, and it even seemed possible that Islam, east of the Nile, might be extinguished. However, in late 1259, the Great Khan Mongke died in China, while campaigning with his brother, Kublai Khan; the other great Mongol leaders had to return east to settle the issue of succession. Sensing weakness, the new Mamluk Sultan of Egypt, Qutuz, had moved against those Mongol troops still in Syria, and even asked permission from the Franks to pass through their territory. Despite the Christians having apparently been favoured by the Mongols in the course of their bloody campaigns, the Franks had been understandably unsettled by the Mongol record of wholescale massacre, and so, for several days, the Mamluk army was permitted to camp peaceably outside the city of Acre, as they prepared for the great confrontation. Indeed, Sultan Qutuz, his deputy, Baibars, and other Muslim commanders were invited into the city as honoured guests. On 3 September 1260, the Mamluks inflicted a crushing defeat on the Mongols at Ain Jalud, the Pools of Goliath. The Mongol leader, the Christian general Kitbuqa, was captured. Mocked by his captors, he boasted that he, unlike the parvenu Mamluk emirs, had always been loyal to his master. They struck off his head.

Ain Jalut was to prove one of the most decisive battles in history, and despite their power, and the extent of their empire, the Mongols would never have an opportunity to reverse its outcome. The Mamluk Sultanate of Egypt became the dominant force in the Near East for the next two centuries, and the fate of the crusader states was sealed, as the victorious Muslims hastened to finish off the enemies of their faith. Having now retaken both Aleppo and Damascus from the Mongols, Sultan Qutuz set off to return to Egypt, covered in glory. Nearing the Nile Delta, he took a break to go hunting hares with some of his commanders. One of them approached him, apparently to make a request, and, as he held the Sultan's hand, Baibars plunged his sword into Qutuz's back, fully justifying Kitbuqa's taunt of disloyalty. It was Baibars who returned to Cairo as the Mamluk Sultan.

Baibars was now nearly 50. A Turk by birth, he was a huge man with brown skin, blue eyes and a loud resonant voice. He had come to Syria as a young slave and had been bought for service in the Egyptian sultan's 'Mamluk Guard'. He had already risen rapidly through the ranks after the Mamluks had seized power, and now that he was Sultan, he turned all his attention and military skill on destroying the remaining crusader presence in Palestine and Syria. In a series of lightning raids, he began to retake castles and towns across the region. The great Hospitaller castle of Arsuf fell, and all the knights were taken into captivity. At Safed, the Templars were offered safe passage if they surrendered. They did so, and they were all seized, bound and beheaded. Emissaries, seeking to negotiate a truce, were received by Baibars at the castle, where the whole area was encircled with the skulls of the murdered Christian prisoners. For the crusaders, the frontier with Islam was now just beyond the gates of Acre.

In 1268, Antioch fell to Baibars, and even Muslim chroniclers were shocked by the carnage that followed. Antioch had been one of the great historical Christian cities, and one of the original Catholic sees. The Principality of Antioch had lasted over 170 years, since its foundation under the southern Norman Bohemond of Taranto, and its loss was another terrible blow to Christian prestige. The crusaders braced themselves for a further onslaught, but for now Baibars paused. There were rumours of another possible Mongol offensive, and of Louis IX preparing to mount a further great crusade from the west. In the event, the Mongol threat failed to materialize, while Louis's crusade to the Holy Land or to Egypt was diverted by his duplicitous brother, Charles of Anjou, to Tunis. Here King Louis IX[6] died of fever, just days before Prince Edward Plantagenet, the future King of England, arrived to join him. Prince Edward went on to Acre,[7] where he was dismayed to find out quite how vulnerable the crusader position had become. He was also horrified to learn that the Venetians, Pisans and Genoese, in addition to fighting each other for control of the Christian sea trade with the Holy Land, were also vying for the benefits of the Egyptian market, including the slave trade. In addition, they were providing the Mamluks with the wherewithal to expand and improve their own navy. Baibar's campaign against the Christian presence resumed, and by 1272, with the fall of the vast fortresses of Crac de Chevalier and Montfort, the crusader presence was almost exclusively confined to the coastal ports. Sultan Baibars died in 1277, in Anatolia, fighting the Seljuks, fellow Muslims, and his death was greeted with huge relief by the Franks. However, while Baibars had not succeeded in extinguishing the Christian presence in the Levant in his own lifetime, he had made its end inevitable. With few of the personal qualities that had won Saladin respect, even from his enemies, Baibars had nevertheless proved to be a brilliant soldier, a subtle politician, a wise administrator and worthy to be ranked among the greatest rulers of his time. According to chroniclers, he either died of wounds, of drinking too much *kumiz* – the fermented mare's milk loved by the Turks and Mongols – or by inadvertently drinking from

a cup of poison, which he had prepared for someone else, and which
he had failed to clean properly.

Mamluk in-fighting, in due course, propelled the Syrian general
Qalawun to the sultanate. Bought by one of the last Ayyubid sultans
for a thousand dinars, Qalawun barely spoke Arabic, but he proved to
be a highly competent commander and, subsequently, ruler. He was
initially diverted by a range of intra-Muslim threats and challenges,
but the Franks did little to take advantage of this situation in order to
strengthen their own precarious position. The massacre of Charles of
Anjou's French garrison in Sicily in 1282[8] ensured that France would
not be in a position to lead any new expedition to the east, and King
Edward of England, who remained well informed and supportive of
the crusader cause, would soon become too heavily embroiled in Welsh
and Scottish politics to offer the strong military leadership that any new
crusade would have required. Groups of military pilgrims periodically
arrived, large enough to be a nuisance, and to destabilize the complex
network of local truces, agreements and accommodations, but always
too small to be of any real military utility. Despite this unpromising
environment, at least the walls of Acre were strengthened and improved,
and a ten-year truce was signed with Sultan Qalawun in 1284. In 1285,
Hugh of Lusignan of Cyprus, the titular King of Jerusalem, died, as
did his eldest son shortly afterwards, leaving a 14-year-old grandson to
be crowned as Henry II by his reluctant and fractious crusader vassals,
who had long favoured an absentee sovereign. A last opportunity to
forge a military alliance with the Mongols, against the Mamluks, was
squandered, and open war erupted again between the Genoese and the
Venetians.[9] Despite all this, large elements of the Frankish population
seemed to have continued to persuade themselves that, for as long as
they did not act in an overtly aggressive manner, the Mamluk Sultan
would tolerate the continued existence of Christian cities along the
coast. However widespread or sincerely held this opinion was, it was
a chimera, and was soon to be brutally exposed as a fatally false hope.

In 1289, succession problems in the County of Tripoli, and in the
fortress port of Tripoli itself, gave Qalawun the excuse he needed
to move against one of the last great centres of crusader presence in

Palestine and Syria. It seems that it was only the arrival of the Sultan and his sizeable army outside the gates of Tripoli that at last alerted the Franks to the seriousness of their situation. Such realization was too late for the defenders. As the siege engines of the Mamluks shattered the walls of the city, the Venetians and Genoese decided that further defence was impossible, and set sail. Panic ensued, and the remaining defenders fled to the boats as Mamluk soldiers poured over the walls. Amalric of Cyprus, King Henry's younger brother, escaped, as did the marshals of the two great military orders, but after that every other man found by the Muslims was killed, and all the women and children taken as slaves. Some refugees did make it to the small island of St Thomas, but Mamluk cavalry forded the shallow waters and finished them off. A Muslim historian tried to visit the island some days later and recorded that he had been driven away by the smell of decaying corpses.

Although a ten-year truce had been agreed between King Henry II and Sultan Qalawun, the precariousness of Acre's position was now painfully clear. The noted soldier John of Grailly, one of the few to have survived the fall of Tripoli, was sent west to try to persuade the Pope, Nicholas IV,[10] to advocate another great crusade. Only some Italians responded to a half-hearted papal call to arms, and, in the hot August of 1290, when the city was full of merchants – Christian and Muslim alike – a band of disorderly, drunken and debauched soldiers arrived in Acre. Short of pay, with no credible commanders, and spoiling for a fight with the infidel, this new crusader rabble caused a riot, and proceeded to slay every Muslim they met. The news of this massacre reached Qalawun in Cairo a few days later, to be swiftly followed by representatives of the government of Acre, who were fulsome in their apologies and in their excuses. The Sultan, understandably, demanded that the guilty parties should be handed over to him for punishment, but despite William of Beaujeu, Grand Marshal of the Templars, arguing the case for appeasement, even at this juncture public opinion in Acre would not countenance handing Christians over to certain death or slavery. Qalawun now deemed the ten-year truce with Acre to have been broken by the Franks, and he determined that the time had come to eradicate the Franks from Syrian soil. His unexpected death as he was setting out from his capital, Cairo, offered only a short respite for the defenders and inhabitants of Acre. His son, al-Ashraf Khalil, swiftly took up his father's cause, summoning his allies from across the region. A last embassy to the

Mamluks was refused an audience with the Sultan, and the ambassadors were thrown into prison, where, reportedly, they did not survive long.

The Muslim armies, from both Egypt and Syria, began to mobilize and march in early 1291, after careful preparation. Nearly 100 siege machines had been built in Cairo and Damascus, and they were moved, with great effort, to the plains of Acre. The weather in early 1291 had been dreadful, and the army from Hama was so heavily laden that it had taken them over a month to reach Acre, having gone via the old Hospitaller fortress of Crac de Chevalier, where they had picked up the constituent parts of an enormous catapult, called *Al-Nasir*, 'The Victorious'. A second great catapult, *Al-Thahir*, 'The Furious', joined it in front of the walls. Al-Ashraf himself arrived with the army on 5 April, having deposited his harem in Damascus. The army he commanded was enormous, and it certainly dwarfed the numbers that the defenders of Acre could muster.

The defences of Acre had been incrementally improved throughout the 12th and 13th centuries. The eastern wall, opposite which Khalil had positioned his great red tent, ran northwards from the Bay of Acre and met the original long northern wall of the city, which ran east from the Mediterranean coast. By the time of the Third Crusade, an outer wall had been added to strengthen the city's defences. Having retaken Acre in 1190, after a three-year occupation by Saladin's army, the crusaders had used prisoners and slaves to construct a new set of double walls around the triangular suburb of Montmusart, which extended up the coast beyond the city's northern walls. These new walls joined the existing northern defences of the city around the St Anthony Gate. The most vulnerable part of the defences was deemed to be in the area of the Accursed Tower, where the eastern and northern walls met, and here Henry II of Jerusalem had built the King's Tower in order to reduce its vulnerability, one of 12 towers that strengthened the landward-facing outer walls. The walls on the Mediterranean and those on the Bay of Haifa were weaker and lower, but the crusaders assumed that they would sustain their maritime superiority. The harbour, often the source of friction between the competing Italian communities, was protected by two long moles, which also kept out silt from the nearby River Belus, with an important defensive feature, the Tower of Flies,[11] at the southern end.

Acre was a rich city, and kings, the Italian communes and the military orders had all invested in it over the course of two centuries, as had the Ayyubids during their three-year occupation, after the battle of Hattin, and just prior to the Third Crusade. The Templars had a large compound and castle, dominating the south-west corner of the city, and they were surrounded by the Italian trading quarters, including the hill which was topped by the Church of St Sabas.[12] With extremely thick walls, the Templar headquarters had an entry gate in its northern wall, with a tall, strong tower surmounted by four turrets, each with a life-size, gilded statue of a lion. There was a further gate and tower to the east, containing the Grand Master's quarters, which looked across the street below into the Pisan commune, and to the house of the nuns of St Anne, which had its own bell tower. There was a further tower, on the sea, which had been built by Saladin, and which housed the Templar treasure, with a series of impressive refectory, arms and stable halls underneath.

The Hospital of St John also had an impressive headquarters, with towers, in the middle of the city, with another centre in Montmusart that included extensive courtyards and gardens. The Teutonic Knights held a widely admired property near the Tower of the Legate, and there was a castle for the garrison troops near St Anthony's Gate, although its fortifications had been neglected. Throughout the rest of the city there were well-endowed churches, and the imposing residences and noble houses of knights, merchants and burgesses. The whole population of Acre in 1291 comprised between 30,000 and 40,000 souls, large by medieval standards, although the number was swollen by refugees. Of these, including the reinforcements that had accompanied King Henry II, there were about 1,000 knights and sergeants, and possibly 14,000 foot soldiers, including those Italian pilgrims who had precipitated the current crisis.

The defenders did not intend to be passive in the face of al-Ashraf's display of Mamluk power, and from the outset they had attempted

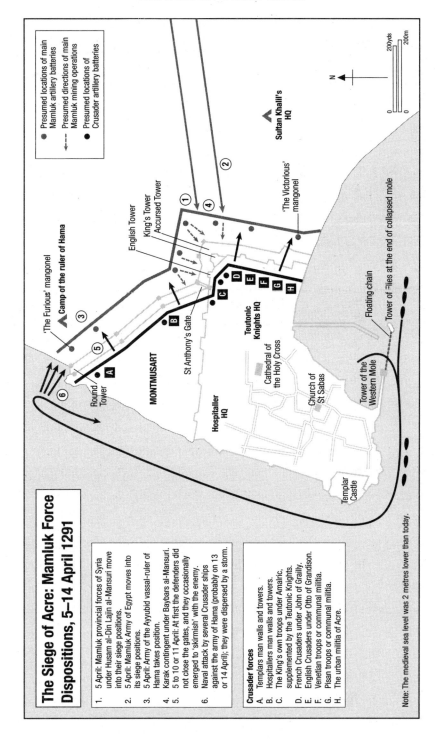

The Siege of Acre: Mamluk Force Dispositions, 5–14 April 1291

1. 5 April: Mamluk provincial forces of Syria under Husam al-Din Lajin al-Mansuri move into their siege positions.
2. 5 April: Mamluk Army of Egypt moves into its siege positions.
3. 5 April: Army of the Ayyubid vassal-ruler of Hama takes position.
4. Karak contingent under Baybars al-Mansuri.
5. 5 to 10 or 11 April: At first the defenders did not close the gates, and they occasionally emerged to 'skirmish' with the enemy.
6. Naval attack by several Crusader ships against the army of Hama (probably on 13 or 14 April); they were dispersed by a storm.

Crusader forces

A. Templars man walls and towers.
B. Hospitallers man walls and towers.
C. The King's own troops under Amalric, supplemented by the Teutonic Knights.
D. French Crusaders under John of Grailly.
E. English Crusaders under Otto of Grandison.
F. Venetian troops or communal militia.
G. Pisan troops or communal militia.
H. The urban militia of Acre.

Note: The medieval sea level was 2 metres lower than today.

Map labels:
- Presumed locations of main Mamluk artillery batteries
- Presumed directions of main Mamluk mining operations
- Presumed locations of Crusader artillery batteries
- 200yds / 200m
- N
- Sultan Khalil's HQ
- 'The Furious' mangonel
- Camp of the ruler of Hama
- English Tower
- King's Tower
- Accursed Tower
- 'The Victorious' mangonel
- St Anthony's Gate
- MONTMUSART
- Round Tower
- Hospitaller HQ
- Teutonic Knights HQ
- Cathedral of the Holy Cross
- Church of St Sabas
- Templar Castle
- Tower of the Western Mole
- Floating chain
- Tower of piles at the end of collapsed mole

to sally out from the gates and towers in order to disrupt the mining efforts, or to try to destroy the siege engines. On 15 April 1291, ten days after the Mamluk forces had been joined by the Sultan, Otto of Grandison had led the Templars on a daring moonlit sortie. They had got deep into the Muslim positions, but the Templar knights and their horses were thwarted by the guy-ropes of the Mamluk tents, and although they had rattled the attackers and destroyed several catapults, they had also sustained a significant number of casualties, as they retreated behind the safety of the walls. A Pisan ship, converted to take catapults, had successfully pummelled the northern end of the Mamluk lines, until a violent storm had destroyed the ship and its weapons of war. A Hospitaller sortie a few nights later also failed, with a Christian knight reportedly finished off, having fallen into a latrine pit. After that, the need to preserve manpower began to trump the desire to take the fight to the enemy. The arrival of King Henry II, who could discern the inevitability of eventual Mamluk success, had led to the last attempt on 1 May to negotiate a settlement with the Sultan. In the stunned silence that had accompanied the impact of the Pisan missile, even that forlorn hope had evaporated.

The Mamluks and their Arab allies now launched attacks along the whole length of the land walls, in order to keep the defending contingents from being able to reinforce each other, but it was in the area around the Accursed Tower that they sensed success was most likely. On 8 May, in the face of increasingly aggressive mining around the clock, the barbican fort in front of the King's Tower was abandoned, and shortly afterwards the towers of the English, the Countess of Blois, and of St Anthony began to crumble. On 15 May the outer wall of the newly built King's Tower collapsed, and the defenders were now forced back onto the inner walls. A major attack on St Anthony's Gate which, if it had succeeded, would have seen the Mamluks inside the city, was only just countered by the reckless bravery of the Templars and the Hospitallers fighting shoulder to shoulder, old enmities and jealousies put aside in the doomed cause of Christian survival in the Holy Land. Al-Ashraf Khalil now ordered a general assault for the morning of Friday 18 May.

Drums beat throughout the night, whipping the attackers into a wild frenzy, and deepening the despair of the defenders and citizens of Acre. As the sun rose on that day, a huge cry went up from the assaulting troops, many of whom had already established themselves between the great double walls. As the missiles from catapults and bows poured through the air and onto the battlements, in what seemed like a solid mass, the Egyptians and Syrians, led by their white-turbaned emirs, surged forward, attacking along the whole length of the walls from St Anthony's Gate to the Patriarch's Tower, close by the harbour. Within this general assault, the main attack – and the focus of the Sultan's attention – was against the Accursed Tower and the surrounding fortifications. The noise around the walls was truly appalling, with the sounds of war overlaid by the battle cries of the assailants, and the noise of cymbals, trumpets and the percussive rhythm of 300 camel-mounted drummers.

The situation within the city was by now chaotic. Bad weather had completely disrupted the maritime evacuation plans, and the poor, weak and needy were being pushed aside by the stronger, and by those who could pay to be saved. Non-combatants and civilians sought the illusory safety of the beaches, the harbour or the Templar compound. The iron discipline of the military orders held, as did that of the French Regiment, but the defence was becoming increasingly incoherent as the Saracens breached the walls in more places. An attempt to staunch the irruption across the ruins of the Accursed Tower was thrown back, even in the face of the Saracen use of Greek fire. A crusader historian recorded an English squire whose surcoat burst into flames and who burned and died, 'as if he had been in a cauldron of pitch'. The Pisan siege machines were burnt, as were their crews, and Saracen horsemen managed to remove the metal spikes that marked the southern end of 'Acre's walls where they met the sea, and drive onto the dock and warehouse areas and into the heart of the city.

William of Beaujeu, on horseback and gathering Templar brethren as he went, headed for St Anthony's Gate. Passing the section of walls held by the Hospitallers, he had encountered Matthew of Clermont, and the Grand Master and the Marshal had both hurled themselves against the Saracen vanguard. The hacking and slashing of close-quarter combat in the narrow streets, alleys and market squares went on until mid-morning, but numbers began to tell, and the Sultan kept feeding fresh troops through the breaches. Locking themselves into a shield wall, the Saracens pressed forward, hurling spears and Greek fire. The Templars and Hospitallers were being slowly pushed back, but they were at least stemming the momentum of the Muslim forces. At that moment, William of Beaujeu, still mounted, but who was neither wearing his full battle armour nor carrying a shield, lifted his left arm and was struck under the armpit by a javelin. Battles can sometimes hinge on such moments, but the crusader cause was almost certainly already lost. Feeling himself mortally wounded, he turned his horse and staggered backwards. Some of the defenders interpreted this as deserting the battlefield, and they too began to retreat.

At this point, Beaujeu's standard-bearer and his household knights closed in around their Grand Master, in order to take him to a place of greater safety, while a group of Italian knights called to him, saying, 'Sire, for God's sake don't leave or the city will fall.' Beaujeu summoned up his failing strength and cried, 'My lords, I can do no more, for I am killed. See the wound here.' At this, he raised his arm so they could see the javelin in his chest, slumped to one side, and started to fall from his horse. The other Templar brethren dismounted, and Beaujeu was placed on a shield and carried, in great pain, to the residence of Amalric, near the German Tower and the beach. There his armour was cut off, while his squires tried to secure a boat for him but were thwarted by the rough seas, and by a Saracen breakthrough at the Tower of the Legate. Still using the shield, Beaujeu was then carried to the Temple compound where more and more of Acre's citizens were fleeing for sanctuary. His last words were to ask what was happening; he died that afternoon, already bitterly conscious that the defence of Acre had failed.

As the resistance of the military orders slowly dissipated, John of Grailly and Otto of Grandison continued to lead a fierce defence of the streets and squares, until Grailly himself was badly wounded, and the two commanders and their followers retreated to the harbour. The Grand Master of the Hospital, John of Villiers, was also wounded, and his knights took him, protesting, onto another ship. His marshal, Matthew of Clermont, having seen his Master safely on board, returned to the fight, where he died in the streets of the Genoese quarter, alongside his remaining Hospitaller brethren, all of them perishing true to their vows of honour, courage and loyalty.

The Patriarch of Acre was rowed out to a Venetian ship, but he allowed so many others to take a place in his skiff that it overturned, and they were all drowned. The Catalan adventurer Roger Flor, who had fought bravely as a Templar during the siege, now turned buccaneer and, having taken command of a Templar galley, founded his great fortune on the blackmail that he extorted from the distressed noblewomen of

Acre. At this stage Henry, King of Cyprus and Jerusalem, and Amalric, Constable of Jerusalem and Lord of Tyre, plainly perceived that neither counsel nor reinforcement were of any further value, and they also embarked to escape. The active defence of Acre was now all but over, and the mighty city and port had fallen to the Muslims nearly 200 years since it was seized in the First Crusade, and almost exactly 100 years since Richard the Lionheart had retaken it from Saladin during the Third Crusade. Sad carnage followed as the Saracens sacked and plundered the city, killing or enslaving all those who had failed to find a berth on the overcrowded galleys and sailing ships of the Italians. In the space of a day, all that remained of the Christian presence in Acre were those knights and the civilians who had found sanctuary within the stout walls of the Temple compound.

Even while Acre was being given over to his soldiers, Khalil had already sent a strong contingent of his army to the fortress port of Tyre, 25 miles of hard marching away, and now the last crusader stronghold of any significance in the Holy Land. Tyre was the strongest city on the coast, and it was potentially impregnable against an enemy that lacked control of the sea. It was from here that the crusaders had sustained their foothold in the Holy Land, when Conrad of Montferrat had been able to defy Saladin over a century earlier. Khalil's plan had merely been to invest Tyre, hoping to get it to surrender, and he had not intended to try to assault the city. However, with Saracen forces once again at the gates, and seeing the pathetic and tragic convoy of ships limping past the city as they struggled from Acre to the ports of Cyprus, the garrison commander, Adam of Caffran, lost his nerve. On 19 May, a mere day after the fall of Acre, he, along with the military, religious and social elite of Tyre, took to the ships anchored and moored in the harbour, and also set sail for Cyprus. The fortress fell without a struggle, and those who had failed to find a ship joined the survivors of Acre in the slave markets of Egypt and Syria, where the price of human misery plunged.

Meanwhile, within the smoking wreck of Acre, the Templars and the remnants of the citizenry still held out in the great Temple compound, tantalizingly close to the sea, where some Italian ships had returned, having discharged their sad cargos in Cyprus. After a week-long standoff, and conscious that an assault would simply cost more lives, Khalil offered the Templar Marshal, Peter of Severy, the opportunity to sail for Cyprus, with all the refugees and their possessions, in return for surrendering the fortress. Peter accepted the offer, and Emir Kitburgha and a force of Saracens entered the compound, while the Sultan's standard was raised over the great entrance tower, with its leonine statues. What was left of the Teutonic Knights had already made a separate deal, and had departed. Reports vary, but undoubtedly the Mamluk soldiers molested some of the women, girls and young men sheltering there, and the crusader knights fell upon them, killing a large number of them, including Kitburgha himself. Having driven out the remainder of the Mamluk soldiers, they hurled down the Sultan's banner. That night, the Marshal sent the treasure of the Templar Order, along with its commander, to Sidon. In due course this treasure would be transferred to Cyprus. The next morning Khalil offered the same terms, deploring the conduct of his men. Peter of Severy, trusting his word, came out of the Temple compound and was promptly taken prisoner. Along with those who had accompanied him, he was beheaded. The last of the Templars now retreated to the treasury and barricaded themselves in. On 28 May, having mined the tower, the Saracens broke in, and the whole structure fell in upon them, killing hundreds of defenders and attackers alike. Any crusader survivors were executed.

By the middle of August, Sultan Khalil, and Emir Sanjar al-Shujai, the commander who had stayed his hand in front of the red tent, had taken Sidon, Beirut, Haifa, and the two Templar castles of Tortosa and Athlit. All that was left of 200 years of the formidable crusader military framework was the lonely island fortress of Ruad, lying some 2 miles off the coast, opposite Tortosa. There the Templars would remain for another 12 years, vainly hoping to act as the springboard for a further crusade, until 1303, when the whole future of the order itself began to be in doubt. By then al-Ashraf Khalil had been dead for nearly a decade, assassinated by his own deputies after only three years as Sultan.

However, in the short time that was left to him, Khalil had proceeded to extirpate the Christian presence in the Holy Land, demolishing castles, converting churches to mosques, destroying irrigation systems and cutting down orchards. The coastline was a scene of devastation, and the effects on trade flows, markets and the economy were to last for decades. Mamluk dominance, so nearly destroyed by the Mongol threat, would last for a further two centuries, until challenged and toppled by the Ottomans in the early 16th century. Local Christians were now treated little better than slaves, and many converted to Islam or fled west. In Cyprus the refugees lived a miserable existence, unwanted and serving as a constant reminder of the failures and the humiliations of the collapse of Outremer. The old easy, confident tolerance of Islam had gone, and, embittered by experience of the long religious wars, a stronger, more pronounced contempt for the infidel now marked the relationship between the Muslim world and Christendom, as they contemplated each other from Spain, through the Mediterranean, to the new battlefields of the Balkans. Two hundred years later, in 1492, the Christians would repay the loss of Acre and the Holy Land by taking the last great Saracen fortress of Granada, and expelling all Muslims – and along with them the majority of Jews – from the Iberian Peninsula.

The crusades did not end with the fall of Acre, but the glamour, the idealism and the certainty were gone. Hattin and the loss of Jerusalem in 1187 had been a colossal shock to the Christian world, but by 1291 everyone knew the crusader states were crumbling. Christians may have been saddened by the loss of Acre, but they could not have been surprised. Apocalyptic visions and preachings no longer inspired large-scale Christian military pilgrimages in the way they had previously, while papal authority had been diminished by the sort of Church scandals that would eventually catalyse the Reformation, and by the politicization of the crusading ideal for narrow, partisan agendas. The great European monarchs were now too busy building up their own authority, and with countering the predatory actions of their own Christian neighbours. In the east, the newly reconstituted Byzantine Empire was too militarily and economically weak, and too beset by multiple threats, to reassume any leadership role in the Holy Land, even if that had been accepted by the Latin Church.

The military orders had mixed fortunes. Acknowledging only the Pope as their superior, they still had great wealth, and great convening power. However, the Teutonic Knights had turned their backs on the Holy Land and transferred their attention to the pagan tribes of the Baltic. Admired, respected, but never liked, the Templars and Hospitallers had set up new headquarters in Cyprus, but they were not made welcome by the Cypriot nobility, nor by the Lusignan kings, and they began to look for new homes. In a long, drawn-out, four-year campaign, the Hospitallers eventually took the island of Rhodes from the Byzantines in 1310, which they would hold for over 200 years, and established a fortress in Smyrna.[13] Their story was far from over.

The Templars were less fortunate. Disliked for their arrogance, wealth, recklessness, and the routine irresponsibility of their policies in the Levant, they had attracted powerful enemies, and in 1307 King Philip IV of France and Pope Clement V, his close ally, moved against them. Using a potent cocktail of accusations, ranging from heresy to sodomy, the order was suppressed, and the last Grand Master, James of Molay, was burnt at the stake in 1314. He died cursing King Philip and Pope Clement, both of whom were dead within months.

The crusading movement was by no means over. Soldiers of God would continue to fight and die 'for the Cross' in Egypt, North Africa, Italy, Spain, Anatolia, the Baltics and the Balkans, and at sea in the Aegean, the Red Sea, the Indian Ocean and the Mediterranean, for centuries. However, with the coming rise of the Ottomans, Christendom would once again find itself on the defensive against a new, powerful, religiously motivated and aggressive Muslim empire. Romantic, chivalric dreams of rescuing the True Cross, and of liberating the Holy City and the Holy Sites would have to wait.

PART THREE

Ruin of an Empire

5

The Walls Fail

Constantinople 1453

On 28 May 1453, there was no debate about when the next assault would come, nor where the eye of this violent hurricane would fall. On the 53rd day of the siege, Sultan Mehmet II's intentions could not have been clearer, and the spies for both sides confirmed this. Fires burned along the ridge opposite the great triple walls of Theodosius. After two days of fasting, the Ottomans were now feasting, feeding an appetite and bolstering a courage that would shortly be tested, yet again, as they prepared to launch a general assault against the landward and seaward defences of Constantinople. The foul weather of the previous week had dispersed, but the ground remained damp underfoot, and the smell of roasting lamb coming from the Ottoman lines only served to remind the defenders, gazing out from the walls, of their own straitened circumstances. The flames of a thousand camp and cooking fires reflected off the low cloud base that lay across the great capital city of Byzantium, across the Golden Horn, across the Bosporus, and across the Sea of Marmara. In the aftermath of the torrential rains that had lashed the opposing forces several days earlier, and of a fog thicker than anything in living memory, a strange light had appeared above that monument to Byzantine greatness, the Church of Holy Wisdom, the Hagia Sophia.[1] Many within the city walls had felt that the ghostly phenomenon marked the departure of the Virgin Mary, the Protector of Constantinople, since its dedication as the imperial capital 1,100 years earlier. However, the Emperor Constantine XI Palaiologos had not been one of them.

Constantine looked far older than his 48 years, as he stood on a small dais within the imperial headquarters tent. This large command tent was hard by the inner walls, and close to the 5th Military Gate, which was situated just north of the River Lycus and between the Rhenium Gate to the south and the Charisius Gate to the north. Seven weeks of close siege had aged him, as it had every man who clustered around him. The constant bombardment from Sultan Mehmet's cannon; the strain of the fighting on the walls; the requirement to constantly arbitrate between Catholic and Orthodox, Greek and Latin, Venetian and Genoese; the paucity of fighting men, and the constant attrition; the shortages of food; the failures of Latin kingdoms and the Pope to send reinforcements; the silence of his brothers in the Morea:[2] all had etched lines in his already gaunt features, all had contributed to his pallor and his greying hair.

Constantine had been a young man in Constantinople during the Ottoman siege of 1422, he had been Despot of Morea for nearly 20 years, and he had served, twice, as a competent imperial regent. In 1439, he had reluctantly acquiesced when his brother, Emperor John, had argued that a renewal of the union between the Catholic and Orthodox churches, in schism since 1054, was the sad but necessary price to be paid for unifying Christendom against the Muslim threat. He was painfully conscious that the Greeks had seen his brother's submission to the Catholic papacy as a betrayal of the Orthodox faith, and he had been horrified to then see the promised crusade by Catholic powers shattered on the battlefield of Varna in 1444.[3] Only dissension within the Ottoman ranks had lifted a subsequent siege of the capital. In 1446, he had been on the Hexamilion walls of the Isthmus of Corinth[4] when Sultan Murad II's new, great cannon had blasted away centuries of confidence in strong fortifications.

By the time of Constantine's accession to the imperial throne in 1449, on the death of his brother, Constantinople was a shadow of its former glory. It had been the Palaiologos family who had re-established the Byzantine Empire in Constantinople in 1261, but the city had never truly recovered from the sacking by the soldiers of the Fourth Crusade in 1204, nor had its population forgotten the traumatizing experience. Instead of the grand and glorious imperial capital that it had once been, with a population of around a million people, 15th-century Constantinople was by now an almost rural network of small population centres, with many of the city's churches and palaces, including the former imperial Bucoleon Palace on the Sea of Marmara, abandoned and in disrepair.[5] The Palaiologos dynasty now used the new Palace of Blachernae,[6] which anchored the northern end of the great walls to the south bank of the Golden Horn. The city's population had declined significantly during the half-century of Latin occupation, and during the Byzantine civil wars of the 14th century, which had done so much to enable Ottoman expansion into south-east Europe. The outbreak of the Black Death had wrought further global devastation from China to the Atlantic, and, by his accession, Constantine's capital had probably contained a mere 50,000 people.

But hardship, disappointments and setbacks had steeled Constantine to his task, and he had grown into an emperor worthy of the times, and worthy of Constantinople's great history. Standing on the dais, clad in imperial armour and regalia, his voice was firm and his shoulders straight, as he prepared to address his audience. To one side of him stood representatives of the last of the great names of Byzantium: George Sphrantzes, who had only recently proposed that the childless Constantine should marry Sultan Murad II's Serbian widow, and Sultan Mehmet II's mother, in order to deflect Ottoman aggression; Lucas Notaras, Grand Admiral of a scarcely existent Byzantine navy, who acted as the Emperor's senior adviser; Andronicus Cantacuzenus, last Grand Domestic of the Byzantine Empire, whose ancestors had once held the imperial purple themselves; and Constantine and John Lascaris, eminent scholars. In front of him were the upturned faces of every man of rank in the city, of church, trade and state, of every Christian nation, and even those of the small band of Muslims allied to Byzantium. There was Cardinal Isidore, former Metropolitan of Kiev and All Russia, who had personally recruited 200 Neapolitan fighters; the Bocciardo brothers, Paolo, Antonio and Troilo, renegades from the Republic of Venice, which had an agreement with the Ottomans; their Venetian bailiff, Minotto, who was technically the guardian of that agreement, but who could not bring himself to contemplate the prospect of the great Christian city of Constantinople falling; Don Francisco de Toledo, a Catalan; Johannes Grant, a German, or possibly a Scot, whose engineering skills had so far thwarted Ottoman attempts to mine the walls; John of Dalmata, a long-term comrade of Constantine's; and Prince Orhan, a 'pretender' to the Ottoman sultanate, whose small band of loyal 'apostates' held the southern end of the walls. Most significant among those assembled was Giovanni Giustiniani Longo,[7] a highly distinguished Genoese soldier of fortune, who had brought with him 700 professional soldiers from Genoa, and from the Genoese island of Chios.[8] These soldiers, along with the Byzantine Imperial Guard, formed the core of the Christian defence and, on his arrival in the city, Constantine had promptly appointed Giustiniani as the commander of the overall defence efforts.

In a clear, confident voice, the Emperor spoke of the gallantry of the defence, of the heroism of the defenders, of the unity of all the contingents, despite their past differences and their rivalries. He recalled Constantinople's great past, and the routine triumph of Byzantium and her allies over great odds and great adversity. He invoked fortune, history and reputation. He compared the great Sultan Murad II with his young, callow successor, Mehmet, and he sought parallels in the Ottoman failures of 1422 and 1444, and their prospects in the imminent assault. The odds were great, but Christ, the Mother of God, the angels and the archangels now raised their swords alongside those of the defenders. He begged every man to seek forgiveness for past wrongs, sins and enmities, and then he raised his hand. 'Listen,' he said, pointing through the canvas of the tent to the walls beyond. There was suddenly profound silence, and everyone knew what that silence signified. Constantine spoke again: 'Those who are to die, be certain your names will live for ever, wreathed in glory. Those who are marked to live, let us meet tomorrow at the Church of Holy Wisdom and celebrate a glorious victory.' At that he raised his hands above his head and roared, 'To your posts – for God, for Christendom … and for Constantinople.' 'Constantinople!' those gathered there roared back, and every man departed for his post, and to his fate.

While the Mamluks had been tearing down the walls of Tripoli, overpowering the fortifications of Acre, and obliterating the Christian presence in Syria and the Holy Land in the late 13th century, another new power had been rising in the Middle East. According to legend, Osman, founder of the Ottoman dynasty, was born on the same day the Mongols had sacked Baghdad in 1258. Little is known of him except that the Seljuk Sultan had granted him and his Turkic tribe lands in Bithynia, adjacent to the fast-ebbing frontiers of the Byzantine Empire. From here,

Osman had taken advantage of the declining Greek imperial power, and the increasing fragmentation of the Seljuk dominions, to expand his own power and reputation. Around the year of Acre's fall, he received the trappings of a sultan, if not the title: a golden war banner; a *mehter*, war drum; a *tug*, a pole with circularly arranged horsetail hairs; and a gilded sword, which would be used during the coronation services of future sultans. He also had a dream, which became embedded in Ottoman mythology. In this dream, Osman saw a moon rise from the breast of a holy man and sink into his own breast. A tree then sprouted from his navel whose shade encompassed the whole world. Beneath this shade there were four mountains, and streams flowed from the foot of each mountain range. Purportedly, the mountains were those of the Caucasus, the Atlas, the Taurus and the Haemus in the Balkans, and the streams represented the Tigris, the Euphrates, the Danube and the Nile. The sun glistened on the peaks and the waterways, on cities, towers and minarets, and on a land of abundant fertility. Birds of every description sang, every leaf of the overarching tree was shaped like a scimitar and, when a mighty wind arose, they all bent to point at the various cities of the world, but especially towards Constantinople, the 'Red Apple' of all Muslim ambition and desire. Osman himself would describe Constantinople as 'that city, placed at the junction of two seas and two continents, seeming like a diamond set between two sapphires and two emeralds, to form the most precious stone in a ring of universal empires'. His successors, not least Mehmet II, would enthusiastically embrace this grandiose ambition.

When Osman awoke and related this story to the holy man, whose daughter he would fortuitously marry, the seer told him, 'God has given the imperial office to you and to your descendants.' This would be the *ur*-myth of the great Ottoman dynasty that would encompass 35 sultans, and which would come to dominate the Middle East, the Mediterranean and south-eastern Europe for the next 500 years.

Byzantine attempts to counter Osman and his aggressive *ghazi* warriors[9] came to nothing. The prospect of a possible Byzantine–Mongol alliance had been shattered by a fresh Egyptian Mamluk victory against the Mongols outside Damascus in 1303, and a Catalan mercenary force under Roger Flor, last seen enriching himself from terrified Frankish ladies during the panicked evacuation from Acre, had ended up turning on the Byzantine Emperor. Osman himself lived long enough to see his son, Orhan, take the city of Bursa in 1326, after a nine-year siege, and establish a new Ottoman capital there. Osman died of gout, which became a genetic disease in the Ottoman dynasty, leaving a will to his son, Orhan, exhorting him to sustain the Turkic *ghazi* tradition of raiding and conquest, to conduct Muslim *jihad* against the Byzantines, and to dedicate himself to spreading the word of Islam.

During Byzantium's civil wars, the predatory Kingdom of Serbia had been able to overrun much of the Balkans and had even threatened Constantinople. In response to this threat, Emperor John VI Cantacuzenus married his daughter Theodora to Orhan, while also employing Ottoman warriors as mercenaries and, fatefully, granting them a base on the European side of the Dardanelles, at Cimpe. After a major earthquake in 1354, the Ottomans had consolidated their position by seizing the important town, port and fort of Gallipoli. From this initial foothold in Europe, the Ottomans had moved rapidly outwards into Thrace and the Balkans, and were soon in direct confrontation and conflict with the Serbs. Sometime during Orhan's reign, the Janissaries[10] had been established, forming the Ottoman Sultan's household troops, and becoming one of the first modern standing armies in Europe. They began as an elite corps, raised through the *devsirme* system of child levy enslavement, by which male children were conscripted from Christian vassals of the Sultan, subjected to forced circumcision and conversion to Islam, underwent intensive training, and were then incorporated into the Ottoman army. Formidably motivated, disciplined and armed, they would participate in all the major Ottoman wars and campaigns, against Christians and fellow Muslims alike, developing into a state within a state until their brutal suppression and disbandment in the early 19th century. It would be a feature of Ottoman rule that many of the most prominent military and civil leaders would be products of the *devsirme* system, which guaranteed a pool of professionally trained soldiers and administrators, whose advancement, and therefore whose loyalty, was totally focused on the Sultan. A determination never to present the Janissaries with a conflict of loyalty underpinned the practice of imperial fratricide, whereby the sultan who succeeded to the throne straightway killed his male siblings, and their male offspring, for the good of Ottoman political stability and unity.

In 1369, the Ottomans took the old Roman city of Adrianople, renamed it Edirne, and made it their new capital. Constantinople, although still linked to the Mediterranean and Black Seas, thanks to its own naval strength, and that of the Christian Italian maritime powers, increasingly began to look and feel like an island in a Turkish-dominated sea. In that same year, presaging Emperor John Palaiologos's efforts a century later, the Byzantine Emperor had travelled to Rome and converted to Catholicism, in an ultimately futile attempt to consolidate a united Christian front against the Muslim threat. In a classic example of Freud's 'narcissism of small differences',[11] the Orthodox Church and the Emperor's Greek subjects bitterly opposed this apostasy, despite the immediacy and proximity of the threat. In truth, after the experience of the Latin Empire, many Orthodox Christians had found the experience of Ottoman vassalage, which allowed them freedom of worship, easier to bear than the arrogance and the doctrinal narrowmindedness of the Church of Rome, and successive Catholic popes.

In June 1389, the armies of Sultan Murad I, and those of Prince Lazar of Serbia, clashed at Kosovo Polje, one of those rare areas of open ground in a region marked by forests, rivers and a multitude of steep, isolated valleys. The Ottoman army may have been as large as 30,000, possibly including numbers of Christian mercenaries or vassals, while the Serbian forces were somewhat smaller, with contingents from Albania and Bosnia, and some Knights Hospitaller from their new fortress city of Rhodes. In a battle whose fortunes fluctuated throughout the day, Prince Lazar and King Teodor of Albania died, while a Serbian knight, taken prisoner, had got close enough to Sultan Murad to kill him in his tent.[12] Both armies withdrew from the battlefield, and Prince Bayezid, summoned from the front line and having been informed of his father's death, immediately slew his younger brother, becoming sole heir to the Ottoman throne. Soon after, as the Serbs realized the scale of their losses, Prince Lazar's daughter was married to now-Sultan Bayezid, while Lazar's son, Stefan, became a loyal vassal of the Ottomans and would play a decisive part in the defeat of the Hungarian–Burgundian Crusade at the battle of Nicopolis in 1396.[13]

By this time the Eastern Roman Empire had lost almost all its Anatolian heartland, less a small toehold in Trebizond on the south coast of the

Black Sea, and most of its Thracian and Balkan hinterland, less the Morea. The great capital city had now become a critical Ottoman objective, but the Byzantines were temporarily relieved when the Turco-Mongol conqueror, Timur the Lame, known in the west as Tamerlane, turned his murderous attention to the Levant and the Middle East. Cut in the mould of his ancestor Genghis Khan, Tamerlane's campaigns against west, south and central Asia, the Caucasus, Persia and the Sultanate of Delhi left the familiar trademark piles of skulls, and desolated, despoiled and depopulated cities and towns. Aleppo and Damascus were taken, and all the inhabitants massacred or enslaved, and in his sacking of Baghdad, Timur demanded that every one of his soldiers produce at least two severed heads.[14] Contemporaries compared Tamerlane's army to 'ants and locusts covering the whole countryside, plundering, ravaging and killing'.

Throughout this period, marked by a parallel tension and antagonism between the Turkic Ottomans and the Egyptian Mamluks, Tamerlane and Sultan Bayezid had been exchanging letters of insult and abuse. At last, Bayezid had over-reached himself and demanded tribute from an emir loyal to Tamerlane. The latter took this as a personal insult, and, in early 1402, his Mongol army invaded Anatolia, driving through the last remnants of the Seljuk Turks and deep into the Ottoman eastern borderlands. On 20 July of that year, Tamerlane, with an army well in excess of 100,000, even allowing for contemporary exaggeration, met that of the Ottomans, with their Christian vassals, outside the town of Ankara. Despite the heroism of Prince Stefan and the heavily armoured Serbian cavalry, who managed to save one of Sultan Bayezid's sons, and the whole Ottoman treasury, and to take them both back to Constantinople, the Ottomans were worn down in the course of a ferocious day's fighting and defeated. Sultan Bayezid took to the hills, which he would have been well advised to have defended from the outset, but was soon captured, and died in captivity three months later. In December 1402, Timur invested the mighty Knights Hospitaller fortress at Smyrna, and, after a siege of 15 days, the Knights took to their ships and set sail for their main base at Rhodes, choosing to fortify their last mainland holding in Halicarnassus[15] by plundering the stones of the Mausoleum, one of the Seven Wonders of the Ancient World, in order to fortify the ramparts of their castle of St Peter.

To Christian relief, Tamerlane's attention was drawn back to central Asia, while Sultan Bayezid's death led to the 1403 Treaty of Gallipoli. This was signed between the Ottomans, Byzantium, Venice, Genoa and the Knights of St John, and it led to the Christian powers ferrying the Ottoman survivors of the battle of Ankara back across the Dardanelles. Further relief came from a bitter, 12-year Ottoman civil war, in which Bayezid's sons battled for the Ottoman succession, and in 1413, when Sultan Mehmet I had emerged as the undisputed Ottoman ruler, he still chose to renew the Gallipoli Treaty, and even referred to himself as 'the obedient son' of the Byzantine Emperor Manuel II Palaiologos. However, the relative positions of power between the Byzantines, the Italian city-states and the Ottomans were soon re-established when Sultan Murad II succeeded his father in 1421. Defeating a 'pretender' to his throne, who had, rather foolishly, been released from comfortable confinement by the Byzantines, Murad II had briefly besieged Constantinople in 1422 before being distracted by a rebellion that threatened the city of Bursa. In the next two decades, while cultivating the powerful image of a *ghazi* king, and reversing the Ottoman losses after Ankara, Murad II would inflict defeats on the Venetians, the Serbs and the Hungarians, capturing further vast areas of the Balkans, including the important city and port of Thessaloniki. He would also lay siege to the great Serbian fortress of Belgrade, which stood on the confluence of the rivers Sava and Danube, and which guarded access to the great plains of the Kingdom of Hungary. In the summer of 1444, Murad II, worried by the apparent rapprochement between the Byzantines and Rome, with its prospect of a new crusade, and challenged by a fresh revolt in Anatolia, offered a ten-year truce to the Catholic Hungarians.[16] On Hungarian acceptance of his offer, Murad II had, surprisingly, chosen to abdicate in favour of his son Mehmet, who was only 12 years old at the time.

The Christian powers breathed another huge sigh of relief, as the great Muslim warlord put aside his temporal responsibilities, and a child ascended the sultanate. However, in another one of those fatal miscalculations that marked western diplomacy at the time, the papacy again chose to overplay its hand. Pope Eugene IV, having effected the reluctant rapprochement and union between the Catholic and Orthodox churches in 1439, now persuaded the young Hungarian king, Vladislaus, that breaking the truce he had agreed and signed with Sultan Murad was not a betrayal, because the Ottomans were 'infidels', and that, given the accession of the new boy-sultan, this was an excellent time to launch a new crusade.

King Vladislaus, and the great Hungarian general and statesman John Hunyadi,[17] therefore led a large Christian army towards the Black Sea, advancing confidently on the assumption that their Italian allies would delay any Ottoman reinforcement from Anatolia, while then proceeding to come through the Bosporus to rendezvous with the main Christian army on the Black Sea coast. To the contrary, the Venetians and Genoese had actually transported the Ottoman armies across the Dardanelles, for both payment and commercial concessions, and subsequently failed to make any link-up with Vladislaus and Hunyadi. The adolescent Mehmet II, now nominal sultan, wrote to his 'retired' father saying, 'If *you* are the Sultan, come and lead *your* armies. If *I* am the Sultan, I hereby order you to come and lead *my* armies.' Murad returned to take command, and he narrowly defeated the Christian coalition, capturing and beheading King Vladislaus, whose body was never recovered. In due course Murad took back the throne from his son and he defeated a further Christian coalition at the Second Battle of Kosovo Polje in 1448. John Hunyadi, taken prisoner and then ransomed, retired to defend the Kingdom of Hungary against further Ottoman incursions, where his own story would be mixed in fatefully with that of Vlad Dracul, the 'Impaler'.[18] Murad himself retired to Edirne, where he died in 1451, and Mehmet II, now 19, had re-ascended the throne of the Ottoman sultans. Hardened by his experiences of both triumph and failure, Mehmet now looked again to the 'Red Apple', and to the fulfilment of Osman's dream, and of Ottoman destiny.

On 6 April 1453, hearing them long before they could see them, the sentries on the 4-mile-long Theodosian Walls watched in awe as the massed *kos* and *mehter* drummers of the Ottoman army, accompanied by the discordant *sevre* pipe-players, crested the ridge in front of them. As their hypnotic, rhythmic beat continued, hour after hour, the fighting men of Mehmet II's legions poured onto the ridge, marching and riding in disciplined silence as they flowed to the left and to the right of the bands. First came the Rumelian Division of south-east Europe, swinging north to the Golden Horn, their ranks filled with the Vlach, Serb, Bulgar and Albanian vassals of the Sultan. Reaching its waters, they halted, turned and settled. Then it was the turn of the Anatolian Division, recruited from Asia Minor and the Arab lands, to pass over the ridgeline, heading south to the shores of the Sea of Marmara. Foot soldiers and mail-clad *sipahi*[19] cavalry from the Ottoman heartlands of Anatolia passed parallel to the walls, turned and stood silent, pennants and war banners flapping in the spring breeze. Despite these enormous numbers, there was still a substantial gap in the centre of the line, opposite the fortifications between the Rhenium and Charisius Gates, where the walls fell into the valley of the River Lycus. As the beating of drums ceased, a heart-stopping yell went up as the *bashibazouks* – those irregulars recruited from the fields and the city slums of the Ottoman Empire – poured over the ridge and ran each way along the armoured fronts of Rumelia and Anatolia. Promised both earthly wealth and religious martyrdom, their role would be to die in huge numbers in the early assaults, hurling themselves against the walls and wearing down the Byzantine defences, and the defenders, while Mehmet waited to deliver the decisive blows that he intended would end Constantinople's 1,100 years of history as an imperial capital and a Christian city.

The running and screaming stopped, and even the *bashibazouks* fell silent, while the gap in the centre remained unfilled. By now Emperor Constantine was on the battlements of the high inner walls, along with Giovanni Giustiniani Longo, and the other battle captains, Greek, Genoese and Venetian. All were staring at the staggering array of Ottoman power. The drums ceased their beating, and now the Janissary *ortas*[20] marched to their battle lines, swaggering down the hill beneath their tall white felt hats, with bronzed shields and breastplates dazzling in the sun, and drawn scimitars resting on their shoulders. They too joined the other elements of the Sultan's army in an almost unbroken line from sea to sea, and they also stood silent and waiting. To their right, the watchers on the wall could also now see another huge Ottoman force march down the north shore of the Golden Horn, with their left flank coming to rest on the walled Genoese enclave of Pera,[21] containing the prominent Galata Tower or Tower of Christ.

At last, a tall young man, dressed in scarlet and armour, mounted on a huge white horse, and wearing an ornate spiked helmet with a turban wrapped around it, rode onto the ridge. He was followed by two poles. On one, green, but almost black with age, was a banner that the Prophet Muhammad had once carried, and on the other were the nine horsetails that befitted a sultan's *tug*. The Emperor and the Sultan could see each other, could almost look into each other's eyes. Constantinople had been subjected to 22 great sieges, and only three had been successful: that of the Latins and Venetians of the Fourth Crusade, and twice during the Byzantine civil wars. Despite their weakened state, and their paucity of fighting men, why should a besieging army not, once again, find itself battered to impotence by the great land walls of Constantine's capital? In the silence, Sultan Mehmet now raised his arm, and the Janissaries parted to reveal a huge pit that had been dug into the hillside, and where the largest cannon ever built was now being positioned: the Basilisk.

Sultan Mehmet II had made his preparations with care. The borders in Anatolia and the Balkans were secure, and there was an uneasy peace with the Mamluks of Egypt. The enmity between the Catholic and Orthodox churches remained as sharp as ever, despite the imperial conversion. The Spanish were still prosecuting the *Reconquista*; the Holy Roman Empire was preoccupied with internecine struggles; while the English and French crowns remained at war, although the English triumphs at Crécy, Poitiers and Agincourt had mostly been reversed. The Hungarians were a chastened force after Nicopolis, Varna and Kosovo Polje; and there were treaties with Venice and Genoa, even though Venetian and Genoese soldiers and sailors were among the defenders of Constantinople. Sultan Murad II had already built a fort on the Anatolian side of the Bosporus, in order to help control the Christian shipping that transited between the Adriatic, the Aegean islands and the trading cities of the Black Sea. In 1452, Mehmet II had rapidly constructed a matching fortress on the European side, known as *Rumeli Hisari*, 'the Roman fort', or as *Bogazkesen*, the 'strait-blocker' or the 'throat-cutter'. The first Venetian ship to attempt to run the blockade had been sunk, its crew members beheaded, and its captain impaled. In cutting off their supply lines to the Black Sea, the Ottomans had effectively declared war on Constantinople.

Ottoman levies and vassals had been summoned from all across the empire, and the foundries of Edirne worked night and day to produce cannon capable of reducing the Theodosian Walls to rubble. In this endeavour Sultan Mehmet had recruited a renegade Hungarian gunsmith, Urban. Urban had previously offered his artillery services to the Byzantine Emperor, but his price-tag was out of the straitened

Constantine's reach. He had now promised to provide Mehmet with the means to breach the great fortifications. The Basilisk, longer than five men lying end-to-end, and firing a stone cannon ball of a diameter larger than the outstretched grasp of the largest man, was his fulfilment of that promise. It had taken 200 oxen to haul the cannon to its huge gun pit on the ridge, over bridges specially reinforced to take its vast weight, and that of its ammunition. In addition to all this activity on the land, Mehmet had also assembled a formidable naval force, whose object was to control the Sea of Marmara, and to deter or defeat any attempt to resupply or reinforce the defenders. Ideally, it would penetrate the Golden Horn itself, threatening the sea walls and stretching the defenders even further, but for now the giant sea chain that stretched between the two shores of the Golden Horn made that impossible.[22]

On 11 April 1453, an enormous explosion signalled the advent of a new era of siege warfare, as Urban's great cannon fired its first shot at the walls near the 5th Military Gate. For the next week the Basilisk, and the other cannon that Mehmet had had hauled before the walls, poured their fire into the Byzantine defences, trying to establish a breach through which the Sultan's army could pour into the great city. At last, on the night of 17 April, the first major land assault was launched.

The Byzantine landward defences of Constantinople, which had been built just over a mile further west of the old, original Constantinian Wall, were in three layers. The main, inner wall, standing 40 feet high and 16 feet thick, was separated from the lower, 30-foot-high outer wall by a 65-foot terrace, the *peribolos*. Between the outer wall and a moat, often dry, there was a further 165-foot terrace, the *parateichion*, while a low breastwork crowned the moat's eastern escarpment. There were 96 battlemented towers along its 3½-mile length, and six main gates, with postern gates at either side that allowed the defenders to reach the *peribolos* and the *parateichion*. However, while the walls of Constantinople were formidable, the defenders of those walls were perilously few in number, and a recent census of the population had revealed only 5,000 men of fighting age and ability, including those of Constantine's household troops. There were more priests and monks in the city than soldiers. With the Venetians and Genoese, the total Christian fighting strength stood at around 7,000, for a walled perimeter, landward and seaward, of over 12 miles. In view of these small numbers, Giustiniani had chosen to fight on the outer walls, and in the *peribolos*, supported by archers, crossbowmen, arquebusiers and his small inventory of cannon, from the inner walls. While there was, as yet, no threat to the sea walls, and the slow reloading of Ottoman cannon allowed the non-combatants of Constantinople to effect running repairs to the damaged walls, Giustiniani felt confident of holding the Ottomans. His initial optimism was right. The massive frontal assault of the 17th broke on the black armour of the Genoese mercenaries, and on the arrow swarms of the Greek archers. The fosse and *parateichion* were filled and covered with the bodies of the *bashibazouks*, and of Mehmet's expendable Christian vassals. Christian morale in the city rose, while the young Sultan's critics, among them his Grand Vizier, inherited from his father, questioned his strategy and urged caution.

During the period preceding the siege, Constantine had sent increasingly urgent messages to western Europe, trying to heighten awareness of the severe plight of Constantinople, and of what was left of the Byzantine Empire, while attempting to elicit support and reinforcements. But only belatedly had the Pope, who was persistently urging Constantine to demonstrate greater commitment to Church union, realized the stark reality of the scale and imminence of the Ottoman threat. Even Venice, involved in its own fights with other Italian city-states, and in treaty with the Ottomans, had begun to debate the wisdom and tenability of their current detached policy towards Byzantium.

On 20 April, the sentries on the sea walls made out, in the distance, the sails of ships. They were three Genoese warships, and a grain supply ship provided by the Kingdom of Aragon, and, as they inched their way towards the safety of Constantinople's harbour, Suleiman Baltoghlu Pasha[23] – Mehmet's Bulgarian-born admiral – launched his naval force against them. To the cheers of the city's inhabitants, who by now packed the walls between the lighthouse and the Acropolis Point, the Christian fleet powered on, as the smaller Ottoman galleys closed in on them. Suddenly, to the horror of the observers, the wind dropped, the Genoese vessels slowed, and, like a pack of hounds, the Turkish ships

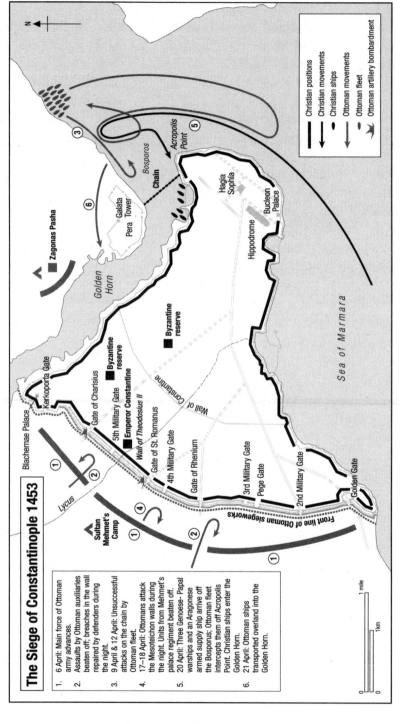

The Siege of Constantinople 1453

1. 6 April: Main force of Ottoman army advances.
2. Assaults by Ottoman auxiliaries beaten off; breaches in the wall repaired by defenders during the night.
3. 9 April & 12 April: Unsuccessful attacks on the chain by Ottoman fleet.
4. 17–18 April: Ottomans attack the Mesoteichon walls during the night. Units from Mehmet's palace regiment beaten off.
5. 20 April: Three Genoese- Papal warships and an Aragonese armed supply ship arrive off the Bosporus; Ottoman fleet intercepts them off Acropolis Point. Christian ships enter the Golden Horn.
6. 21 April: Ottoman ships transported overland into the Golden Horn.

Christian positions
Christian movements
Christian ships
Ottoman movements
Ottoman fleet
Ottoman artillery bombardment

Zagonas Pasha

Sultan Mehmet's Camp

Front line of Ottoman siegeworks

Blachernae Palace

Kerkoporta Gate

Gate of Charisius

5th Military Gate

Emperor Constantine

Wall of Theodosius II

Gate of St. Romanus

4th Military Gate

Gate of Rhenium

Pege Gate

3rd Military Gate

2nd Military Gate

Golden Gate

Wall of Constantine

Byzantine reserve

Byzantine reserve

Hippodrome

Hagia Sophia

Bucleon Palace

Lycus

Golden Horn

Galata Pera Tower

Bosporos

Chain

Acropolis Point

Sea of Marmara

N

0   1 mile
0   1km

pulled alongside them. As grappling irons flew across the closing gap, the Christian crews threw themselves at the boarding parties, using the greater height of their decks to stab and fire downwards. Meanwhile, the Ottomans tried to bind their own ships together, in order to allow more soldiers to cross on the bridge of boats and, in doing so, to overpower the crews of this relief fleet. In response, the Genoese manoeuvred their own ships together, in order to form one great wooden fighting platform, centred on the supply ship, allowing them to surge soldiers and sailors to wherever the danger was greatest.

Mehmet had already been alerted to this new situation. Every day he, too, watched for evidence or indication that the western powers were marching or sailing to the aid of Constantinople. He knew that members of his own close entourage were sceptical of this whole endeavour. As the walls absorbed all that he could throw at them, and as the increasingly frenzied assaults of his troops were thrown back, he knew that a new Muslim failure to seize Constantinople could well lead to his own deposition – and death by a silken bowstring. Seizing a horse, he cantered across the pontoon bridge that linked both sides of the Golden Horn and, riding through the troops of Zagonas Pasha, he took his horse into the shallows by the walls of Pera. As the sea battle reached its crescendo, Mehmet became more agitated, until he could be seen from the walls opposite riding his horse into the Golden Horn, up to his stirrups, hurling insults and imprecations at his hapless admiral. Suddenly, battered and beset as they were, the Genoese and Aragonese sensed the wind rise again. Under a continuing, relentless hail of missiles, the sails, furled to avoid being set on fire, were rapidly unfurled again, and axes swiftly cut the Ottoman galleys from the Christian ships, and the Christian ships from each other. The vast chain boom across the entrance to the Golden Horn was lowered, and the great vessels sailed into safe berths under the covering fire of the cannon on the sea walls, and to the joyful pealing of bells throughout the city. Still screaming, Mehmet, with a face like thunder, wrenched his horse around and galloped back to the ridge overlooking Constantinople. That night, Admiral Baltoghlu Pasha, his right eye shot out in the fighting, lay prostrate in the Sultan's tent as Mehmet berated him for his failures, threatening to take him outside to be beheaded. Baltoghlu Pasha was a popular officer. While he had failed, he could not be accused of cowardice. Sensing uneasiness among his commanders, Mehmet commuted his sentence to 100 lashes, demotion, and the division of his wealth among the Janissaries. Mehmet's close friend Hamza Bey was promoted to be *Kapudan Pasha*, the new Admiral of the Fleet.[24]

Constantine had hoped that this minor miracle presaged the arrival of a much bigger western fleet, but the Genoese captains brought no such news. Therefore, the Emperor had despatched a small, fast brigantine, under cover of darkness, with orders to sail as far as the Aegean Sea to scout for a larger relief force. On 22 April, the recent joy of Constantinople turned to sour despair as Sultan Mehmet unveiled his master counterstroke. As those on the walls of the city, and on those of Pera, were looking to the east, they saw, to their amazement, a sail appear on the top of the hills that rose up on the northern side of the Golden Horn. Shortly afterwards, they were able to discern the shape of a galley hull, with oars gently 'rowing' in the air, to the accompanying beat of drums. As they watched, the galley crested the hill, and then slowly came down the slope on a bed of timber rollers, its weight held by hundreds of soldiers straining on ropes. To the cheers of the Ottomans, on both sides of the Golden Horn – a cheer that grew as the news passed down the line to the Sea of Marmara – the first galley slid into the water, just as a second sail appeared above the tree line. All day this process continued, until the Ottomans had assembled 80 craft of various sizes in the northern end of the Golden Horn. Suddenly, the assumptions of the defenders about their capacity to hold the defences were threatened, as they now had to guard the sea walls. Death and wounding, fear and fatigue, hunger and anxiety, all were sapping the capacity of the defence to hold the line in the face of constant bombardment, and relentless attrition. A spirited plan to deal with the new threat from the Turkish fleet by sending fire-ships among them was thwarted by rivalry between the Genoese and Venetians, by delay, and ultimately by the betrayal of a warning light in the Tower of Christ. As the survivors of this enterprise were impaled on the beaches, Constantine ordered that his own Ottoman prisoners be hanged, one by one, from the city walls.

Mehmet also sought to undermine the walls, an Ottoman specialization, and all through April and May his Serbian miners dug and toiled underground. John Grant meanwhile led a ferocious counter-mining campaign, listening for the vibrations that told of Ottoman tunnels, and then digging his own tunnels that intercepted those of the Serbs. This had led to hellish close-quarter combat underground, with short-bladed weapons, shovels, maces and fire. The chance capture of two Turkish commanders, and their subsequent torture, led to the rapid discovery and destruction of all the attackers' mining efforts.

The siege had now gone on for over six weeks. Casualties had been high, but the stakes were higher, and both sides recognized that a climax was approaching. On 22 May, sentries saw a single brigantine tacking its way across the Sea of Marmara. It sported Ottoman colours, but as it approached the walls the recognition flash of a white sheet on its port side revealed it to be Constantine's reconnaissance ship, sent out nearly four weeks earlier. Shortly after it had darted across the entrance to the Golden Horn, the bleak news that it brought was widely known. They had encountered no great relief fleet bringing ships, grain and soldiers to the aid of those who defended Christendom's historic eastern capital city. They were alone in this last, titanic struggle between the followers of the Prophet and the guardians of Orthodox Christianity. Hard on the heels of this news came a final offer of honourable surrender, from the young Sultan to the old Emperor. It was couched in courteous language, commended the bravery of the defenders and offered generous terms. Constantine, equally courteously, rejected the offer. As a Byzantine emperor, inheritor of more than a millennium of greatness, he could do no other.

On the evening of 28 May, with bells ringing mournfully from every church tower in Constantinople, a last service was held in Hagia Sophia. Candles drenched the church in light as incense and prayers rose into the night air. The whole population of the city seemed to be there, Catholic and Orthodox, for the first time, confessing and taking communion, as the chanting of the Patriarch, the priests, the monks and the choirs implored God for salvation, and the Virgin Mary for protection. As the service drew to a close, Constantine gave his own benediction to the worshippers, and, accompanied by a bodyguard of imperial troops, he galloped west back to the walls, while those who were going to fight rode or marched back to their positions on the ramparts. The Emperor had first gone to the Blachernae Palace, where he asked his household to forgive him for any wrongs or insults he may have committed against them. Then, bidding the emotionally shattered men and women of his personal household farewell, he had ridden into the night and to the 5th Military Gate, where his command tent was filled with his companions and his commanders.

With the cry of 'Constantinople' on their lips, Giustiniani, with his black-armoured Genoese and those Byzantine troops selected to be the bulwark on which the Ottomans dashed themselves, marched through the postern gates into the *peribolos* between the inner and outer walls. Few in number, they were sustained by faith in God, their leaders, the fortifications, their armour and their training. Emperor Constantine XI then resolutely marched through the postern gate with them, and the gates were shut behind them, and locked, the keys being held by the defenders of the inner towers. Their backs were now, quite literally, to the wall. There was to be no retreat. Above them the archers and arquebusiers clustered on the battlements and in the towers. They were readied to kill those beyond the outer wall, or to direct their fire on those breaches in the walls where the Ottomans would be forced to concentrate as they sought to puncture and peel back the skin of the 'Red Apple'.

Sometime after midnight, in a chillingly disciplined display of centralized command, the fires along the ridgeline were extinguished in a rippling movement from the Golden Horn to the shores of the Sea of Marmara. The breath of history hung in the air. Hope, despair, desperation, fear, anticipation, greed, all the timeless competing emotions of conflict down the ages hovered for a moment in the stillness of the early hours of 29 May 1453. Then, with an almighty cry, the surviving *bashibazouks* – that multitude of irregular, unreliable, lightly armed, poorly trained Muslims and Christians – once again hurled themselves at the fortifications, while the Ottoman guns pounded the walls and Ottoman arrows fell like a snowstorm on the defenders. Wave after wave poured over the moat and across the *parateichion*, carrying flares to light the battlefield, and scaling ladders to mount the walls, while the massed Ottoman drums filled any gap in the bombardment with their relentless thumping. Mehmet's vast cannon had shattered the fortifications, and whole stretches of the wall had fallen, but their very success had created a landscape of piled rubble that could favour a defender, but only if there were enough of them to sustain this intensity of fighting for long enough. The Sultan's regular troops continued to stand silently on the ridgeline, ready to turn back, or to execute any of those in the initial attack who sought refuge from the carnage.

Giustiniani's men rotated to man the breaches, the professional men-at-arms, and seasoned killers, massacring the *bashibazouks* as they crested the piles of brick, stone, mud, timber and dirt-filled barrels that constituted the defensive line, and as they tried to establish some form of foothold in the city. The dead fell, and their bodies joined the makeshift defences, while the Christian wounded were propped up against the inner wall, awaiting death or preparing to return to the fighting after rudimentary medical care. The gates remained shut and locked.

After two hours or so, those *bashibazouks* who had survived the bloodbath on the walls fell back. Although their attack had failed, they had worn down the defenders. There were no reinforcements to replace those who had fallen. There was to be no respite for the wounded and the dog-tired, or for those whose shoulders ached from drawing on their bows, those whose exhausted sword-arm could hardly be raised, and those whose armour was dented and broken from repeated blows. Archers from the inner wall lowered ropes and descended to harvest the field of arrows in order to replenish their own quivers. A few stayed to fight alongside their friends and compatriots. The attacks along other parts of the great walls, and upon the sea defences, made it impossible for the Emperor and his battle captains to re-allocate troops, and the single set of uncommitted reserves had to be ready to counter a breakthrough in the most obvious areas of danger. They simply could not be fed into the desperate fight too early, while those in the front line could still persevere.

Next came the Anatolian troops of Ishak Pasha. Regulars, many of them had both military and combat experience and had fought for the old Sultan in the wars against the Persians, the Serbs and the Hungarians. Now, they too tried to storm the stockades, clambering over the collapsed walls and the bodies of the irregulars, and they came up against the valiant and adamantine courage of the defenders. The Ottoman troops, conscious they were fighting under the gaze of 'God's shadow on earth', fought tenaciously, bravely, desperately even, to break through the compact ranks of the Christians, but the narrow area in which they were fighting helped the defence. Their sheer numbers told against them, trapped as they were between the steel wall of Genoese armour, and the press of their comrades behind them. Fighting with mace, axe and sword, the defenders could hack and slash to their left and right, while the attackers could hardly wield a weapon, and those on the inner wall could pour fire into the mass of Ottomans while hardly having to aim. At last, a group of attackers crashed through a gap in the fighting and tumbled onto the *peribolos*. Battles hinge on such moments. However, once again Giustiniani's men surged up the collapsed walls to fill the gap, and to cut off the Anatolians, while the Emperor himself led the assault that killed them all. As dawn began to break across the Balkans, and a new sunrise began to reflect off the waters of the Golden Horn and the Bosporus, and to glint off the towers and cupolas of the city, Constantine knew that the 1,100-year history of Constantinople as a Christian capital city now rested on a finely honed knife-edge.

Constantine was not despairing. The fortifications were holding. The young Sultan's soldiers had suffered immense casualties and had not breached the defences anywhere. The defenders themselves were exhausted but were not defeated or downhearted. Indeed, the extraordinary heroism they had displayed through the 53 days of the siege gave them both pride and the hope that maybe, against all the odds, they could add further lustre to the glory of Constantinople, and add a further chapter to her great and glorious history. But now came the Janissaries – those disciplined, professional, superbly trained and ruthless warriors – prepared to succeed for the Sultan where other, lesser soldiers had failed, or die in the attempt.

The guns once again thundered out, hurling shot after shot of stone, marble and metal against that section of the walls identified, from the outset, as Constantinople's point of weakness. The barrage only lifted as the Janissaries reached the outer wall and pushed their way over the bodies of dead and dying Muslim and Christian soldiers. With the most tremendous effort, the Greeks and the Italians continued to resist, and to repulse the enemy. The hopes of defenders were rising when, totally unexpectedly, a group of Ottomans entered the killing zone between the walls, next to where the walls of the Blachernae Palace met the defensive triple walls of the city. Whether by accident or treachery, the Janissaries found that a small sally port, called the Kerkoporta, had been left open, and they poured through. Panicked defenders, few in numbers, who had thought the main threat and assault was several hundred yards to their left, were suddenly confronted by soldiers from the cream of the Ottoman military establishment. Not wanting in courage, they fought to kill those who had entered, and attempted to slam and re-bolt the door.

At that very moment, by another of those accidents of history upon which great events turn, a shot, fired by a culverin, a small arquebus, hit Giustiniani, the rock of Constantinople's defence. The shot pierced his fluted, Milanese-made breastplate, and entered his chest. He fell to the ground. Shaken by his wound, and already emotionally and physically exhausted after the relentless pressure and bloodshed of weeks of combat, his indomitable fighting spirit collapsed. Giustiniani's presence among the defenders was worth a battalion of troops, and his worthiness as a commander and example as a warrior had been beyond praise. Acre had been lost by the time Beaujeu had been fatally wounded, but the fate of Constantinople still lay in the balance. Win or lose, live or die, Giustiniani's place among military history's heroes would have been assured, if he had held his position. But now, tragically, and deaf to the personal pleas of the Emperor not to leave his post, as they had all agreed to before being locked inside the *peribolos*, the Genoese commander ordered his men to take him from the battlefield. To the cries of the Genoese, the key to the postern gate was thrown down from the inner wall, and his soldiers carried their stricken commander inside the walls of the city. Those soldiers who were still hacking and slashing away at the Janissary attackers now saw the gate open, and their comrades carrying their leader away to safety. Thinking that the defences had been broken, the Genoese all rushed to escape through the same gate, leaving the Emperor and the Greek fighters alone between the walls.

———

Like the good commander that he was, Sultan Mehmet now 'sensed' the battle beginning to flow in his favour. He sensed the Christian defence slacken and buckle. This was his own moment in history, the chance, as foretold in Osman's dream, for him to fulfil his own destiny, and that of the Ottomans, by taking Constantinople. He moved as far forward as his bodyguard, charged with preservation of the Sultan's life, would let him go. Frantic orders were rushed forward to urge the Janissaries to redouble their efforts, and to concentrate their attack on the weakened position. Thousands of fresh troops, and those of earlier assaults, rushed to the area and poured across the battered stockade that topped the remnants of the Theodosian Walls. The motivations of God, glory and gold drove them on to conclude this one, last great effort. In the face of numbers, it was now the Greeks who had problems wielding their weapons, as their previously coherent defence was broken into smaller and smaller groups, and more and more of them fell beneath the Muslim blades.

Meanwhile, Janissaries, men from the Anatolian and Rumeilian divisions, and maniacal bands of *bashibazouks* were pouring through the Kerkoporta gate, where the defenders had not been able to eliminate the initial incursion. They surged up the steps of the towers, eager to place the banners of Islam on the battlements, for the glory of God, and for the huge monetary prizes that the Sultan had promised. A great, historical city, a treasure-house of wealth beyond their dreams, was now almost in their hands, ripe for all the rapine, killing and destruction that the three days of unrestricted plunder promised them. Soon the first enemy flags were seen on both the outer and inner walls. The Emperor and his commanders frantically tried to rally their troops, but it was too late. Triumphant Ottoman soldiers were already mixed in with fleeing Christians as the gates of the inner wall were broken open, and the fields and orchards of the west of the city were revealed and, beyond them, the glories of Constantinople itself.

Constantine had always been determined to defend the city to the last, or to die in the attempt. Surrounded by the last of his Imperial Guard, he paused for one final moment to consider his fate and that of his city. History relates that he removed his imperial insignia, and closely followed by his cousin, Theophilus Palaeologus, along with Don Francisco de Toledo and John of Dalmata, was seen to charge into the ranks of the enemy, laying about him with his sword. He was never seen again, and his body was never identified or recovered, although legend had it that he was spirited away by angels and turned into marble, awaiting the moment when he would lead a Christian recovery of Constantinople.

———

Thousands of Ottomans now poured into the city, as gate after gate was taken and opened. Ottoman flags were seen on tower after tower, and the news of the breaching of the great landward walls spread like proverbial wildfire through the city. Civilians poured into the churches, futilely convinced that God would not desert His people in their hour of need. Others locked themselves, fruitlessly, in their houses, while others fell fighting in the streets as they tried to preserve their properties and their families. Many rushed for the harbour areas, to try to escape on the Italian ships that had already hoisted their anchors and their sails. The Genoese traders, across the Golden Horn in Pera, sternly warned by the Sultan not to try to intervene, watched in helpless fascination as the Ottoman hordes engulfed Constantinople, setting fire to houses and toppling crosses, while the screams and wails of the inhabitants drifted across the narrow waters. Perhaps Giuliani Giustiniani Longo, lying in agony on his bed, on a Genoese ship that was pulling away into the Sea of Marmara, also heard the cries of a dying city. Great commander that he was, he must have been horribly aware that on his moment of weakness had turned his own reputation, and the fate of the heroic defence of Constantinople. He died on the island of Chios, three days later.

The excesses that followed the early hours of Ottoman victory have been well chronicled. Even allowing for exaggeration, for attempts to blacken the Ottoman name, and that of the Sultan, and for the development of a narrative that might inspire a new crusade, the realities were appalling. Houses, homes and shops were looted and destroyed, and the inhabitants massacred. Monasteries and convents were broken into and monks and nuns raped and enslaved. Many, to avoid dishonour, killed themselves. Blood ran from the hills of Constantinople into the Golden Horn. Those who sought sanctuary in the churches, including the hundreds in Hagia Sophia, were killed, or bound as slaves, and everything that could be taken from the splendid secular and religious buildings was taken. Icons were destroyed, precious manuscripts were lost forever, and within days Mehmet had ordered the whitewashing of most of the magnificent Orthodox churches' mosaics, murals and frescos. Death and enslavement did not distinguish between social classes. A breakdown of discipline in the Ottoman navy, by those not prepared to let the land forces monopolize the opportunity for enrichment, meant that more ships, crews and refugees escaped than might have, while local 'deals' by commanders away from the main actions allowed others to flee, or some churches to escape destruction. Prince Orhan's Muslim troops died fighting to the last man, while the Cretans bargained for their lives and their freedom by surrendering the three towers near the entrance to the Golden Horn.

Sultan Mehmet, who would rightly go down in history as *Al-Fatih*, 'The Conqueror', entered Constantinople on the afternoon of the first day of occupation, escorted by the finest of his Janissary guards. He wore a cloak of deepest crimson, trimmed in ermine, and a gilt-inlaid silver helmet. He rode slowly through the streets, threading his way between his looting soldiers, to the Church of Holy Wisdom. Here he picked up a handful of earth and poured it over his turban, as an act of humility towards his God. Entering the church, he stood silently for a moment, before reprimanding one vandal for his destruction of the marble flooring: 'I gave you the contents of the city, but its buildings are mine!' He then went with Hamza Bey to the old, deserted Bucoleon Palace, where he is said to have murmured the words of a Persian poet: 'The spider weaves the curtains in the palace of the Caesars; the owl calls the watches in Afrasiab's towers.' All around he saw desolation, death in the streets, ruins and desecrated churches. Although a city that had been taken by storm, not surrender, was traditionally handed over to the soldiers for three days, it was too much for Mehmet, and he halted the killing. Moved to tears at the damage wrought to the city that would swiftly become the new Ottoman capital, it is reported that he whispered, 'What a city we have given over to plunder and destruction.'

The next day, the booty was collected and distributed, including to those soldiers who had not been able to take part in the sack of the city. Noble ladies were freed, while many youths, boys and girls, were taken into the Sultan's harem, or offered positions in his army or household if they renounced their religion. Many refused, and they were executed. Mehmet sent hundreds of slaves to the rulers of Egypt, Tunis and Granada. Lucas Notaras, the former confidant of the Byzantine Emperor, was reputed to have been offered the governorship of Constantinople if he gave his son to Mehmet, 'for his pleasure'. Notaras refused, and both father and son were beheaded.

On 21 June, Mehmet departed for Edirne, leaving behind the blackened and ruined shell of the former Byzantine capital. The Hagia Sophia was already a mosque, but the old Church of the Holy Apostles now became the Patriarchal Church of the newly appointed Patriarch, Gennadius, while the Orthodox Christians became a 'protected class', or *millet*,[25] under the Ottomans. Mehmet himself soon returned to live in Constantinople, and to make it his capital. He was the heir to the Roman and Byzantine emperors; where else could he reside? Long before his death in 1481, Constantinople was once again a thriving, bustling metropolis, where new buildings rose on an almost daily basis, where the markets and workshops buzzed with activity, and where traders came and went in ever-increasing numbers. Within a century the population stood at half a million people, ten times the number who had sheltered behind its walls on the final days of its existence as a Christian capital.

PART FOUR

The Struggle for the Middle Sea

6

The Knights at Bay

Rhodes 1522

Sultan Suleiman landed on the island of Rhodes on 28 July 1522. Born in Trabzon, on the Black Sea coast, he was just 26 years old, but he already carried himself like an Ottoman ruler. Not yet known as 'the Magnificent', by western observers, nor as 'the Lawgiver', by his Turkish subjects, he already had a formidable reputation. On his accession to the throne in September 1520, the Venetian ambassador to the Sublime Porte described Suleiman as 'tall and slender but tough, with a thin and bony face. Facial hair is evident, but only barely. The Sultan appears friendly and in good humour. Rumour has it that Suleiman is aptly named, enjoys reading, is knowledgeable and shows good judgement.' His opinion was prescient. At the age of seven, Suleiman had already begun his studies in science, history, literature, theology and military tactics. This was the man who would dominate the thoughts and actions of rulers and peoples from China to the Atlantic for much of the next 46 years. In his first significant military campaign, he had already demonstrated his intent to continue the expansionary policies of his father, Sultan Selim I, by, at last, taking the great fortress city of Belgrade, thereby opening the way for even greater Ottoman inroads into eastern and central Europe. For 1522, he had now looked to root out the menace of the Knights Hospitaller from Rhodes, that last major crusader bastion in the eastern Mediterranean, from which island Christian forces had been able to harry and attack Ottoman and Mamluk navies and merchant traders for over 200 years.

Suleiman's arrival was marked by great fanfare, and as his galley hove into view, after its short voyage from the port of Marmaris, on the Anatolian coast, all the other Turkish ships in the Bay of Kallithea[1] hung banners from their yardarms and unfurled their sails. He disembarked, mounted a horse and rode to his pavilion, set up some 4 or 5 miles south of the great fortress and port city of Rhodes. He was surrounded by a unit of Janissaries who, accompanied by their band, marched alongside him, singing loudly and firing their handguns. It was a magnificent sight, and the sound of the procession could be heard on the distant city walls. There could be no doubt as to its significance. In his pavilion, Suleiman's commanders awaited his arrival, abased themselves as he dismounted, and stood in silence until commanded to give their reports.

The Ottoman advance fleet had anchored in Kallithea Bay on 26 June, on which fell that year the Christian Feast Day of Corpus Christi. Troops had begun disembarking immediately, with slaves and labourers put to work unloading vast quantities of victuals, arms, armour, cannon, gunpowder, tents and all the paraphernalia of war. It was a huge scene of carefully organized chaos, orchestrated by an army full of veterans of campaigns in Serbia, Hungary, Persia and Egypt, and a navy whose size and professional competence were growing by the year. As each vessel was unloaded, it pulled back from the shore to be replaced by another skilfully manoeuvred galley, while it made its own way back to the Turkish mainland for more supplies and more soldiers. Such a process was repeated over and over again between 26 June and 10 July. Estimates of the size of the fleet vary widely, but the overall number of ships, of various types and classes, probably began at around 250, and rose to nearly 400, as Suleiman brought in his naval forces from Syria, to join those that had sailed from Constantinople and from the naval base at Gallipoli.

By leaving the Levant and Middle Eastern coast largely unprotected, Suleiman made it clear where his priorities lay, and the watchers on the walls of Rhodes would have easily been able to see this restless passage of maritime traffic. By mid-July 1522, a force of around 165,000 men had been assembled for the assault on Rhodes, including 100,000 soldiers, 15,000 sailors and up to 50,000 labourers who would undertake mining operations, the digging of trenches, the erection of huge siegeworks, and the carriage of supplies and ammunition to the front lines. It was a formidable enterprise, and a contemporary inventory of the fleet lists: cuirasses, coats of mail, helmets, gauntlets and shields in large numbers;

pikes, cannon, handguns, bows, crossbows, arrows and bolts, bombs, powder flasks; tools and materiel for masons, stonecutters and diggers; and 3,700 wicker baskets that would be filled with soil to act as defence works for the artillery.

Suleiman had begun his planning in the wake of his victory in Belgrade but had kept the target of his preparations a secret. Was he going to strike north into the Hungarian plains, east again against the historical Persian enemy, with its heretical Shia leanings, or against one of the last major western presences in the eastern Mediterranean? Back in 1517, during the reign of Suleiman's father, Selim the Grim, the Christian powers had assumed Rhodes was the target, only for the knights to have watched the great Ottoman fleet sail past them to support the Ottoman army in its overthrow of the Egyptian Mamluk regime. Indeed, fresh from their success, the Ottoman naval commanders had actually sailed into Rhodes's harbour on their triumphant return to Constantinople where they had been treated as honoured guests. Now, in June 1522, all became clear as Suleiman had once again despatched his naval fleet from Constantinople, while he led a sizeable portion of the army overland. Mustapha Pasha, the Second Vizier,[2] commanded the fleet and sailed the 375 miles to Marmaris, via Gallipoli and the island of Chios. Suleiman and his forces had been ferried across the Bosporus and then marched the 185 miles to Kutahya, where he was joined by Qasim, the Beylerbey of Anatolia; Bali Pasha, the agha of the Janissaries; and Ali Bey, agha of the Ottoman irregulars, or Azab, from an Arabic word literally meaning 'unmarried' or 'bachelor'. His other key commanders, Ayas Pasha and Ferhad Pasha, joined him in the following days. They then marched a further 185 miles to Marmaris, with Suleiman himself travelling at the rear, leaving enough time for all preparations for the siege to be complete before his carefully staged arrival on 28 July. His Grand Vizier Piri Pasha, who had persuaded Suleiman to make Rhodes his objective for 1522, would join him on the island.

The Ottoman and Muslim worlds had been transformed since Mehmet the Conqueror had breached the Theodosian Walls in 1453 and captured Constantinople. With its capture, Sultan Mehmet felt he had also inherited the historical destiny of the Romans, and the right to

Godfrey of Bouillon and the soldiers and pilgrims of the First Crusade achieved an extraordinary victory by taking Jerusalem in 1099. However, the bloodshed and destruction they then inflicted had a long-lasting impact on Christian–Muslim relations. (Getty Images)

Godfrey of Bouillon, Protector of the Holy Sepulchre after the crusaders took Jerusalem. (Getty Images)

Salah ad-Din bin Yousef bin Ayyub, better known to history as Saladin. His forces defeated the crusader army of King Guy of Lusignan at Hattin in 1187. (Getty Images)

Crac de Chevaliers. This castle of the Knights Hospitaller, guarding the Homs Gap, is possibly the best known of a series of castles that helped the crusaders to dominate Syria and the Holy Land. (Gianfranco Gazzetti / GAR, CC BY-SA 4.0)

Above In July 1187, King Guy of Lusignan staked the future of the Kingdom of Jerusalem on a battle with Saladin at Hattin, which led to the destruction of the crusader army, and the loss of the Holy City. (Alamy)

Opposite Matthew of Clermont defending the walls of Acre against the Mamluks in 1291. The fall of Acre led to the final destruction of 200 years of crusader presence in Syria and the Holy Land. (Getty Images)

Assault by the forces of Sultan Mehmet II on the Theodosian Walls of Constantinople in May 1453. The conquest of the city marked the final episode in the fall of the Byzantine Empire. (Alamy)

Hagia Sophia, the Church of Holy Wisdom, was the centre of the Christian Orthodox religion for nearly 1,000 years. Converted to a mosque in 1453, and a museum in 1935, it became a mosque again in 2020. (Getty Images)

Sultan Mehmet II enters Constantinople. After the taking of the city, Mehmet took the title *Al-Fatih*, 'The Conqueror'. He moved the Ottoman capital from Edirne to Constantinople, where it remained until 1923. (Getty Images)

Suleiman the Magnificent, also known as 'the Lawgiver', ruled the Ottoman Empire from 1520 to 1566. He inherited an empire that had doubled in size under his father, Sultan Selim the Grim, and with it the title of Caliph. (Getty Images)

In 1522, Sultan Suleiman besieged Rhodes in an attempt to stamp out the last crusader presence in the eastern Mediterranean. After a siege that lasted over six months, Suleiman offered the Knights of St John generous surrender terms. (Alamy)

The d'Amboise Gate was part of Grand Master d'Aubusson's ambitious plans to strengthen the defences of Rhodes after the failed Ottoman siege of 1480. It formed an integral part of the defence of the city in 1522. (Getty Images)

Map of Malta in 1565, showing the fortified peninsulas of Senglea (left) and Birgu (right). Mount Sciberras and the Fort of St Elmo are at the top of the picture. (Alamy)

The Ottomans finally overwhelmed the defences at St Elmo on 23 June 1565. Dragut's severing of the fragile logistic link between St Angelo (top right) and St Elmo had eventually doomed the defenders. (Alamy)

In September 1565, after an heroic defence of three and a half months,
the Knights of St John and their Maltese allies were relieved by the Spanish forces
of Don García de Toledo. (Alamy)

Jean Parisot de la Valette was 70 years
old when he led the defence of Malta, and
his personal example was vital in defeating
the Ottoman assault.
(Sparrow (2019), CC BY-SA 4.0)

Dragut, the great Barbary corsair, was
80 at the time of the siege of Malta.
His late arrival, and untimely death, were
pivotal in the outcome of the siege.
(Getty Images)

Above These views of Lepanto give a useful depiction of the order of battle of the opposing fleets of the Holy League and the Ottomans. However, they cannot capture the sheer violence, bloodshed and chaos of this massive sea battle, which saw perhaps 40,000 lives lost in the space of four hours. (Top: Alamy; bottom: Getty Images)

For commanders, soldiers, sailors and oarsmen, Lepanto was a visceral, large-scale, close-quarter fight. Many galleys were burnt to the waterline, and little quarter was asked, or given. (Alamy)

The heroes of Lepanto. Don Juan of Austria (left) commanded the fleet of the Holy League. Among his key subordinate commanders were Marcantonio Colonna (centre) and the irascible Sebastian Veniero (right). (Getty Images)

INFELIX KARA
MAGNI TURCARUM
MINISTER
Poſt acceptam cladem ante
Juſſu Imperatoris Supremo dicti

MUSTAPHA BASSA
IMPERATORIS
PRIMARIUS;
Viennam ab Eodem obſeſſam,
Albá Græcá Strangulatus et decollatus.

J. Gole

Ex Formis Nicolai Viſſcher, cum Privil: Ordin: Gen: Belgii Fœderati.

Above The Holy Roman Emperor, Leopold I, was a cold, unimaginative, and ungracious figure, but he did just enough in 1683 to pull together a coalition that would defeat an Ottoman army on the verge of taking the city of Vienna. (Alamy)

Opposite Kara 'Black' Mustapha's ambition to take Vienna in 1683 was bold but realistic; however, his arrogance and complacency cost him the siege, and this defeat marked the start of the long Ottoman decline from imperial greatness.
(Rijksmuseum, RP-P-1894-A-18289)

King John III Sobieski of Poland shifted his allegiance to the Habsburgs as the Ottoman threat to Central Europe became more insistent. A very seasoned warrior, he made a major contribution to victory at Vienna. (Getty Images)

Duke Charles of Lorraine was a much-admired professional soldier, and a gifted diplomat. His subtle handling of Emperor Leopold I and other senior commanders was key to success at Vienna. (Getty Images)

The battle for the Burg Bastion. During the siege of Vienna almost all of Kara Mustapha's energies were poured into breaching the defences of Vienna between the Burg and Löbl bastions. (Getty Images)

This scene shows the Ottoman siege of Vienna in 1683 continuing
(note the siege trench network), while the forces of King John and Duke Charles pour
down the slopes of the Wienerwald to overwhelm Kara Mustapha's hastily positioned
defences. (Getty Images)

When King John and his cavalry, including the famous 'winged hussars', poured onto
the battlefield from the Wienerwald, the Ottoman forces on the west flank were
overwhelmed and destroyed. (Getty Images)

Kaiser Wilhelm II, the aggressive King of Prussia, and Emperor of the new German Empire, sought closer relations with the Ottoman Empire. In 1898, as part of this policy, he visited Jerusalem, where the Jaffa Gate had to be partly demolished to facilitate his entry. (Getty Images)

General Edmund Allenby entered Jerusalem on foot on 11 December 1917, in deliberate contrast to the Kaiser's flamboyant entry in 1898. Ottoman defeat in World War I signalled another period of Christian dominance in the Holy Land and Near East that lasted until World War II. (Library of Congress, LC-USZ62-93094)

Sultan Mehmet VI was the last Ottoman sultan. When the new Turkish Republic of Mustapha Kemal Ataturk abolished the sultanate on 1 November 1922, Mehmet was declared *persona non grata*. He is shown here arriving in Malta on a British warship later that month. (Alamy)

sovereignty over all their former lands, including even the imperial and papal city of Rome itself. Although they would never reach or conquer Rome, the city became the new 'Red Apple' of Ottoman ambition. Mehmet had followed up his great victory by taking Trabzon, the last Byzantine outpost in Anatolia, all the Genoese colonies in the Black Sea, the Kingdom of Serbia, and most of the Greek Peloponnese, and by forcing Vlad Dracul, ruler of Wallachia, to submit to Ottoman rule. He had failed to take Belgrade in 1456, due to a spirited defence by John Hunyadi, but by 1466 the territories of the Kingdom of Bosnia and the Duchy of Hercegovina were also under Turkish rule, resulting in waves of conversion to Islam among the native Christian communities.

At the same time, the Ottomans had embarked on a war with Venice that lasted until 1479, mocking Venetian pretensions in Greece and the Balkans, and exposing their vulnerability in Italy, as Turkish armies ravaged Venice's northern mainland territories. At this stage, Venice had to concede that it simply could not afford to be both a maritime empire and a major land power. In 1480, Mehmet had landed a 70,000-strong army on Rhodes, intending to destroy the crusader stronghold and its supporting fortresses on the island of Cos, and at the mainland port of Petronium. The army had been led by Mesic Pasha, a Greek renegade, and a Palaiologan kinsman of Constantine XI, the last Byzantine Emperor. He had been Constantine's young nephew and, if Constantinople had not fallen, may even have succeeded the childless Constantine as Emperor. The siege had lasted two months, but neither bombardment nor mass assaults had managed to overcome the fortifications and the defenders of Rhodes, and Mesic Pasha had withdrawn as quickly as he had come, having suffered up to 25,000 casualties and the loss of vast quantities of materiel. The Ottomans had invaded southern Italy in the same year, taking Otranto and beheading the 800 Christian captives who refused to convert to Islam, and some western leaders suspected that the Sultan, even then, had plans to take Rome itself. However, the Ottomans had withdrawn from Italy in May 1481, when news reached them of Sultan Mehmet's death on campaign in Anatolia.

Much of the extraordinary Ottoman expansion in the 14th and 15th centuries had been fuelled by the synergy of the Islamic concept of *jihad*, the martial struggle to defend Islam, and the Turkish tradition of *ghazi*, the nomadic raiding psychology that, successfully applied, offered land, slaves and booty to a leader's followers. Therefore, a successful commander needed to pursue an almost constant state of war against non-believers and heretics, both as a religious and moral duty, and as a way of rewarding his soldiers and his supporters. Only by continual, imperial expansion could a sultan create the landholding opportunities that allowed him to impose obligations on his commanders to provide soldiers and resources. In addition, the excellence of the Ottoman administration and bureaucracy, largely populated by picked, educated and trained slave-converts, meant that successful sultans could embark on major campaigns, east or west, on an almost annual basis.

In this period, the Ottoman armies advanced remorselessly with their mix of highly motivated and incentivized levies, disciplined and ruthless Janissaries, and increasingly professional artillery forces. In contrast, the western, Christian armies they were pitted against were either furnished by mercenaries, or were raised from societies in the middle of a long process of transitioning from late feudalism to much more professional bodies of soldiers, salaried and equipped by increasingly centralized states, like France and Spain. The long-standing assumptions of heroic, chivalric individualism had been tested to destruction in the Hundred Years War, and again at Nicopolis and Varna. This western transition would accelerate throughout the 16th century as the riches of the 'New World'³ poured into Europe, and into the coffers of the kings. This, in time, allowed for the proliferation of firearms and the development of an increasingly effective combination of cavalry, artillery, and the infantry combination of pikes and muskets, that would be used to such powerful effect by the Spanish *tercio*⁴ formations. Before this transformation, the Venetian envoy to Constantinople, Daniello de Ludovisi, could rightly complain that 'the Lord Turk can count on good soldiers because they are not mercenaries ... nor given to him for aid by other princes ... instead, the troops of the Lord Turk are his own'. That applied to all the elements of the Sultan's army and navy, and to the commanders, all of whom owed their loyalty to none but the Sultan and the Ottoman state.

The end of the 15th century was an extraordinarily dynamic, challenging and unsettling time across Europe and the Middle East. The death of Sultan Mehmet II had been met with huge relief and satisfaction by Christian powers, including the papacy, and the

Ottoman state was deeply fractured by the immediate outbreak of civil strife between Mehmet's two sons, Bayezid and Cem. Bayezid eventually won, with the backing of the Janissaries, while his brother had sought sanctuary with the Knights of St John, initially in their castle of St Peter in Petronium, and then on the island of Rhodes. Cem became a pawn in the confrontation between the Ottomans and the west, with Bayezid paying substantive sums to the Knights of Rhodes, and subsequently to the papacy, and then the French king, to keep him incarcerated, and away from any chance of stirring up a further insurrection. Pope Alexander VI, from the Borgia family, used much of this Ottoman money to finance the painting of the Sistine Chapel, and Cem himself died in Capua in 1495.

Initially, Sultan Bayezid had largely left the Christian powers alone, although always concerned about the prospect of another major crusade. He watched with unease the culmination of the Christian *Reconquista* in Spain,[5] and the elimination of the Muslim presence there, and then with incredulity the subsequent expulsion of the Jews, whom he warmly welcomed into the Ottoman Empire, where they thrived.[6] Instead, he found the early part of his reign distracted by the long-standing rivalry with the Sunni Mamluks of Egypt. However, with the death of Cem, and under pressure from his professional soldiers, who aspired to glory and gold, Bayezid embarked on a new war with Venice for control of the eastern Mediterranean, made further inroads into Hungary, and even defeated a large Polish army in Moldova.

In 1502, Bayezid was, once again, forced to turn east, and to confront the persistent challenge of the Persians who, under Shah Ismail, the first ruler of the Safavid dynasty,[7] had decisively adopted Shi'ism as their state religion. Shah Ismail had made a rapid conquest of much of Iran, Mesopotamia and the Caucasus, and he was now actively promoting Shia heterodoxy in Ottoman Anatolia, where many Turcomans of the border regions resented the rule from Constantinople. Things came to a head in 1511, when there was a significant Shia rebellion in the east that was only just supressed. In confronting this Shia threat, Bayezid had at first attempted to appease the Safavids, but this approach had ultimately provoked his son, Selim, into open revolt. Sultan Bayezid had abdicated in early 1512, and he died a month later, on his way into internal exile. Selim was largely assumed to have had his father poisoned.

Sultan Selim I has rightly earned the sobriquet 'the Grim'. A seasoned commander by his accession, he rapidly showed that he was cut from a different cloth to his father. Gathering a list of the Shia in eastern Anatolia, he had around 50,000 of them rounded up and executed. In 1514, he had attacked and defeated the Safavids at the battle of Chaldiran, where his artillery, and his musket-equipped Janissaries had swiftly despatched a Persian army, whose armament and tactics were still rooted in the Middle Ages. In 1516, he had taken up the Ottoman challenge to the Mamluks and decisively defeated them outside the gates of Aleppo, and again, the following year, outside the walls of Cairo. He had now conquered Syria and Egypt and, by overthrowing the Mamluks, he also became the Custodian of the Holy Cities of Mecca and Medina. In due course, the last Abbasid 'shadow caliph' was moved from Cairo to Constantinople, along with the sword, cloak and banners of the Prophet Muhammad.[8]

With the death of the last 'shadow caliph' in 1543, and the subsequent assumption of his title by the Ottoman sultans, the transfer of the religious leadership of the Sunni Islamic world shifted from the Arabs, and from the Al-Quraysh tribe, who had held it for nearly 900 years, and moved to the Turks and the House of Osman. The Ottomans would hold the caliphate, and with it the loyalty and regard of all Sunni Muslims, for the next 400 years, until the abolition of this great, historical institution by Ataturk in the wake of the defeat and collapse of the Ottoman Empire at the end of World War I. No one would have the temerity or confidence to claim the title of Caliph again until the leader of Islamic State, Abu Bakr al Baghdadi,[9] proclaimed himself the successor of the Prophet Muhammad from the *minbar* of the Grand Mosque of Mosul in 2014.

With the defeat of the Mamluks, Sultan Selim had almost total control of the eastern Mediterranean coastline from Egypt all the way round to

Greece. He now wanted to secure the lucrative pilgrim and slave routes, and the sea lanes and maritime trade highways between Constantinople, the Levant and Alexandria in Egypt. The Knights Hospitaller, with their fortress in Rhodes, their castles in Petronium and Cos, and with their predatory galleys patrolling the seas, challenged this monopoly. They had to go, and the lingering crusader presence in the region that they also represented must be extinguished. Expelling those duplicitous, vacillating commercial partners and rivals, the Venetians, with their fortress trading ports in Crete, Cyprus and on the Peloponnese, could wait.

Selim never had the time to fulfil this ambition, and he died in 1520, after ruling for only eight years. However, his reign had been one of great significance. He had transformed the balance of power in the Middle East, in the eastern Mediterranean, and within the Islamic world. He bequeathed an uncontested throne to his son, Suleiman, an empire that had doubled in size, and now contained all three of Islam's Holy Cities. Now, for the first time, the Ottoman Empire encompassed a majority of Muslim subjects. Selim also bequeathed the legacy of war with Persia, which would roll on for a further 200 years, a set of ambitions for further conquests in Europe, which Suleiman had rapidly realized with his taking of Belgrade in his first year, and the plans and the wherewithal to conquer Rhodes. This great legacy, however, would inevitably leave Sultan Suleiman with a 'crisis of orientation', in terms of prioritizing east, west, and now the Mediterranean. Emperor Constantine the Great would have readily recognized the strategic tensions that this situation posed, and the strain that it would put on the allocation of resources. In addition, the Ottoman assumption of the Mamluk lands and responsibilities would now take them into confrontation with the Christian powers in the Red Sea and the Indian Ocean, as a result of western exploitation and expansion in the wake of Vasco da Gama's great voyages of exploration. But, in 1522 the Ottoman objective was Rhodes.

Philippe Villiers de L'Isle-Adam, the Grand Master of the Knights Hospitaller, stood on the battlements of the Italian Tower on the eastern walls of the city. He had his back to the commercial port, where the Naillac and French Towers guarded the entrance, although Ottoman ships were already blockading the approaches. Further north was the Mandraki, the military harbour, where the order's great war galleys sat low in the water under the protection of the guns of the Tower of St Nicholas. Across the entrance to the commercial harbour was a substantial defensive chain, while a combination of the guns of St Nicholas and 'block ships' protected the Mandraki. Along both moles stood a line of windmills, built to produce grain, but which also served to shelter the moorings of the galleys and the merchant ships. He was looking south to where the Ottoman labourers continued to dig their trenches towards the great defensive moat of Rhodes, and to raise ever-higher mounds of earth on which to put the formidable array of cannon that Suleiman had brought with him. The work had by now been going on, unremittingly, for more than two weeks, despite some night sorties by the defenders, and some well-aimed artillery fire from the massive bastions of Rhodes that thrust out from the defensive walls. The Grand Master had been sparing with his permission for attacks outside the walls, despite the pleas of his younger knights to act offensively. He knew that every available man who could hold a weapon would be needed to stand and fight on the defensive walls when the Great Turk ordered his soldiers to surge forward in those massed assaults that were the terror of Christendom.

De L'Isle-Adam stood silently, while his companions, watchful, and fearful for his safety, waited for his orders and instructions. It was hot, and he was wearing heavy siege armour that offered a greater degree of protection as he had proceeded along the whole length of the defences, from his palace complex in the north-west of the city, to his current place of observation. The Grand Master had been here before, when Mehmet the Conqueror's forces had besieged the city, over 40 years earlier.

In 1478, aged 18, de L'Isle-Adam had joined the Hospital, and had sailed for Rhodes to join the *langue* of Auvergne. The order was divided into eight *langues*, or chapters. That of Auvergne, along with those of Provence and of France, made the French the largest contingent among the 500 or so Knights of St John, and the 2,000 squires and sergeants. Alongside the French were the *langues* of Italy, Germany, England, Aragon and Castile, and Portugal. The French, by virtue of their numerical strength, held the greater part of the high official positions of the order, but the other *langues* held other important appointments, and therefore provided balance in the Council of the Grand Master.

Each *langue* had a bailiff, and responsibilities for the great offices of the order were divided among them. The Bailiff of Provence was nearly always the Grand Commander and he controlled expenditure, superintended the stores, and was governor of the extensive arsenal. The Bailiff of Auvergne was the commander-in-chief of all the forces, army and navy. The Bailiff of France was the Grand Hospitaller, with supreme direction of the hospitals and infirmaries of the order, the founding purpose of the Knights of St John half a millennium earlier. The Bailiff of Italy was the Grand Admiral of the galleys, the primary offensive capability of the order since the loss of the Holy Land, and the Bailiff of England was chief of the light cavalry, the turcopoles.

In 1478, the Grand Master had been Pierre d'Aubusson, also from the *langue* of Auvergne, and, in the siege of 1480, de L'Isle-Adam had found himself fighting alongside this great Hospitaller knight, during the assaults on the Tower of St Nicholas and again among the rubble and wreckage of the Italian Tower. It was here that the Ottoman commander Mesic Pasha had launched his most bloody and concerted attacks, and it was here that the young knight had stood over the Grand Master, who had been wounded for the third time that day, wielding a mighty two-handed sword as his fellow knights scaled the stones of the collapsed defences to push the Janissaries back into the moat and beyond. Days later, as Mesic Pasha suddenly chose to abandon the siege, he had sallied forth with the defenders to chase the Ottomans to their ships, and to help loot the great Ottoman red tent on St Stephen's Mount. Throughout the siege, the knights had looked, in vain, for any relief operation from other Catholic powers, but their own gallant and dogged defence of Rhodes had bought them a further 40 years in the eastern Mediterranean. In surviving three months of close and bitter siege, the young de L'Isle-Adam had learned a great deal about the Turks, about the fighting spirit of the Knights of St John, and about the conduct of siege warfare, both as an attacker and as a defender. He had stayed long enough in Rhodes to see d'Aubusson[10] begin the huge new defensive works that had transformed the fortifications of Rhodes, making the city into one of the most well-defended fortresses in the world.

The original dry moat had now been widened to between 30 and 50 yards, and huge *tenailles*[11] had been constructed within areas of the moat to break up attacks on the walls. The walls themselves had been thickened and strengthened, both to counter the increasingly powerful and effective Ottoman artillery, and to be able to mount the Order's own new large cannon. Powerful bastions, thrusting out from the original line of walls, allowed the knights to fire down the length of the moat, in support of other towers. The work had transformed the defensive capability of Rhodes.

After the fall of Acre in 1291, the Knights of St John, like the Knights Templar, and anyone else who had survived the Mamluk siege, had gone to Cyprus. From there they had carried out desultory attacks on Muslim maritime trade, Ottoman and Mamluk, for several years, while waiting to see if Christian Europe would raise another crusade to retake the Holy Land. No such enterprise was to be forthcoming, and the Lusignan rulers of Cyprus did not welcome their presence. The 'crusading ideal' had been badly tarnished by a century of successive compromises and failures, and the papacy had increasingly politicized the concept of a 'crusade', in order to pursue its own power struggle with the Holy Roman Emperor, or with doctrinal challenges to Catholic orthodoxy. These struggles would only get more visceral in the succeeding decades. In the early 14th century, the Order of the Temple had been formally suppressed. The Hospitallers had avoided a similar fate, and indeed had benefitted significantly from the fall of their long-time rivals. There was also little hope of assistance from Constantinople, because of the visceral antipathy between Catholic and Orthodox churches, the Byzantine civil wars, and the threat to Constantinople from the rising power of the Ottomans. In the meantime, the Christian rulers of Spain and Portugal were continuing to pursue their relentless *Reconquista* in the Iberian Peninsula, while the kings of England and France were either engaged in internal struggles or were conducting open warfare with each other.

In 1306, disappointed by their situation in Cyprus, the Hospitallers had come to the island of Rhodes and, after a four-year campaign, they had taken the port and city of Rhodes from the Byzantines. They had thrived in Rhodes and had developed from a land-based military organization into one of the finest proponents of medieval sea power, using their great galleys, powered by Muslim slaves and criminals, as highly effective maritime fighting platforms. With these they patrolled the sea lanes of the eastern Mediterranean, sometimes sailing as far as the Barbary Coast, and the Muslim pirate lairs of Algiers, Tunis and Tripoli. Sometimes their lasting enmity with the Mamluks even led to tactical cooperation with the Ottomans. Sometimes they would enter into arrangements with the great Italian maritime city-states of Venice, Genoa and Pisa, whose competition and rivalry they knew well from their shared history in the Holy Land. By 1522, they had been on the island for over 200 years. Now, 40 years after the last great siege, Ottoman power was once again focused on Rhodes and, once again, the Knights of St John would look in vain for reinforcement or relief from fellow Christian powers.

On 29 July 1522, the day after he had disembarked, Sultan Suleiman went into the forward trenches, with his commanders, to oversee the start of the assault. The Ottoman positions made it evident where the main blows would fall: against those ramparts defended by the Knights of Italy, Provence, England and Aragon. Piri Pasha, the Grand Vizier for this overall campaign, commanded those forces facing the eastern parts of the walls, from the sea to where the Grand Master now stood on the Tower of Italy. Golden embroidery on a field of green marked his command tent. Next to him was Qasim Pasha of Anatolia, facing the defences as far as the Gate of St John, his tent sporting silver embroidery on a blue background. Suleiman's Second Vizier, Mustapha Pasha, was described as 'facing a difficult and unsurpassable locality, of difficult access to the walls and the boulevards that fortified it', certainly meaning the walls from the Gate of St John to the Tower of Spain, which were well protected by extensive *tenailles*. As the Sultan's brother-in-law, his tent was of gold and red. Finally, on the west and north sides, all the way to the sea, were the forces of Ahmed Pasha, and those of the Beylerbey of Rumeli, Ayas Pasha. The Janissaries, led by Bali Agha – described in a letter back to Constantinople as, 'the principal commander of the soldiers of the religion, so valorous that he is like a roaring lion' – appear to have been positioned among all the other soldiers, in order to inspire them if they became weary or discouraged during the siege. The tents of the battalion commanders were also bedecked with colour, although not with silver or gold embroidery, while the mass of the soldiers' and labourers' tents were earth-coloured, making those of the commanders stand out even more prominently.

Admiral Kurtoglu commanded the fleet of warships, ready to attack from the sea when, and if, the Sultan commanded, but also to guard the supply ships that went to and fro from Marmaris, and to watch for a Christian naval resupply or relief force. Kurtoglu was a former corsair, who had wreaked havoc across the Mediterranean and along the coastlines of Italy and Spain. In 1516, he had been offered the appointment of an Ottoman admiral for Selim the Grim's expedition against the Mamluk Empire. After the overthrow of the Mamluks, Kurtoglu had sailed down the Nile, and he had then established the Ottoman Red Sea and Indian Ocean fleets, which aimed to confront the growing naval power of the Portuguese. He had a deep loathing for the Order of St John, which had killed two of his brothers, and now held a third one as prisoner on Rhodes. He had already attempted to ambush de L'Isle-Adam in 1521 and had again attempted to intercept him on his way back to Rhodes in early 1522. He was a formidable and committed enemy.

Within days, the Ottoman labourers had dug trenches to the scarp of the moat and had constructed a huge network of earthworks for their artillery positions. Despite the impressive effectiveness of the defenders' own artillery, the sheer numbers of the attackers, and of their labour force, meant that any pause in their activities was short-lived, and casualties were rapidly replaced.

The Knights of St John manned the walls by *langue*. The French defended the sector from the Naillac Tower to the Palace of the Grand Master; they were succeeded by the Germans, around the d'Amboise Gate; those from Auvergne around the Bastion of St George; the Spanish by their own tower; the English, east from the Tower of the Virgin to the Gate of St John; and the Provençals and Italians from there to the sea, and along the windmill-lined mole to the Tower of France. Each of these forces were commanded by their bailiffs, and each *langue* also contributed soldiers to the Grand Master's reserve forces within the city, and to the defence of the towers that guarded the harbours. The Grand Master had written to the Doge of Venice, on the eve of the siege, seeking help and reporting that he only had some 16,000 men for the defence of Rhodes, of which around 700 were Hospitaller Knights. He was most certainly not trying to exaggerate his numbers in seeking to elicit sympathy and support. He had 8,000 troops stationed around the four corners of the city: 2,000 to serve as mobile forces to plug gaps and to respond to emergencies, and 6,000 to act as a reserve,

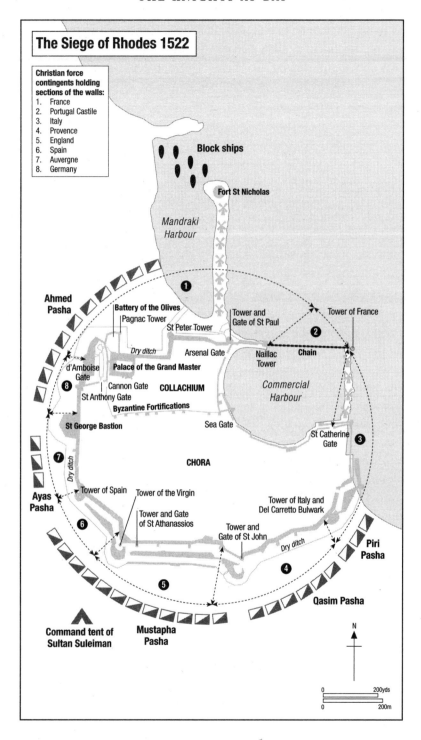

The Siege of Rhodes 1522

Christian force
contingents holding
sections of the walls:
1. France
2. Portugal Castile
3. Italy
4. Provence
5. England
6. Spain
7. Auvergne
8. Germany

Block ships

Fort St Nicholas

Mandraki Harbour

❶

Ahmed Pasha

Battery of the Olives
Pagnac Tower
St Peter Tower
Dry ditch
Arsenal Gate
d'Amboise Gate
Palace of the Grand Master
Cannon Gate COLLACHIUM
St Anthony Gate
Byzantine Fortifications
St George Bastion

Tower and Gate of St Paul
Naillac Tower Chain
Tower of France

❷

Commercial Harbour

Sea Gate

St Catherine Gate

❸

❽

❼

Dry ditch

Ayas Pasha

Tower of Spain
Tower of the Virgin

Tower and Gate of St Athanassios

CHORA

❻

❺

Tower and Gate of St John

Tower of Italy and Del Carretto Bulwark

Dry ditch

Piri Pasha

❹

Qasim Pasha

Command tent of Sultan Suleiman

Mustapha Pasha

N

0   200yds
0   200m

based in the centre of town, and under his direct command. Runners would report back to him constantly from the walls, as the various assaults ebbed and flowed. Of these 16,000, the number of professional fighters was probably not much greater than during the siege of 1480, with perhaps 5,000 locals, or mariners from the galleys, who could be relied upon to bear arms competently. The rest were largely available as a last resort and were normally used to carry supplies to those fighting on the walls, to rebuild fortifications destroyed by Turkish artillery, or to remove the wounded to the infirmaries.

The artillery bombardment of 1480 had convinced d'Aubusson to completely restructure the defences of Rhodes, but that of 1522 also showed how far the Ottomans had come in mastering the power of gunpowder since they had shattered the Theodosian Walls in 1453. Sultan Suleiman had 74 great pieces of ordnance with his forces, as well as innumerable smaller guns and arquebuses and muskets. His artillery pieces were mostly dug in no further than 200 yards from the walls, and often they were manhandled to as close as 40 yards.

On the evening of 31 July, an arrow carrying a letter with the Sultan's seal was shot into the Tower of England. It was immediately taken to the Grand Master, who summoned his knights to attend him in the garden of the Grand Palace. De L'Isle-Adam read out the letter himself. Suleiman wrote, 'Despite having urged you three times to surrender, I have yet to hear a sensible reply. I, Sultan Suleiman, will therefore commence hostilities at sunrise tomorrow.' The Grand Master thereupon demanded that all the knights parade on the ramparts the following morning, in full battle armour, to await the opening of the Ottoman offensive.

Suleiman was as good as his word, and, at daybreak, the Turkish artillery opened fire along the length of the fortifications, starting from the Italian positions and rippling down the line to those of the Aragonese and Castilians, stationed near the Spanish Tower. On the defensive side, 700 Knights of St John were arrayed in the towers and bastions, and along the ramparts and *tenailles*, armour shining silver in the morning sun. While each knight's armour was marginally different, reflecting the varied wealth of the wearer's family, what they all had in common was the white cross on a field of red adorning their breastplates and their capes. The tips of lances, rapiers and the great two-handed swords reflected the sun. Every *langue* flew its own arms and colours, while the Grand Master himself stood on the Aragonese rampart, enveloped by the smoke of the cannonade, with the battle standard of the Order of the Knights of St John snapping in the morning breeze. As the cannon balls thumped into the walls and bastions of Rhodes, their reputation from 200 years as defenders of the Holy Land, and from a further 200 years as the most aggressive and militant 'corsairs' in the eastern Mediterranean, hung over them like the aura of courage, personified.[12]

The evident strength of the fortifications in the early days of the bombardment gave the defenders and civilians some confidence that they could endure this siege, as they had done in 1480. In addition, the dismal failure of Kurtoglu's attempt to capture the Fort of St Nicholas also raised their morale, as both harbours remained secure while that garrison prevailed. Not only were Turkish ships hit and sunk, but poor seamanship led to two ships colliding, and the crew of a merchant vessel being captured. However, while Mesic Pasha had made the assault on the Tower of St Nicholas the centrepiece of his earlier operation, Suleiman, after attempting to batter it into submission for ten days, then ignored this fortified strongpoint, except to demonstrate against it in order to tie down Hospitaller manpower. Meanwhile, demonstrating the Sultan's impressive grasp of modern warfare, the Ottoman navy continued to supply the huge army, seemingly endlessly, from the huge depots of foodstuffs and gunpowder amassed in the port of Marmaris.

Day and night the Ottoman guns shook Rhodes's defences. Huge bronze cannon battered the towers and bastions, as the Turks attempted to fill in the extensive moats. Meanwhile, howitzers and mortars contributed to the civilian chaos and panic by lobbing incendiary and explosive rounds into the close-packed houses of the city. The Hospitaller guns were equally well served, and Suleiman sent a report back to his vizier in Istanbul, commenting on both the accuracy and power of the Christian gunners. But even the death of the Ottoman master gunner, Mehmet, whose legs were blown off by counter-fire from the walls of the Tower of England, did not discourage the Turks. Suleiman had quickly decided that the early artillery offensive had failed to produce results because his cannon had been situated on the same level, or slightly lower, than the new, thicker, remodelled defences of Rhodes. Work to build elevated platforms for his guns had already begun, and these were ready by mid-August. However, despite the rising casualty levels among the defenders of Rhodes, it soon became apparent that this would not be a decisive development in itself, so Suleiman ordered a higher daily rate of fire. The destruction first became noticeable in the outer wall of the English Tower, where collapsing brick, stone and earth began to fill the moat.

On the last day of August, a single ship sailed into the harbour of Rhodes, as the defenders lowered the great chain, flouting the Turkish blockade. Coming from Naples, it only carried four knights and a handful of mercenaries, but it was also packed with gunpowder. Like the Genoese flotilla that had braved the blockade of Constantinople in 1453, it provided a huge, temporary boost to the morale of the defenders, but it would prove to be another false harbinger of further relief from the Christian powers. In a further echo of 1453, Suleiman had his naval commander, Kurtoglu, tied to his own ship's mast and flogged, *pour encourager les autres*.

No more help for the defenders of Rhodes would arrive. The Hospitallers were a monastic military order solely answerable, from their inception, to the Pope. The Grand Master could make a personal appeal for assistance to the great monarchs and lords of Christendom, hoping to exert moral pressure, but only the Pope could make a formal request or a demand for military assistance to the order. Even had a king or queen been anxious to plan for, or to declare, a crusade, such plans could not proceed without the approval of the Pope, in whose gift lay the vital 'papal indulgences'. Nor would monies be raised or provided by the church, without papal endorsement. In 1513, Leo X, a member of the influential Florentine Medici family, had been elected as Pope. Although credited with the flippant remark, 'God has seen fit to give us the papacy, so let us enjoy it', he had been a conscientious supporter of the Knights of St John, whose important but precarious position in the eastern Mediterranean he acknowledged. However, from the start of his papacy, he had faced two other major challenges. The first was the obvious and growing threat from the Ottomans in the Balkans, as they increased their expansionist pressure. The second, arguably the more pressing for a pope, was his attempt to preserve the unity of Catholic Christendom in the face of rising tensions between the Valois kings of France, and the Habsburg monarchs of Spain and of Austria. This had been exacerbated when the Holy Roman Emperor, Maximilian I, had died in 1519 and his grandson, young Charles Habsburg, already ruler of the Netherlands and King of Spain, had now also succeeded him in his German and Italian possessions. The Habsburg position, already strong, was now considerably enhanced by its access to all the wealth that was flowing from the nascent Spanish colonies in the newly discovered Americas. Born in 1500, Charles was only 19 when he came into this enormous accumulation of wealth and power. The Valois of France, sandwiched between Spain and the imperial territories of Germany, the Netherlands and Italy, and acutely nervous of their own royal position, saw a potential confrontation with the Habsburgs as a greater 'clear and present danger' than the distant threat from the Ottomans.

Since the French had invaded the Italian peninsula in 1494, France and Spain had been in brisk and bloody competition for nearly a quarter of a century. The Balearic Islands, Sicily, Naples and south Italy had already been taken as Spanish territories, but the French and Spanish powers were now struggling for control of Milan, Genoa and the north of Italy. Florence remained fully in France's shadow, while the Pope and the Papal States, trapped between these power blocs, did what they could to retain their freedom of manoeuvre. The Republic of Venice, despite its routine, cynical, mercantile compromises, remained the only genuinely independent state in Italy at this time, although even its great maritime empire was being threatened by Ottoman ambition. This Valois–Habsburg confrontation, now expanding into a continent-wide clash, would shape European politics for the next century.

Christian disunity had already existed for centuries between the Catholic and Orthodox churches. The growing struggle between the Catholic Valois and Habsburgs put additional pressure on Christian unity and loyalty, and now Catholicism itself, both papal and monarchical, was being challenged by the growing Protestant movement. In 1517, a priest, Martin Luther, had published his Ninety-Five Theses, and nailed them to the door of All Saints Church in Wittenberg. This comprehensive list of complaints against the papacy had been primarily aimed at the egregious sale of papal indulgences in order to raise money for the building of a new basilica in Rome, and to give the Pope the wherewithal to fund a fresh crusade against the Ottomans.[13] However, the list also addressed a whole range of other issues to do with the Catholic Church and its shortcomings. At its heart was the contention that man was justified by 'faith alone', and that the Pope and the Catholic Church did not have the exclusive right to interpret scripture. This brought into question the whole role of the Catholic Church in Christian society, including the significance of relics, icons, saints and the whole paraphernalia of Christian worship at that time. It is difficult to exaggerate the effects of Luther's teaching on the development of the western world, and the subsequent split of England from Rome, under the Tudor King Henry VIII, would be but an early indication of the problems and challenges to come.

After a concerted effort to bring the renegade priest back into the fold, Luther had been excommunicated by Leo X in 1520. This had only bought temporary respite, however, and before he could revert to confronting the Ottoman threat, Pope Leo himself had died from pneumonia in 1521. Emperor Charles V's former tutor, Adriaan Boeyens, a Dutch priest living in Spain, was now, to universal surprise, elected as his successor. However, he could not formally be acknowledged as Pope Adrian VI until he had travelled to Rome for his coronation, and the Habsburg Emperor, Charles V, the Valois French king, Francis I, and the English king, Henry VIII, all wanted him to proceed to the Eternal City via their own kingdoms. The new Pope, Adrian VI, anxious to avoid such pressure so early in his papal tenure, had therefore secured passage to Genoa, but he had only landed there on 17 July 1522, as the Ottoman navy and army were about to concentrate in Marmaris. Now delayed for a further month, he arrived in Ostia, the port city of Rome, on 28 August, and his coronation service at last took place on the 31st, a month after the Ottoman guns had opened fire on the walls of Rhodes. Adrian VI was painfully aware of the twin, existential challenges to Christendom, but, due to all these delays, there would be no inaugural declaration of Church policy at the College of Cardinals until well into September. The Knights of St John, all 700 of them, therefore remained on their own in the defence of Rhodes, the last crusader bastion in the eastern Mediterranean.

Meanwhile, the bombardment continued, the defensive walls shivered and cracked, and the casualties rose. The Turks now began an extensive programme of tunnel digging and mining, in order to bring down the great defensive bastions and walls. Within the thousands of labourers recruited and conscripted from across the empire were hundreds of professional, Christian engineers and miners, drawn from the silver mines of the Balkans, as the Ottomans had advanced into south-east Europe. On 4 September, beneath the outer wall that girded the English Tower, the Turks had exploded their first significant mine, trying to take advantage of the damage their guns had already done. At the same time, they increased the intensity of the artillery barrage and, for the first time since the siege had begun, Turkish infantry poured down into the moat, braving the enfilade fire from the Spanish Tower, and placed scaling ladders against the ramparts of the inner wall, or scrambled up the rubble and fallen masonry. Mustapha Pasha, no 'chateau general', could be seen issuing orders from the rim of the moat as he commanded the attack. One-third of the outer wall had been blown apart, revealing the earth foundations of the English Tower, and exposing the 6-foot-wide tunnel the miners had dug.

The defenders kept firing arquebuses and crossbows until the last minute and then fell back to the inner fortress wall, hoping to draw the Turks into close, hand-to-hand combat, where their armour and their superior training gave them the advantage, as the Ottoman artillery was no longer firing for fear of hitting their own soldiers. De L'Isle-Adam himself was everywhere, always accompanied by his private secretary, a French knight, Jean Parisot de la Valette. Inspired by his memories of d'Aubusson's leadership 40 years earlier, he urged, he encouraged, he cajoled, he ordered, he took his place on the towers and the boulevards, he charged at the head of the reserves, he helped comfort the wounded in the hospital, and he led the prayers in the chapel. Like all the best commanders, de L'Isle-Adam had an instinctive feel for where he should be, where the most dangerous threat was, and where his presence would have the greatest, and the most positive, effect.

The English knights were now contesting every inch of their wall, but the Grand Master was again alongside them, and French and Castilian knights surged along the walls, and up from the town below, to reinforce them. As the sun set, the first great Turkish assault faded and the survivors fell back across the moat, pursued by fire from the defenders. Although the attackers had been repelled, the Turkish success with the mine had deeply unsettled the defenders.

The man charged with overseeing the Hospitaller defences against the Ottoman attacks was Gabriel Tadini di Martinengo, a Brescian engineer previously under Venetian employ in Crete. With the Turkish siege impending, the Grand Master had written to the Cretan authorities asking for his assistance. Such assistance had been 'officially' rejected, since Venice, conscious of the precariousness of its own positions in Crete and Cyprus, had a peace treaty with the Ottomans.[14] However, Tadini had been spirited away from Crete, and he had arrived in Rhodes a few days before Suleiman. Tadini, who had already made a significant contribution with his work on the defences, now, like John Grant at Constantinople, took command of the anti-mining operations. He began a campaign of tunnel detection, counter-mining and the 'venting' of the fortifications, to ensure the explosive power of successful mines was, at least, partially dissipated. A trench was dug behind the walls and covered with planks, under which the children of the city stretched thin sheepskin hides, hung with small bells or corks, which helped detect the slightest vibrations set off by digging. With such simple methods, 12 mines were exposed in September alone, and the Serbian miners, despised as traitors to their religion, were killed in their own tunnels.

In the absence of any new intelligence on the enemy since his landing in late July, the Grand Master determined to send spies into the Ottoman camp. Two Italian-born knights were selected by the Grand Council. One was Giambattista Orsini, a member of the powerful Roman family, and a descendant of both a pope and a former Grand Master; the other was a knight from Puglia who was fluent in Greek. They slipped out of the military harbour on a small boat that night, threading their way through the Turkish fleet, disembarking near the Hospitaller fortress of Lindos,[15] and discreetly joining the polyglot ranks of the labourers near the city walls. Given the size of the Turkish camp, and the chaos and the casualties, neither their presence nor subsequent absence was noticed. They returned, as they had come, bringing news of more tunnels and mines, particularly in the area of the English wall, and also reports of a traitor and spy within the walls. More cities and castles had fallen to treachery than to assault over the centuries, and the Grand Master feared betrayal as much as he feared the Ottoman artillery. The English bailiff, Sir William Norfolk, a man who had served as a galley slave for the Ottomans until ransomed, was entrusted with the investigation. Meanwhile, the Turkish preparations for a new assault intensified, as the artillery thundered, and mines were detonated, night and day.

Suleiman made little attempt to disguise the timing of his next attack, and it was believed that the main weight of the enemy would fall somewhere along the walls between the Tower of Italy and the Tower of Spain, which had already taken a battering. On 21 September, Suleiman ordered his whole army to rest and to fast, including those Christian levies in his ranks. At daybreak on the 24th, any peaceful dawn silence was shattered as the drums, flutes and bugles of the Ottoman army struck up, first in front of the walls the English *langue* held, and then spreading in an arc to encompass the whole of the landward fortifications of Rhodes. After five major assaults on various sectors of the walls, it was clear that, on this occasion, Suleiman was attempting an attack on all fronts, compromising de L'Isle-Adam's ability to move his reserves around, or to reinforce the most threatened positions.

The bells of all Rhodes's 44 churches began to ring the alarm, matching the cacophony of sound coming from the Turkish trenches, and knights, soldiers and citizens – already weary from weeks of vigilance, wall repairs and fighting – rushed to their defensive positions, painfully conscious of the gaps in their numbers. Those Castilian and French knights assigned to the seaward walls also now piled onto the landward defences, their vacated posts being filled by the crews of the merchant vessels trapped in the harbours. The Grand Master positioned himself with the English knights, alongside the great battle flag of the order, and he watched as a smaller gold tent was erected opposite the Tower and Gate of St John, from where Suleiman would direct and observe the battle. His four viziers, now mounted on conspicuous white horses, took up their positions near the edge of the moat.

The attack opened, along the whole landward side, with Muslim and Christian irregulars, drawn from the mass of labourers, their enthusiasm for this assault reinforced, where necessary, by Janissaries with drawn swords. Screaming, with martial fervour or terror, they poured into the moat and up the rubble, killing or wounding enough of the defenders to make their enormous sacrifice worth it, certainly in the eyes of their commanders. As the sun rose in the sky, they fell back. Their retreat and withdrawal were watched in silence on the ramparts, as to continue to fire at their backs would be a waste of the ammunition that would be needed to counter the next major assault. This began with hardly a pause in the fighting.

This time it was the turn of the veteran Turkish regulars from Anatolia, inspired by devotion to the Sultan, and to their religion. On they came, clambering up ladders and rubble along the length of the walls, as the knights fired everything at them, then threw everything within reach at them, including fire-pots, basins of pitch and rocks, and then engaged them face to face, and hand to hand, with mace, axe, dagger and sword. A cry went up: 'Ottoman banners on the walls of the Spanish Fort!' De L'Isle-Adam and La Valette gathered up their reserves and raced through the narrow streets to repel the attackers there, just as news reached them that the situation on top of the Italian wall had become almost as desperate. This was the same wall which de L'Isle-Adam had almost died defending in 1480. As Suleiman's runners brought him reports from the walls, the Sultan sensed that the deterioration in the defences between the Spanish and English towers offered a decisive opportunity, and, like Napoleon's Old Guard some centuries later at Waterloo, he ordered in the Janissaries.

Incredibly, the Rhodian defences held up, although the Spanish Tower changed hands three times in the course of the afternoon. After more than six hours of combat, the attackers fell back yet again, leaving the moat filled with the dead and the wounded. Not a cry of triumph was heard from the walls and, when the Turks began to remove their casualties, not a shot was fired at them. The defenders lay on the battlements, or in the streets and the hospital, stupefied by their efforts, and pole-axed by their exertions. Meanwhile, in his battle tent, Suleiman was exploding with rage at the six commanders who knelt on the carpets, heads bowed. The 28-year-old master of the Ottoman Empire, inheritor of the 'Red Apple', guardian of the last Abbasid Caliph, custodian of the Two Holy Cities, and conqueror of Belgrade, could hardly contain his fury at the failure of the day's assault. Mustapha Pasha was sentenced to death, and when Karim Pasha intervened on his behalf, he too was condemned to death. Shocked and quivering with fear, the other commanders dared to remonstrate that the army would disintegrate if these commanders were executed. As Suleiman calmed down, and his own good sense prevailed, he came round to their way of thinking. Karim Pasha would retain his position, but Mustapha Pasha was demoted to Governor of Syria and would depart the next day.

The Turkish attacks intensified in October, being launched at ten-day intervals, and allowing little respite for the defenders. On 11 October, Tadini had removed his helmet while inspecting the defences, and a random arrow had hit him in the right eye. Although it did not kill him, and he continued to direct his counter-mining and repair operations from his hospital bed, his wounding came as an unpleasant shock for the Grand Master and the knights. By 20 October, the defences on the Spanish wall had had to be repaired with hastily constructed wooden fences, which were immediately burnt down by the Turks. On 26 October, William Norfolk, still searching for the traitor and spy, caught a Jewish doctor red-handed, trying to fire an arrow with a letter attached, from the walls around the Fort of St George, into the Ottoman camp. Under torture, he said he was simply a messenger, and he identified Diaz – the Portuguese servant of the Bailiff of the Chapter of Castile, Andrea del Mare – as his co-conspirator. Diaz, in turn, claimed that he was simply carrying out the orders of his master. The council were both astonished and deeply upset. Del Mare was also Lieutenant Grand Master of the order. He was arrested, but under both questioning and torture he absolutely refused to say anything in defence or explanation. There were neither pleas nor words of denial. On 4 November, the Jewish doctor and Diaz were hanged, while del Mare was beheaded, having refused the offer of last rites. Their heads were put on pikes facing the enemy from the Fort of St George, but there is no record of any Turkish response.

By November, while the Ottoman bombardment and attacks continued, their morale was suffering, and their numbers had been heavily depleted. Rain had fallen, and the battlefield – already torn up by the presence of 100,000 men, their engineering works, their detritus and their dead and wounded – was now a quagmire. But while Suleiman could still use his naval superiority and his base at Marmaris to mitigate his losses, and to provide some respite for his soldiers, the defenders were increasingly running out of options, other than Suleiman's departure or the arrival of a Christian relief force. However, Adrian VI, installed as Pope in late August, had still not managed to convene the full College of Cardinals, and an outbreak of plague had further delayed the possibility of this taking place. At the same time news also reached them of a fleet from their English Chapter, sailing to their aid, which had foundered off the coast of Spain with the loss of all hands. Near the end of November, the Grand Master, at last, called in the garrisons of Cos, Petronium and Lindos, relinquishing fortresses held for over 200 years.

The siege had now lasted for five months, since Rhodes was invested, and it had been four months since the first artillery bombardment. Morale and fighting spirit had remained remarkably high throughout this period, among both the Catholic Knights of St John and the majority Orthodox Rhodians, despite all the sacrifices, death and hardship. However, with the near-certain knowledge that there was now no relief coming, and all the indications that the Ottomans were going to sustain the siege through the winter, this common purpose and sense of joint endeavour began to crack, and such knowledge clearly found its way across the walls. On 29 November another arrow with a message was shot into the city. It contained a letter from Suleiman urging surrender on good terms but promising death to all if they persisted in their defence. On 4 December, a Genoese man carrying a white flag climbed out of the trenches and down into the moat, asking to speak to the Grand Master. The guns fell silent as he delivered the same message to a gaunt, stony-faced de L'Isle-Adam, whose one-word reply was, 'Leave.' Similar approaches were made on the 6th and the 8th of the month, but this time the guns continued to fire.

On 9 December, in the middle of a powerful Mediterranean storm, another council meeting was held in the Grand Master's Palace. The Orthodox bishop, and the spokesmen for the common people of Rhodes made the same point. If the knights would not negotiate, then the people of Rhodes, who had stood by the Grand Master throughout the siege, and through the whole occupation of Rhodes by the order, would. They said that they believed the Sultan's offer was made in good faith, and that he would provide protection for those citizens who chose to stay, and permission to depart for those who chose not to. Their words were heard in resigned silence, except for Jean de la Valette, who argued that abandoning Rhodes meant relinquishing the order's *raison d'être*. The Hospitallers existed to fight the infidel, as well as to guard and tend pilgrims, and to pursue the release of Christian captives. To surrender, or to make a treaty with the Muslim

Sultan, was to fly in the face of everything that 400 years of their order's existence had taught them, or had been handed down to them as an example. Compromise would put them on the same level as the despised Venetians. On 12 December, two high-ranking Ottomans appeared before the Gate of the Tower of St John and handed over a further letter for the Grand Master.

Despite La Valette's intervention, Philippe Villiers de L'Isle-Adam now decided to make an initial offer of a three-day truce. Orsini was chosen again for this mission, and on the following day he, and a companion, passed through the d'Amboise Gate and, crossing the moat and the Turkish siege lines, they entered the tent of Ahmed Pasha. Meanwhile, as hostages, the nephew of Ahmed Pasha and another high-ranking Ottoman commander entered the city through the Gate of St John. The knights were treated with astonishing hospitality, staying until late in the evening. In lengthy discussions, conducted in Greek, they learnt that the Turks had suffered over 40,000 casualties, had detonated over 50 mines, and had fired around 85,000 cannon balls. It was clear that, given this expenditure of men and materiel, only the Sultan's personal presence during the siege had ensured its continuation. The peace terms with which Orsini returned were strikingly generous, given the relative strengths of attacker and defender. Suleiman promised to adhere strictly to the following conditions, if Rhodes was surrendered:

- The Knights of St John to have the right to remove from the island everything they want, including holy articles, battle flags, and sacred statues.
- The knights to have the right to leave the island with their battle gear and possessions.
- In the event the order's own ships are insufficient to carry these articles, the Turkish navy will provide as many ships as are necessary.
- Everyone will be allowed 12 days to prepare for departure.
- During that period, the Ottoman army will withdraw one mile from the front line.
- During that period, all the order's bases outside Rhodes must surrender.
- All inhabitants of Rhodes who wish to leave the island will be allowed to depart freely, if they do so within three years.

- Those who decide to stay will be exempt from the obligatory tax levied upon all non-Muslims living in Ottoman-controlled territory for five years.
- All Christians remaining on the island will be guaranteed complete freedom of worship.
- Contrary to the long-standing custom of the Ottoman Empire, the children of Christian residents of Rhodes will be exempt from recruitment into the Janissaries.

The Rhodians were jubilant at this set of concessions, while many of the knights were relieved and gratified by the leniency and courtesy of the terms. However, the Grand Master, buoyed up by the arrival of a Venetian blockade runner, procrastinated, and the ceasefire period lapsed. On 16 and 17 December, in foul weather, the Turks resumed their attacks, and the fighting on the walls was as vicious and brutal as at the height of the siege. On 18 December, the Ottomans launched a ferocious assault on the half-destroyed Aragonese section of the walls. Knights were summoned from all the other sectors of defence, and the Grand Master himself was again right at the epicentre of the fighting.

By the afternoon the moat was once again filled with corpses, but the Janissaries kept on coming, trampling over the bodies of their comrades, in an attempt to break the resistance on the walls and to, at last, bring this hellish siege to a victorious conclusion. As the day came to an end, the Turks were still in possession of a section of the ruins of the Spanish Tower. There were now no longer the forces or the energy, among the defenders, to remove them. The attack resumed the next day, once more against the area either side of the Spanish Tower, but also against the Italian Tower to the east. The Grand Master was once again on the front line, with La Valette, and once again, quite miraculously, he survived the fighting unscathed. That evening he handed down his decision, his alone, to surrender the fortress and to accept the Sultan's terms. A Knight of St John, and two representatives of the civilian population, entered the Turkish camp on 20 December, while the Turks removed their dead from the moat. Not a shot was exchanged.

A new tentative three-day truce was agreed, and while 25 knights and a further 25 commoners were accommodated in the Turkish camp,

400 Janissaries laid down their weapons and entered the city. The surrender document was signed in Ahmed Pasha's tent. Ahmed Pasha signed for Sultan Suleiman, and an Auvergnese knight, the successor to del Mare as Lieutenant of the Order, signed on the defenders' behalf. The agreement was dated 25 December. While this was taking place there was a commotion within the walls when the Janissaries began to behave arrogantly towards the locals. De L'Isle-Adam, trying his best to avoid an outbreak of violence on the birthdate of Christ, appealed directly to the Sultan, claiming the truce was being broken. Suleiman immediately withdrew the Janissaries and, as promised, also withdrew the whole army a mile from the city.

The following day, an invitation arrived for the Grand Master to visit the Sultan and, that afternoon, De L'Isle-Adam crossed the bridge at the Tower d'Amboise, on horseback and in full armour. He was accompanied by La Valette carrying the great battle flag of the order, and all the bailiffs of the chapters, and their lieutenants. This deliberate act of defiance and pride had a marked effect on the Turkish soldiers, including the Janissaries, those forcibly converted former Christians, and on the other Christian levies of the Sultan, and they instinctively stepped aside as the Grand Master and his entourage approached the great golden tent of the Ottoman Sultan. Their welcome was courteous and dignified, but the meeting was clearly one between the victors and the vanquished, and no amount of politeness could disguise this fact. As the conversation, again conducted in Greek, came to an end, with the Grand Master declining any period of grace for the order to depart the island, the young Sultan calmly fixed the older man with a stare: 'I have won,' he said. 'Despite that, I cannot help but feel heartfelt sadness that you and your followers, who are so courageous and upright, are being forced from your homes.' It was the most remarkable meeting and exchange between avowed enemies, both bolstered by their own conviction of religious certainty. If Suleiman had looked beyond the Grand Master, as he brought the meeting to a close, he may have seen the steely glint of iron determination in the eyes of Jean Parisot de la Valette that said, 'This is not yet over.'

The Sultan had entered Rhodes on horseback by the Gate of St John on 29 December, accompanied by an honour guard of 100 immaculately turned-out Janissaries. He went no further than the civilian harbour, and made no attempt to approach the Grand Master's Palace, or the residences of the knights. Around 5,000 Rhodian citizens would join the exodus, accompanying the 400 or so surviving knights, and their sergeants and servants. They would require a total of 50 ships for their departure, and there were not enough galleys of the order, or merchant ships from the Italian maritime states, to accommodate them all. As promised, the Turkish navy made up the difference, but the civilian population were terrified of embarking to find they had been enslaved and consigned to life as a galley slave, or worse, and initially refused to board the Ottoman vessels. The knights themselves, as warrior monks, had few personal possessions, other than their armour and their weapons, but the order had any number of relics, statues and artefacts from the 400 years of their existence. Forced to abandon Palestine, Cyprus and now Rhodes, they needed a new, secure home, and they would spend the next several years seeking one, amid the shifting alliances and fortunes of Christian Europe. With reverence, the right hand of St John, in its magnificent silver reliquary, was placed in the cabin of the order's flagship, the *Santa Maria*. Alongside it was placed the shard from the cross upon which Christ had been crucified, two thorns from the crown Christ had worn before his crucifixion, and the mummified body of St Euphemia.[16]

Departure was set for New Year's Day, 1 January 1523. The Grand Master paid a farewell visit to the Sultan, to offer parting formalities, and to receive the official travel documents from Suleiman. These guaranteed all who were leaving safe and free passage throughout the Ottoman Empire. They spent longer together than previously, and no doubt de L'Isle-Adam spoke of his youth, fighting in 1480 alongside Grand Master d'Aubusson, against Mehmet the Conqueror's army, on the same walls. He would later describe the Sultan as, 'a knight, in the truest sense of the word'.

Slowly the civilian harbour filled with the noise of oars being run out and sails being half-raised. Venetian, Genoese and French flags fluttered from the mastheads of the merchant vessels, and friends and family made their tearful, and sometimes fearful, goodbyes. Turkish merchant ships stood by to take on board those who could not find a berth with Christian crews, but the Turkish war fleet itself had discreetly withdrawn. In the military harbour, 25 assorted galleys and sailing ships stood ready to depart, a meagre enough force for an organization that had dominated the eastern Mediterranean for over two centuries. The order's flagship was captained by an English knight, Sir William Weston, and it led the convoy out of the harbour. One by one, the other ships followed in its wake, while the church bells began to chime in unison within the newly conquered Ottoman fortress of Rhodes. If Suleiman was minded to order the tolling to cease, he did not do so.

The battle flag of the order cracked in the chill wind, as it flew defiantly from the main mast of the *Santa Maria*, and as it did from the mast of every ship and galley. The knights' shields, with their white crosses on red, were arrayed down the sides of every ship, and the knights stood behind them, clutching their lances. Their eyes were stinging with tears, although, if you had asked them why, they would have said it was caused by the cold and by the sea breeze. The windmills that stretched along the breakwaters were creaking in the wind, and then, as the flagship passed the Fort of St Nicholas, cannon fire could be heard echoing from the fortress. Suleiman had ordered a salute, to a worthy and doughty foe. The Grand Master and his knights were speechless and silent, as they watched their island home recede into the distance.

They Shall Not Pass

Malta 1565

The knights, their sergeants, and those soldiers from the Spanish and Italian contingents nearest the gates when they were opened, surged over the bridges crossing the deep, dry moats that protected the peninsulas of Birgu and Senglea. Forming up in three, largely ad hoc divisions, they advanced up the low hills to confront the Ottomans. On 22 May 1565, three days after disembarking, the advance guard of the Turkish army had now drawn itself up to the south of the Grand Harbour and its fortifications. The ridge was crowned with rich standards, and brilliant with the robes and jewelled turbans of the Ottoman commanders. Triangular banners of silk floated at the head of the different detachments, and the caparison of the horses was as colourful as the clothes and armour of their masters. Francisco Balbi da Correggio, the 60-year-old poet, soldier of fortune, and member of the Senglea garrison throughout the great siege of Malta, wrote, 'the whole, at a distance, seemed an infinite multitude of flowers in a meadow or luxuriant pasture; nor delightful only to the eyes, but also to the ears, from the various instruments, melted down by the air into exquisite harmony'.

Swiftly dressing their ranks, the defenders of Malta moved rapidly forward, sun glinting off weapons and armour. The Knights Hospitaller were wearing their famous surcoats of red with the white eight-pointed cross. Cannon from the Bastion of Castile and the Fort of St Michael began to fire over their heads as they advanced, with the Mediterranean Sea to their left reflecting the early morning sun of a day in late May.

Watching them from an exposed position on the battlements of the Bastion of Provence was their commander, the Grand Master of the Order of the Hospital of St John, the redoubtable Provençal soldier Jean Parisot de la Valette. He had not ordered this attack, but neither had he sounded the recall. He was now 70 years of age, the same as that of Suleiman the Magnificent, the Ottoman Sultan who had ordered this assault on Malta, and that of Mustapha Pasha, the commander of the Turkish army, whose troops had debouched onto the island seeking further Ottoman triumph and glory. La Valette had stood at the right-hand side of Grand Master Philippe Villiers de L'Isle-Adam during the siege of Rhodes 43 years earlier, protecting him with his shield and sword, as the two of them had stood in the breached fortifications of the English wall. Ice-cold himself, he also understood the fire and the impetuosity of youth.

When Don García de Toledo, Philip II's viceroy in Sicily, had swept down to visit him in March 1565, he had given La Valette three valuable pieces of advice: 'restrict your Council to the bare minimum, and let them all be well tried veterans; husband your limited strength, and resist sorties and skirmishes; above all, take care of your own person. The death of the commander has too often been the cause of defeat.' He had departed, leaving his young nephew behind with La Valette, and promising a relief force of up to 25,000 by the end of June. La Valette had willingly embraced the first of these admonitions. A small decision-making body was consistent with his own experience and his own instincts, although, in the coming months of trial and tribulation, he would regularly communicate and explain his decisions to wider groups, while not leaving them open to debate. He also knew the wisdom of the second. The Ottoman force was four times larger than his garrison, split as it was between the forts of Birgu, Senglea, and St Elmo, and the fortified town of Mdina.[1] However, on this first day he chose to resign himself to the inevitable and to let his young men, many of whom had never been in combat before, accustom themselves to this enemy, and to 'blood themselves' early in the confrontation. As to the last piece of advice, sound though it was, La Valette, with his fanatical faith and imperious nature, would routinely neglect it. Indeed, as he stood on the Bastion of Provence that first day, a soldier next to him had been shot dead by a Janissary musket, and his own page had been wounded in the neck.

This initial struggle went on for six hours or so, until La Valette, seeing the weight of Turkish numbers beginning to tell, ordered the signal to retire. The defenders streamed back as the gates were opened, while the gunners held off the advancing Turks. Only 21 Christians had been killed, but although several hundred Turks were left dead on the field of battle, a further 150 defenders had been wounded. The action had served to raise the morale of his troops, but La Valette knew he could permit no further sallies. A captured Turkish standard was brought to him for his inspection, and a Navarrese knight, Jean de Morgut, showed him a golden bracelet, taken from the arm of a richly dressed Turkish officer. The Arabic inscription read, 'I do not come to Malta for wealth or honour, but to save my soul.'

As the sun set, Mustapha Pasha ordered his troops to withdraw, and they established three main divisions: their left wing on the Marsa, at the western end of the Grand Harbour; their centre against the ridge of Corradino; and their right wing facing Senglea, the western of the two fortified peninsulas. Two days earlier, in a skirmish with Christian cavalry scouts, Adrien de la Rivière, a young Knight of the Order, and his companion, Bartolomeo Faraone, had been taken prisoner. Under torture, they had told the Ottoman commander that the weakest point in the Christian defences was the Bastion of Castile. Fully aware of the fate that awaited them, La Rivière and Faraone had lied, and it was now painfully clear to the Turks that the Bastion of Castile, and indeed the whole of the landward defences, were, in fact, strong, well defended and protected by a large number of cannon. A vengeful Mustapha Pasha had the two captives taken out and bastinadoed to death in front of his soldiers.

When the Knights of St John had sailed from Rhodes on that first day of 1523, they had sailed into an uncertain future. In many ways, the politics of the eastern Mediterranean had been easy for the order, if increasingly precarious. They had a long-standing and well-established base, a clear mission and purpose as maritime warriors and defenders of Christendom, and sufficient resources, until Sultan Suleiman had focused the full force of the Ottoman power on their extinction. They had spent the subsequent seven years homeless. They were respected for their military prowess and religious dedication; indeed, Emperor Charles V, referring to their defence of Rhodes, and conscious that none of the Christian powers had come to their assistance during the six-month siege, had declared, 'Nothing in the world was ever so well lost as was Rhodes.' However, they were not liked. At a time of growing nationalism, state centralization and religious fragmentation, a multi-national order owing its loyalty to an increasingly discredited papacy was beginning to look like an anachronism. Their single-mindedness in confronting the infidel had not only made life difficult for the Mamluks and the Ottomans, but also for those commercial maritime agnostics, the Venetians and Genoese. In addition, their wealth, arrogance and haughtiness, deriving from a strict recruitment criterion, based on aristocratic descent, did not make them easy company.

Having first sailed to Crete, de L'Isle-Adam had spent the next years trying to hold the order together, to nurture their resources and to establish a new base. Minorca, Ibiza, Ischia and, under pressure from the Pope, innumerable other islands and ports, had been considered as potentially available for the knights by European sovereigns. However, for one reason or another, all the most prosperous and fertile islands had been deemed, by their owners, as unsuitable or unfeasible. At last, in 1530, the Maltese archipelago had been presented to the order by Charles V, Holy Roman Emperor and King of Spain, 'in order that they may perform in peace the duties of their Religion for the benefit of the Christian community and employ their forces and arms against the perfidious enemies of Holy Faith'. In return, the knights were merely required to make an annual presentation of a falcon to the Viceroy of Sicily, which island was part of the Kingdom of Spain, as was most of Italy south of Rome, and to give a guarantee that they would never make war on the kingdom.[2]

Still pining for their home in Rhodes, one of the most fertile and fruitful islands in the Mediterranean, de L'Isle-Adam and his knights were even less enthusiastic about this gracious imperial gift when their reconnaissance party reported back to them. The island of Malta, they said, was merely a rock of soft sandstone, barely covered by more than 3 or 4 feet of earth, with almost no wood, and poorly provided for water. It was about 18 miles long by 9 miles wide, lying about 50 miles south-west of Sicily, and broadly equidistant from both Gibraltar and Cyprus. Despite its obvious geographical significance, sitting astride the maritime routes from both ends of the Mediterranean, neither Spain nor the Ottomans seem to have afforded it the importance it deserved. It had one significant town, Mdina, on high ground in the middle of the island, and a population of perhaps 12,000. There were no ports of any note on the western side of Malta, but to the east and south there were several useful coves and inlets, as well as two spacious harbours, which were capable of accommodating the largest of galley fleets, but which were currently poorly protected. Gozo, the smaller island to Malta's north, was no more than 8 by 4 miles, with a small citadel in the centre, and around 5,000 inhabitants.

With the Emperor's gift of Malta and Gozo also came responsibility for garrisoning and defending the important seaport of Tripoli on the North African coast. This was a lonely Christian outpost, flanked by Tunis and Algiers, the hostile Muslim pirate states of the notorious Barbary Coast. It had been an unappealing package, but after seven years of futile search for a new home, de L'Isle-Adam and his Grand Council felt they could not reject the Emperor's offer. In the autumn of 1530, de L'Isle-Adam and the officers of the order stepped ashore at the small fort of St Angelo. Although the Grand Master initially set up his headquarters in Mdina, the order, as a maritime power, soon set about establishing itself on Birgu, and around what would become known as the Grand Harbour. In doing so they sought to recreate the urban model of Grand Palace, Conventual Church, hospital, *langue auberges*, harbour facilities, and fortifications that they were familiar with from their long stay in Rhodes.

Well known as they were, the order's quest for a new permanent base had not been high on the priority list of any of the great powers of Europe. The invasion of the Italian peninsula by Charles VIII of France in 1494 had set in train a colossal, Europe-wide struggle for power between the French Valois monarchy and the Austrian and Spanish branches of the Habsburg family that would last until the extinction of the Valois dynasty in 1589.[3] Neither the threat from the expanding Ottoman Empire nor the growing challenge to Christian unity presented by Protestantism and the Reformation would be enough to unite the Catholic powers. Throughout this period, the papacy itself, as an institution and as an individual, would remain an integral element of both this dynastic confrontation and this theological competition.

Although the French had taken Naples, their war objective, they had been evicted soon afterwards, during the War of the Holy League. In this war, Catholic France had found itself pitted against a Catholic coalition of the Papal States, the Holy Roman Empire, Spain, Milan and Venice. A further Italian land grab by Charles's successor, King Louis XII, was robustly countered by another anti-French coalition. The early decades of the 16th century saw a bewildering realignment of politics around the whole of Europe, the Mediterranean and the Near East. In the same year that Martin Luther had nailed his Ninety-Five Theses to the door of Wittenberg Cathedral, Sultan Selim the Grim's armies, fresh from military success against the Persians, had defeated the Mamluk Empire of Egypt. In this historically decisive campaign, Selim the Grim had almost doubled the size of his empire, and he had also inherited the three holiest cities of Islam. The Ottomans had thereby assumed leadership of the whole Sunni Muslim world. At around the same time as these extraordinary successes by land, the great corsair Khair ad-Din, better known as Barbarossa, had become the ruler of the great slave and pirate entrepot of Algiers. He had then sailed to Constantinople, accompanied by a huge cargo of rich gifts for Sultan Selim, where he had put his bases, galleys and wealth at the service of the Ottoman Empire. At a stroke, the combined Ottoman maritime power could now compete with the Christian powers throughout the Mediterranean.[4]

———

On the Christian side, the consolidation of Habsburg power under Emperor Charles V in Spain, Sicily, Naples, Burgundy and the Netherlands had coincided with the rapid and bloody acquisition of additional rich colonies in the 'New World'. In 1525, deploying this new wealth against a backdrop of widespread peasant revolts across all central Europe, Emperor Charles V had defeated and captured King Francis I of France at the battle of Pavia. Francis was held as a hostage for several months in Spain, until he signed the humiliating Treaty of Madrid[5] with the Emperor, and his response to this humiliation, along with the long-standing Valois fear of Habsburg encirclement, had been to open secret talks with the new Ottoman Sultan, Suleiman. In December 1525, his envoy, John Frangipani, had travelled discreetly to Constantinople, to propose a formal alliance against the Habsburgs.

Avoiding imperial spies and assassins, Frangipani had returned to King Francis in early 1526 with a letter from Suleiman which ended with this flourish: 'Night and day our horse is saddled, and our sabre is girt. May God on high promote righteousness. May whatsoever He will, be accomplished! For the rest, question your ambassador and be informed. Know that it will be as said.' The Valois hopes of putting pressure on the Habsburgs came to fruition later that year when, encouraged by this evident Christian disunity, Suleiman had launched a major campaign against Hungary. His shattering victory over King Louis II and the Hungarian nobility at the battle of Mohacs in August led to the partition of the Kingdom of Hungary for the next several centuries, and an Austrian and Hungarian competition for power and status, that the Ottomans would skilfully exploit.

King Louis II had only been ten years old when he had ascended the throne, and was only 20 when he died, drowning in a small stream in his armour as he fled the battlefield. At his premature birth, he had been kept alive by being wrapped in the warm skins of freshly slain animals. In 1520, on the accession of Sultan Suleiman, Louis had recklessly ordered the execution of the Ottoman ambassador who had come to his court demanding Hungarian tribute for the new Sultan, and he had sent the unfortunate envoy's head back to Constantinople. It had not been a wise diplomatic gesture, and his death at Mohacs, and the destruction of the Hungarian army, had been the Ottoman answer.[6]

Emperor Charles V had already ceded rule of Austria to his brother, Ferdinand, and Ferdinand now took advantage of the death of King Louis II and the destruction of the Hungarian nobility to annex a substantial slice of Hungary for the empire. Victory at Mohacs had brought the Ottomans, for the first time, to the frontiers of the Holy Roman Empire, and the death of King Louis II had also marked the end of the Jagiellonian dynasty, whose dynastic claims in central Europe had previously trumped those of the Habsburgs. Meanwhile, within this potpourri of cynical alliance-making, and acutely conscious of French diplomatic manoeuvring in Sunni Ottoman Constantinople,

Emperor Charles V had also sent his own emissaries to the Safavid capital of Ctesiphon in 1525, and again in 1529. Although nothing would come of it, the Emperor had hoped to counter the Valois–Ottoman coalition with a parallel Habsburg–Persian alliance that would, in its turn, threaten the Ottomans from the east, and thereby take pressure off the Habsburg Empire. Meanwhile, the bloody sack and destruction of Rome, by underpaid Christian imperial troops in 1527, led to Pope Clement VII having to barricade himself within his fortress of St Angelo and, in his anger, choosing to side with the French. This chaos in Christendom could only contribute further to Ottoman confidence, as they looked to advance further into Europe. In 1529, only appalling weather, and the consequent loss of his heavy artillery, had thwarted a Turkish assault on Vienna, thereby narrowly robbing Sultan Suleiman of yet another stunning victory, and one that would have opened up all of Europe to his armies.

Described as 'the sacrilegious union of the lily and the crescent', the Franco–Ottoman alliance would last, intermittently, for more than two and a half centuries, until the Napoleonic campaign against Ottoman Egypt in 1798 shattered a relationship that had proved so useful to both parties. In July 1532, as the Hospitaller Grand Master was starting work on the new fortifications of Malta, King Francis I had sent an ambassador, Antonio Rincon, to Belgrade to present the Ottoman Sultan with an extraordinary and magnificent four-tiered helmet-crown, which had been fashioned in Venice.[7] In 1533, Barbarossa had made a visit to France, and in support of his visit, Sultan Suleiman had ordered him to put his fleet under French command for an attack on Genoa. In August 1534, Philippe Villiers de L'Isle-Adam was found dead in his lodgings in Mdina. In his hand was a report that suggested that the Ottoman objective for the campaigning season in 1535 would be Malta. As a veteran of the great 1480 and 1522 sieges of Rhodes, the elderly de L'Isle-Adam had known exactly what such an assault would mean, in terms of scale and ferocity, and he also knew how unprepared the Knights of St John were to meet such an attack. The rumour proved to be false, and the knights, although locked in persistent conflict with the Ottomans, would have another 30 years to prepare their new sandstone island fortress, before Sultan Suleiman determined, again, to destroy this chivalric order of warrior monks.

In 1535, the Ottomans had moved to formalize further their relationship with France, and a French embassy and chapel were established in Pera, the old Genoese settlement across the Golden Horn from Constantinople. With this had also come a range of important commercial and trading rights and privileges. In addition, Sultan Suleiman now sent letters to the new leaders of Protestantism in Germany and the Netherlands, encouraging them to ally with King Francis against Emperor Charles, and to fight against the Habsburgs. For the remainder of the decade, French ships routinely sailed with Ottoman fleets and their corsair allies, bringing destruction to Habsburg territories across the Mediterranean, although they stood back from participating in the horrific slave trade pursued, at an industrial level, by the Muslim navies. In 1538, during a further Valois–Habsburg war, Barbarossa achieved a significant victory against a Spanish–Venetian fleet off Prevesa[8] in the Ionian Sea.

In 1541, a papally sanctioned Habsburg 'crusade' against Algiers came to grief in the face of a massive and unseasonable storm, while the assassination of the French ambassador, Antonio Rincon, as he travelled through Italy, provoked increased Franco–Ottoman collaboration. In the ensuing conflict, King Henry VIII of England – who had divorced Emperor Charles V's aunt, Katherine of Aragon, in order to marry Anne Boleyn, and who had formally broken with the papacy in 1534 – was this time allied to the Holy Roman Empire. In his breach with Rome, Henry had also decreed the spoilation of the English branch of the Order of the Knights of St John. Among the most heroic defenders of Rhodes in 1522, there would be no English *langue* to contribute to the defence of Malta.

The Valois–Habsburg fighting in the Netherlands had been expensive and inconclusive, while that in the Mediterranean had not been that much more productive, although Barbarossa, with his 110 Ottoman galleys and 30,000 men, had combined with 50 French galleys to besiege Nice in 1543. They had managed to take the city but not the citadel. Later in that year, after the siege had been concluded, King Francis had offered the Ottoman fleet and army the opportunity to winter in Toulon, in order that they could continue to harass the coasts of Spain and Italy in the following year. During this stay, Toulon Cathedral was converted into a mosque, and the call to prayer was heard across the city, five times a day. According to one observer: 'To see Toulon, one might imagine oneself at Constantinople.' At the same time, France had artillery units supporting the Ottomans in their renewed campaign in Hungary, and advisers alongside the Ottoman army in their long-running war with Persia. Whatever one's view of this supreme exercise in realpolitik, the Ottoman alliance certainly aided France in escaping the grasp of the Habsburgs and, as a by-blow, it significantly helped the development of Protestantism in northern Europe. However, it did nothing for Catholic unity in the face of the challenges from Lutheranism and Calvinism, nor for Christendom in the face of continuing aggressive Ottoman expansion in the Mediterranean, and in central Europe.

Grand Master Jean Parisot de la Valette was that rare beast, a completely single-minded man, totally dedicated to the order. He was descended from the first hereditary Counts of Toulouse, crusade leaders and founders of the County of Tripoli in the Holy Land. He had joined the order at 20 years old, had fought at Rhodes in 1522, and had never revisited his family estates, or returned to his native country. He was described as 'a very handsome man, tall, calm and unemotional, speaking several languages fluently – Italian, Spanish, Greek, Arabic and Turkish'. The last two he had learned when, suffering a fate that was not uncommon in those days, his ship, the *San Giovanni*, had been destroyed and he had been captured and made a Turkish galley slave by Abdulrahman Kust Ali. He survived a year in the hellish world of a galley slave before being liberated in the type of prisoner exchange that often characterized this period.

The great Barbary corsair Dragut, who had been born a Christian in 1485, within sight of the great Hospitaller fortress of St Peter at Petronium, saw La Valette when he was a slave and secured better conditions for him. Some years later, La Valette was present when Dragut himself was captured after he had sacked the island of Gozo. He sympathized with the corsair's anger and remarked, 'Monsieur

THE HOUSE OF WAR

Dragut – it is the custom of war', to which Dragut had wryly replied, 'and change of fortune'. When Barbarossa besieged Genoa in 1544, he had demanded the release of Dragut, and had gone ashore to dine with the famous Genoese admiral Andrea Doria[9] in his palace at Fassolo, where they discussed a ransom, eventually set at 3,500 gold ducats. Dragut straightaway launched another raid on Gozo and returned to raid Malta again in 1547. In 1550 he was almost captured again, when he was repairing his galleys on the island of Djerba. Blockaded by Andrea Doria, the recipient of his ransom money, he had all his ships dragged overland through hastily dug canals and on heavily greased tracks to the other side of the island, from where he had blithely sailed away to Constantinople, capturing two Christian galleys along the way.

During his long service as a Knight Hospitaller, La Valette had held nearly all of the most important positions in the order. He had filled the onerous post of Governor of Tripoli from 1546 to 1549 and was then selected to be Lieutenant to the Grand Master, at that time Juan de Homedes. The year 1551 would be a dire one for the order, when Dragut descended on Malta yet again, landing with about 10,000 men in the eastern bay of Marsamuscetto, and marching across the Marsa to besiege the still-incomplete fortifications of Birgu and Senglea. The corsairs then went north to besiege Mdina, but realized they did not have enough force to capture the whole island. Instead, they moved to Gozo where, after bombarding the citadel for several days, they enslaved almost the whole of the island's population, taking them to the slave market of the Algerian inland city of Tahuna. Dragut then moved swiftly against the Hospitaller base at Tripoli, capturing the fortress, and taking prisoner the commander and several prominent Spanish and French knights, although the intervention of the French ambassador in Constantinople led to the early release of the latter.

The continuing vulnerability of Malta had been starkly exposed by these recurrent corsair raids, and it was only their campaigns in the Balkans, and against the Persians, that had stopped the whole weight of Ottoman power being thrown against the knights on their small, but important, island. In 1554, La Valette was elected to be General of the Galleys, an appointment normally considered an Italian monopoly.

It was given to La Valette in recognition of his expertise and experience as a master of galley fighting and tactics. Almost his first achievement as General of Galleys was to capture Abdulrahman Kust Ali and, in his turn, send him to the oars. Kust Ali would die soon after, still shackled to them.

The order had been enlarging and improving the defences of Malta from the moment they had taken possession of the island. Although the threat of imminent invasion was real, progress had been intermittent, and the resources of the knights were hit by the Spanish and imperial wars, the French alliance with the Ottomans, the effects of the Reformation, and sporadic papal interest. However, the demoralizing events of 1551 had focused minds, and in 1552, Grand Master Juan de Homedes set up a formal commission to report in detail on the state of the island's preparedness for an assault, and to draw up plans for a rapid improvement of the defences. The first and most obvious weakness was the fact that the main entrance to the Grand Harbour was undefended on its northern side. Here, where the rocky headland of Mount Sciberras comes to a point, it was decided to build a fort, to be called St Elmo. At the same time another fort, called St Michael, was to be built on the Senglea peninsula,[10] in order to give crossfire over Dockyard Creek, where the order's galleys were moored. The defences of Mdina were also to be strengthened, although there was only so much that could be done with its medieval walls.

St Michael was quickly completed, the sandstone rock of the island being easy to quarry, but the fort at the end of Mount Sciberras was a more difficult undertaking. On the site of an old watchtower, a new defensive structure was built, in line with the new military architectural developments on the continent and informed by the experiences of the Ottoman siege tactics at Rhodes. It not only commanded the entrance to the Grand Harbour, but also to Marsamuscetto, the bay in which Dragut had landed the year before. Small, and in the shape of a four-pointed star, the fortress of St Elmo had 875 yards of high defensive walls, made from sand- and limestone. Deep ditches were built around it, and on the landward side, facing Mount Sciberras, a counterscarp or ravelin had also been built. The whole structure rested on solid Maltese rock, so it could not be mined, an Ottoman speciality. Unfortunately, it had been built in a hurry, and there were both design and construction faults. Its biggest weakness, however, was that, being at the tip of the peninsula, it could be dominated by the artillery of an enemy holding the higher ground of Mount Sciberras.

It was the unanimous election of Jean Parisot de la Valette as Grand Master in 1557 that turbo-charged work on the defences, on the restoration of Hospitaller finances, and on the morale of the knights and brethren of the order, the 'Religion'. La Valette was a strict disciplinarian. He would not tolerate lax behaviour, or any of the abuses that had sapped both the spirit and the reputation of the order. Edward Gibbon wrote, 'The Knights neglected to live, but were prepared to die, in the service of Christ.' La Valette was determined to address this. Out went private duels, living outside the confines of the *langue auberges*, drinking and dicing. In came religious observation, military exercises and weapon drill. He cultivated the good opinion of the local Maltese, conscious of their disdain for the knights, but also of the critical importance of their active support in any forthcoming siege. An unknown Maltese historian gave this account of the Knights of St John when they arrived on the island:

> By the time the Knights came to Malta, the religious element in their foundation had fallen into decay. Their monastic vows were usually regarded as mere form, and they were remarkable for their haughty bearing and worldly aspirations. The Maltese, on the other hand, grown accustomed to be treated as freemen, greatly resented the loss of the political liberties that had been conceded to them … It is not, therefore, surprising that there was little love lost between the Maltese and their new rulers.

However, the depredations of the last decades had left neither knight nor Maltese in any doubt about the consequences of a successful Turkish invasion. Shared peril gave both sides the incentive to cooperate closely and to make defensive plans together, and for the knights to spend some time examining their own attitudes and behaviour.

The work on properly fortifying Malta continued, but the Christian powers remained divided in the face of Ottoman ambition. The prospect of another Catholic crusade in the Balkans had always been viewed with a deep-rooted ambivalence by those of the Orthodox faith. 'Better a sultan's turban in Hagia Sophia than a pope's mitre' had been a Greek cry well before the fall of Constantinople in 1453, and so it remained.

When the Turkish and Arab armies of the Ottomans marched, they did so alongside Christian, or newly converted Serbs, Bosnians, Wallachians and Croatians. In the wake of Charles V's abdication as Emperor in 1556, Spain, the Netherlands, the Habsburg holdings in Italy, and the colonies of the New World went to his son, King Philip II of Spain, while his German domains went to his brother, Archduke Ferdinand Habsburg, who now also became the Holy Roman Emperor. In 1558, Queen Elizabeth I ascended the throne of England, confirming that country as a Protestant power, and strengthening the cause of Protestantism across northern Europe. In 1559, mutual exhaustion led to the Treaty of Cateau-Cambrésis,[11] which largely ended the Valois–Habsburg dynastic struggle, especially when the French king, Henry II, died in a freak jousting accident that year, and his son, Francis II, died the year after. With Catherine de Medici as regent for her young, and mentally unstable, son, Charles IX, France entered a disruptive and bloody period of religious wars, which would continue well into the 17th century, through to the fall of the House of Valois, and the rise of the House of Bourbon.

Suleiman, like the Roman and Byzantine emperors his dynasty had supplanted, was always torn between the security demands of both east and west, and in his attempts either to expand or to defend the empire. From 1533, the Ottomans had conducted a long series of bloody, expensive and indecisive wars against the Safavids, whose Persian and Shia identity constituted a dynastic, ethnic and ideological threat. Accepting the title of Caliph in 1543 – the year the last 'shadow caliph' had died – had only added to Suleiman's consciousness of his religious responsibility to confront the infidel and the heretic. The Peace of Amasya of 1555 defined the boundary between the Ottoman and Safavid empires, and this still broadly marks the borders between modern Turkey and Iran, and modern Iraq and Iran. Further east, the Ottomans had inherited from the Mamluks another long-running war in the Red Sea, Persian Gulf and Indian Ocean, this one against the Portuguese and other western powers who were increasingly competing for the rich trade in spices and silk, which had previously come along the Silk Routes, and whose wealth fed the Ottoman coffers in Constantinople.

Sultans, however grand, are human, and the success of Suleiman's armies and navies, the splendour of his court, the power he wielded, the wealth he controlled, the titles he claimed, could not spare him from the personal vicissitudes of life. Historian Marc Baer wrote that Suleiman is remembered for 'his passion for two of his slaves: for his beloved Ibrahim when the Sultan was a hot-blooded youth, and for his beloved Roxelana when he was mature'. Both brought him heartache. The same age as Suleiman, Ibrahim had been taken as a Christian slave and rose to be Grand Vizier by the age of 28, and commander-in-chief of all the Sultan's armies. Caught up in the power struggles of the Ottoman court, Ibrahim went from, '*Makbul*, the Beloved, to *Maktul*, the Executed', in 13 momentous years. His nemesis had been Roxelana, the Sultan's favourite concubine and eventually, to the horror of the Ottoman court, his legal wife. Roxelana mistrusted the ambition and arrogance of Ibrahim, and also his influence over Suleiman. In due course she conspired to convince the Sultan that his Vizier was planning to usurp the throne and, in 1536, having dined amicably together, Suleiman had Ibrahim strangled as he went to bed.

Suleiman had one son by Roxelana, Selim, but he had three sons by other concubines: Mustapha, Bayezid and Cem. Mustapha was widely assumed to be the heir and was universally admired for his personal qualities and warrior spirit. However, jealous tongues reported to Suleiman that his eldest son coveted the throne, and that the army, in particular the Janissaries, favoured the young prince as Sultan. Returning from campaigning in Persia in 1553, Suleiman had summoned Mustapha to his tent at his camp in central Anatolia, where his mute eunuchs killed him with a bowstring. Soon after, Prince Cem was said to have died of grief at his stepbrother's murder, while Princes Selim and Bayezid were both given commands in different parts of the empire.

Within a few years, however, civil war had broken out between the two brothers. Roxelana had died in 1558, and Suleiman now backed her son, Selim. Prince Bayezid was defeated near Konya in 1559, and he sought refuge, along with his four sons, in the court of the Safavid Shah, Tahmasp I. This was double treason, and Suleiman was unrelenting. He demanded that Bayezid either be extradited back to his father or be executed. In 1561, in return for a large payment of gold, the Shah allowed a Turkish executioner to travel to the Safavid capital of Qazvin, and to kill, by garrotting, Bayezid and all his young sons.

In 1560, the Spanish, the Papal States and the Knights of St John had organized an expedition to retake Tripoli, this time under the command of Giannettino Doria, nephew and adopted son and heir of the great Genoese admiral Andrea Doria.[12] Disease delayed the fleet's departure, and bad weather and lack of water made them abandon their plans for Tripoli, falling back on the island of Djerba, which they quickly took, and on which they rapidly built a defensive fort. To their surprise, the Turkish Grand Admiral, Piali Pasha, son-in-law of the Sultan, alongside the irrepressible Dragut, arrived with a large fleet and instantly attacked them. The naval battle was over in a few hours, with about half the Christian fleet destroyed, and with the loss of around 10,000 men, many of them irreplaceable skilled sailors and marine arquebusiers. Piali and Dragut then besieged the fort, while Giannettino Doria himself escaped in a small boat. After three months the defenders surrendered, and around 5,000 of them were shipped back to Constantinople, including their commander, Álvaro de Sande. Sande was ransomed two years later and made his way back to Spain. He would join the Knights at Malta for the next, inevitable, clash-of-arms. The Ottomans, reportedly, erected a pyramid from the skulls of the defeated Spanish soldiers, which stood on the site of their victory until the late 19th century.

After the disaster at Djerba in 1560, Malta lay open, but the Ottomans failed to seize their chance to take the island, which would have allowed them to threaten Sicily, the Italian peninsula, and even Spain itself. La Valette now called upon all the Knights of St John, from their commanderies across Europe, to join their brethren in Malta. St Elmo was further strengthened, with a raised 'cavalier' on the side facing the Bay of Marsamuscetto, and with an additional separate ravelin to the front. This was largely constructed from wood, which had had to be imported from Sicily. St Angelo also had two new artillery platforms added, to enable the fort to be able to fire across the Grand Harbour in support of Fort St Elmo, while a channel was cut between St Angelo and Birgu, where the order's smaller ships could dock. Birgu itself was surrounded by a line of continuous defences with an overall length of 2 miles. Where the defences of Birgu and Senglea faced the south, or landward, side, a high rampart wall was constructed, containing two large bastions, as well as two demi-bastions at either end. Beyond these formidable defence works, a large ditch had been carved out of the solid rock.

Spies and merchants took news of these preparations back to Constantinople, while other spies and merchants brought back news of Sultan Suleiman's own preparations. The galleys of both sides continued to raid across the Mediterranean, seizing ports, ships and slaves. In early 1564, the great maritime hero of the Knights of St John, Mathurin d'Aux Romegas,[13] seized the Barbary stronghold of Peñón de Vélez, opposite the Spanish port of Malaga. Shortly after, near Cephalonia at the other end of the Mediterranean, Romegas, with several galleys of the order, attacked and, after a very bloody battle between knights and Janissaries, captured a large Ottoman galleon. Owned by the Chief Eunuch of Suleiman's harem, it was carrying a vast wealth of merchandise, belonging to him and to a large number of the Sultan's ladies, including Mihrmah, Suleiman's favourite daughter by Roxelana.

At Sultan Suleiman's Grand Council in October 1564, held to decide the military objectives for the next year's campaigning season, the Sultan was not short of advocates for an assault on the island of Malta. However, others argued for a further major drive into the heart of Europe, in order to redress the failure to take Vienna in 1529. Still others spoke for an invasion of Sicily, or a descent on the coast of Spain itself, to assist the growing rebellion by the Moriscos, those Spanish former Muslims forced to recant their faith after the *Reconquista*. Suleiman would also have listened to his concubines crying for vengeance against the knights, and to his imam, reminding him of his Islamic duty to suppress the enemies of the Faith, and to rescue those members of the Faith who languished in infidel dungeons, or who pulled at infidel oars. He would have been conscious of the demands of *jihad*, of the continuing requirements of *ghazi* leadership to keep his followers loyal and motivated, and of the need for a sultan, and a caliph, to sustain the prestige of his own position, and that of Islam. In addition, he would no longer have been under any illusion about the strategic significance of Malta and its harbours, nor the challenge the Knights Hospitaller continued to pose to his reputation and credibility.

Therefore, the edict went forth. In 1565, the might of the Ottoman Empire was to be deployed against Malta, and against the Knights of the Order of St John. The Sultan himself had spoken: 'Those sons of dogs whom I have already conquered and who were only spared by my clemency at Rhodes, forty-three years ago – I say that now, for their continual raids and insults, they shall be finally crushed and destroyed.' The Sultan's direction was not to be gainsaid. The arsenals at Constantinople and Gallipoli started outfitting the war fleet of galleys and cargo vessels; the foundries began casting new and bigger cannon and mortars; gunpowder was prepared and packed in vast stockpiles of barrels; supplies of every description began to be gathered in; the corsair commanders began to assemble; the Janissaries increased the tempo of their training; and the call went out to Anatolia and the Balkans for the *sipahis* and their levies to start moving towards the embarkation ports in early 1565. However, this was not to be like the assault on Rhodes, where Sultan Suleiman and his armies had had the Anatolian mainland nearby, from which to ferry supplies and reinforcements, and to where the wounded could be evacuated. Although the Barbary Coast offered some strategic depth, the army and navy would have to transport the vast bulk of what they needed to subdue Malta and its defences across a thousand nautical miles of capricious sea. If the great siege of Malta was to be primarily a land operation, it would begin as a vast seaborne invasion.

The Sultan, now 70 and painfully suffering from gout, went down to the shipyards on the Golden Horn to inspect the work. Mustapha Pasha had been given command of the army. He too was 70, and he was reputed to be descended from the standard-bearer of the Prophet Muhammad, whose body was buried at Eyup, at the head of the Golden Horn. He had already fought against the knights at Rhodes, where he had been condemned for his failures, reprieved, sent to Syria, and brought back into royal favour. He was a veteran of the campaigns in Hungary and Persia, and he possessed a fanatical attachment to both the Sultan and to Islam. As co-commander, Suleiman had appointed Admiral Piali Pasha. Piali Pasha was only 35 years old, but he was one of

the heroes of Djerba, and, importantly, he was married to a daughter of·
Prince Selim, the son of Suleiman who had emerged triumphant from
the succession struggle. These two campaign leaders were supported
by some other outstanding, proven commanders, Ulich Ali, a notable
corsair, and Ulich Ali Fartax, a former Dominican brother, and
Hassem, the Governor of Algiers. Aware of the potential complications
of a split command, Suleiman had given orders that the two supreme
commanders must work together in everything. Piali he ordered to
'reverence Mustapha as a father', and Mustapha to 'look upon Piali
as a beloved son'. He also gave further instructions that both of them
should await the arrival and advice of that venerable, renowned corsair,
Dragut, before launching the main assault.

In early April 1565, to the sound of time-keeping drums, the shrill
whistles of the overseers, and the creak and groan of several thousand
great oars, the bulk of the Ottoman fleet made its way out of the
Bosporus and the Golden Horn, under the eyes of Sultan Suleiman,
and turned into the Sea of Marmara. The armada was composed of 181
ships, not counting a large number of smaller vessels. Of these, 130
were the long-oared galleys, and around 30 were the larger galleasses,
able to carry up to 1,000 men. A further 11 large merchant ships
accompanied the fleet, one of which alone carried 600 fighting men,
6,000 barrels of gunpowder and 1,500 cannon balls. Laden with men
and supplies, the fleet made its way sedately into the Aegean, picking
up further ships as it passed the dockyards of Gallipoli. They were also
joined by individual corsair and pirate craft, which trailed the fleet, like
jackals, anticipating the rich pickings of Malta. The embarked army
was around 30,000 strong, including a force of over 6,000 Janissaries,
perhaps 9,000 *sipahis*, 5,000 irregulars, and another 10,000 volunteers
and levies. More men would join them from the corsair bases on the
Barbary Coast. Another 25,000 sailors and volunteer oarsmen were also
available to support the soldiers, if conditions permitted. They came
well prepared for the austere conditions of Malta, and for a siege and
assault that their spies assured them should not take more than a few
weeks. The two commanders were in the vanguard. Mustapha's huge
and ornate galley was a gift from the Sultan, called *Sultana*. Piali sailed
in a galley described as 'the largest and most beautiful ship that ever
sailed on the Bosporus'. Above the High Admiral's stern quarters was
set the personal standard of the Grand Turk: a beaten silver plaque, 10

feet square, surmounted by a crescent moon and a golden ball from which floated a long horsehair plume.

La Valette knew of their coming. As he demolished all the buildings which lay outside the settlements of Birgu and Senglea, and called in all the civilian farmers, with their animals, vegetables and spring crops, he recalled Don García's promise of a relief force by the end of June. Grain was poured into silos, bread was baked, vast quantities of water were stored in casks, although Birgu did have its own spring, and powder and weapons were distributed. Two of the order's galleys were north in Messina, on Sicily, but of the remaining five, three were put in the new channel between St Angelo and Birgu, while two were sunk in a manner that would allow them to be raised again later. The great merchant ship of the Chief Eunuch was left in full sight in Dockyard Creek, moored alongside the west flank of Birgu. A great chain, like that which had guarded the Golden Horn, was stretched across Dockyard Creek, secured on the Senglea side, and operated from a capstan on St Angelo. It rested on small boats, which acted as pontoons, and it was covered by a battery of cannon, set low in the fortress near the slave quarters. Well aware that the two peninsulas may have to fight separate or simultaneous battles, La Valette had also put a pontoon bridge across Dockyard Creek, in order that the garrisons could provide each other with mutual support and reinforcement.

La Valette had around 9,000 men under arms. He had collected nearly 700 knights, along with their servants, although more continued to make their way to Sicily and might be expected with the relief force. He had maybe 2,000 soldiers from King Philip II's Spanish and Italian dominions, and around 1,000 oarsmen and Christian convicts released from the galleys. Importantly, he could call on around 5,000 Maltese to fight, and the rest of the population to help with repairs to the defences, to carry food and water, and to tend to the wounded. It seemed likely to La Valette that the Ottomans would land and attack from the Bay of Marsasirocco in the south-east, although they might prefer, if they could, to force an entry and disembark in the harbour of Marsamuscetto, as Dragut had done in 1551, or even in the Grand Harbour itself. It was therefore possible that St Elmo might have to bear the first onslaught, and the size and leadership of that garrison was therefore of the utmost importance. The fort was normally manned by six knights and 600 men, under the command of the veteran Chevalier Luigi Broglia. La Valette now sent the younger Chevalier Juan de Guaras as his second-in-command, with a further 200 Spanish infantry under Don Juan de la Cerda, and a further 46 knights, who had volunteered from the seven *langues*. The Protestantism of England in 1565 meant that the English *langue*, once 'so rich and noble a mainstay of the Order', was now represented by only one knight, Sir Oliver Starkey, the Grand Master's secretary and close friend. In recognition of Starkey's valour and long service, and in memory of the English contribution to the order for over half a millennium, Starkey was assigned a reserve detachment, drawn from all the other *langues*. La Valette now sent Marshal Copier, along with all the order's cavalry, to Mdina, under the command of Chevalier Don Mesquita, accompanied by as many non-combatants as he could persuade to go.

The first Ottoman ships were sighted from the battlements of St Elmo and St Angelo on the morning of Friday 18 May, and immediately the alarm bells began to be rung, signal cannon fired, and beacons lit. The Maltese population moved into the fortifications, on both Malta and Gozo, bringing everything with them, and poisoning the wells behind them. As the huge fleet headed for the south of the island, cavalry followed them along the coastline, while Romegas took four small vessels out to reconnoitre the size and capacity of the armada, and its destination. Passing up the west coast, Piali had anchored off the small inlet of Mgaar. La Valette had feared that the Ottomans planned to disembark in the north, take Mdina, having battered down its weak walls, and thereby break his communications with Sicily. It was therefore with a sense of relief that he heard reports from his scouts that the fleet had retraced its steps and, by midday on 19 May, was beginning to disembark in Marsasirocco, where the advance guard moved rapidly to the village of Zeitun. It was here, in this first clash, that La Rivière and Faraone had been captured, and the first major miscalculation of the Ottoman command had been made.

La Valette had feared that the Turks would initially seize the north of the island, making any relief operation hazardous, and, after their setback at the Bastion of Castile, that was exactly what Mustapha Pasha had wanted to do. However, his plan was overruled by Admiral Piali Pasha, who was unsatisfied with Marsasirocco as an anchorage, although he overestimated the dangers from bad weather of that harbour. He wanted first to secure Marsamuscetto for his fleet, before Mustapha Pasha expanded the land operation, and to do so safely and effectively, Fort St Elmo must be taken and neutralized. Assured that the fort had been hastily and poorly constructed, the Ottomans therefore now hauled their heavy artillery across the Marsa, and onto the slopes of Mount Sciberras, anticipating that their fleet would be safely docked in Marsamuscetto within the week. At the same time, La Valette – clear where the next blow would fall – sent the French knight Pierre de Massuez Vercoyran, known as 'Colonel Mas', with a further 64 knights and 200 enlisted men, and the Spanish Captain Miranda, to join St Elmo's garrison. On 24 May, Mustapha Pasha ordered his batteries to open fire, and his snipers to harass the defenders. Under this intense bombardment, the lime- and sandstone blocks of the landward wall of the fort began to crumble. As the Ottomans opened fire, La Valette received a discouraging note from Don García de Toledo in Sicily, setting out his problems in assembling a relief force of sufficient size to come to his aid.

'St Elmo is the key to Malta,' La Valette had told Colonel Mas, and every day it held out would weaken the Turks, and would give him more time to continue preparing the defences of Birgu and Senglea. In order to support the garrison, he built an additional rampart on St Angelo, which allowed him to fire on the Turkish gunners on Mount Sciberras, while Marshal Copier's cavalry routinely sallied forth from Mdina to harry the enemy's foraging and watering parties, and their outposts and labourers.

With the walls of St Elmo subject to intense bombardment, Broglia was clear that only a nightly influx of reinforcements would allow him to hold the fort, and La Valette despatched a further 50 knights, all volunteers, 400 Spanish soldiers under Chevalier de Medran, and 60 former galley slaves. On 29 May, the defenders of Birgu and Senglea were woken by the rattle of musketry as Colonel Mas and de Medran led a sortie against the Turkish positions, and they watched as the banners of the defenders advanced up Mount Sciberras towards the gun positions. 'Janissaries forward!' cried Mustapha Pasha as he saw the labour battalions collapse and fall back, and the warrior monks of the Sultan and the Order of St John fell upon each other. Slowly,

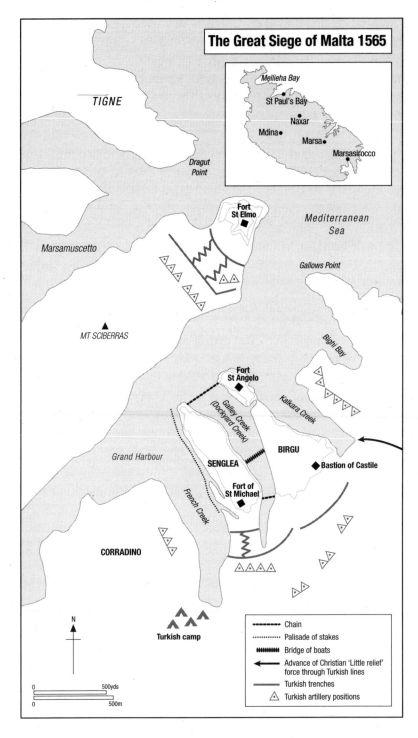

The Great Siege of Malta 1565

TIGNE

Mellieha Bay
St Paul's Bay
Naxar
Mdina
Marsa
Marsasirocco

Dragut
Point

Fort
St Elmo

Mediterranean
Sea

Marsamuscetto

Gallows Point

MT SCIBERRAS

Bighi Bay

Fort
St Angelo

Galley Creek
(Dockyard Creek)

Kalkara Creek

BIRGU

Grand Harbour

SENGLEA

Bastion of Castile

French Creek

Fort of
St Michael

CORRADINO

N

Turkish camp

Chain
Palisade of stakes
Bridge of boats
Advance of Christian 'Little relief'
force through Turkish lines
Turkish trenches
Turkish artillery positions

0   500yds
0   500m

numbers began to tell, and the defenders of St Elmo were pushed back, yard by yard, until they regained the safety of the gates, while their guns fired over their heads at the advancing Turks.

On 31 May, to great fanfare, that most illustrious of the Barbary corsairs, Dragut, arrived at Malta. Known as a 'living chart of the Mediterranean' by the Christians, and 'the drawn sword of Islam' by the Muslims, he had proved himself to be one of the finest seamen, and land commanders, of the era. Eighty years old when he landed at what is still known as Dragut Point, he had been present at almost every major naval engagement of the 16th century, had raided Malta six times, had taken Tripoli from the knights, and had, himself, served as a galley slave. He was scornful of the decision to assault St Elmo first, instead of securing the whole island, but now that this operation was in full swing, it must be brought to a successful conclusion, and he accepted the assurances that this would take only a matter of days.

Dragut, rightly, assessed that the fort's strength lay in its capacity to be reinforced from St Angelo, and he gave orders for new batteries to be constructed on Tigne, at Dragut Point and Gallows Point. The artillery fire on St Elmo doubled, and cannon balls pounded the fort from all sides, as Admiral Piali also brought his galleys in close to fire against the seaward walls. St Elmo was described as being 'like a volcano in eruption, spouting fire and smoke', but still it stood, and still, by night, the wounded were recovered to St Angelo, and more volunteer knights and soldiers were ferried across to bolster the garrison. On 4 June, the ravelin fell to the Ottomans, and for six hours the battle raged on the landward walls, and around the bridge between the ravelin and the main defences. Clad in plate armour, and using muskets, swords, maces, grenades, and tubes and firework hoops of Greek fire, the knights, soldiers and Maltese tenaciously held their positions as Dragut, and Mustapha Pasha hurled wave after Janissary wave at the small fort. When the troops were eventually called off, it was estimated that the Turks had lost upwards of 2,000 soldiers. To their mind it was worth it; Balbi da Correggio, who was present on the island throughout the siege, noted: 'Shorn of its outworks the Castle of St Elmo stood like some bare and solitary trunk, exposed to all the fury of the storm …' The sun shone, the heat rose, and still no relief force was in sight, or in prospect.

On 7 June, another Ottoman attack was launched, with guns opening up again from all sides, as the walls of St Elmo shattered and crumbled, with debris cascading and sliding into the surrounding ditches. But still the defence held. De Medran crossed to brief La Valette and the Grand Council. St Elmo was now nearly untenable: Would it not be better to evacuate it, in order to reinforce Birgu and Senglea? La Valette needed more time: 'We swore obedience when we joined the Order. We swore also on the vows of chivalry, that our lives would be sacrificed for the Faith whenever, and wherever, the call might come. Our brethren in St Elmo must now accept that sacrifice.' That night, 15 volunteer knights and 50 soldiers from the Mdina garrison, along with de Medran, rowed back across the black waters of the Grand Harbour to St Elmo.

At midnight the following day, at the end of another Turkish assault that again seemed certain to overwhelm the garrison, La Valette received an extraordinary message. Fifty-three young knights of the order had signed a letter, stating that St Elmo was now indefensible, and demanding his permission to sally forth from the wreckage of the fort, and to end their lives in a last burst of chivalric glory. La Valette sent three knights to assess the situation, and to report back. Despite their complaints, Chevalier Costantino Castriota was not convinced that St Elmo was about to fall, and he offered to raise a relief force of 600 new volunteers, which he did. Upon seeing this, La Valette wrote to the 'mutineers', telling them that they would be relieved that night, and that he would feel more confident in the defence of St Elmo, when 'it is held by men whom I can trust implicitly'. The 'mutiny' collapsed immediately as the young knights, whose names have gone unrecorded, were confronted with shame and dishonour. They pleaded for the Grand Master's forgiveness. They would stay and die in St Elmo.

On 10 June, over three weeks after the invasion, the Turks attempted a night attack, which was repulsed with heavy loss. On the 14th, they offered safe passage to the garrison, if St Elmo was surrendered; the messenger was driven back by arquebus fire. On the 16th, another frenzied assault went in, led by imams and dervishes. Fired up by the prospect of death in a holy cause, and seeing, 'only the line of battlements before them and Paradise beyond', they too dashed themselves upon the mounds of shattered sandstone and their equally shattered defenders. The agha of the Janissaries was killed, as was de Medran, alongside 150 Christians, and a further thousand Turks.

On 18 June, a cannon ball fired from St Angelo hit the stony ground of Mount Sciberras, and a splinter of rock struck Dragut above his right ear. Mortally wounded, he had only been saved from instant death by his turban. Many years before, when his brother had been killed in Malta, he had prophesied that 'I, too, shall die in the territory of the Knights.' His removal from the battlefield was a disaster for the Turks.

In Birgu, the knights went in solemn procession to the Conventual Church of St Lawrence. It was the Feast of Corpus Christi, which fell that year on Thursday 21 June, marked with full honour by the order ever since the days of their foundation in the 12th century. Even as they paraded in the dark formal robes of the order, and knelt in prayer, the guns of the Turkish artillery continued to thunder and, at last, the cavalier of St Elmo was overrun by the Ottomans. On the evening of the 22nd, a Maltese swimmer brought the last message from St Elmo. The garrison's discipline still held, morale remained high, de Guaras, Miranda and Colonel Mas were all severely injured, but every man would fight to the last. As dawn rose on 23 June, every Ottoman gun, at sea and on land, opened fire, and Mustapha Pasha ordered a general assault. To his amazement, St Elmo held out for a further hour. De Guaras and Miranda, too wounded to stand, were placed in chairs in the breach, each with a large two-handed sword by his side. As the Turkish lines burst on the fort, De Guaras was hurled from his chair and his head cut off, while Miranda and the gallant Colonel Mas were also struck down and hacked to pieces. One by one the last defenders perished, as Chevalier Lanfreducci lit a signal flare to tell La Valette that St Elmo was, at last, and after 31 days of siege, lost. A Janissary officer flung the flag of St John at Mustapha Pasha's feet, while the banner of Sultan Suleiman the Magnificent was raised in the ruins. Dragut finally expired on hearing the news, while Mustapha Pasha gazed across the waters of the Grand Harbour at the looming fortress of St Angelo. 'Allah,' he cried, 'if so small a son has cost us so dear, what price shall we have to pay for so large a father?'

With the summer temperatures continuing to rise, the Turks now began to move their artillery from Mount Sciberras to the Corradino Heights, overlooking the Bastion of St Michael at the head of the Senglea peninsula. The final chapter of the defence of St Elmo had been played out when the Ottomans nailed the beheaded corpses of the Knights of St John to wooden crosses, and set them adrift to float across the Grand Harbour to bump against the base of Fort St Angelo. La Valette's response was prompt and brutal. All Turkish prisoners were taken to the ramparts, executed, and their heads struck off, loaded into cannon, and fired across the waters into the Turkish camp. La Valette had made it clear to the knights, the soldiers and the Maltese: they would either prevail, by their own efforts or those of a relief force, or they would die, fighting to the end. Meanwhile, at last, the Ottoman fleet sailed into Marsamuscetto Harbour, as Piali Pasha had wished for, and the crews disembarked to add to the numbers of the attackers.

On 30 June, Mustapha Pasha made a further attempt to negotiate a surrender, promising La Valette the same terms that de L'Isle-Adam had accepted at Rhodes in 1522. He may have been driven to this gesture by the news that Chevalier de Robles, a famous soldier of the order, had managed to land 700 soldiers in the north of the island, and had made his way, undetected, to the shores of Kalkara, and thence into Birgu. De Robles had initially sent scouts ashore, who had learnt of the fall of St Elmo. Ordered by Don García de Toledo to withdraw if the garrison of Malta had looked to be doomed, de Robles had kept this information from the Spanish naval commander, and he had disembarked with this small, but significant, band of reinforcements, while the galleys sailed back to Sicily, none the wiser. Whatever the reasons for the Ottoman offer, La Valette sent Mustapha Pasha's emissary back with a blunt rejection, but not until he had been paraded past the fortifications and their grim-faced, armour-clad defenders. La Valette's Maltese allies were equally blunt and defiant when approached to desert him. They were staunch Christians, and they knew, all too well, the history of Ottoman rapine and destruction. 'The Maltese would rather be the slaves of St John, than the companions of the Grand Turk,' they defiantly proclaimed.

Some days later, the lookouts on the spur bastion in Senglea saw flares at the landward end of Mount Sciberras, and heard the creak and groan of wood, and the crack of whips. Like the Byzantines in Constantinople 100 years earlier, they watched as the Ottoman ships from Marsamuscetto were hauled across the land on rollers, to be launched into the Grand Harbour. As the fleet began to grow, one of La Valette's knights saw an individual on the far shore gesticulating, and clearly offering to desert. As boats were launched to pick him up, the Turks also saw him, and he plunged into the Grand Harbour, where he was rescued by Maltese swimmers.

The 'deserter' was from the noble Byzantine Lascaris family, who numbered three emperors among his ancestors. Captured, converted and raised by the Ottomans, he had risen high in their ranks; but now, seeing the heroic courage of the defenders of Malta, he had determined to return to the religion of his origin. He advised La Valette and his commanders that, when the fleet was complete, the Ottomans would simultaneously assault Senglea from the land and from the sea. On his advice, La Valette constructed a lengthy stockade of stakes along the northern shore of Senglea, relying on the great chain across Dockyard Creek to protect the southern side, along with the pontoon bridge that would allow reinforcements to cross from Birgu. When the initial blows fell, at the end of the first week of July, it would be Maltese swimmers who gallantly defended the maritime palisade, on three separate occasions.

At last, on 15 July, Mustapha Pasha ordered the first major attack. The invasion fleet was led by boats containing imams proclaiming holy war, and they were followed by boatloads of Turks, Egyptians, Balkan levies, and new, enthusiastic arrivals from Algeria and the Barbary Coast. As the boats closed on Senglea, the assault went in on the landward walls and, despite the gallantry of the defence, Ottoman banners began to appear on the walls, until La Valette felt confident enough to send his reserves across the pontoon bridge from Birgu, and once again the fortunes of war tipped in the Christians' favour. Mustapha now committed his own reserve, ten boatloads of soldiers, who powered across the Grand Harbour, aiming to disembark near the tip of Senglea, while everyone's focus was on the southern shoreline. It was a gamble that may well have paid off, if La Valette had not sited the gun battery in the base of Fort St Angelo, just above the waterline. As the Turkish troops neared their objective, ball and shrapnel from the five guns, no more than 200 yards away, scythed through their boats and their ranks, hurling 800 of them into the water, where the survivors were finished off by the arquebuses and muskets on St Angelo. As Mustapha Pasha – the conqueror of St Elmo and hero of a hundred other battlefields, from the Balkans to Persia – gave the order to break off the action, the Maltese swimmers returned to the water to strip the Turkish dead of their jewels, rings and ornamented daggers and swords.

With options for another waterborne assault limited, Piali was now put in charge of operations against Birgu, while Mustapha Pasha continued to concentrate on taking Senglea, hoping that, by sealing off the knights from further reinforcement, and by stopping the two peninsulas from reinforcing each other, he might stretch La Valette's defences to breaking point. On 2 August, every Ottoman gun opened fire, while five major attacks went in on the Bastion of St Michael, to no effect. The sound of the artillery barrage could be heard in Sicily. At the end of a bitter, exhausting and violent day, the banner of St John still flew over the beleaguered battlements. Mustapha Pasha now ordered a five-day bombardment, in order to give the defenders no rest, and on 7 August he renewed his assault. Piali's troops made it over the main defences of Birgu and then found themselves confronted by a well-made, and well-defended, inner wall. Trapped between two defensive barriers, they were hacked down as they tried to retreat, and as the defenders now became the attackers. Things were, however, going better for the Turks at Senglea, and the elderly Mustapha Pasha moved forward to the walls at the head of his bodyguard. La Valette could only watch and pray, unable to extract any of his soldiers from the frenetic and bloody struggles around the walls of Birgu.

Every man in Senglea was now committed to the defence of St Michael's, and the knights were inexorably having to move back, step by step, as the pressure increased and their own numbers diminished. The fight for Malta was at its most critical moment when, suddenly, clear above the noise of battle, they heard the Turkish signal to retreat. It seemed a miracle, as soldiers who just minutes before had been locked in mortal combat now grounded their arms and dashed the sweat from their brows. La Valette, watching this unbelievable turn of events, and seeing the Turks stream north to the Marsa, could only imagine that Don García de Toledo's relief force had at last landed on Malta. This was exactly the news that a panicked messenger had brought to Mustapha Pasha, but it was false.

In Mdina, Chevalier Don Mesquita had surmised from the crescendo of artillery fire that the Turks were launching a full-blooded assault on both peninsulas. He had gambled that in order to mass as many troops as possible, the Turkish commanders would have left their logistic base in the Marsa only lightly defended. He was right, and he had launched Marshal Copier's cavalry force, which had swept through the Turkish lines causing havoc, seizing or hamstringing horses, destroying stores, and massacring the sick and the wounded, of whom there were many. They were long gone by the time Mustapha Pasha had realized his error and was tearing his beard, vowing death and destruction on the Knights of St John, and pledging to bring Jean Parisot de la Valette in chains before the Sultan. The best chance to take Malta had been squandered and lost.

As La Valette and his battle captains had been giving thanks to the Almighty for their salvation, a further letter had arrived from Don García. Always cautious, as befitted a subordinate of King Philip II, and always conscious that an ill-planned or ill-executed relief would leave Sicily open to the Ottomans, Don García had procrastinated for weeks, as he built up a credible force and awaited news from Malta. Under huge pressure from his own commanders, and particularly from those members of the order who had not made it to Malta before the Turkish landings in May, he now told La Valette that a force of 16,000 would come to the relief of Malta before the end of August. However, La Valette was understandably sceptical of this new promise, and he made it clear to his Grand Council that they should only rely on themselves for their salvation. It was a grim but necessary message, which he leavened by publicizing Pope Pius IV's 'Bull' that granted plenary indulgence to any who fell in war with the Muslims. It was the same plenary indulgence offered to the knights, soldiers and pilgrims of the original crusades and, among people of strong faith, it had the same impact. In the meantime, the defenders of Malta had reason to be grateful for La Valette's personal leadership and inspiration, and for his earlier, comprehensive arrangements for the defence of the island. Battered they may be, but there was still food, water, arms and ammunition for the defenders, and they were united in their determination to fight to the end.

The Turks had now resorted to mining, a siege specialization of theirs, and, although the soil of Malta was shallow, they could still make slow but steady progress through the sandstone. By 18 August, Mustapha Pasha was told that a credible mine had been developed underneath the Spanish-held Bastion of Castile. He intended to use this mine in conjunction with an old-fashioned siege tower, of the type employed against Jerusalem in 1099. He would open the attack with another assault on St Michael's Bastion, in the hope that La Valette would send troops from Birgu to reinforce Senglea. At that stage, he would set off the mine underneath the Bastion of Castile, and Piali's dervishes and Janissaries would surge over the walls to overwhelm the defenders.

La Valette did not fall for this strategy, and he did not commit his reserves to the defence of Senglea. Mustapha Pasha ordered his engineers to spring the mine anyway. While not unexpected, the mine still had a devastating effect, as a great section of the wall collapsed into the ditch, and as the Turks appeared through the dust and debouched into the town. The cries went up: 'All is lost; retreat to St Angelo!' La Valette, unarmoured, seized his sword and a light helmet, and charged towards the breach. The Maltese went forward with him, and then the knights clustered around him as he led the counter-attack. Wounded in the leg by grenade fragments, La Valette fell and rose again. Urged to retire, he limped forward and climbed up the rubble slope to the top of the battlements. The defenders surged after him, and within minutes the walls were cleared, and the ruins of the Bastion of Castile reoccupied. Only then did La Valette allow his wound to be dressed. There was to be no rest. The assault went on through the night, with explosions and Greek fire lighting up the sky, the combatants, and the wreckage of the fortifications. La Valette could be seen silhouetted in the breach, urging the defenders to ever-greater effort and sacrifice and, in the morning, the defences were still in Christian hands. Don García's nephew had already been killed in the fighting, and now La Valette's own nephew, conspicuous in his splendid armour, was struck down as he led an assault on the siege tower. Consoled by friends, La Valette said, 'These two young men have only gone before us by but a few days. For, if the relief from Sicily does not come, and we cannot save Malta, we must all die. To the very last man, we must bury ourselves beneath these ruins.' It was a rare note of hopelessness from this most courageous and inspiring of commanders.

Amid the destruction around the ramparts of Birgu, La Valette now urged Maltese workmen to open a gap in the base of the defensive walls, opposite the Turkish siege tower. As the Turks were approaching the walls and firing down on the defenders, a dark hole appeared in the defences at the foot of their tower. A cannon, loaded with chain-shot, often used in naval combat to bring down masts, was thrust through the opening and fired. As the tower collapsed and crashed to the ground, the cannon was withdrawn, and the gap hastily refilled. Meanwhile, at Senglea, a vast explosive device, devised by Mustapha Pasha's engineers, was manoeuvred through the rubble, and hurled among the knights and soldiers. The fusing on the bomb was too slow and, with remarkable courage, the defenders seized it and managed to roll it back over the wall, where it exploded among the attackers. A day that had started so dismally for the defence had ended in something resembling a victory.

Both sides were now confronting the prospect of defeat. The conditions within Birgu and Senglea were horrific. Almost every survivor, military and civilian, was wounded, the hospitals were full, the dead lay unburied, while women and children worked tirelessly to reinforce the walls and defences, and to keep the fighting men supplied. Meanwhile, despite their better camp discipline, dysentery had broken out among the Turks and, with hundreds of rotting corpses littering the battlefield, there was a danger of an outbreak of plague. While La Valette and his commanders and knights remained of a single mind and purpose, the tensions between Mustapha Pasha and Piali Pasha had broken out again, as they faced the prospect of failing to subdue Malta before the weather made conditions hazardous for the fleet. Casualties had been high, and they had even begun to run out of ammunition and gunpowder, so great had their artillery expenditure been. How would failure be viewed in Constantinople? Meanwhile, the pressure on Don García to launch his relief force was overwhelming, as the story of the knights' heroic defence reached as far as Protestant England. Even Queen Elizabeth I, no supporter of the arrogant papal military order, and locked in confrontation with the Catholic powers herself, commented, 'If the Turks should prevail against the Isle of Malta, it is uncertain what further peril might follow to the rest of Christendom.'

At the Grand Council meeting on 23 August, the mood was one of grim, fatalistic determination. They had just seen off a further Turkish attack, there might yet be a relief force, and the advance of the seasons might yet force the Turks to withdraw or to suspend operations. The best course of action might be to abandon Birgu and withdraw into the fortress of St Angelo. La Valette stood alone against this consensus: Birgu and Senglea must prevail together or Senglea would inevitably fall; the water supply in St Angelo was not adequate; divided defence also kept the attackers and their artillery divided; the loyal Maltese must not be abandoned. Unchallenged in his leadership, and unyielding in his determination, La Valette's opinion prevailed. Not only would the knights not retreat into St Angelo, but La Valette ordered the destruction of the bridge linking Birgu to the fort. Even the order's most sacred relics were to stay in Birgu.

Mustapha Pasha, who was contemplating keeping his army in Malta over the winter, even if Piali withdrew his fleet, at last decided to try to take Mdina in the centre of the island. The enterprise was a farce. Don Mesquita had only a small garrison, but he equipped every man, woman and child with some item of armour and a weapon. Mdina stood on a steep rocky outcrop, and as the already demoralized Turks advanced uphill in the sun, the defenders opened fire with cannon and muskets. To the Turkish soldiers and commanders, Mdina's walls looked packed with alert, well-armed soldiers, while their artillery fire convinced them that the garrison had ammunition to spare. Mustapha Pasha called off the attack, and his army returned to invest the two peninsulas again.

On 25 August, unbeknownst to La Valette, Don García de Toledo had at last set sail from Sicily, with 10,000 troops in 28 ships and galleys. The Spanish formed the bulk of the force, but there were individuals and small contingents from all over Europe. Don Juan of Austria had tried to join the expedition, and only a direct order from his half-brother, King Philip II, had thwarted his ambition. The Regiment of Naples was commanded by Álvaro de Sande, the Spanish commander who had been taken prisoner at Djerba and ransomed from Sultan Suleiman. Despite poor sailing conditions, Don García's fleet eventually reached the island of Linosa on 4 September, where he received La Valette's latest communiqué, advising him to land in the bay of Mellieha in the north of the island. Don García hesitated again, and any vigorous action by Piali's galleys could easily have destroyed or dispersed the fleet, or have persuaded Don García to give up his disembarkation plans. Inexplicably, no Ottoman attempt was made to intercept the fleet, and on the morning of 7 September the long-expected, long-delayed relief force began to stream ashore at Mellieha, anxious to be assured that the defenders of Malta still held out.

The news of the landing reached Mustapha Pasha and La Valette at about the same time. Although the relief force was significantly smaller than expected, the Ottoman army was no longer the powerful organization that it had been three months earlier. Reduced by death and disease, and dismayed by the tenacity of the knights, the soldiers and the Maltese, it had been demoralized by repeated failures to breach the defences. Disheartened by the whole conduct of the siege, and aware that some of his troops were already on the verge of mutiny, Mustapha Pasha ordered the immediate evacuation of Malta.

All through the night of 7 September, the Turks moved their wounded, supplies and artillery to the ships waiting in Marsamuscetto. Meanwhile, the relief force had advanced swiftly to Mdina and to the high ground around Naxar. When dawn broke on 8 September, the defenders of Birgu were confronted with rows of empty trenches, and a scorched and cratered landscape, filled with the detritus of war. Across the Grand Harbour, they could no longer see the Sultan's banner flying over the shell of St Elmo. La Valette ordered the gates to be opened, and, for the first time in months, the soldiers and civilians streamed out into the Maltese countryside. Knights quickly reoccupied St Elmo, re-hoisted the white cross of St John, and deployed cannon to harass the departing Turkish fleet.

As Mustapha realized the modest strength of the relief force, he regained his confidence and bravado and demanded that his troops disembark again, while Piali's fleet sailed and rowed up to St Paul's Bay. It was another blunder. The relief force, especially the newly arrived Knights of the Order and the Mdina garrison troops, were in no mood for caution, while the Turks had little fighting spirit left, and little appetite for combat. At the sight of the Christians charging down the slope of Naxar at them, many broke and fled for the beaches. Mustapha Pasha had two horses shot from under him, but he stood his ground, rallied his troops and tried to stem the rout. It was to no avail. Relentlessly, the Ottomans were driven into the sea. While small boats attempted to rescue as many as possible, taking them out to the war galleys that hovered just off the coast, those who could not get on board were massacred in the shallows. By the evening of 8 September, the knights had regained full possession of their island, and a north-westerly breeze was blowing the Ottoman fleet towards Greece, and towards the judgement of the Sultan in Constantinople.

Suleiman was merciful. Advised of the defeat, he had overcome his gout to stamp on the letter that carried the news and vowed that he would lead an expedition against Malta, himself, the following year. He never did so and, instead, died of apoplexy at the siege of Szigetvar in the Balkans, furious at yet another epic resistance by a Christian garrison.[14] Piali Pasha and Mustapha Pasha both regained imperial favour under the new Sultan, Selim II.[15] Piali captured the island of Chios in 1566, thereby ending the Genoese presence in the eastern Mediterranean, and he and Mustapha Pasha would brutally complete the conquest of Cyprus in the war with Venice in 1571. Piali and Ulich Ali would go on to be the architects of the renaissance of the Ottoman fleet in the wake of the maritime disaster of Lepanto in the same year.

Malta was in ruins, but the victory had been as decisive as it had been costly. La Valette had lost nearly half of his knights, and almost all the survivors were wounded, maimed or crippled. Of the Spanish, the foreign soldiers and the Maltese defenders, nearly 7,000 were dead. Of an original garrison of around 9,000, La Valette had only 600 left who were capable of bearing arms. The total Ottoman losses, allowing for the Algerians and Barbary corsairs who joined the initial invasion force, have been estimated at around 30,000. Probably only 10,000 of the great fleet and army that departed Constantinople in May 1565 made it home. The news of the victory was carried, at lightning speed, all over Europe, and even in Protestant lands services of thanksgiving were held. The age of chivalry may have been drawing to a close, but the heroism of the Knights of St John in defence of the island of Malta inspired universal admiration.

Don García was taken to see where his nephew had been killed. He was a gallant soldier, conscious of the consequences of failure or miscalculation, but, although raised to be Duke of Fernandina, and subsequently Prince of Montalban, he was pursued to his death in 1577 by accusations of cowardice and pusillanimity. Before his death, however, he would prove to be an excellent correspondent and mentor for Don Juan of Austria in the lead up to the battle of Lepanto. La Valette became the hero of the age. There was no more talk of moving the order's headquarters. Birgu and Senglea were renamed 'the Victorious City' and 'the Unconquered', and a new, fortified city, Valetta – named for the illustrious commander and funded by a cornucopia of donations from across the Christian world – began to be built on the slopes of Mount Sciberras. It was known as *Superbissima*, 'Most Proud', and construction was guarded by 15,000 Spanish soldiers of King Philip II, stationed on the island in the event of another Ottoman invasion. Unlike Grand Master d'Aubusson before him, La Valette turned down the Pope's offer of a cardinal's hat and concentrated on the construction of 'his' city. In July 1568, after a day's hawking in the sun, he succumbed to a stroke, and he died in the Magistral Palace in Birgu on 21 August, on which fell that year the Feast of Corpus Christi, the great feast day of the order. He was eventually laid to rest in the crypt of the impressive Co-Cathedral of St John in Valetta, alongside his great friend, Englishman and fellow knight, Oliver Starkey. His tomb is inscribed with the words: 'Here lies La Valette, worthy of eternal honour. He who was once the scourge of Africa and Asia, and the shield of Europe, whence he expelled the barbarians by his holy arms, is the first to be buried in this beloved city, whose founder he was.'

The Ottomans never again tried to break into the western Mediterranean, while the absolute strategic importance of Malta was to be demonstrated yet again, nearly four centuries later, during World War II. For the heroism of the Maltese people, in that second 'great siege', King George VI awarded the whole island the George Cross, the highest British award for civilian valour. As for the Knights of St John, the siege of Malta was the apogee of their existence as an order, although they had an important 'cameo role' in the 1571 battle of Lepanto. In the succeeding centuries both their medical and their military *raison d'être* declined and atrophied, while their income slowly dwindled, as nationalism, Protestantism and secularism eroded regard for this papal military order, and the behaviour and morals of the knights themselves diminished European regard for them. In 1789, the French Revolutionary Government seized the assets and property of the order in France, and in June 1798, Napoleon, on his way to Egypt, invaded Malta and negotiated a surrender with the Grand Master. The fighting was not even the palest of a shadow of the heroic actions of 1565.[16] In 1814, as part of the Treaty of Paris, Malta officially became a colony in the British Empire. It became independent in 1964, but Malta and the Maltese would forever be associated with the great siege of 1565.

8

'There Was a Man Called John'

Lepanto 1571

To the steady, rhythmic beat of the drums, the two great fleets slowly advanced towards each other, every galley and ship skilfully using their oars and sails in order to manoeuvre into their agreed battle formations. On the Christian side, the great, heavily armed, but slow Venetian galleasses[1] were having to be towed by other galleys, in order to get them into their positions ahead of the main body of the fleet of the Holy League. The coast of Greece was on their port side, with the prominent headland of Skoupas, and the fleet had passed in column through and around the Curzolari islands of Koutsilaris and Oxia. They had, then, majestically, pivoted on their left flank, in order to swing into battle formation as they entered the Gulf of Patras. At the front and centre of this mass of over 300 vessels, slowly fanning out into three distinct, large fighting formations, and a reserve, was the flagship of the fleet, the imposing *Real*,[2] carrying the overall commander of this huge Catholic maritime force, Don Juan of Austria.[3] Coming up along his port side was the flagship of the large Venetian naval contingent, painted all red, including the oars, and only flying, as yet, the blue banner that marked all the ships of the central division.[4] Standing proud on his afterdeck was the Venetian admiral, Sebastiano Veniero, 75, irascible and quick to anger. Not five days earlier, the whole fleet had been on the verge of destroying itself as a result of his explosive temper and actions. On Don Juan's starboard side, the straining oarsmen of the galley *Capitana Pontificia* brought the flagship of the small, but effective, papal squadron alongside. As it drew level, Pope Pius V's naval commander, Marcantonio Colonna, grinned broadly at Don Juan.

The day before, in thick fog, the 300-ship fleet of the Holy League had anchored off the island of Petalas. As it moved cautiously out of the harbour and bay, just before daybreak on the morning of 7 October 1571, Don Juan had sent light galleys ahead, in order to disembark scouts who could get up on the high ground of the Greek mainland and look down into the Gulf of Patras and the Bay of Lepanto. As it was a Sunday, the Lord's Day, the whole fleet had heard mass and taken communion, even as they moved out into open sea. The fast vessels had returned not long after first light, breathless with the news that the whole Ottoman fleet appeared to be in and around Lepanto, and that it was clearly preparing to weigh anchor and move out into the Aegean. They had counted 200 warships but claimed to have seen many other smaller ships grouped around them. It was what the commanders of the Holy League had both feared, and hoped, for their news confirmed that Ulich Ali's Algerine corsair force, of around 100 fast galleys, was not poised out of sight and preparing to swoop on their flank. This report confirmed that Ulich Ali was grouped with the regular Ottoman fleets of Ali Pasha – Sultan Selim III's *Kapudan Pasha*, High Admiral – and that of Mehmet Pasha, Bey of Alexandria, known as 'Sirocco' after the ferocious hot wind that blew up from Africa. Experienced sailors that they were, the scouts estimated that it would be around three hours before the fleets clashed, if they both kept advancing at their current rate. With galleys still deploying in a forest of masts and oars, Don Juan ordered his crew to 'back oars' and halted his flagship. As fresh reports of the Ottoman deployment reached him, he ordered a green banner to be unfurled on the mainmast of his ship, and a single shot to be fired. It was the signal to be ready for battle, and a nervous, anticipatory, collective shudder rippled across the fleet.

Don Juan summoned a rapid conference on the *Real* to confirm the best course of action. He first addressed Sir Mathurin d'Aux Romegas, the most renowned naval commander of the Knights of Malta, whom Pope Pius V had recruited as an expert adviser for the inexperienced Admiral Colonna. Despite his affliction of nerves, Romegas remained as redoubtable a warrior and commander as he had been during the siege of Malta, six years earlier. Now, when asked by Don Juan what he thought, he was forthright. 'What do I think? That if the Emperor, your father, had seen such an armada as ours, he would not have stopped until he became emperor of Constantinople, and done so with ease.' Slightly disingenuously, Don Juan asked, 'You mean we must fight, Monsieur Romegas?' 'Yes, Sir,' replied the knight. 'Then, let's fight.' He asked Colonna himself, who answered laconically in Latin, paraphrasing the Gospel: 'Even if I should die, I will not deny you.' Venetian opinion hardly needed to be canvassed, given the Ottoman invasion of Cyprus the previous year, and the shocking news they had learnt about the fall of Famagusta, and the fate of its garrison and its commander. Only Don Juan's own Spanish advisers tried to remind him of King Philip II's instructions regarding preserving the safety and integrity of the fleet, and the dangers of betting all on one throw of the dice, but Don Juan cut them short: 'Gentlemen, this is not the time for discussion, but for fighting.'

In the meantime, with a skill and competence born of long practice, the galleys were being prepared for war. The decks and bridges were cleared, and some of the rowers' benches were covered over with planking to allow the soldiers more room to move and to wield their weapons, whether arquebus, pike or sword. Sand was scattered to soak up blood, and to give the soldiers' feet greater grip in the fighting. Offensive and defensive weapons were stacked in prescribed areas of each vessel, as men checked their arms and helped each other to don their armour. Light breastplates and short swords were given to the volunteer oarsmen of the Venetian vessels, as they were expected to fight alongside the regular soldiers when the opposing galleys were alongside each other. Christian convicts were also released and armed, as Don Juan had promised a general amnesty if his fleet was victorious, but the Muslim galley slaves remained manacled to their benches and oars. While the two sides were evenly matched in vessel numbers, although both commanders had underestimated the size of the opposing fleet, the Holy League had an almost two-to-one advantage in cannon. These were now being loaded with a mix of round, chain and canister shot, while fire-pots and fire 'trumpets' were also being prepared.

The conference over, Gian'Andrea Doria, commander of the right wing and admiral of the Genoese contingent of the King of Spain's navy, informed Don Juan he would be moving towards the open sea, in order to give the Catholic fleet more room to deploy. The prince asked him to ensure that his left-hand galleys did not lose contact with the right-hand galleys of the centre division, those of the Knights of Malta, thereby leaving a gap in the line which the Ottomans might exploit. Don Juan, still unarmoured, then went across to Veniero's flagship where, conscious of the enormity of their shared endeavour and the scale of what was at stake, he embraced the older man, putting aside any previous animosity. He then returned to his frigate in order to visit several other galleys as they manoeuvred into their allocated positions, clasping hands and exchanging words with mariners and soldiers, while distributing medals, coins, rosaries and souvenirs of every kind. When he had nothing left to give, he handed one man his hat, and to two others his gloves, who promptly pinned them to their own hats. Accompanied by his chaplain and his aides, his presence raised morale wherever he went, and he was loudly cheered as he proceeded down the line of battle. At one stage he passed Admiral Colonna and hailed his stocky colleague, cheerfully punning, 'a warm welcome to the stoutest column of the Church'.

When Don Juan returned to the *Real*, the complex and complicated deployment was almost completed. The left wing, of 63 galleys, 59 in the front line and four in immediate reserve, was under command of the Venetian *provveditore*, or 'overseer', Agostino Barbarigo, a skilled seaman whose calm personality had been deliberately chosen by the Venetian doge to help mitigate the character deficiencies of Veniero. He was liked and trusted by Don Juan, and he put his own ship close to the Greek shore, at the far left of the left wing, in order to stop the Ottomans turning that flank of the League's fleet. The right wing of this contingent was anchored by the galley of the commander of the Venetian Cretan fleet, Marco Querini, and a Neapolitan fleet of ten galleys, sent by the Marquis of Santa Cruz and commanded by the Spaniard Pedro de Padilla, hovered behind, coving the gap between left and centre.

The centre division, under Don Juan's direct command, consisted of 62 galleys, with a further two galleys positioned directly behind the *Real*, commanded by his Spanish adviser Luis de Requesens, and with orders to offer immediate assistance to the commander, if he and his ship appeared to be threatened. Inevitably, in addition to the Venetian and papal flagships, the centre division also contained the flagships of several of the smaller contingents, including those of the Knights of

Malta and of the Duke of Savoy. Gian'Andrea Doria, commanding the King of Spain's Genoese contingent, held the right flank with a mixed division of 53 galleys, including a large Venetian contingent. Like Agostino Barbarigo on the left flank, he had stationed himself on the very far right of his division, well out into the Aegean Sea, and prepared to counter any attempt by the Ottoman division of Ulich Ali to outflank the Christian forces from the open sea. Under advice from Don García de Toledo, almost all the Holy League galleys had removed the traditional ramming spike from their prows, in order to be able to mount additional centre-line cannon, and to be able to fire at lower elevations than was possible with the rams fitted. In front of each of the three divisions, confusing for the commanders of the advancing Ottoman fleet, were two of the enormous Venetian galleasses, designed and equipped like maritime fortresses, with thickened hulls and a mighty array of guns, facing forward, aft and arrayed along their flanks. Manoeuvred primarily by sail, they presaged the transition from the armed galley, dominant in the Mediterranean for nearly 3,000 years, to the 17th-, 18th- and 19th-century multi-sail and multi-gun 'men-of-war' that would dominate maritime warfare until the advent of steam. Lastly, the Marquis of Santa Cruz held a further fleet reserve of 30 galleys, which were to be committed to reinforce whichever section of the line was most threatened. He also had under command another 40-odd smaller vessels, filled with soldiers whose role was to attack the enemy's 'light craft', doing as much damage as possible, or to provide reinforcements for the larger galleys.

For their part, the Ottoman fleets had been lurking in the shadow of the fortress of Lepanto since 27 September, retreating there after a report of Holy League presence in the Adriatic had forced them to abandon their operations against the strongly defended Venetian port of Kotor. Ali Pasha and his fellow admiral, Mehmet Pasha, had come there after bringing the siege of Famagusta to its bloody conclusion in early August 1571. In doing so they had completed the conquest of Christian Cyprus – an island held by the Venetians since 1489, by crusader kings for 300 years previously, and by Byzantine emperors for 900 years before that. Despite a long-standing truce between Venice and the Ottoman Empire, Sultan Selim II, who had succeeded his father, Suleiman, in 1566, had determined to complete the subjugation of the eastern Mediterranean early in his reign. Rhodes may have fallen to the Ottomans in 1522, but the Venetians had continued to hold great fortresses in Cyprus and Crete, and along the Greek shoreline of the Adriatic Sea. Scarred by his father's defeat at Malta, Selim had concluded a peace treaty with the Hungarians in 1568, bringing a prolonged period of war with the Habsburgs to an end, and freeing him to look south. In mid-1570, a great invasion force had landed at Larnaca, in southern Cyprus. Although they took the capital, Nicosia, fairly quickly, killing or enslaving the 20,000 defenders and civilians, the fortress port of Famagusta had held out gallantly and bravely for a further 11 months, waiting in vain, like the defenders of Constantinople and Rhodes before them, for a relief operation that would never come. In August 1571, the siege had concluded in a surrender by the garrison on terms similar to those offered at Rhodes half a century earlier. However, in the handover of the city, and the planned execution, something had gone horribly wrong, resulting in the massacre of most of the defenders and the population. The fate of the Venetian commander, Marcantonio Bragadin, was particularly barbaric and gruesome. Whether planned, or in a fit of spontaneous rage, Lala Mustapha Pasha, the Turkish army commander, had cut off Bragadin's ears and nose. Torturing him for several days, he then had him flayed alive, parading his skin around the island before sending it, and Bragadin's head, back to Constantinople. This was the shocking news that had reached Don Juan and his commanders, including the Venetians, just four days earlier.

Although Ali Pasha knew about the sailing of the fleet of the Holy League from Messina in Sicily, he had been uncertain in what direction it would go, particularly now that Cyprus had been taken. As a result, victuals, munitions and reinforcements had been sent to several locations that might be vulnerable to a Christian attack, and the *Kapudan Pasha* himself was therefore short of supplies and men. Believing, after Cyprus, that the campaigning season was over, many mariners and soldiers had been released to go home, and the Ottoman ships themselves needed repair and overhaul, having been at sea for the last six months. Now, the news of the enemy fleet's approach resulted in the rapid conscription of men from the local fortresses and towns. Ali Pasha had also received a series of conflicting and ambiguous directives from Sultan Selim.

An inexperienced maritime commander, he had been exhorted to display, 'all his courage and intelligence', then to 'winter' at Kotor, which he had not taken, or 'another port'. In the same letter he was ordered to attack the Christian armada 'after getting reliable news about the enemy' and after consulting the other commanders of his three fleets, 'all in perfect agreement and unity, in accordance with what is found most suitable'. In this there were shades of Raglan's direction to the Light Brigade in the Crimean War.

Ali Pasha held his own council on 6 October, in the castle of Lepanto. Present were: Mehmet Pasha Sirocco, the Algerine corsair; Ulich Ali Pasha; Hassan Pasha, Bey of Algiers, and the corpulent son of the great Barbary corsair, Barbarossa;⁵ the noted naval commander, Kara Hodja; Second Vizier, Petrev Pasha; and many others. Kara Hodja reported a Christian force of around 150 galleys, short of water, undermanned, and riven with the divisions that often marked Christian coalitions. Petrev Pasha, although not a maritime expert, was less confident. He believed the Christian force to be nearer 200 galleys, and he worried about the presence of the Venetian galleasses. The Ottoman fleet might have been larger (it wasn't), but it too had deficiencies. Moreover, the Christians were more heavily armed, and armoured, and had gained experience fighting at sea since their disaster at Preveza in 1538. He also worried about the many enslaved Christian oarsmen in the Ottoman fleet, who could cause trouble if they managed to free themselves in the course of a major maritime battle.

On balance, the bulk of the Council erred on the side of caution. However, Ali Pasha demurred. The Christian fleet was smaller and was clearly rent with dissension; Gian'Andrea Doria was reported to be away with his ships on another mission; the galleasses were overrated; the Ottoman mariners and soldiers might be green, but they had always been victorious, even without armour; bows were better than arquebuses, because they had a higher rate of fire; the Christian slaves would be locked below deck once the fighting started. Ali Pasha was adamant that they must engage the fleet of the Holy League: 'For what shall the world say if we, used to provoking the others to battle, now challenged by such despicable enemies should refuse to fight?' Besides, were the Ottomans victorious in this maritime clash, all Italy would be theirs to invade. The Council moved in his favour, 'either because they were convinced', as it was reported, 'or in order not to be accused of cowardice'. Late that evening the Ottoman fleet inched out of the Bay of Lepanto.

As darkness began to fade on the morning of 7 October, the Ottomans, too, deployed into a three-division formation, and a reserve. Despite his bravado the previous evening, Ali Pasha was beginning to have doubts. A huge flock of crows, flying over and around Lepanto, had been taken as a bad omen by many of the sailors; Gian'Andrea Doria's galleys were now revealed to be present with the main body of the Holy League fleet. As he realized that Doria's move to the right was an integral part of Don Juan's battle plan and was not an attempt by some of the Christian ships to flee west, Ali Pasha began to grasp the relative sizes of the two fleets. In addition, he could still not fathom the role of the Venetian galleasses, while he knew that many of his commanders were, at heart, unconvinced by his decision to initiate this fight. Nevertheless, the Ottoman fleet was now slowly advancing to the mouth of the Gulf of Patras.

Ulich Ali's Algerian contingent, 67 galleys strong, was on the left, opposite Doria, while Mehmet Pasha Sirocco, with 55 galleys, had the right wing and was deploying close to the Greek shore, and confronting Don Juan's left flank, under Barbarigo. Although they had no option, some of the more experienced captains were certainly worried that, in the heat of battle, the closeness of the shore might tempt some crews to desert their ships. Ali Pasha commanded the centre, from his great flagship *Sultana*,[6] with 91 vessels, and a small reserve was to the rear, under Murad Dragut.[7] There were also several smaller ships, packed with soldiers, which, like their counterparts in the Holy League, were to contribute additional fighting men to the larger galleys whenever necessary or possible. The Ottoman fleet was deployed in a crescent shape, with the wings thrust forward in the hope of being able to turn either, or both, Christian flanks. If this happened, then Don Juan would be forced to commit his fleet reserve left or right, while the Ottoman centre crashed through the opposing force. This very noticeable crescent formation was noted by the Holy League captains, as military commanders, and commented upon by them, as Christians. Ali Pasha called his two young sons to him and reminded them of who they were, and of their duty, before they were placed on another galley. Having listened to their father with humility, they took their leave, with the promise to bring back the papal flagship, and the simple words, 'blessed be the bread and salt you have given us'.

On his flagship, Don Juan was helped into his mirror-polished armour. He left his helm off for the present. He then heard mass, and priests from the newly formed orders of the Jesuits[8] and Capuchins[9] heard confessions from sailors and soldiers across the fleet, while the Muslims performed their own ritual ablutions. This was a papally endorsed crusade, so Pius V's bull of general indulgence and absolution for all those who died in fighting the infidel was read out on each of the League's ships. Every Christian, from prince to galley oarsman dropped to their knees. This was a crusade, and they were fighting for the glory of Christ the Lord, and for the salvation of Europe. The Muslims did not need such reassurance; under *jihad*, dying in battle for their faith guaranteed their entry into heaven.

It was around eleven in the morning and although, thanks to their oars, the two fleets were closing with each other, the League were hampered by a light headwind. Both flagships opened fire with single shots, to gauge range. Trumpets sounded, and the great banner of the League was hoisted on the *Real*'s mainmast. At that, alongside the coloured flags denoting their divisions, the fleet exploded with the colours of Spain, Venice, Genoa, Naples, Florence, Milan, the papacy and the Knights of Malta. The Ottoman fleet, previously drifting forward at a leisurely pace, under sail, now found the wind had turned against them, and they had to transition to oars. From the mast of *Sultana* flew the Ottoman battle standard, presented to Ali Pasha by Sultan Selim himself, on which the name of Allah was embroidered 29,800 times. With multi-coloured robes, turbans and banners, sun glinting everywhere off polished armour and weapons, and accompanied by the sound of massed drums, the Ottoman fleet was an impressive and daunting sight.

The Christians took the change of weather as a sign of divine favour. Apparently calm and relaxed, Don Juan watched the fleets close from the poop deck of *Real*. He had earlier listened to musicians on Admiral Veniero's flagship, and now he summoned his own. He descended to the main deck and there, in a supreme example of what the Italians call *sprezzatura*, 'studied nonchalance', he danced the *galliard*, in full armour, with two other Spanish gentlemen. A total of 500 ships, and 170,000 men were now poised on the brink of the largest sea battle in over a millennium.

Don Juan's journey to be commander of the fleet of the Holy League, at 24 years of age, had been an extraordinary one. He had been born in Regensburg in 1547, the issue of an affair between his father, the Holy Roman Emperor, Charles V of the House of Habsburg, and Barbara Blomberg, the daughter of a burgher of the city. Kept unaware of his parentage, he was handed into the care of Luis de Quijada in Valladolid in Spain, at the age of seven. In that same year, 1554, Emperor Charles V wrote a codicil to his will, in which he recognized Juan, also known as Geronimo, as his 'natural' son. Although Charles had inherited his vast empire largely through peaceful, dynastic good fortune, he had then spent much of his long life and reign waging war, and exhausting his royal revenues, including those that had poured in from the New World territories. He would leave huge debts to his successors as a result of his attempts to defend the integrity of the Holy Roman Empire from both the Protestant Reformation and the expansion of the Ottoman Empire, and as a result of having to wage a series of debilitating wars against his fellow Catholic, the King of France. In 1556, Charles had laid down the overwhelming burden of his mighty imperial project. He had divided his hereditary and imperial domains between the Habsburgs of Spain, headed by his son Philip, who now became King Philip II of Spain, and the Habsburgs of Austria, headed by his brother, Archduke Ferdinand, who now also became Emperor. Charles himself retired to the Monastery of Juste in Spain where, before he died in 1558, the year the Protestant Queen Elizabeth ascended the throne of England, he officially acknowledged Juan as his son.

King Philip II, now 32 years old, and aware of his father's updated will, returned to Spain from the Netherlands in mid-1559, and he summoned Luis de Quijada to bring Juan to a hunt near the Monastery of Santa Maria de La Santa Espina. When the King appeared, de Quijada told Juan to dismount as a sign of respect. Juan, still oblivious to the significance of this meeting, did so and the King asked him if he knew the identity of his father. Juan declared that he did not. Only at this point did King Philip embrace the 12-year-old boy and explain that they shared a father and were thus brothers. Juan was now to be known as Don Juan of Austria, but he was to be addressed as 'Your Excellency', not as 'Your Highness', and although he received a generous stipend from the Royal House, he did not live in the palace, and in public ceremonies, of which there were many, Juan stood, walked or rode ahead of the grandees, but always behind the royal family.

Juan grew up alongside his cousins, the deeply troubled Don Carlos, King Philip's son and heir, and Alessandro Farnese, the son of Charles's other acknowledged illegitimate child, Margaret of Austria. Farnese became a great friend of Don Juan. He would go on to be the Duke of Parma, and King Philip's most able commander in the wars in the Netherlands. It was his army with which the Spanish Armada was supposed to rendezvous in 1588. At Lepanto, Farnese would command the three galleys provided by the Duchy of Parma. In 1565, when the Ottomans had attacked the Knights of St John in their island fortress of Malta, Don Juan had disregarded Philip's instructions to remain in Madrid and made his way to Barcelona in order to try to join the Spanish relief fleet of Don García de Toledo, which was to help lift the siege of Malta in September of that year. Only a direct letter from the King, reaching him on the dockside and ordering him to return 'under pain of his displeasure', had caused him to abandon his attempt. This disobedience was forgiven by King Philip when, in 1567, Don Juan revealed to the King that his increasingly deranged son, Don Carlos, was planning treason. Arrested, Don Carlos was incarcerated; he died the following year, pursued by rumours that he had been poisoned by his father.

Don Juan now got his wish to go to sea, and in 1568 he had been appointed commander of the Mediterranean fleet, although also provided with a highly experienced maritime subordinate, Luis de

Requesens, and Álvaro de Bazan, the Marquis of Santa Cruz. Both of them would be with Don Juan at Lepanto. His mission was not simply to challenge the Barbary corsairs who tormented the coasts of Spain, Italy and the Balearics, from their pirate bases in Tunis, Tripoli and Algiers. It was also to stop Muslim support for the Morisco rebellion that had broken out in southern Spain when these Catholics converts, of Moorish descent, had been forced, by decree, to abandon their customs, language, clothing and religious practices.[10] It had been a most brutal and bloody campaign of unrestricted warfare. It was driven by deeply felt ethnic and religious antipathy, but also by a genuine Spanish fear that the next great Ottoman campaign by the new Sultan Selim might be an all-out assault on the Iberian Peninsula, notwithstanding the Christian victory at Malta three years earlier.

It was the Ottoman–Venetian War, which had opened with the Turkish invasion of Cyprus in June 1570, that had catalysed the formation of the Holy League under Pope Pius V,[11] an ascetic cleric known as the 'hound of God'. The Holy League was formed with the intention of relieving Cyprus, which it failed to do, and trying to break Ottoman control of the eastern Mediterranean, in which it was to be more successful. The Holy League included the major Catholic powers of southern Europe, but a condition of the Spanish Empire's participation was that Don Juan of Austria be designated supreme commander. Although it was riven from the outset by political and personal frictions, and by conflicting objectives, the Holy League was formally stood up on 25 May 1571, as, unbeknownst to the participants, the siege of Famagusta was approaching its sanguinary conclusion. The Protestant states had no intention of joining, and nor were they welcome. Indeed, in 1570 Pope Pius V had excommunicated Queen Elizabeth I, and had declared her to be a heretic, along with many of her Protestant Dutch allies. The Holy League did keep membership open for the Holy Roman Empire, France and Portugal, but none of them joined. The Emperor had only just concluded a ten-year truce with Sultan Selim, in order to take the pressure off his Hungarian frontier, and many of his own imperial states and subjects were Protestant, while the French had had an active anti-Habsburg alliance with the Ottomans since the 1520s, and they too faced internal problems from the Protestant Huguenots. Portugal had no forces to spare, owing to its own debilitating campaigns against the Muslims in Morocco, and its exhausting maritime confrontations with the Ottoman fleets in the Red Sea and the Indian Ocean.

Don Juan had departed from Madrid in late July 1571, after a final audience with King Philip, who remained ambivalent about committing the Spanish fleet, including those contingents from his territories in Sicily and Naples, to a maritime campaign in the eastern Mediterranean. He still, and rightly, had concerns about the ever-present threats from North Africa. Don Juan's Spanish maritime advisers were therefore there to remind him not to hazard the King's ships.

At Barcelona, Don Juan had received a letter full of useful advice from Don García de Toledo, as to how to conduct himself and how best to exercise command in a coalition fleet, where so many of his subordinates would be older, and often far more experienced than he was. Among Don García's practical suggestions was that the League's galleys should remove their rams, and that the fleet should aim to hold their fire until ships were almost touching: 'In my judgement the correct course is to do as the cavalry troopers say, and to fire the arquebus so close to the enemy that you are splashed by his blood.' The other Spanish elements of the fleet sailed into Barcelona port led by the Marques Álvaro de Bazan of Santa Cruz, aboard his own personal galley, named *La Loba* (the 'She Wolf') after her golden figurehead, and Don Juan hosted the captains and commanders on his flagship. Another of King Philip's admonitory letters now reached him, stressing the need for him to comport himself with dignity and modesty. Given the reports of the splendour of his reception at Genoa on 26 July, and of his extravagant behaviour wherever he disembarked, it was clear that Don Juan had not been minded to take much heed of this advice. His original fleet of 47 galleys had now swelled to 84, and at Spezia he embarked several thousand Genoese and Italian troops. On 9 August he arrived in Naples, again to huge enthusiasm and welcome, and on the 14th he went to the Church of Santa Clara, in full polished armour, where he received the Pope's 'baton of command' from Cardinal Granvella, the Papal Nuncio, and the banner of the Holy League, with its embroidered image of Christ, over the arms of the Pope, Spain and Venice.

When he departed for the Sicilian port of Messina the next day, it was with a crystal capsule, given to him by the Cardinal, containing a splinter of the True Cross.

There had been tension at Messina, as everyone knew that the Venetian contingent of the Holy League fleet was both undermanned and disorganized. Only the emollience of the papal commander, Marcantonio Colonna, had persuaded the irascible Veniero to accept Spanish and Italian Habsburg soldiers on board his galleys, but the fiery Venetian would not embark any of the imperial German troops. Don Juan held his first combined council on the *Real*, with his 70 subordinate commanders. He had already spoken to each of the major contingent commanders separately, another piece of Don García's wise advice, in order to judge their characters and to ascertain their motivation. Meanwhile, unbeknownst to them, one of Ali Pasha's own light galleys had sailed among the fleet at night, garnering information for his own commander.

While in Naples, Don Juan had already sent Gil de Andrade, a distinguished Knight of Malta, east with four fast galleys to try to locate the Ottoman fleets, but no word had been received before the fleet of the Holy League departed from Messina on 16 September. They sailed in the formation in which they would fight, with three large divisions and a substantive reserve. Don Juan had already made the decision to mix the contingents within the squadrons, in order to ensure that no single contingent could refuse to fight or depart the battlefield. It also ensured that every individual commander felt responsible for the honour of his own country, state or city.

On 26 September, the fleet reached Corfu and surveyed the damage to the town and to the churches inflicted by Ali Pasha's soldiers and sailors in the previous month. Don Juan now sailed to Gomenizza, a port on the mainland, leaving Veniero and Colonna in Corfu to make their final arrangements, including embarking more soldiers on the Venetian ships, which Veniero failed to do. Here, one of Gil de Andrade's scouts reported that Ali Pasha, with his 200 galleys, had anchored in Lepanto, but that Ulich Ali, possibly with another 100 Algerine galleys, appeared to be on a detached mission to take the sick and wounded to Modon.

At this news, Don Juan closed up the fleet and conducted a full-scale rehearsal of battle drills, with some uncomfortably close live firing. At the council that evening there was rare unanimity that the fleet should sail south to the Curzolari islands and offer battle. At the same time as they were making this decision, a despatch had arrived in Messina for Don Juan, from King Philip, telling him to remain in Sicily for the winter. The battle of Lepanto would be long over before Don Juan read the message, thanking God that he had sailed well before this direction from his royal half-brother.

Held in the bay by strong winds, Don Juan ordered a further review on 2 October, as a thinly disguised reason for, once again, checking the battle-worthiness of the Venetian ships and crews. He rather tactlessly sent the Genoese admiral, Gian'Andrea Doria, to conduct this inspection of the Venetian galleys, pushing Veniero to the edge of his self-control. With this personal dislike between the two commanders, and the historical rivalry between Genoa and Venice as the backdrop, a major incident had then broken out between Captain Alticozzi and his Habsburg soldiers, and the Venetian crew of the galley on which they were embarked. Veniero sent emissaries to sort out the altercation, who were literally thrown overboard, and then shots were fired. Veniero, by now incandescent, demanded the surrender of the 'mutineers', and then he hanged Captain Alticozzi, already badly wounded in the melee, and three other Italian soldiers, from his yardarm. Within minutes, Venetian and Spanish ships were ready to fire on each other, while embarked soldiers were prepared to fight with the crews of their ship. An outraged Don Juan summoned a council. Emotions were running high, and there was little love lost for the Venetians. Some demanded that Veniero be punished, while others spoke of returning to Messina, leaving the Republic of Venice to face the Ottomans on their own. At last Colonna spoke. Veniero was a loose cannon, and a disruptive element in council, but the importance of the Holy League, and its holy enterprise, was too significant to be allowed to fall victim to personal grievances, especially with the infidel fleet so near. His suggestion was that Veniero's place in the fleet council be taken by his deputy, Agostino Barbarigo, but that the Venetian flagship retain her position to the left of the *Real*. This pragmatic solution was seized upon by Don Juan, and by the other contingent commanders. News of this incident somehow found its way to the Ottoman high command, confirming them in their belief in the fragility of the Christian coalition. What Ali Pasha did not know was that a despatch from the Governor of Crete had reached the fleet that same night, detailing the capitulation of Famagusta, the massacre that had followed, and the gruesome end of Bragadin. A cold rage silenced any bickering on board, and a flaming desire for revenge gave the fleet of the Holy League a unity of purpose it had not enjoyed before, and would not again.

The music ceased on the *Real* and Don Juan bowed to his fellow dancers, as an esquire passed him his open-faced helmet and his sword. The impromptu dance floor was now occupied by Pietro Doria, with 50 pikemen and arquebusiers, while other professional soldiers from the famed Spanish *tercios* manned the other platforms and decks. Miguel de Cervantes,[12] who was crewing on a Spanish galley, and who would be badly wounded in the battle, wrote that there was barely 2 square feet of space per man on the fighting platforms, and that they were 'bound and locked together' in the face of enemy guns, 'not a pike's length away'. Scarcely believable courage was required of the men at these posts. Don Juan's own battle station was astern behind a huge royal banner on its own flagpole, with other notables claiming places of honour next to their king's half-brother. A large crucifix was hoisted to the top of the mainmast and secured above the banner sent to Don Juan in Naples by the Pope.

The danger to the Christian fleet was becoming more apparent, as Doria discerned Ulich Ali's double line of galleys facing him on the Christian right flank which, operating like sliding doors, could open up and extend to engulf his wing of the Holy League's fleet. Don Juan had been warned of the terrifying noise that accompanied an Ottoman attack, but his interspersing of naval and troop contingents had also meant that there were few concentrations of the inexperienced or the panicky. The record of the battle holds few examples of ships or crews who did not do their duty, and the spirit of motivation across the fleet is a testament to the mental preparation orchestrated by Don Juan, to his planning and organization, and to his own personal example. In his polished armour he stood out prominently on the deck of the

Real, providing precisely that very visible leadership against which his cautious royal half-brother had warned him.

After the protocol of the opening rounds, it seems that it was the forward guns of Francesco Duodo's galleass – one of the Venetian pair of ships positioned about half a mile ahead of the *Real* – that opened fire first and, to the joy of the Christian observers, their opening salvo broke the backs of two Ottoman galleys. The main Ottoman fleet surged on, driven forward by the whips of the slave masters, parting their formation to pass either side of the galleasses, and thereby exposing themselves to the galleasses' broadside guns. The scene was wreathed in gun smoke from the cannon, but the vast battle formation of the Turks had already been disrupted, and instead of advancing in a menacingly disciplined, unbroken line, opening up to let the second echelon move smoothly into the battle line, they came on as discrete detachments, vulnerable to being enveloped or outflanked, as would happen. No less importantly, instead of the fleet opening fire in a massed volley on the orders of the *Sultana*, a series of ragged and uneven salvos whistled over the mastheads of the Holy League. The anticipated initial shock of battle had been dissipated by poor gunnery, and it steadied the nerves of soldiers and sailors alike. In contrast, the Holy League captains held their nerve and, under strict control from the *Real* and the squadron flagships, discharged a massive first volley from their forward guns – low, and at very close range – which Spanish poets unanimously likened to 'the crack of doom'. The whole Ottoman line shuddered under the onslaught, and the breeze, which had favoured the Christians, now blew the gun smoke across the opposing ships. In doing so, it unsighted the massed ranks of highly trained Turkish bowmen as they prepared to launch an avalanche of arrows. By the time this inadvertent smoke screen had begun to clear, the Turkish ships, and the archers, were well within the musket and arquebus range of the Holy League ships.

The battle of Lepanto lasted around four hours from first contact, and although the Ottoman battle line had flattened as it advanced,

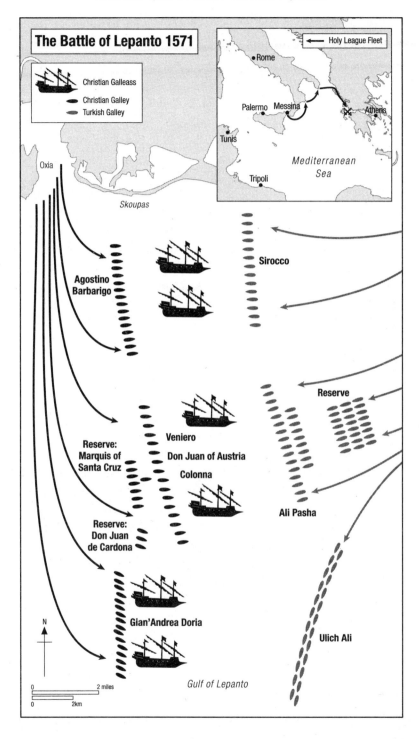

241

the wings closest to the shore probably clashed first, while those to seaward manoeuvred for longer before engaging, as Ulich Ali tried to draw Doria further out to sea while he sought to exploit any gap that he could create between the Christian right wing and Christian centre. In due course, the Christian left wing under Barbarigo was bunched up against the shore, in a close melee with Sirocco, while the right wing, under Doria, was extended far out into the Aegean.

Sirocco had attempted, as anticipated, to turn Barbarigo's left flank, and at one stage Barbarigo found himself alone, and facing north-west, as he attempted singlehandedly to prevent this manoeuvre. Four Venetian galleys rapidly moved to support him, and a desperate fight close to the shore ensued, during which Barbarigo raised his visor so that his orders could be better heard. As he did so, he was hit in the face by an arrow, mortally wounded, and taken below decks to die. Galleys from Naples came to add their weight to the fighting, and the balance of advantage began to shift in favour of the Christians. Sirocco had by now overloaded his own right flank, thereby allowing himself to be pinned to the coast by the galleys of Querini and Padilla, and opening up his own gap with the Ottoman centre. He too was hit, and with his flagship sinking, the mortally wounded Sirocco was plucked from the waters, and as much in mercy as in vengeance, he was beheaded on the deck of Barbarigo's galley. Now, the worry that proximity to the shore might encourage crews to look to their own safety was proved correct, as the surviving galleys of the Ottoman right wing sought to beach themselves on the mainland and the nearby islands. At this stage, the feared uprising among the Christian galley slaves further hampered the Turks and added to the chaos. The Venetians, with relentless savagery, had taken to their small boats and mercilessly pursued, and cut down, the fleeing crews and soldiers. Meanwhile, a papal galley, and three Genoese ones, punched through the gap created by the Venetians and turned south to attack the flagships of the Beys of Negroponte and of Rhodes. It was during this fierce engagement that Cervantes had received a crippling arquebus wound to his hand.

Ali Pasha had anticipated that the Holy League would not keep advancing into his trap if both their wings collapsed, but he and Ulich Ali had hoped that, by smashing into the Christian centre, Don Juan would have to commit all the Marques of Santa Cruz's reserves, while Ulich Ali, with a reinforced left wing, would be able carry out a great enveloping movement in the Aegean Sea, allowing him to attack the rear of the Holy

League fleet. In the event, Ali Pasha's attack on the centre was neither as strong nor coherent as was required to lock down the Christian centre, while Ulich Ali's careful and masterful manoeuvrings on the left flank came too late to decide the battle in the Ottoman favour. As it was, there was little scope for tactical finesse as the central squadrons of the two battle lines, almost 150 galleys, crashed together. It was every man for himself, as the battle increasingly became one of soldiers fighting across the wooden platforms of galleys locked together in a series of death struggles. The noise was indescribable, and the waters of the Gulf of Patras were already full of sinking or burning vessels, the galley slaves still manacled to their benches, and hundreds of dead or drowning soldiers and sailors.

The *Sultana* had slammed into the port side of the *Real*, rearing up over the banked oarsmen, but the *Sultana*'s complement of Janissaries had been decimated in the first violent salvo of cannon and arquebus, and it was the Christians who had boarded the Ottoman flagship. The fighting on the decks went on for more than an hour as both the great warships received a steady flow of reinforcements from supporting galleys, clambering through their stern companionways. The commanders were as exposed as their soldiers and crews. Ali Pasha wielded an exceptionally powerful bow that reportedly pierced both the breast and back plate of a Spanish soldier, while Don Juan wielded a great double-handed sword, which he used to punch and parry like a quarterstaff. At one stage he was clearly close enough to the action to receive a knife wound to his ankle, which he was not wise enough to attribute to an arrow in his subsequent report to King Philip. To the north, his cousin Alessandro Farnese almost singlehandedly took on a Turkish galley, leaping on board with only one other soldier, and fighting his way the length of the vessel to effect its surrender.

Spanish troops had twice fought their way to the mainmast of the *Sultana*, only to be forced back onto the *Real*, but on the third assault, Ali Pasha was killed by a bullet to the forehead. His head was hacked off by a soldier and presented to Don Juan who, dismayed by this lack of respect to a worthy foe, had it thrown in the water. As the fighting around the *Sultana* subsided, the galley carrying Ali Pasha's two young sons was captured and the boys put into Don Juan's cabin on the *Real*.

Meanwhile, on the Ottoman left, Ulich Ali had succeeded in drawing Doria's galleys further and further to the right, opening up just the gap between the Christian squadrons that Don Juan had warned him against. Santa Cruz, with his powerful 20-galley reserve, was a shrewd tactician, and an able and brave commander, but he had failed to assess the threat to the right flank correctly, and he had allowed himself to be drawn into the fight in the centre too early, before he was really needed. It was an uncharacteristic error by a skilled seaman. It was to be England's good fortune that Santa Cruz would die in Lisbon in early 1588 and was therefore unavailable to command the Spanish Armada later that year.[13] Fortunately, Juan de Cardona had held back his initial vanguard force, and he now plunged in where the fighting was fiercest, helping to plug some of the gap, but suffering an extremely high casualty rate as a result.

In stretching the Holy League's right flank, Ulich Ali had succeeded in forcing the various blocks of galleys in the division – Venetian, Genoese, papal and Sicilian – to break away from each other, leaving each of them vulnerable to being pounced upon by a section of the stronger Ottoman left wing. After the battle was over, galley upon galley was found with not a single living soul upon them, testifying to the intensity and brutality of the fighting. At one stage, the Venetian galleass, *Christ over the World*, with its many cannon and large amounts of gunpowder, caught fire and blew up, taking several Turkish galleys with it. The Venetians would come in for a great deal of criticism after Lepanto, being accused of indiscipline, selfishness and opportunism, and the taking in tow of Turkish ships that had been defeated by other contingents. In addition, while a Venetian attack in the centre had certainly helped save the ships of Cardona and of the Knights of Malta, who were under pressure, the outer group of Venetian galleys had defied Doria's orders to hold their position and had turned back. They were savagely punished for their actions by Ulich Ali and his son, Kara Bey, and their frantic attempts to retrieve the situation imposed only a little delay on the Ottoman plans. Meanwhile, Pietro Bua, captain of the *Gold and Black Eagle*, surrendered, and his galley was towed back to Lepanto where he suffered the same ghastly fate as Bragadin at Famagusta. Despite these successes, Ulich Ali's engagement had begun possibly as much as two hours after that of Sirocco and Barbarigo to the north, and maybe an hour after the *Real* and *Sultana* had clashed in the centre. Later reports claimed that the Ottoman captains on the far right could already see that by this stage Ali Pasha's grand plan had failed, and some of them turned for home.

Doria, too, was later sharply criticized, although much of the criticism came from the Venetians, keen to draw attention away from their own deficiencies, and their own, mostly inadequate, showing on the right wing. Luis de Requesens wrote a report to King Philip of Spain that damned Doria with faint praise and pointed out that Doria's galley had been one of the least damaged in the fleet. He sweetly added that no weight should be attached to this fact for, as he admitted, even the great Duke of Alba had said, 'One cannot die in despite of God's will.'

<hr />

At this stage the *Real* came back into action, having re-benched the rowers after the horrors of the fight with the *Sultana*, and she and several other galleys manoeuvred in order to reinforce the embattled right wing. Piero Giustiniani had been the last survivor of the Maltese flagship, and he had only managed to save his life by offering the Algerine boarders a large sum of money to spare him. Now, as Ulich Ali saw that the battle was lost and tried to retreat to Lepanto, the Ottomans had cut adrift their prizes. The Knights of St John reboarded their flagship, killed the prize crew, released Giustiniani and, to his joy, reunited him with his ransom money, although the Ottomans had made off with the great banner of the order. Ulich Ali and his surviving galleys were forced to escape to the west, but they were skilfully and aggressively flanked and shepherded by the squadrons of Doria and Padilla. Of the 30 or so galleys that had followed Ulich Ali's lead, only eight were able to round the southern point of the island of Oxia, while the remainder were forced to surrender or run aground.

The battle had been intense and bloody. One anonymous diarist wrote:

> The greater fury of the battle lasted near to four hours and was so bloody and horrendous that the sea and the fire seemed as one, many Turkish galleys burned down to the water and the surface of the sea, red

with blood, was covered with Moorish coats, turbans, quivers, arrows, bows, shields, oars, boxes, cases and other spoils of war, and above all many human bodies, Christian as well as Turkish, some dead, some wounded, some torn apart, and some not yet resigned to their fate struggling on the surface in their death agony, their strength ebbing away with the blood flowing from their wounds in such quantity that the sea was entirely coloured by it, but despite all this misery our men were not moved to pity for the enemy ... although they begged for mercy they received instead arquebus shots and pike thrusts.

Most accounts agree that 8,000 were killed outright in the Holy League fleet, of whom 5,200 were Venetians, 2,000 were Habsburg Spanish, Italian and German soldiers and sailors, and 800 were from the papal contingent. A further 4,000 would die of wounds, and around 10,000 others were wounded but recovered, including Cervantes. The majority of the casualties were on the 21 galleys that had been completely overwhelmed in the fighting, with the almost total loss of their crews and their embarked soldiers. These losses represented about 20 per cent of the manpower of the fleet of the Holy League. Only about 40 of the Ottoman galleys escaped back to Lepanto, with around 84 galleys destroyed, and around 130 vessels captured. Possibly 25,000 Turkish commanders, crew, soldiers and rowers were killed, with around 3,500 declared captured, and nearly 12,000 Christian slaves released, many of whom would rapidly join a series of Greek uprisings in the Peloponnese. It was suspected that many more Turkish prisoners were, in fact, taken, as the price of slaves across the Mediterranean in the next few years plummeted. The butcher's bill for four hours of fighting in the eastern Mediterranean was therefore in the region of 40,000 killed, possibly the largest single day's death toll since the battle of Cannae in 216 BC.

As the shattering noise of the battle began to fade, an enormous sense of post-conflict melancholy spread across the fleet. However, there was little time for reflection, or even rest for the shattered and exhausted crews and soldiers. That evening, the fleet was driven to shelter from a strong southerly wind and had withdrawn to Petalas. The unity that had compelled Don Juan to embrace Veniero at the end of the battle, and to call him father, soon evaporated. In a gross breach of protocol, Veniero sent a highly partisan report to Venice, announcing the great victory at Lepanto, and thereby securing the prominence of the Venetian version of events. Thus, the King of Spain heard of the victory through the Venetian network of couriers, on 29 October, and only received a report from Don Juan himself on 29 November. King Philip's reply was both effusive in its praise of this great military feat of arms and slightly frosty about Don Juan's own rather cavalier approach. Pope Pius V also heard the news of Lepanto from the Venetians, but it is a well-recorded story that he had been kneeling at prayer in the Vatican on 7 October, the day of the battle, when, around midday, he rose and, summoning his cardinals and priests, declared, 'Let us pray together, for I have just seen the Virgin Mary lead us to a great victory.' True or false, Pope Pius was so exhilarated by confirmation of the victory at Lepanto, and the prospects of recovering the Holy Land from the infidel, that he began to compare Don Juan to St John the Baptist. He would die in May 1572, before witnessing either the massacre of St Bartholomew's Day, in which the French Catholics attempted to extirpate the French Protestants, or the dismal collapse of the ideals of the Holy League, which he had been so instrumental in forming.

Ulich Ali sent his first despatch about the Ottoman defeat at Lepanto on 8 October, and it reached Constantinople and the Grand Vizier, Mehmet Sokollu Pasha, on 24 October. It simply stated, 'The Imperial Fleet encountered the fleet of the wretched infidels and the will of God turned the other way.' Sultan Selim II had received a fuller report from Petrev Pasha the day before, which was far clearer about the extent of the catastrophe. However, Sultan Selim, buoyed up by the fall of Cyprus, was far more philosophical than his surviving commanders might have expected, and Petrev Pasha received a reply reassuring him that 'a battle may be won or lost. It was destined to happen this way according to God.' Muslim fatalism could be useful in the face of disaster. In a tense interview with a nervous Venetian ambassador, Mehmet Sokollu Pasha compared the Venetian loss of Cyprus to the amputation of an arm, while the loss of the Ottoman fleet was the equivalent of a shave, after which the beard would grow back stronger. He was almost as good as his word, and within five months the French ambassador reported that Ulich Ali, the new *Kapudan Pasha*, had already built and fully equipped a new fleet of 150 galleys: 'I should never have believed the greatness of this monarchy, had I not seen it with my own eyes.' In fact, the wars for the Mediterranean were now essentially over until the 19th century. Then the British and the French would challenge each other for supremacy and redraw the map of the region, as the Ottomans continued to decline from the high-water mark of their siege of Vienna in 1683.

———

Disappointment pursued Don Juan, the gallant prince who had danced the *galliard* on the foredeck of the *Real*, in shimmering armour and with a westerly breeze in his fair hair, and who had secured one of the greatest sea victories in history. Addressed by his subordinates and his admirers as 'Highness' and 'Prince', there is no evidence that his mean-spirited half-brother ever gave him these honours. Within weeks of his triumph, he was writing to Don García de Toledo of his sadness, and of his acute consciousness of being under-appreciated by King Philip. However, his valour and his gallantry were recognized and acknowledged in Constantinople. In 1573, Selim II's niece, the daughter of Ali Pasha, wrote to Don Juan asking for the release of her surviving younger brother, the other having died of influenza. She accompanied this request with rich and valuable presents. He returned the youth to her, along with several other high-ranking prisoners, and her gifts, saying he would do so again in the future, if the opportunity presented itself. In response to this gallantry, Sultan Selim sent Don Juan a further munificent and magnificent cargo of gifts, with a gracious letter addressing him as 'a captain of unique virtue'. This virtue, he continued:

> has been destined to be the sole cause, after a very long time, of greater harm than the sovereign and ever-felicitous House of Othman has previously received from Christians. Rather than offence, this gives me the opportunity to send you gifts ... they come from one who, being the greatest among men, makes himself almost your equal by his present generosity. Pray God to guard you against our anger.

Don Juan equally affably replied that he was mindful of the Sultan's generosity but that it was his intention 'to make perpetual war upon you'.

———

It was not to be. The Christian victory at Lepanto did confirm the de facto division of the Mediterranean between the Ottomans and the Spanish, and it halted further Ottoman encroachment in Italy, ending their ambitions to take Rome. However, the Holy League had formed too late to save Cyprus, and it did not regain any of the territories that had been lost to the Ottomans prior to Lepanto. In 1572, the Holy League fleet re-formed, again with Don Juan as supreme commander. However, there were fresh dissensions among the Christian leadership; the new, untested Turkish fleet, under Ulich Ali, successfully avoided a confrontation, and the opportunity for a further Christian naval victory was squandered. Pope Pius V had died in the same year. The Holy League fleet failed to sail at all in 1573, and in the meantime, Venice concluded a separate peace with the Ottomans, an act which led to the Holy League being disbanded. Don Juan, with a Spanish and Italian force, attacked and took Tunis in the same year, only for the Ottomans to retake it in 1574.

When Luis de Requesens, Governor General of the Low Countries since 1573, died suddenly in 1576, Don Juan was appointed as his successor. It was a significant but thankless role and task, and in late 1578 Don Juan contracted a fever, and he suffered a miserable death at the age of 31. English domination of the Channel meant that his body could not be transported back to Spain by sea. Instead, his body was dismembered, the constituent parts packed in salt and returned to Madrid, overland, carried in four large leather saddlebags. There, the body of the 'last crusader' was reassembled and buried in the chapel of the Escorial.

PART FIVE

The Marches of Central Europe

9

'Like a Flood of Black Pitch'

Vienna 1683

At sunrise on 12 September 1683, the crest of the Kahlenberg, the 'Bleak Mountain', was concealed by a light autumnal mist, which promised a fair, possibly sultry day, and which, clinging to wooded flanks of the feature, grew denser as it descended, until it rested heavily on the shores and the stream itself of the River Danube. From here, two nights earlier, Duke Charles of Lorraine's[1] scouts had watched the fiery distress signals rising from the tower of Vienna's St Stephen's Cathedral, and had been able to send up their own flares to tell the beleaguered defenders of Vienna that, at long last, a relief force was on its way. As the hours wore on, and the mist began to disperse, the watchers on the Kahlenberg began to make out the city of Vienna itself. They would have been able to discern the walls and fortifications of the ancient capital of the Habsburgs, and they would have seen that, from the Burg Bastion to the Scottish Gate, there was a long and shapeless mass of rubble and ruin, through which it looked as if a battalion, marching abreast, could have entered.

In front of this scene of desolation, they would also have seen a labyrinth of overlapping, cross-hatched lines, which were the Ottoman siege trenches, and which looked, to some writers of the time, like the scales of a fish. In these trenches, the Turkish miners were still digging, and the storming parties were still awaiting the Grand Vizier's orders to launch yet another assault on Vienna's shattered walls, and its exhausted defenders. The huge Ottoman tented camp behind these siegeworks had been emptied of fighting men, but the harems of the pashas remained, as did the mass of Christian prisoners, still in chains and awaiting death. Camels, horses and donkeys, along with their drivers, and a mass of camp followers, still peopled the long streets of tents, all in a confusion of fear and suspense.

Nearer to the base of the Kahlenberg, and along the length of the Wienerwald feature, imposing numbers of the Turkish army were beginning to draw up in battle array, in order to dispute the descent of the Christian armies from the mountain passes, and to prevent their deployment onto the plains leading to the great Habsburg capital. Further to the west, on the reverse slope of the Wienerwald range, tens of thousands of Christian troops might have been seen toiling up the ascent, the cavalry dismounted and leading their horses up the steep, wooded incline, while the artillery dragged their guns and ammunition through the woods and across the ravines that marked the feature. Near the crest of the Leopoldsberg, troops had gathered in a half circle around the Kahlenberg chapel of the Margrave and, when the bell for matins chimed, the clang of arms and the noises of the march were silenced. On a space kept clear around the chapel, a large standard with a white cross on a red background was unfurled – a defiant riposte to the blood-red flag planted in front of the tent of Grand Vizier Kara Mustapha, the Ottoman commander of the siege of Vienna. There was a shout of acclamation as the crusader emblem of holy war was displayed, and again all was hushed as a small procession of the leaders of the Christian relief force moved towards the chapel. The procession was led by a small, wiry man with a tonsured head and a large beard. This was the famous Capuchin monk Marco d'Aviano, who was a friend and confidant of both Pope Innocent XI, whose money was subsidizing the Christian campaign, and the Holy Roman Emperor, Leopold I, who was wisely and tactfully still with his Habsburg court some miles to the west.[2] Close behind Brother Marco was a large, imposing man, his dark hair part-shaved, dressed in sky blue, riding a bay horse. This was the great military commander King John III Sobieski of the Poles, victor of numerous battles against the Ottomans and their Tartar allies. He was flanked by his young son, Prince James, and by Duke Charles of Lorraine, the experienced and diplomatically sure-footed commander of the imperial forces. The short mass was accompanied by the voices of a small choir and the continuing thunder of artillery from the walls of Vienna and the trenches of the Ottomans, and at its conclusion Prince James knelt to be knighted by his father. Sobieski addressed his Polish retinue:

> Warriors and friends, today we fight the infidel on foreign soil, but we fight for our own country, and under the walls of Vienna we are defending those of Cracow and Warsaw. Today we have to save, not a single city, but the whole of Christendom, of which that city of Vienna is the bulwark. The war is a holy one, and you fight not for your sovereign, but for the King of Kings. I have but one command to give, follow me.[3]

As the commanders and their staff moved swiftly back to their contingents, the crack of five cannon shots gave the signal for the general advance.

In 1676, the Ottoman Grand Vizier, Faizal Koprulu, had died of complications associated with heavy drinking, and he had been succeeded by his step-brother-in-law, Mustapha Pasha, known as Kara, 'Black'. Kara Mustapha was of Albanian origin, and had been adopted by, and had married into, the great Koprulu family. A dedicated Muslim, he was known to dislike alcohol and European Christians. He was variously described as greedy, humorous but terse, intransigent, perfidious, covetous but unwilling to accept bribes, and completely devoted to the Ottoman state. However, he was also clearly a clever and highly competent man, and well trusted by the Sultan. He had served as his step-brother-in-law's deputy on several occasions, commanded in the war against the Poles, negotiating a settlement with John Sobieski, who would be elected King of Poland in 1674, and he had led several successful expeditions into the Cossack regions of Ukraine. At the Great Council meeting, held in the Second Court of the Topkapi Palace[4] in the summer of 1682, his opinion and his decision, on the Sultan's behalf, was final. In the campaigning season of 1683, notwithstanding that a 20-year truce with Emperor Leopold was still in effect,[5] the Ottoman army would again march west against the Habsburgs and, just as significantly, Sultan Mehmet IV would be leading the army himself.

Consequently, on the evening of 6 August 1682, Mehmet IV's gardeners dug a narrow trench beside the Imperial Gate. At intervals they planted seven long crimson poles, each as thick as a man's arm, and from the golden globe at the apex of each hung a cascade of black and coloured horses' tails, the traditional Sultan's *tug*. To the inhabitants of Constantinople, and to the European ambassadors who resided there in various states of 'house arrest', the meaning was clear: the Sultan, God's 'shadow on earth', was going on campaign. The direction of the campaign was yet to be revealed, and the ultimate objective had yet to be decided, but as the news filtered back to the capitals, courts and chancelleries of Europe, the assumption was that the Habsburgs were again in the firing line of Ottoman ambition.

Through the winter of 1682, the Cyrpreci Meadow, outside the old Theodosian Walls of Constantinople, was transformed into a vast military camp, with a command post of ornate pavilions at its centre, and row upon orderly row of tents erected around them. This was the Ottoman way of war, and every function of the court had its travelling counterpart. There were audience chambers, reception rooms, dining facilities, and even a tent for ceremonial executions. For the 1683 campaign, the Imperial Corps of Tent Pitchers and Tent Makers had provided more than 15,000 tents. No possible requirement for the army was neglected, as those who had been at the sieges of Rhodes and Malta could testify. The infantry did not carry their own weapons on the march; swords, spears, bows and arquebuses went on camels, or were stacked in carts pulled by oxen. Fresh supplies would be waiting for the soldiers each night, and flocks of sheep and goats would be driven ahead of the army. The whole administrative competence of the operation contrasted starkly with the haphazard, chaotic and unhygienic nature of the European equivalent.

Lined up wheel to wheel in the artillery enclosure were guns of every size, including the great siege guns, whose progress was so dependent on the weather and terrain, unless they were being moved by river, which carried its own complications. However, the Ottomans also had a formidable engineering capability, both for bridging and mobility, and for assaulting and undermining enemy fortifications. While the Holy

Roman Emperor had to cajole, persuade or even bribe his subordinates to produce troops and materiel for war, constantly watching for treachery or betrayal by his fellow Christian leaders, an Ottoman sultan could summon up an army of 100,000 by simple decree. In due course the heart of the Ottoman army assembled. The *sipahi*, the gorgeously arrayed feudal heavy cavalry, with their silks and brocades, their chain mail and their plumed helmets, masters of the mace, sword and battle axe, and of the powerful recurved bow. The *akinjis*, the dowdily dressed, highly effective irregular cavalry, who served for slaves and loot, but who might inherit *timar* landholdings if the empire continued to expand, raising them to the position of *sipahis*. The Janissaries, the professional infantrymen, the *ghazi* warriors of the Sultan, inspired by military excellence and by a devotion to the Faith encouraged by the Bektashi[6] dervish preachers attached to each unit. Discipline, training and motivation marked the professionalism of the regular Ottoman army, and they combined their individual courage with the adoption of new military technology, particularly firearms, and bombs called 'grenades', from the Spanish *granata*, because they looked like pomegranates.

By 6 October Kara Mustapha was able to inform Sultan Mehmet that all was ready, and the Sultan left the Topkapi Palace to take up residence in his war tent. At every stage elaborate ceremony was observed, and the Habsburg envoy, Count Capara, was now in no doubt that this campaign was aimed at his master, Emperor Leopold. The next day the Sultan and his advance guard set out for Edirne, 150 miles north-west of the capital, taking a leisurely pace, in order that Mehmet IV could indulge in his favourite occupation, hunting. Not for nothing was he known as *Avci*, 'the Hunter'. A merchant wrote to his friend in London regarding the Sultan's departure, saying that the Grand Vizier's procession was led:

> by the Vizier's guard covered over with skins of lions, bears, tigers and leopards; next came six horsetails, carried before the Vizier by eighteen men, then fifty of the Vizier's pages. Behind him came two huge camels, the greatest to be found in the Empire, carrying the clothes of the Prophet Muhammad, which he wore in his lifetime, and the Koran, as it was delivered by Muhammad to his successors. Sultan Mehmet rode on a milk white horse, covered over with invaluable jewels.

Behind the Sultan rode his sons, Princes Ahmed and Mustapha, clad in plain clothes, and then bodyguards, pages and bowmen, all splendidly dressed, followed by some 5,000–6,000 *sipahis*. The parade had lasted some six hours. When the Sultan left Edirne for Belgrade, the procession had more than doubled in size.

Meanwhile, word had gone out across the Ottoman lands, to subjects and vassals alike, from Egypt and Syria, throughout Anatolia, to the Balkans and to the Ukraine, demanding, or asking, that they fulfil their oaths of allegiance or friendship, and produce the soldiers and the tribute that they owed, or had promised, to provide the Sultan as his subjects, vassals or allies. One of these carefully worded messages was taken by an envoy, in a fast galley, to the Black Sea and on to Crimea, where it was delivered, with honeyed words and lavish presents, to the Khan of the Tartars, with whom the Ottomans had been in alliance since the 15th century. Hardy and fast-moving superb mounted archers, the Tartars were an indispensable adjunct to the Ottoman professional army, fulfilling a vast range of functions that freed the regulars to fight the set battle, or to conduct a lengthy siege. Implacable in their savagery, reckless of danger, tireless and bold, what they did, like no one else, was to spread terror among civilian populations.

On 15 March 1683, the Sultan set up his war tent in Edirne, but when they departed for Belgrade a couple of days later, in foul weather, the soldiers were dismayed to see Mehmet's elaborate turban blown off by a sudden gust of wind. Battling torrential rain, which lowered morale and slowed the artillery train, the army reached Belgrade, midway between Constantinople and Vienna, on 3 May. Only now did the Sultan and his Grand Vizier reveal to key commanders that the campaign's objective was, in fact, to be the Habsburg capital. Motivations are difficult to fathom, but Sultan Mehmet, whose namesake had taken the Byzantine capital in 1453, was certainly inspired by the idea of being hailed as the Conqueror of Vienna, and Kara Mustapha, adopted son of the great Koprulu family, may have felt it was his own destiny to achieve something glorious. Both of them felt that the massive expenditure of resources warranted a worthy objective. Taking Vienna would be the fulfilment of Osman's dream about the Ottoman dynasty and would show the world who was the true heir to the Roman Empire, and the imperial Roman destiny. If Constantinople had been the 'Red Apple', Vienna was the 'Golden Apple'. Maybe the subjection of Rome itself would follow. This was heady stuff. However, most of the Ottoman commanders had assumed, and wanted, a more limited campaign; possibly capturing the two powerful Habsburg fortresses of Gyor and Komarom on the rivers Raab and Danube, and adding them to the two fortresses of Esztergom and Neuhäusel that the Ottomans already held. Properly garrisoned over the winter, they would be in an excellent position to take Vienna the following year, and then push out far enough to defend it, a strategy that might possibly lead to the collapse of the Habsburgs. Ibrahim Pasha, the elderly and experienced commander of Buda, certainly thought so, and had made his opinions very clear to the Grand Vizier.

However, although the symbolic value of taking Vienna was clearly more compelling to the Sultan and the Grand Vizier than just straight military logic, the plan was by no means merely a megalomanic whim. Certainly getting to Vienna, and taking it, in the remaining months of the campaigning season was a tall order, but Europe was divided, and the Emperor was focused as much on France as he was on his eastern borders. Leopold's position in the empire, and particularly in Hungary, was brittle because of his treatment of the Protestants. The imperial army was weak, much of it remained in the west, and Leopold might find it difficult to raise new forces, or to attract allies. The plague of 1679 had left Habsburg finances in a poor state, and the defences of Vienna itself were reported to be in an equally poor condition. Overall, it was a compelling set of reasons for making a bold move against the Christians.

On 13 May, a full-scale parade was held on the banks of the Sava. The Sultan came down from the fortress of Belgrade, and, with his sons Ahmed and Mustapha sitting alongside him, he ceremonially handed over command of his army to the Grand Vizier. He would now await the outcome of this great endeavour. He also entrusted his Grand Vizier with one of the three banners of the Prophet that Sultan Selim the Grim had taken from the Mamluks in 1517. Kara Mustapha, now *seraskier*,[7] possessing the untrammelled power of life and death, knelt before the Sultan and kissed the earth on which he trod. By this act the Sultan would share in any success, as he had done in Crete and in the Ukraine, but he would disclaim any responsibility for failure.

On 20 May, Sultan Mehmet visited his Grand Vizier's tent for the last time, before watching the Janissaries march off to the crossing point of the River Drava at Osijek. They would not meet again.

———

In August 1526, Suleiman the Magnificent, urged on by King Francis I of France, keen to put pressure on his Habsburg rivals, had invaded the Catholic Kingdom of Hungary, and he had defeated the Hungarian boy-king, Louis II, at the battle of Mohacs. In doing so, he had paved the way for the Ottomans to gain control of south-eastern Hungary. At this stage there were two contenders for the precarious throne of Hungary. One was a Hungarian noble called John Zapolya, and the other was Archduke Ferdinand of Austria, soon to become Holy Roman Emperor on the abdication of his brother, Emperor Charles V. Although, in the wake of Mohacs, the Ottomans had sacked the royal capital and fortress of Buda, which lay across the Danube from the riverine port and town of Pest, Suleiman had withdrawn back to his own territory, choosing not to impose direct Ottoman rule at this stage. Therefore, conscious of the dangers of imperial overstretch, given the relative weakness of the Ottoman position in the lands of Bosnia and Serbia and Wallachia, Suleiman had accepted the offer from John Zapolya to become his vassal. In 1529, Sultan Suleiman's armies made an attempt to take the Austrian capital of Vienna. The attempt failed. The campaign was poorly planned, it was too late in the season for such ambitions, and the weather was foul. As a result, the Sultan had made peace with the empire in 1533, and he had formally ceded western Hungary to Archduke Ferdinand of Austria, to the anger of the Hungarians. In 1541, Sultan Suleiman helped John Zapolya defeat an Austrian army outside the city of Buda, but this time Suleiman chose to secure the city for the Ottomans.[8] They would hold the fortress, on and off, until 1799.

———

Archduke Ferdinand of Austria became Holy Roman Emperor in 1556, and when he died in 1564 he was succeeded by his son, Maximillian II. The new Emperor inherited the long-standing confrontation with the Ottomans, including the complexity of relations with, and within, Hungary, and he also inherited the animosity of the Valois kings of France on his empire's western frontier. In addition, he was forced to confront the growing, and increasingly divisive, issue of Reformation politics and of Protestantism. However, pressure in the east did diminish for a while in 1566, when the seemingly indomitable 72-year-old Sultan Suleiman died while on campaign in Hungary. His death was kept a close secret from the army,[9] as a courier was despatched to his son, Selim, to prepare him for his accession. Under Selim II, the Ottomans had taken Cyprus from the Venetians in 1571, but they had also suffered the catastrophic naval defeat at Lepanto in the same year.

Sultan Selim's own son, Murad III, had begun his reign by strangling his five younger brothers, overseeing a deteriorating position in both the Balkans and in Hungary, and then foolishly initiating a new series of bloody and exhausting wars with the Safavids, although they ended with the advantageous Treaty of Constantinople in 1590. Murad also entered into correspondence with Queen Elizabeth of England, since both shared an adversary in the Habsburgs, and he entertained the notion that Islam and Protestantism had 'much more in common than either of them did with Roman Catholicism, as both rejected the worship of idols'. Elizabeth and her spymaster, Francis Walsingham, had seriously contemplated trying to initiate joint operations with the Ottomans during the outbreak of war with Spain in 1585, although the execution of Mary Queen of Scots in 1587, and the subsequent defeat of the Spanish Armada in 1588, had significantly reduced the direct threat to the English crown. The French had already set the precedent for such a realpolitik arrangement with the infidel Turk, as had the Habsburgs with the Persians.

Sultans Selim II and Murad III never left Constantinople and, for two years, Murad never left the Topkapi Palace itself, fearful of plots against his life by the Janissaries. Mehmet III, not to be outdone by his father, murdered 19 male siblings on his own accession in 1595. Ahmed I inherited the 'Long War' with the Habsburgs but brought it to a close in 1606, having captured the great Danube fort of Esztergom, east of Vienna. His successors presided over a period of palace intrigue, mental instability, harem politics, Janissary disloyalty and Anatolian peasant uprisings. To the relief of Christendom, and all central Europe, from 1623 to 1639 the Ottomans conducted a further debilitating war with the Safavids, which ended with Sultan Murad IV, who had commanded the army himself for the latter years, as opposed to delegating authority to his Grand Vizier, taking Baghdad. In the Treaty of Zuhab that followed the war, the Persians irrevocably lost the lands of Mesopotamia, and the borders that had been set by the previous Peace of Amasya in 1555 were largely confirmed.

Whereas Suleiman the Magnificent had lived to 72, from the death of Selim II in 1574, to the accession of Mehmet IV in 1648, none of the intervening sultans had lived beyond 38 years, while two had been deposed, two were clearly mentally disturbed, and two had been murdered.

Meanwhile, Europe entered into a sustained period of religious warfare between Protestants and Catholics that would ultimately descend into the appalling horrors of the Thirty Years War. In 1552, after three decades of religious civil war within the empire, often inflamed by French interference and cynical French support for the Protestants, Emperor Charles V had concluded the Peace of Passau.[10] In doing so he effectively surrendered his lifelong quest for European religious unity, by guaranteeing the Protestant Lutherans religious freedom within the empire. This was further confirmed in the 1555 Peace of Augsburg, which officially ended the religious struggle, making a legal division of Christianity permanent. The Peace of Augsburg was significant for elaborating the principle of *cuius regio, eius religio* (whose realm, his religion), which broadly permitted individual rulers of the multitude of polities within the empire to choose either Lutheranism or Roman Catholicism as the official religion of the state. Those believers of either faith, who did not wish to conform to their ruler's choice, were considered free to emigrate to another region within the empire. Calvinism, which was despised by both Catholics and Lutherans, would not be recognized as a legitimate choice until the Peace of Westphalia in 1648, which brought the Thirty Years War to a conclusion.

These agreements were implemented against the backdrop of the papacy's Counter-Reformation[11] programme, which continued throughout the long confrontation with the Ottomans in the Mediterranean, and Roman Catholicism had received a huge boost to its moral and religious authority in the wake of the victories at Malta and Lepanto. However, the gloss of these military triumphs had been significantly tarnished in 1572 by the massacre of St Bartholomew's Day, when the French Valois monarchy had sought to extinguish the French Protestant Huguenots. Attitudes on both sides hardened, and the Valois did not outlast this political crime for long, dying out in 1589. They were succeeded by the Bourbon dynasty, who would inherit the competition and confrontation with the Habsburgs, and who would pursue it just as aggressively and relentlessly as their Valois predecessors.

Meanwhile, the achievements of Passau and Augsburg in bringing peace to the empire were progressively undermined in the succeeding decades, first, by the expansion of Protestantism into those areas that had been previously designated as Catholic, and second, when rulers themselves underwent a religious conversion that threatened the internal stability of their states, and sometimes the imperial, and even European, balance of power. When Emperor Matthias had died in 1619, the Catholic monarch of Austria, Ferdinand II Habsburg, had been elected as his successor. However, by the time of his election, a Protestant revolt in Bohemia had already initiated a series of sub-conflicts and confrontations that swiftly expanded into a more general religious conflagration.

Emperor Ferdinand II was unable to confine this contest to Bohemia, and very soon the French, Spanish, English, Danes, Poles and Swedes were progressively drawn into the conflict. Across three decades, but particularly so after the Swedish intervention in 1630, no part of Europe was immune from the inflamed religious passions of the time, and plague, disease, famine and rapine followed hard on the heels of the rampaging armies. Historians assess that, by the time the Peace of Westphalia was signed in 1648, there had been over a million military casualties, and that the population of the empire alone had fallen from around 19 million to around 12 million.[12] Such a scale of depopulation had not been seen since the period of the Black Death in the 14th century. The early 17th century was a period of civilizational trauma, at a time when Christendom – a now badly damaged, brittle and fragile concept – still confronted an existential threat from the Muslim Ottomans and their allies.

Differences in religion would continue to remain a major issue for Christian Europe throughout the 17th and 18th centuries, but the Thirty Years War was the last major war in continental Europe in which religion can be said to have been a primary driver. It created the outlines of a Europe that would persist until the Napoleonic Wars and beyond: the nation-state of France; the beginnings of a unified Germany and a separate Austro-Hungarian bloc; a diminished but still significant Spain. Centralized states, like France and Spain, better able to sustain standing professional armies, with impressive artillery trains like those of the Ottomans, and the growing influence of the concept of nationalism, would increasingly be the drivers for conflict.

While the urge for religious conflict may have largely begun to burn itself out within Europe, it had most certainly not yet exhausted itself in the confrontation between the Catholic Habsburgs and the Muslim Ottomans. As the Habsburg Empire slowly recovered from the great struggle in central Europe, so too did the Ottomans from their long period of dynastic weakness. Sultan Mehmet IV had ascended the throne in 1648, at the age of six, just as the Peace of Westphalia was being signed. His father, Ibrahim the Mad, had seized him from his mother's arms, as an infant, and thrown him into a cistern, from which harem slaves had had to rescue him. Sultan Ibrahim had himself been strangled by executioners, sent by his own mother, shortly after his extravagantly corrupt Grand Vizier, Ahmed Pasha, had been torn to pieces by the mob, earning the posthumous nickname of *Hezarpare,* 'A Thousand Pieces'. When he was only nine, the young Sultan Mehmet had been encouraged to sign the death warrant of his own grandmother. In among this Ottoman court intrigue and chaos, Mehmet's mother's lasting contribution to the early stability of his long reign had been to grant Koprulu Mehmet Pasha full executive power as Grand Vizier. Mehmet Pasha may have been already 80 years old when he was persuaded to assume this enormous responsibility, but he persuaded the Sultan to move back to Edirne, away from direct involvement in the imperial administration in Constantinople; he crushed an internal military uprising; he stabilized the economy and the Ottoman finances; and he ruthlessly purged, or executed, those who abused their positions, or who failed in their responsibilities.

Under the Koprulus, Mehmet Pasha and then his son Faizal Pasha, the Ottomans took the remaining Aegean islands off Venice and, in a siege that had lasted from 1648 to 1669, they finally took the fortress port of Candia, and with it the island of Crete. Thus, at last, the Ottomans completed the total domination of the eastern Mediterranean. They also fought a successful war in Transylvania, pushing the Ottoman border closer to Austrian lands, and another against the Poles. When they accepted the vassalage of the Cossack Petro Doroshenko in the early 1670s, Ottoman rule extended as far as the right bank of the River Dnieper in Ukraine. The Ottoman Empire was now at nearly its greatest territorial extent (see map on p.16). Faizal Pasha's only great failure had been against the Habsburgs at the battle of St Gotthard in 1664, where, in another abortive attempt to march on Vienna, he had allowed his army to become divided, crossing a river, and the imperial forces had inflicted a major defeat on him. To the disgust of some parties, the young Emperor Leopold I did not use this victory to secure the liberation of all of Hungary, but instead he concluded a new 20-year truce with the Ottomans, convinced that the long-standing threat from France remained Austria's primary risk, and he used the intervening time to try to strengthen the defences of Vienna. That Ottoman–Habsburg truce was due to expire in 1684.

If Sultan Mehmet and Kara Mustapha could be accused of being overambitious, then Emperor Leopold I and his counsellors appear to have been equally over-sanguine. Having been given a false sense of security and superiority by the victory of St Gotthard over the Ottomans, nearly 20 years earlier, they had more recently appeared to be mesmerized by the growing power of France under the 17th-century Bourbon kings, Louis XIII and Louis XIV. However, a new and growing Ottoman threat could not be ignored, and Emperor Leopold sent envoys out to all the electors and states of the empire, seeking aid, while eagerly accepting the money that the crusade-minded Pope Innocent XI offered. Crucially, he pushed for an alliance with John III Sobieski, now

King of Poland. Late in the day, the Habsburgs also began to upgrade the defences of Vienna, and to strengthen the garrisons in the eastern fortresses that protected the empire and its capital city.

Born in 1640, Leopold I had been proclaimed Emperor in 1658. Possessing the classic Habsburg lower jaw, he had been a bright and studious youth, interested in literature, languages and music. Destined for an ecclesiastical career, he succeeded to the imperial throne when his elder brother, Ferdinand IV, had died unexpectedly early of smallpox. He also inherited his brother's prospective wife, Margaret Theresa of Spain, who was inevitably, in the manner of dynastic marriages, both his niece and a Habsburg first cousin. With a Jesuit upbringing, he was a deeply religious and pious monarch, and quite unyielding in refusing to seek compromise on denominational issues. This had unhelpfully served to alienate many Protestants in Hungary and within the empire. An English visitor to his court described him thus: 'His gait was stately, slow and deliberate; his air pensive, his address awkward, his manner uncouth, his disposition cold and phlegmatic.' He was competent, and he was diligent, but he was not an inspiring leader, and he was prone to both indecision and stubbornness.

Nor was he surrounded by noticeably talented men, but one of his best decisions was to choose Charles, Duke of Lorraine, to be his field commander. Now in semi-retirement, the Duke of Lorraine had fought against the Turks in the 1664 campaign, including at the battle of St Gotthard. Exiled by the seizure of his lands in France, he had a fierce resentment against encroaching French power, and he had distinguished himself many times in the imperial wars against the Bourbons. He was heavily scarred by smallpox and had a long aquiline nose, 'almost like a parrot'. John III Sobieski of Poland, who admired him as a fighting soldier, offered this honest description: 'He wears grey, unadorned, a hat without a feather and boots which were polished two or three months ago, with cork heels. His wig (a rotten one!) is fair in colour. His horse is not bad, with an old saddle and trappings of worn and poor quality. He is obviously little concerned about his appearance. But he has the bearing of a person of quality.' He walked with a pronounced limp, the result of a broken leg at the siege of Philippsburg in 1676.

In a period that valued swagger and style, Charles, with his aristocratic lineage and his military record, did not feel he had to play to the crowd. In the forthcoming campaign, when there would be panic, poor intelligence, fear and hard fighting, his reputation would count for much. His greatest attribute as a commander was the affection and trust he inspired in soldiers, in an age when the social gap between leaders and their followers was often vast. In battle he was frequently found in the thick of the fiercest fighting, and he often discarded his 'rotten wig' to reveal close-cropped, dark red hair. His other great attribute was his diplomatic skill in managing the royal and aristocratic commanders of those contingents that would march to Vienna's aid.

Early in 1683, the Catholic Elector of Bavaria, Maximillian Emmanuel, already betrothed to Emperor Leopold's eldest daughter, Maria Antonia, agreed to commit 8,000 troops to the defence of the empire in the east. His Franconian allies had also committed to contribute troops. The Hanoverians – Protestant and unhappy with Leopold's stance on denominational issues – shared his concern about the intentions of France and Louis XIV. But, although sympathetic to the imperial cause in the east, Elector Ernest Augustus would eventually send a mere company of infantry to Leopold, albeit under his son, George, who would, in due course, become King George I of England. The Saxons, another Protestant state, would eventually despatch nearly 10,000 troops, under their elector himself, but the personal relationship between the Protestant John George III, and the Catholic Leopold I, was never close.

However, Leopold's diplomacy had failed with the Hungarian Protestants, who were led by the nobleman Emeric Thokoly. Although there was a long-standing frontier 'truce' between the empire and the Hungarians of the south-east, Thokoly, like John Zapolya before him, saw a better path to independence for Hungary by being a vassal of the Ottomans, who had offered to make him 'King of Upper Hungary', than by accepting Austrian overlordship. The Habsburgs remained naively positive about Thokoly's position and continued to try to lure him into neutrality, right up until 21 July 1683, when Thokoly had unilaterally discarded the 'truce' with the empire, and he and his troops had openly declared for the Ottomans and had begun to operate alongside them.

Conversely, Leopold's diplomacy with the Poles bore dividends that were crucial to the outcome of the fight for Vienna. Kara Mustapha had initially been so successful in disguising the objective of the 1683 Ottoman campaign that he had alarmed both Austria and Poland enough to force them into partnership, and an accord had been secretly negotiated between Leopold and Sobieski in late 1682. It was a complex but comprehensive agreement, covering a range of potential threats and offensive options, but the key element was a commitment by both sides to support the other if either Vienna, or the Polish city of Cracow, were laid under siege. While Leopold, as Emperor, could make this commitment unilaterally, Sobieski, as an 'elected king', had to put the agreement to a fractious Polish Diet, where French influence was strong and active, where the simultaneous threats from Russia and Sweden also needed to be factored in, and where the grubby issue of money, and who paid for what, needed to be agreed. At last, on 18 April, after an agony of waiting by the friends of the Habsburg alliance, the Polish Diet agreed to Sobieski's plan. Whether to deter, defend, operate separately, or to march to the aid of Vienna, 48,000 troops were now to be raised, mustered and ready to move by 1 July. Emperor Leopold had also directly hired 3,000 experienced Polish cavalrymen, under the command of Prince Lubomirski, who had moved immediately to join the Duke of Lorraine on the Danube.

On 6 May, as Sultan Mehmet and Kara Mustapha had revealed to their senior commanders that the campaign objective of 1683 was not merely to be the outer bulwarks of the Habsburg Empire, but Vienna itself, Leopold and his court left the capital, in a long procession of coaches, for the plain of Kittsee, on the south bank of the Danube, opposite the modern city of Bratislava. There, the core of the army that would defend Christian Europe was drawn up in field array for the Emperor's inspection. Compared to the mass of the Ottoman army coming to confront them, it was not an imposing force. There were only just over 32,000 Austrian and Bavarian soldiers, paraded regiment by regiment, with 72 guns and a mere 15 mortars arrayed in front of them. At eight in the morning, the Emperor and the Empress, and their 14-year-old daughter and her newly betrothed, Maximillian Emmanuel, knelt before the soldiers, while the Archbishop of Gran celebrated mass. Field chaplains passed through the ranks distributing communion, while each officer and soldier was issued with a papal indulgence, to sustain them in the forthcoming fight with the hereditary enemy and infidel. Leopold also promised his troops an additional month's pay although, to few people's surprise, this was never to be paid.

At last, on 14 June, Kara Mustapha himself crossed the River Drava at Osijek, and his Tartar horsemen surged ahead of the main body, returning periodically with intelligence reports and prisoners, and with saddlebags stuffed with plunder or decapitated heads. On 27 June, the Grand Vizier set up his camp in the old Hungarian royal capital, the White City, and called a further council of war. Ibrahim Pasha of Buda, 40 miles to the east, had not been invited, as he was known not to favour the attack on Vienna. The next day the army began its march towards the fortresses of Gyor and Komarno, the heart of Habsburg defence against invasion from the south-east.

The Austrians still remained unclear about the ultimate Ottoman intentions, and complacent about the strength of their network of defences. The Duke of Lorraine, like so many coalition commanders, was daily subject to conflicting advice and direction, and he marched on the Ottoman fort at Esztergom, and then back again, crossed the Danube to the north, moved towards Neuhäusel, and them came back south of the Danube once more. Leopold maintained a reassuringly calm composure and, as preparations to improve the defences of the capital city moved slowly forward, he decreed that prayers should be said continuously, night and day, in the great Cathedral of St Stephen. Going hunting from 2 to 6 July, Leopold's only public concession to the fast-deteriorating situation was to order that the ancient crown of St Stephen be brought from Bratislava to Vienna for safekeeping.

On Saturday 7 July, as the Emperor was hearing early morning mass, as usual, the sheer scale and immediacy of what was about to overwhelm him became alarmingly clear. A stream of messengers brought a set of ever-worsening reports from the Hungarian border. The news was catastrophic. The Ottoman army was already approaching Gyor, like a river in full spate. Tartars were already through the supposedly impassable marshes that surrounded the fortress, and were moving fast, burning villages and cornfields as they went. Only now was it patently clear that the main army was set on besieging Vienna itself. By chance, the Duke of Lorraine, after his frustrating weeks of aimless marching, had based the bulk of his army astride their axis of advance, but rising smoke told him that the Ottoman advance guard, and the Tartar raiders, were already between him and the capital. After several decades of having patronizingly dismissed or stereotyped the Ottomans and their army as weak, dissolute and ineffective, the Christian powers had been rudely awoken.

Duke Charles was a professional, seasoned soldier. He was now confronted with three important tasks. First, he must regroup the army, currently on both sides of the Danube. Second, he must slow down the Ottoman advance in order to give time for the capital to complete its defences. Third, and most sensitive, he needed the Emperor to acknowledge that, if his army was to be the core of any serious relief operation, he could do little to prevent the siege of the imperial capital, even if he could provide some reinforcement for its defence. As he was making his assessment, rumours flooded into Vienna that Gyor had already fallen, that the Tartars were beyond the capital, and that the Ottomans were on the doorstep of Vienna. These rumours were all premature, but by six o'clock in the evening, Emperor Leopold formally announced that the royal family and the court were going to depart, leaving a shadow war government to manage the defence of the city. Although this was criticized at the time as a craven act, Leopold had no brothers, or living uncles, and only two small sons and a pregnant wife. Killed or captured by the Turks, his loss to the empire could spell the end of the Habsburg dynasty. At eight in the evening, Leopold, leading a long procession of coaches and carts, departed by the Palace Gate, crossed to the north bank of the Danube and, accompanied by a strong cavalry escort, set out for Linz. His stepmother, braving possible Tartar ambush, set out on the shorter southern route, via the great fortified monastery of Klosterneuburg. It was reported that 60,000 Viennese citizens followed in their wake.

At this stage there were only about 1,000 trained soldiers available to man the walls of Vienna, and the man chosen to lead the defence, Ernst Rüdiger von Starhemberg, a tough and battle-hardened soldier, was still with the army on the far side of the Danube, but he was summoned back. Duke Charles, now clear that the main Ottoman army was going to stay south of the Danube, had already sent the infantry north and told them to undertake a forced march to the capital, while he tried to put some distance between his own cavalry and Kara Mustapha's *sipahis*. The arrival of Duke Charles and Starhemberg in Vienna helped calm the situation, damped down the incipient panic, and brought order and purpose to the defensive preparations. Starhemberg was another experienced Habsburg officer. Resilient, calm and impenetrable, he was tall and wiry, with a long, thin nose, like an eagle's beak. Always favouring attack over defence, he was exactly the type of commander that the Viennese garrison needed, and his energy, judgement and bravery would be a lodestar for the defenders, military and civilian alike, over the increasingly desperate weeks of the forthcoming siege.

Under Starhemberg, the garrison and the remaining citizens set about repairing those walls and bastions in the south-west section of the city, the most likely focus of the Turkish assault, and hauling artillery pieces into position. An outer earthen palisade, beyond the main walls and a deep moat, had been allowed to deteriorate over the years. This was urgently built up again, and long timbers, ships' masts and tree trunks, evenly spaced, were hammered deep into the ground. These were then secured by cross-beams, and stood some 6–8 feet tall. Earth was piled up behind this palisade, and the area in front of it was cleared. Held by disciplined, trained and well-motivated soldiers, plentifully equipped with arquebuses, pikes and grenades, the palisade would prove to be a deceptively formidable obstacle. In addition, while the palisade still stood, the guns of the bastions, the ravelins, and the inner walls could fire over it, in support of its defenders.

With an energy fuelled by fear, carpenters constructed strongly roofed passages out of planks, logs and wicker gabions that would allow the easy movement of defenders as they rotated on the defences or moved to the areas of greatest danger. This vital work continued far into the long summer night, illuminated by the light of flares, torches and bonfires. Vienna had only just survived Sultan Suleiman's siege of 1529, because Turkish mining and breaching of the walls near the Carinthian Gate had taken longer than anticipated, and the early onset of winter had forced a premature Ottoman retreat. Given its position on the Danube, with a canal that served the port of the city, and with tributary rivers south and north, there was only so much that could be done. However, since that siege, the ancient 13th-century ramparts had been encircled with a girdle of squat, solid, angular bastions, shaped like broad arrowheads and mostly surfaced with brick, rather than stone. Designed to absorb the shock of cannon fire, they jutted out from the curtain walls, in order to allow the heavy artillery pieces placed on them to provide supporting fire to each other, to cover the moat that surrounded the city, and to allow the artillery to fire beyond the palisade. In the moat itself stood a series of massive detached additional triangular firing platforms, the ravelins, each more than 20 feet high, again providing supporting fire to the other elements of the defence. While improvements had been made in artillery and handguns in the intervening decades, the concept behind the fortifications would have been totally comprehensible to the knights of Rhodes and Malta in the previous century, as would have been the siege expertise of that Ottoman army that was now rapidly closing in on the city.

As the population of Vienna had grown, the building works within the city, including those in the imperial quarter, had expanded right out to the walls. Then the buildings went up in height until, at last, the wealthier citizens had begun to build parks and houses outside the walls. Vienna had been built on the south bank of the River Danube, and the land to the south-west of the city sloped gently down to the city walls and, apart from a few streams, was flat and dry. It was here that the main expansion of the city had taken place. By contrast, the land to the north-west was more broken, and it rose more steeply to the imposing and forested Wienerwald feature, whose foothills had increasingly become used for farming and for vineyards. Military logic would dictate that the ground in front of fortifications should be cleared for several hundred yards, in order not to give an attacker any advantage, but all plans to include the new developments to the south-west, and those constructed on the Leopoldstadt Island on the eastern side, within an extended defensive wall, had been derailed by cost and complacency. The ground where the Ottoman miners would eventually focus their efforts had already been helpfully dug up for Vienna's vegetable gardens.

The fortifications on the south-west sector of the city were strong, but they were also compromised. Comprising the reinforced palisade, and the moat, with its substantive new ravelin, the smaller Löbl Bastion was not properly aligned with the larger Burg Bastion, and the wall between them was both longer and less robust than sound planning should have allowed. These defects constrained the movement of the defenders, and left some areas in the moat less well covered by fire than they should have been. Immediately behind these defences were the Imperial Palace, and then a maze of narrow city streets with their high buildings. In the event of a breach in the defences, Starhemberg and his siege expert, Georg Rimpler, intended to fight inside the city, where every road would be blocked with chains and barricades, and where every house would be turned into a strongpoint for which the Ottoman soldiers, without the direct support of their artillery, would have to fight.

The city's arsenals were already well stocked, and more ammunition and powder came in before the Ottoman arrival, as did vast quantities of timber for the defences. The capital was also well supplied with artillery pieces, but it was short of manpower. To Starhemberg's relief, the advance guard of the retiring imperial infantry arrived on 10 July, and more arrived the next day, just as the Turks took the town of Hainburg, slaughtering the garrison and sending the heads back to the Grand Vizier. By 13 July the main body of the Ottoman army was only 7 miles from Vienna, while the Tartars were raiding on a wide arc, from north to south, 20 miles ahead of them and already well beyond the capital. In the city, determination was mixed with panic, and when a youth, inexplicably dressed in women's clothes, was found starting a fire near the arsenal by the western Scottish Gate, he was hacked down and ripped to pieces. Hungarians, suspected of sympathy to the Ottomans, were also attacked and killed. The fear of spies and saboteurs never went away throughout the siege.

That same day the mass of General Alexander Leslie's[13] infantry command completed their long, tiring march from Gyor and, passing Lorraine's dragoons and cuirassiers on the Prater Island, they marched over the canal bridge and through the city gates. It was not a moment too soon, and a delay of just a single day would have made their entry impossible. Starhemberg now had some 11,000 regular troops for 3 miles of wall, although many were suffering from dysentery, and he also had a number of other armed bands, some drawn from the city's militia and police, and others raised by the city's guilds. That night, seeing the rising smoke of the Ottoman advance on the eastern horizon, Starhemberg ordered the forcible clearing of the glacis, burning down everything in the south-west residential and park areas outside the palisade and counterscarp that might hinder the defenders or aid the attackers. At the same time Duke Charles led his cavalry north of the Danube, and away to the west.

On 14 July, any Viennese hope of salvation or relief evaporated as the Ottomans paraded past the walls, at a measured pace, and well within sight of the defenders, swiftly encircling the city. In the south-west, they had marched through the still-smoking, burnt-out remains of the formerly graceful suburbs. The Grand Vizier had a formal letter to surrender delivered to the gates of Vienna: 'Accept Islam and live in peace under the Sultan. Or deliver up the fortress, and live in peace under the Sultan, as Christians; and if any man prefer, let him depart peacefully, taking his goods with him. But, if you resist, then death, despoilation or slavery shall be the fate of you all.' Starhemberg just as formally rejected the letter, and continued walling up the gates of Vienna. Kara Mustapha had expected no less. Wading across the northern canal, the Ottoman cavalry now occupied Prater Island and Leopoldstadt and, bringing the guns across on pontoons, began bombarding the city's northern walls and gates almost immediately. To the south-west, the vast legions of Ottoman miners wasted no time in beginning their work and, within two days, had dug 6-foot-deep trenches to within 50 yards of the palisade, although Starhemberg did organize some early, nighttime sorties to disrupt their work, and to steal cattle.

This smooth start to his campaign may have made Kara Mustapha complacent and overconfident. He, too, made the mistake of underestimating his opponent and applying outdated stereotypes. He had experience of war, but he seemed so focused on the city in front of him that he made little use of his cavalry to tell him what was happening to the west. Not only did he not secure the high ground of the Wienerwald, but he did not even fortify the open, western flank of his own vast, tented camp. The defences of Vienna looked weak, and his cannon, miners and Janissaries should easily overcome them. In the middle of July 1683, he assessed that the chances of the Habsburgs gathering a relief force of any significant size looked remote. The Grand Vizier had ambition, he had a plan, and he had time. He planted his palatial tent among the still-smoking ruins of St Ulrich, and he also built a new, fortified forward command post, just 500 yards from the city's fortified palisade, and well within cannon range. From here he could watch the entrenchments advance and be able directly to command the repeated assaults. Although the Ottomans had troops all around the city, both defenders and attackers knew that the point of main effort was to be the sector between the bastions of Löbl and Burg. As the miners continued to drive their saps forward, long, deep trenches sprouted out on either side, parallel to the outer rampart and, as the guns pounded the earth and timber palisade and the stone and brick walls of Vienna, the Ottoman troops began to fill those trenches, ready for the initial assaults.

<hr />

At last, on 23 July, and on an order from the Grand Vizier himself, the Ottoman soldiers rose out of the trenches and rushed across the short distance of open ground, scaling up the steep slope of the palisade and attempting to climb over the stout timber fence. Ranks of musketeers rose up to meet them, stepping forward, firing through the timber walls, then stepping back to reload, allowing another musketeer to move forward, thereby keeping up an almost continuous volley of deadly, close-range fire. Around the musketeers, other soldiers wielded lethal 13-foot-long pikes – made famous in Europe by the Spanish *tercio* formations – or short boar spears, while yet others launched showers of grenades. Meanwhile, the guns on the Löbl and Burg bastions, and those on the ravelin, fired whenever they could do so, in order to break up the next wave of attacks. The fighting was savage, and without quarter, and it went on day after day. Ten days after the first assault the palisade had still not been breached, and the Turks reverted to mining underneath it, and to building up mounds either side of their saps, to be able to shoot down on the defenders. A significant mine exploded, creating a huge pile of earth and a great pit, but the Ottoman infantry who tried to take advantage of this were, in the words of one of the defenders, driven off by 'Count Sereni and St Croy, Lieutenant Colonel of the Regiment of Dupigni, coming to our succour, with a hundred fresh men armed with grenades; soon they got the better of the Turks and cutting off many of their heads, fixed them on the stakes of the palisade and counterscarp in sight of the enemy'. Mining and counter-mining now became a major feature of the siege.

On 7 August, the 25th day of the siege, with mines, artillery and grenades, the Janissaries at last managed to push through an open space created in the rampart and to dig in on the edge of the moat. On the following days the Turks brought their guns nearer the wall, while their miners, now in the moat, proceeded to dig towards the two bastions. On the afternoon of the 12th, amid a sense of expectation, by defender and attacker alike, another huge mine went off, creating a causeway from the counterscarp to the ravelin. The Turks surged forward, and some eight Ottoman banners were fixed there, excellent targets for the Habsburg gunners but a grim marker of a new reality: the Ottomans held a section of the ravelin, and they could not be driven off.

Starhemberg, wounded early in the fight and routinely racked by dysentery, was always to be seen on the walls, or even in the breaches, fighting alongside his soldiers. His letters to Duke Charles – routinely smuggled out of the besieged city by brave messengers[14] – painted a vivid picture of the scale and intensity of the fighting, the state of the defenders, the artillery duel, and the situation with regard to powder, water, food and money. He was amazed at how unimaginative Kara Mustapha's plan of attack was, and its almost total focus on the south-west meant that he had been able to take risks in other sectors of the city, in order to reinforce and rotate the defenders of the Löbl and Burg bastions. For 37 days, 10,000 men would battle over the narrow strip of land separating these bastions from the Ottoman lines. Whatever the horrors of the Thirty Years War, no battle or siege had been fought on such a scale, or for such stakes. The intensity of the daily, yard-by-yard struggle in the moat, around the bastions, and on the walls of Vienna reflected the significance of a possible Ottoman victory.

Constantinople had been the extinguishing of the last flickering flame of the Byzantine Empire. Taking Vienna would possibly, even probably, be the destruction of the Holy Roman Empire, leading to death and enslavement on an unimaginable scale, mass conversion to Islam, and the opening up of all Christian Europe to the forces of the Ottoman Sultan and Caliph. Even as the soldiers of Starhemberg and Kara Mustapha fought and died for possession of the 'Golden Apple', the Tartars, and the other irregular forces that accompanied the Ottoman army, were giving central Europe a ghastly foretaste of what a Habsburg defeat would look like.

On 25 August, Starhemberg launched another desperate sally into the moat, with soldiers debouching from the sally ports by the Löbl Bastion, and by that of the Carinthian Gate. Designed to slow down the relentless Ottoman advance on the city walls, it cost soldiers he could ill afford to lose, and achieved nothing. Two more mines went off the next day, and the day after. On 27 August, a small party of artillerymen climbed the tower of St Stephen's Cathedral and fired 40 rockets into the air, a signal to Duke Charles to send 'speedy relief'. Every evening after that the rocket party made the same journey, although there was, as yet, no hint of a relief force. The ravelin was now just a towering mass of earth, brick and stone, where the defenders kept a last, precarious foothold. A torrential downpour slowed the fighting on the 28th, and Starhemberg sent soldiers from his own regiment, under his adjutant, Captain Heisterman, to garrison this forlorn hope. Heisterman was already a known figure among the defence, having wrestled with and killed a Janissary soldier, carrying both his head and his sword back up the walls, and presenting them to his commander. Given permission to withdraw if the fighting became too intense, he and his 50 soldiers held the position for a further 48 hours until, at last, on the night of 3 September, Starhemberg ordered Heisterman and the last 20 survivors to withdraw, and the whole ravelin fell into the hands of the Turks.

The following day, at precisely two in the afternoon, when the watch was being changed among the defenders, the most powerful mine to date exploded under the north, inner, face of the Burg Bastion. Thirty feet of bastion wall collapsed, making the artillery positions there unusable. With both sides deafened by the explosion, a thousand Janissaries poured out of the trenches and surged up the rubble of the shattered bastion as the smoke and dust billowed around them. Defenders and attackers alike moved towards the new breach. The situation was desperate. If the Ottomans could not be dislodged from the walls, the defence of Vienna would stand in the balance. Starhemberg and all his commanders rushed to the scene. Once again, the musketeers formed up, protected by pikes and spears, and despite the chaos, noise and carnage around them, they established a ragged rhythm: fire, step back, reload, step forward, fire, step back, reload, step forward yet again. On it went; fear of an Ottoman breakthrough, and faith in their commanders and comrades, kept the soldiers in the line, as men fell on either side, and the Turks kept pressing bravely forward. Smaller cannon were manhandled onto the debris, firing grapeshot into the moat, while showers of grenades were hurled into the solid mass of the attackers. As a late, warm dusk fell, the defenders still held the walls, but only 4,000 of the original garrison still stood, and there were no more trained soldiers in reserve.

Labouring all night and the following day, the defenders made what they could out of the debris and shattered remains of their fortifications. On 6 September, three more mines went off under the Löbl Bastion, throwing down a great section of the 20-foot-thick walls, destroying the artillery emplacements, and leaving a further huge gap. Only the difficulty of scaling the rubble stopped the Ottomans' furious assault succeeding. A summer marked by heat and torrential rain was beginning to sap Ottoman morale, as were the casualty levels and the resilience of the defence. Reports from the camp spoke of an untypical breakdown of discipline and administration, and of camp rumours about a Christian force being prepared to the west. However, reserve troops from Buda were now coming in, as were new supplies of weapons, ammunition and food. One last heave, and there would be gold and glory for all. No one wished to contemplate the prospect of failure.

Wednesday 8 September was the Nativity of the Blessed Virgin Mary, and in the cathedral and throughout the city the day was celebrated with intense fervour. That night the rocket party ascended the tower of St Stephen's yet again and launched their flares. As the rockets soared into the air and died, the small party, at last, saw five answering flares burst high over the Kahlenberg, on top of the Wienerwald feature to the west. Help was at hand, but in the Duke of Wellington's words, 'It would be a close-run thing.'

———

Since the middle of July, increasingly concerned for the defenders of Vienna, Duke Charles had husbanded his cavalry force, blocking off every advance by the Ottomans and their Hungarian allies along the north bank of the Danube. He was also doing what he could to deter the Tartar marauders, and to defend the routes to the west, where the royal family and court were, and from where allied contingents were marching to Vienna's aid. Now, nearly two months later, and still only partially aware of conditions in the capital, the Habsburg allies gathered. Maximillian Emmanuel of Bavaria was there with his 11,000 troops, including five battalions of infantry, and John George of Saxony with a further 10,000. The Franconians and Swabians had brought an additional 9,000 troops. By the end of August some 30,000 infantry were bivouacked on the plain north of the Danube, screened by the imperial cavalry and the Poles of Prince Lubomirski. All now awaited the arrival of John III Sobieski, King of Poland. Count Raymond Montecuccoli, the victor of St Gotthard, had once said, 'Three things are required to wage war: money, money, and more money.' Soldiers were vital, but so was cash, and the enormous cost of this enterprise had been underwritten by Pope Innocent XI, who was obsessed with the Ottoman threat, and who had wished to resurrect the Holy League that had been so stunningly successful at Lepanto under the patronage of Pope Pius V. The 'army of liberation' for Vienna, Catholic and Protestant alike, was bankrolled by the Vatican.

At last, on 31 August, the Poles arrived, after a long and tiring journey, and Duke Charles rode out to meet King John, who was riding at the head of 3,000 light cavalry. The bulk of the Polish force, 15,000 strong, arrived shortly afterwards, preceded by some 2,000 hussars, the famed Polish 'winged horsemen', heavily armoured in their plate and chain mail, and resplendent in leopard skins and plumed helmets. A holdover from the great days of the medieval knights, their days might be numbered on a western European battlefield, but against an Ottoman army, in the right circumstances, they held all the advantages of their crusading forebears, and of the knights of the papal military orders. It was a magnificent display, and although no one was unaware of the odds that they faced, it was a sight to raise the morale of all who saw it.

———

Duke Charles of Lorraine was beholden to Emperor Leopold, and ranked lower than King John and the electors of both Bavaria and Saxony. His military reputation and his personal qualities were therefore vital in determining a proper chain of command and getting full agreement to a plan of attack, while always conscious of the imminent prospect of Vienna falling to Ottoman assault. Emperor Leopold had favoured a cautious approach, going around the Wienerwald and approaching Vienna from the south, but Duke Charles, knowing that time was of the essence, had disregarded his sovereign's advice and had persuaded the assembled commanders that the force of 60,000 cavalry and infantry should go directly across this imposing feature. On 8 September, the army drew up in review order on the plain at Tulln, with the Poles having crossed to the south bank on two pontoon bridges, wary of a Tartar attack to disrupt their movement. Lorraine had already despatched Colonel Heissler with 600 dragoons to ride towards Vienna, to confirm that the Turks were not holding the Wienerwald in any strength, and if possible to take up a defensive position on the Kahlenberg. It had been Heissler's rockets that had told Vienna's defenders that relief was on its way.

Tulln was no more than 15 miles from Vienna, but there was only a single high road winding up through the Wienerwald. In 1683 the whole feature was a wilderness, and largely uninhabited. Lorraine did not know this ground, nor were there any detailed maps. It stretched like a narrow peninsula of high ground from the eastern Alps to the bend in the Danube west of Vienna, and was a huge, forested area of beech and oak, rocky underfoot and cut by many small streams and ravines. The western flank was very steep, but it looked manageable, even to cavalry and artillery, given enough time. The Vienna side was less precipitous, but it was still very broken ground, and the small settlements and vineyards would make it very difficult for both the infantry and the cavalry to maintain formation, or for contingents and commanders to communicate. Along the

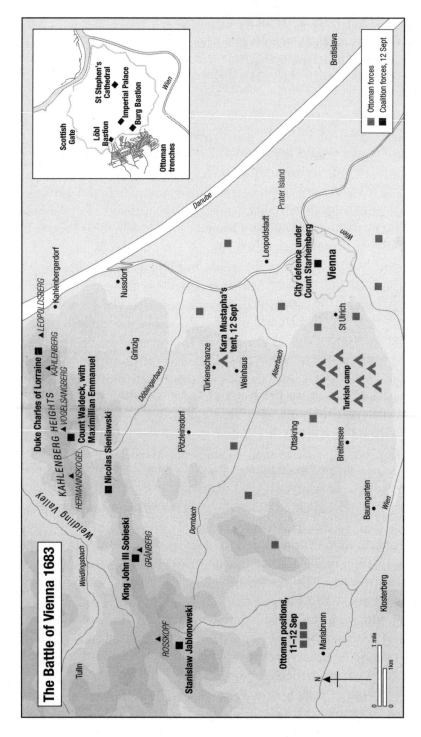

5-mile ridge were a set of named high points, from Rosskopf to the Hermannskogel, the Vogelsberg, and the Kahlenberg, with an average height between these landmarks of around 1,000 feet, until the ridge dropped to the Danube.

───

Duke Charles would be in overall command of the left flank, closest to the Danube, with all the imperial infantry and cavalry, and with the large Saxon contingent, although the elector would retain direct authority over his own troops. The centre was composed of the Bavarian and Franconian infantry, under the command of Count Waldeck, with Maximillian Emmanuel riding with his own cavalry. King John III Sobieski held the place of honour, on the right. In simple terms, the infantry was concentrated on the left, and the bulk of the cavalry on the right. The army intended to descend from the hills in a huge arc, stretching from the Danube to beyond the River Wien, and attacking the whole western face of the Ottoman camp.

By dusk, Duke Charles's forces were largely in position, but the Polish cavalry were having understandable problems getting large numbers of horses up the steep slopes, while the cavalrymen, when they had to dismount, were not ideally equipped for clambering over rocks and wading through streams. The artillery were having an equally tough time of it. The complicated and difficult deployment of the 60,000-strong force went on all of 10 September, and that night some volunteer Savoyard mountain troops, including Prince Eugene of Savoy[15] – the great commander of the later Duke of Marlborough's wars – overran the small Ottoman outposts near the Kahlenberg. They killed most of the Turks, but some escaped to report to Kara Mustapha Pasha that an infidel Christian relief force was now assembling on the hills to the west. By mid-afternoon on 11 September, most of the contingents were camped from one end of the Wienerwald to the other, although the Polish cavalry were still struggling to get to the area under the Rosskopf peak. By now, the Ottoman siege trenches threatening Vienna were clearly visible, as were the shattered walls and bastions of Starhemberg's beleaguered fortifications, and as were the tents of the great Ottoman camp and their urgent preparations to meet this new threat.

Duke Charles and King John had ridden to a vantage point on the Kahlenberg and viewed the slopes down to the plain with some dismay. The country bore little relation to the maps they both carried: flat land was, in fact, very broken; the gradients were steeper than anticipated; the fields were full of vineyards, not corn and wheat; and the small villages and hamlets could be easily fortified by the Turks. Both men may have been buoyed up by martial ardour and religious fervour, but they were also professional soldiers, and they both knew that this would be a difficult, uncertain fight, and that the nature of the ground meant that the musketeers and pikemen could not necessarily advance in good, disciplined order, nor the dragoons, hussars and cuirassiers form up and charge in neatly organized echelons. Duke Charles decided to move five additional infantry battalions across to King John, in order to provide greater protection for the Polish cavalry in the advance, but despite their concerns there was to be no resiling from the overall structure of the agreed plan.

Kara Mustapha had learned on 9 September that the relief army was gathering at Tulln, and he had called a council of war on the morning of the 10th. It was decided that the siege would continue, but that the mass of Ottoman cavalry, hitherto largely, and inexplicably, unused, would move to meet this new threat from the west. The Grand Vizier and his commanders rode in a sweep along the base of the Wienerwald. It was evident that the main attack would centre on the area close to the Danube, along the road that led from Klosterneuburg, and then push down through the village of Nussdorf, to the twin villages of Unter and Oberdöbling. The main Ottoman defensive position would therefore have to be around Oberdöbling, while Kara Mehmet, Pasha of Diyabakir, would move quickly to secure and fortify Nussdorf. A small force would join the Tartar cavalry on the left in covering – what to him seemed to be – the less likely line of approach from below the Rosskopf peak. The Polish cavalry in fact only got into position there after nightfall on the 11th. Although they were masters of siege warfare, in only a few places did the Turks attempt to construct any type of proper defensive positions. Guns and Janissaries were drawn from the siege trenches, and the reinforcements from Buda, under the still-sceptical Ibrahim Pasha of Buda, marched through the great camp to the new Ottoman lines facing west. It was a perfectly respectable plan, but it was based on complacency, arrogance and an underestimation of the Christian forces. As the left flank of his new western defensive line continued to appear to be largely unthreatened, Kara Mustapha pushed more and more men into the positions on the right, opposite those areas from where he expected the main Christian assault to come. Some of his personal bodyguard took up positions above the village of Gerstdorf, on a steep bluff, still known as the *Türkenschanze*, the 'Turk's Redoubt', and Kara Mustapha planted his own red battle tent there, along with the Prophet's standard.

At 5am on the morning of 12 September, the Habsburg infantry, coming under fire from Turkish skirmishers, moved to attack the village of Nussdorf. The dawn mist was clearing, and it was clearly going to be a hot day, with the early morning sun shining in the faces of the attackers. Visible to the defenders of Vienna, they marched purposefully downhill, bearing a huge white flag emblazoned with a scarlet cross. The Saxon battalions next to them also began to advance. This had not been Lorraine's plan, and he quickly moved to regain control, by sending cavalry to ensure he was not outflanked on the banks of the Danube, and by directing the Bavarian infantry to support the Habsburg advance. The whole northern slope was now alive with men. Ottoman diaries later reported that, on the morning of the 12th, a 'huge army of Christians advanced upon the Ottoman camp. It looked as if a flood of black pitch was pouring downhill. Thus they attacked, in the vain hope of encircling the fighters of Islam from both sides.' It might well have been 'in vain', if the relief army had only planned to fight on the banks of the Danube.

By 11am, having steadied his infantry, and as they moved remorselessly forward to take the village of Nussdorf, trying, with difficulty, to keep formation in the broken country, Duke Charles rode across to confer with King John. Around noon, with the sun now high, the advance of the Christian left flank began to slow. To the east, both sides could hear the sounds of the continuing siege. Vienna could still fall at any time.

It was now that a huge cloud of dust from thousands of horses' hooves appeared above the Wienerwald, as the 20,000 cavalrymen of the Polish army moved into position. On the far right was Stanislaw Jablonowski, who had fought against the Swedes, Cossacks, Russians, Turks and Tartars, then the King himself, just under the Granberg feature, and finally Nicolas Sieniawski, another experienced and trusted commander. In front of the cavalry were the Polish infantry, stiffened by the German pikemen and musketeers sent by Lorraine. Twenty-eight guns, laboriously hauled up the mountain, were in support.

At 1pm, the three columns of the Polish force began to make their way slowly downhill, over treacherous broken ground. In the hour that it took them to negotiate the terrain and to begin to take up their battle positions, the Ottomans could see the Polish cavalry transform from a great cloud of dust into line upon line of mounted, armed men. Both sides now faced a dilemma. Given the terrain, and their assumptions about the Ottomans, Lorraine and Sobieski had both believed that progress would have been much slower on 12 September and that, despite the threat to the city, the day would have been spent beating off Ottoman attacks, while forming up and preparing for a fully coordinated attack on the 13th. The terrain, while looking bad, had in fact been easier to manoeuvre across and around than expected, and they had pushed forward further and faster than they had expected. It was now mid-afternoon, and Lorraine called a brief battlefield conference on the left, asking his commanders whether they should sustain the momentum of their current advance or pause to regroup properly. Legend has it that the Saxon general, von der Goltz, said that God was giving them this victory, and that they must fight on to achieve what He had ordained for them. Besides, he added, he was an old man and fancied a comfortable bed in Vienna that night. The ensuing silence was broken by explosive laughter: 'We march on,' said Lorraine. On the other side of the battlefield, Sobieski had come to the same conclusion.

Kara Mustapha was in a dreadful situation. Continuing the siege and holding off Duke Charles and his Habsburgs on the main Danube route was eminently doable, but the appearance of massed Polish cavalry further to his south-west presaged a disaster. Against the odds, and against advice, the Grand Vizier had gambled that weakness and division among the Christian powers had made Vienna vulnerable. He had been proved right, but he had then squandered the opportunity for a rapid assault and capture of the city by his lack of imagination and urgency, allied to arrogance and complacency. Just a few more days' delay in the Habsburg relief, better preparation, better coordinated assaults on the Viennese walls, or a serious attempt to guard and defend his western flank, may have brought him the time to achieve his mighty objective. Kara Mustapha had been on the cusp of joining the ranks of Islam and the Ottomans' greatest heroes, but he now faced total defeat. Just after 3.30pm, the Habsburg, Franconian, Bavarian and Saxon infantry, closely supported by their light horse artillery, renewed their assault along the line. By 5pm, the Unter and Oberdöbling villages had fallen, and Lorraine ordered the victorious troops to concentrate on the Türkenschanze, from the north.

As they attacked, they could see, to their south, the Poles begin a series of magnificent cavalry charges. The Turkish defenders had moved some artillery and a mass of *sipahis* to meet this threat, but there were no fortifications for them to rally or manoeuvre around, or from which to defend. Sobieski opened his offensive with a glorious charge by a large company of his armoured 'winged' Polish hussars. The splintering of their lances could be heard over the noise of battle and, although few returned, Sobieski had noted their effect on the Turks, and he prepared to launch all three of his mounted columns against their positions. He would not have done this on a European battlefield, but on 12 September 1683 he was not facing disciplined western pikemen and well-trained musketeers, but an increasingly demoralized Ottoman army that had sustained a gruelling siege for two months, and which now saw all prospect of victory and personal enrichment evaporating before their eyes.

Kara Mustapha, who by now had retreated to his great tent in the middle of the camp, could also see his own dreams and ambitions going up in smoke. Seeing him depart from the Türkenschanze, thousands of Ottoman troops had also joined in the withdrawal. Paralysed by fear and confusion, the Ottoman commanders could not bring any order to the defence of the Ottoman camp, and at around 6pm, Sobieski gave the order for a general advance. With the sun at their backs, almost 15,000 armoured horsemen went from a walk, into a trot, a canter and then, as they closed with the Ottomans, a gallop, as the front ranks lowered their lances, and the remainder drew their long, slashing cavalry sabres. In the face of this great armoured cavalry charge, the bulk of the Turkish opposition were swept aside, crushed or melted away, and vast numbers began to stream east. Kara Mustapha himself had rallied his spirits, and he even tried to lead a sortie against the flank of Jablonowski's troops, but most of his bodyguard were killed, and he was urged to leave the battlefield with the banner of the Prophet.[16] He needed little encouragement, and he departed the battlefield swiftly, taking his personal wealth with him and giving orders for the siege of Vienna to be abandoned. The Polish cavalry pursued the retreating Turkish army for some miles, then turned back to help systematically loot the vast treasure trove of the Ottoman camp.

Just 12 hours after the battle had begun, it had ended in total victory for the relief army. Lorraine, now on the Türkenschanze, sent a message to Starhemberg and the citizens of Vienna: the city was relieved. The garrison of Vienna had been watching all day as events had unfolded, even as they continued to battle among the rubble and the ruins of the Löbl and Burg bastions, terrified that a last Ottoman assault might make their heroic defence of the last weeks in vain. From the first flares over the Kahlenberg to Lorraine's formal message, four days later, their desperate defence had been bolstered by the prospect of relief. Now Starhemberg and all the dignitaries of the city emerged from the Scottish Gate to receive and greet some of the victorious commanders, while the Bavarian cavalry rode through the streets to 'the happy tunes of kettle drums and trumpets'. General von der Goltz spent one further night under canvas, as Lorraine and Sobieski ordered elements of the relief army to remain vigilant against the return of the Grand Vizier and his army. It never came. Vienna, the Holy Roman Empire and Christendom had been saved.

At sunrise on 13 September, the Viennese citizens poured out of the city via the Stuben Gate, after two months of close and anxious siege, clambering over the rubbish of the ramparts and the trenches, and wandering through the remains of the Ottoman camp. Among them was the gallant architect of the city's defence, Starhemberg, who made his way to receive the congratulations of the relief force commanders, who themselves were meeting for the first time since the mass at Kahlenberg. In the meantime, the Emperor had advanced as far as Dürrenstein in order to receive the most up-to-date reports, while the sound of a 300-gun salute from the ramparts was enough to convince people in the wider countryside that the preceding hours of silence heralded victory, not the fall of the city. However, as King John III Sobieski eventually made his way into Vienna, the Polish monarch was made painfully aware that demonstrations of Austrian gratitude were already being heavily constrained by Habsburg precedence, protocol and jealousy. A *Te Deum* was sung at the Augustine church and the sermon preached from the famous text, 'there was a man sent by God, and his name was John', plagiarizing Pope Pius V's words about Don Juan of Austria and the victory at the battle of Lepanto. However, there was little else in the way of official recognition for Poland's contribution, or indeed for that of any of the other monarchs, electors and princes. The Protestant Elector of Saxony was already marching north again within three days of the relief of the city, while King John, in his very candid letters to his French wife, Queen Marie, was soon complaining of a range of deliberate or casual snubs and obstructions to himself, personally, or to his soldiers.

While Polish and imperial cavalry continued in pursuit of a well-conducted withdrawal by the Ottomans, King John moved his headquarters to Schönau, about 15 miles from Vienna. This was both to avoid a protocol embarrassment with the arrival of the Emperor in his capital, and to escape the possibility of plague and disease. At last, on 15 September, to Leopold's evident distaste, a stilted meeting, conducted in Latin, took place between the Emperor and the King. While Austrians reported on the Emperor's cordiality, the King's private letters made it clear that Leopold, both as Emperor and man, did not enjoy being in debt to the Poles and that, in his inspection of the Polish soldiers, he neither deigned to thank them, 'even by raising his hat', nor did he give the King any mark of imperial favour. 'I am glad, Sire, to have rendered you this small service,' said King John pointedly at the conclusion of this awkward occasion, and the Emperor did at least have the grace to send the present of a sword to the newly knighted Prince James a few days later. Among his own commanders, including Duke

Charles of Lorraine, the Emperor was equally ungracious, and only Starhemberg received an appropriate reward in the form of 100,000 crowns, the Order of the Golden Fleece, and the rank of Field Marshal.

Despite such slights, animosities and jealousies, the perennial bane of Christian coalition armies, the decisive Ottoman defeat at Vienna offered an extraordinary opportunity for the Habsburgs and their allies to reverse the relentless Turkish advances of the last centuries. In addition, Emperor Leopold had by now developed an almost messianic vision of himself as a Christian leader against the infidel, and he sought daily pictorial reminders of his great imperial forebears as the exemplars of crusading prowess. Despite the continuing threat to his western borders from a predatory France, who had willed an Ottoman victory at Vienna, Leopold chose to sustain his papally subsidized coalition in the field against the Ottomans. On 17 September, the Polish army broke camp and marched east.

In the next months, despite setbacks, which included an over-enthusiastic John Sobieski and his son almost being captured by Ottoman cavalry, the Christian forces retook the great Ottoman-held fortresses of Gran and Esztergom. The latter had been taken by Sultan Suleiman himself, and it had heroically withstood a sustained siege in 1595. Now, in early December 1683, in return for exceptionally favourable conditions, the Ottoman commander surrendered the fortress a mere six days after the opening barrage. The loss of this potential future bridgehead for a renewed Ottoman offensive cost Kara Mustapha his life.

The Grand Vizier's first halt, after he had fled the battlefield, had been with his besieging troops at Raab. Here, he sought to reassert his authority by executing those he accused of treachery or cowardice. The victims included the sceptical Ibrahim Pasha of Buda, whose advice, if it had been followed, might have saved both Kara Mustapha and the Ottoman army. With him were executed, by beheading or strangling, two other pashas, the agha of Janissaries and 50 other lesser commanders. The Vizier then departed for Buda, sending messages ahead of him to Belgrade, in order to alert the Sultan to the 'setbacks' at Vienna, while attempting to distribute the blame for his own failures. When Kara Mustapha heard of the fall of Gran, he moved quickly to Belgrade, to try to intercept the Sultan, only to find that Mehmet had already departed for Edirne, where he was when he heard the news of the fall of Esztergom. Although the Sultan had only recently sent his Grand Vizier messages and gifts of royal approbation, this latest news was the final straw. Two court officials now went north to Belgrade, and on 25 December, at the time of the midday prayer, they showed Kara Mustapha the warrant from the Sultan demanding the return of his emblems of office, the Seal, the Holy Standard of the Prophet and the key to the Kaaba at Mecca. His fate was to be executed.

Kara Mustapha died well. Removing his fur-lined cloak and his turban, he handed them to a servant. Asking that the carpet be removed so that his body might fall on the earth, assuring his entry to Paradise, he knelt, arching his head and raising his beard. With practised ease, two executioners wound the soft silken bowstring around his neck, pulling steadily with all their strength until the Grand Vizier, with hardly a tremor, died. His body was lowered to the ground, his head severed from the corpse, and the skin of his skull expertly removed and stuffed with straw. Within an hour of their arrival, the little party was on its way back to Edirne, bearing with it the stuffed head of Kara Mustapha in a silk bag.

Throughout the winter of 1683–84, the Habsburgs worked feverishly to assemble a new army for the conquest of the east, and on 5 March 1684, Emperor Leopold, King John III Sobieski and the Doge of Venice signed an agreement to establish a new Holy League and to wage 'unceasing war' on the Ottomans, underpinned and subsidized by Pope Innocent XI. This was to be a pan-Christian enterprise, and the Orthodox Russians and even the Calvinist ruler of Brandenburg and the Prussians, Elector Fredrich Wilhelm, offered troops for this 'holy war'. On 14 June 1684, the coalition army, once again under the command of Duke Charles of Lorraine, and accompanied by the newly promoted Field Marshal Ernst Rüdiger von Starhemberg, was under the walls of the city of Buda, taken by the Ottomans in 1541, and held ever since. The city was not to finally fall until 1686.

In the intoxication of victory at Vienna, the Christian powers had wilfully discerned a collapse in Ottoman morale and fighting competence. Their fevered imaginations had been seized by the idea of more swift battlefield successes, which might even take them as far as the glittering waters of the Bosporus, with a Christian army once more marching through the gates of the great Theodosian Walls. They should have been warned by the tenacity of the Ottoman resistance during their march to Buda, but in 1684 no one was anticipating that this new stage of an old conflict would last for over 15 years, or that a debilitating succession of wars with the Turks would not be ended for another century. Although the failure of the siege of Vienna was rightly to be seen as the 'high-water mark of the Ottoman Empire', the ebbing of the Turkish tides was to prove to be a long, slow and hard-fought process.

PART SIX

The World Remade

He Stoops to Conquer

Jerusalem 1917

On 7 December 1917, the British and imperial troops of General
Edmund Allenby[1] had taken the city of Gaza, after a brilliant deception
operation that had totally misfooted the Turkish army, along with their
German and Austro-Hungarian allies and advisers. Having seized the
Ottoman positions from Gaza to Beersheba, supported by Captain T.
E. Lawrence[2] and his Arab irregular forces on his right, and open, desert
flank, Allenby, despite some understandable reservations, intended to
advance a further 60 miles to the Jaffa–Jerusalem line. It was late in
the year, but in a series of manoeuvres, conducted in foul weather and
fraught with operational risk, Allenby had succeeded in pushing the
Turks ever further north, taking the port of Jaffa on 16 November. His
advance produced scenes of panic in Jerusalem, where Field Marshal
Erich von Falkenhayn[3] had his headquarters. From Damascus, Djemal
Pasha,[4] one of the architects of the Ottoman entry into the war on the
German side, and of the subsequent Armenian Genocide, demanded
the expulsion of all Jews from the city, and the dynamiting of Christian
buildings. The Germans demurred, and Colonel von Papen[5] pleaded
with Falkenhayn to evacuate Jerusalem which, for all its religious
significance and importance, had no military strategic value. Papen
asked Falkenhayn to imagine global headlines reading, 'Huns blamed
for razing Holy City'. With bombs dropping around his headquarters,
and opium cigarettes being dropped by British aircraft in the hope
of intoxicating the Turkish soldiers, Falkenhayn finally moved his

headquarters to Nablus, taking a portrait of the Kaiser with him. On 4 December, the British bombed the Ottoman headquarters in the Russian Compound, while Turkish officers debated whether to fight or surrender, Turkish soldiers began to desert, and the last cartloads of the wounded made their way out of Jerusalem. On the evening of 7 December, the first British troops saw the city, although a heavy fog lay over Jerusalem, and rain was darkening the surrounding hills. At 3am on the 9th, the German forces withdrew, and by 7am the last Turk had departed by St Stephen's Gate.[6] At 8.45am, British soldiers approached the Sion Gate, the point from where Raymond St Gilles had launched his assault on the city in July 1099.

It was at this stage that the liberation of historic and holy Jerusalem somewhat descended into farce. Hussein al Husseini, the Mayor of Jerusalem, had been given a document by the Ottoman governor, with the declaration of the city's surrender. Declaring Jerusalem to be an 'open city' in order to avoid the destruction of the Holy Sites, the letter exhorted the British to 'protect Jerusalem the way we have protected it for more than five hundred years'. It was, in fact, only 400 years since Selim the Grim had taken control of Jerusalem from the Mamluks, along with the responsibility for the Holy Cities of Mecca and Medina, and the Turkish track record of municipal care and inter-faith harmony had been decidedly mixed. Notwithstanding this, al Husseini tore through the streets trying to find a white flag with which to formally surrender the city, although such a banner traditionally denoted the home of a marriageable virgin. A proffered white blouse was deemed to be inappropriate, but a bedsheet, taken from the Colony Hotel and tied to a broom handle, seemed to fit the bill. At last, the mayor set off to hand over Jerusalem, riding through the Jaffa Gate accompanied by a small, multi-faith retinue. However, this historical mission proved to be harder to fulfil than he had anticipated. The first British soldiers he came across were cooks. They were scavenging for eggs in a hen coop, and their commitment to providing breakfast for their commanding officer proved to be more compelling than the attractions of accepting al Husseini's surrender. Gathering an ever-greater 'comet-tail' of followers, he next encountered Sergeants James Sedgewick and Fred Hurcombe of 2/19th Battalion, the London Regiment, who were equally reluctant to seize their moment in history, but who consented to be photographed with the mayor and his party, and to accept some cigarettes.

Al Husseini was further rejected by two British artillery officers, who turned down the honour of taking the surrender of Jerusalem, but who swore that they would inform their headquarters. The mayor then met Colonel Bailey, who informed Brigadier Watson, who summoned General Shea, who, galloping to the Tower of David, accepted the surrender on behalf of General Allenby, who, in his turn, eventually heard this news in his tent near Jaffa, where he was talking to Lawrence of Arabia. Meanwhile, a squadron of the Westminster Dragoons, a British Yeomanry cavalry regiment, rode into the city to help secure the key establishments; they were the first formed body of Christian soldiers to enter Jerusalem since the crusader garrison had been bloodily evicted by the Khwarezmians in 1244.

Accompanied by the sound of his artillery still pursuing the retreating Turks, Allenby rode to the Jaffa Gate. Prime Minister Lloyd George[7] had hoped to deliver the news of Jerusalem's surrender as 'a Christmas present for the British people', weary at the close of the fourth year of the world war. Allenby had allowed him to fulfil this wish. 'The capture of Jerusalem has made a most profound impression throughout the civilised world,' Lloyd George wrote shortly after hearing the news. 'The most famous city in the world, after centuries of strife and vain struggle, has fallen into the hands of the British Army, never to be restored to those who so successfully held it against the embattled hosts of Christendom.'

In October 1898, Kaiser Wilhelm II, Emperor of the newly formed German Empire,[8] had visited Jerusalem as part of an extensive trip around the increasingly frail Ottoman Empire. In a style typical of the man and his imperial pretensions, the Kaiser chose to enter the Holy City mounted on a large white horse and wearing a white uniform, a golden neck covering and a helmet surmounted by an impressive golden eagle. He was flanked by German soldiers who carried mock-crusader banners, summoning up images of the medieval Teutonic Knights, whose reputation for military prowess and ruthlessness had been adopted as part of the ethos of the powerful modern Prussian state. To permit this cavalcade into the city, without the Kaiser having the embarrassment of having to stoop or duck his head, the Ottoman authorities had been prevailed upon to remove the gate of the Jaffa Gate, and to blast an opening in the Old City walls. Such actions may have achieved their diplomatic task of fatally solidifying the relationship between Germany and the Ottomans, but the locals – Muslim, Jewish and Christian alike – were shocked.

In December 1917, despite a hubristic British press and cartoonists drawing parallels between Allenby and Richard the Lionheart, the Foreign Office telegraphed the General, advising him to avoid such 'Kaiserine' grandiosity: 'Strongly suggest dismounting,' said the telegram. Allenby did not need any such advice. Although he went by the nickname 'the Bloody Bull', he was a well-read man, of considerable sensitivity, whose soul had been tempered by the recent death of his only son on the Western Front. He too warned his own staff against using crusader analogies, imagery or language in their reports and negotiations. At last, in the late morning of 11 December 1917, General Allenby, Commander-in-Chief of the Egypt Expeditionary Forces, rode to the walls of Jerusalem on his horse, Hindenburg, where he dismounted and, in contrast to the Kaiser, walked through the still gate-less Jaffa Gate. He was accompanied by the American, French and Italian legates, and by Lawrence of Arabia, who was clearly overwhelmed by the historical significance of the moment. They were met by all the patriarchs, rabbis, muftis, imams and consuls of the city, while a mounted guard of honour, provided by the Australian 10th Light Horse Regiment, kept watch.

Allenby and the official party now climbed the steps of a platform erected near the Citadel of David and, to a hushed audience, Allenby read out his statement acknowledging the importance and uniqueness of 'blessed Jerusalem':

Since your city is regarded with affection by the adherents of three of the great religions of mankind, and its soil is consecrated by the prayers and pilgrimages of devout people of these three religions for many centuries, I make known to you that every sacred building, monument, holy spot, shrine, traditional site, endowment, pious bequest or customary place of worship, of whatever form of the three religions, will be maintained and protected according to the existing customs and beliefs of those to whose faith they are sacred.

His proclamation was then repeated in French, Hebrew, Arabic, Russian, Greek and Italian, and those inhabitants who still remained in the city applauded loudly, while remaining understandably apprehensive about the future.[9]

Mayor al Husseini now made a seventh, and finally successful, formal surrender of Jerusalem. Despite his own instructions, as Mayor al Husseini at last handed over to him the keys of the city, Allenby is supposed to have said, 'The Crusades have now ended.' Allenby then marched back out of the Jaffa Gate and remounted his horse, while the cheering of the crowds was accompanied by the sound of German aircraft firing in support of a local Turkish counter-attack. Allenby was at this stage unaware of the recent signing of the Balfour Declaration[10] that stated, 'His Majesty's Government view with favour the establishment in Palestine of a national home for the Jewish people.' Nor was he fully aware of the profound differences between the provisions of the Sykes-Picot[11] Agreement, which had divided the post-war 'spoils' of the Ottoman Middle East between Britain and France, and the promises made by Great Britain to the Sharif of Mecca in the McMahon-Hussein[12] correspondence, of which Lawrence of Arabia considered himself the guardian. At lunch, following the surrender ceremony, Georges Picot, the French envoy, turned to Allenby. 'And tomorrow, my dear General,' he said, 'I'll take the necessary steps to set up civil government in the town.' Lawrence reported the incident in his magisterial book, *Seven Pillars of Wisdom*: 'A silence followed. Salad, chicken mayonnaise and foie gras sandwiches hung in our wet mouths unmunched while we turned to Allenby and gaped. His face grew red, he swallowed, his chin coming forward (in the way we loved) whilst he said grimly: "The only authority is that of the Commander-in-Chief – MYSELF."'

The administration of Jerusalem proved to be a bureaucratic and diplomatic nightmare from the start, and when the brilliant, immaculate and fastidious Sir Ronald Storrs arrived on 20 December as Military Governor he was horrified to discover the squalid reality of the city. His predecessor, General Barton, assured him that the only tolerable places in Jerusalem were 'bath and bed'. Meanwhile the Ottoman–German defences were hardening to the north, and the bad weather that Allenby had feared was significantly hampering his operations. He had wanted to advance to the Beirut–Damascus line, but for this he required an additional 16 or 18 divisions. Instead, the Germans launched their last great offensive on the Western Front in March 1918,[13] and Allenby found himself having to provide 60,000 urgently needed reinforcements for Field Marshal Douglas Haig. It was only in late summer 1918, after the Germans had been roundly pushed back in France and Flanders, that Allenby was able to continue the advance that would lead to the eventual capitulation of the Ottoman Empire. This was effected with the signing of the Armistice of Mudros[14] on 31 October 1918, 11 days before the guns, at last, fell silent on the Western Front.

The failure of the siege of Vienna in 1683, and the eventual fall of Buda in 1686, had precipitated the fall of Sultan Mehmet IV. His early reign had seen victories in Crete and against the Poles and the Russians, but in the wake of his defeats in Austria and Hungary, he seemed to become indifferent to the fate of the empire, ignoring the Janissary demands to give up hunting, and neglecting his army, his subjects and his religious obligations. Retreating to Constantinople, his image as a *ghazi* commander, or as a champion of *jihad*, was fatally compromised. The imperial treasury was empty, and the customary incentives of God, gold and glory for his soldiers seemed over. As Ottoman territory contracted, the land grants that subsidized the *sipahis* and gave them the means for social advantage became fewer. The new Grand Vizier imposed swingeing new taxes on an increasingly restive religious class, and when, in 1687, the new Holy League had inflicted a further defeat on the Turks at Mohacs – the scene of Sultan Suleiman's great victory of 1526 – jurists and Janissaries alike rounded on the Sultan. The execution of the Grand Vizier did not assuage their anger, and they marched on the capital, gathering in Hagia Sophia for as long as it took to establish a case for deposition. At this point they had dethroned Mehmet IV and had pulled his terrified, younger brother out of the harem and placed him on the throne, as Sultan Suleiman II.

With the Ottoman Empire in a state of turmoil, the Holy League had continued to make progress in central Europe. In 1697 they destroyed an Ottoman army, led by the Sultan himself, at the battle of Zenta. The subsequent 1699 Treaty of Karlowitz, known as 'the Austrian Treaty that saved Europe', established the enlarged Habsburg

Empire as a dominant power in European politics. It was a watershed moment in history, whereby the Ottomans lost substantial amounts of territory, after three and a half centuries of expansion into Europe. Although the Ottoman borders would wax and wane over the next 100 years, never again would they acquire territory on the scale of Mehmet the Conqueror, Selim the Grim, or Suleiman the Magnificent (see map on p.16).

While the Ottoman, Safavid, Habsburg, French and Spanish empires were clearly defined by their religious identity and culture, the wars between them were losing their distinctively religious character, as they became part of a more modern competition for power, territory and wealth. Despite the opportunities presented by a major revolt of the Janissaries in 1703, from 1703 to 1714 all the European powers were preoccupied with the War of the Spanish Succession, where both Catholic Austria and the Protestant British and Dutch were at war with the French to thwart their attempts to put a Bourbon candidate on the throne of Spain. These were the great days of Marlborough[15] and Eugene of Savoy,[16] of the battles of Blenheim and Ramillies, and of the British seizure of Gibraltar, and they marked a major check on French ambitions in Europe. However, despite the continuing threat of France, and the obvious weakening of the Ottomans, the Habsburgs remained pathologically fearful of a Turkish revival, and continued to pour much of their imperial wealth into fortifying their eastern borders.

The 1739 Treaty of Belgrade fixed the imperial demarcation line between Ottomans and Habsburgs on the rivers Danube and Sava, while Ottoman treaties with the dying Safavid dynasty in 1748 largely confirmed the borders that had been agreed between the Sunni sultan-caliphs and the Shia shahs in the mid-16th century. These agreements gave the Ottomans nearly half a century of relative peace and calm, and during this period there was a significant growth in economic, cultural, diplomatic, intellectual, academic and social engagement between the Ottomans and the Europeans. However, the baton of Christian confrontation with the Islamic world was now being taken up by the Russian tsars. Two growing internal challenges, which were confronting all empires of the time, added to the pressure that this burgeoning new external threat posed to the Ottomans. The first was that of tension between the social and religious conservatives, who sought imperial renewal in a return to the values and mores of the early empire, and the political and technical reformists, who feared that without change there would be revolution or further military defeats. The second was that of nationalism, which would increasingly challenge the multi-cultural, multi-ethnic foundations of the Ottoman Empire and state.

The foundations of the new Russian Empire had been laid by Tsar Peter the Great's remarkable reform programme of the early 18th century, which significantly altered the political and social structure of this hitherto medieval country, and by military success in the Great Northern War against Sweden, which strengthened Russia's standing on the world stage. At the signing of the Treaty of Nystad in 1721, Peter accepted the title of 'Emperor of all Russia', ushering in the transformation of the country from a tsardom to an empire. In 1722 he had fired the opening shots in a long war with the weakening Persian Safavids, aimed at establishing Russia as a power in the Caucasus and on the Caspian Sea. His successor, Empress Anna, subsequently took up the long-standing struggle with the Ottomans in Ukraine and on the Black Sea, and severely weakened the Crimean Khanate, the Ottomans' long-time vassal. The Seven Years War,[17] involving all the major European powers in a conflict of global proportions, did give the Ottomans some breathing space for reform and regeneration, but in 1768 Sultan Mustapha III was both provoked and urged into initiating a war with the Russian Empire. The Russians were spoiling for a fight, and it was a long, bloody and expensive six-year disaster for the Turks, in which they lost territory, soldiers and reputation. At one stage, they feared that a Russian fleet, which had sailed to the Mediterranean from the Baltic Sea, might even bombard or take Constantinople.

At the 1774 Treaty of Kucuk Kaynarca, the Ottomans made a lame claim to be allowed 'protector status' over the Muslim inhabitants of their lost territories, giving the Russians the excuse to demand a similar status with regard to all Orthodox Christians within the Ottoman Empire. The Russians would soon use the provisions of the treaty as a rationale for extending their power, and their pretensions, even further. In 1783 the Russians annexed Crimea, and under Catherine the Great there were growing calls for the conquest of Constantinople, the re-establishment of the former Byzantine Empire under the Russians, and the re-consecration of Hagia Sophia as the main church of Christendom. The Russian tsars were clearly looking to inherit the mantle of the Roman and Byzantine emperors, as the Ottomans had done before them.

The start of a long process of Muslims retreating to the heartlands of the Ottoman Empire, which would accelerate throughout the 19th century, was also beginning to gather pace. The outbreak of the Revolutionary and Napoleonic Wars had again consumed the attention of the great European powers, but Bonaparte's expedition to Egypt had led to the end of the Franco–Ottoman alliance that had been in active, sometimes passive, operation since the 1520s. It also accelerated the detachment of the Arab and North African provinces, of which Egypt was the most important, from the Ottoman centre. Meanwhile, the French revolutionary calls for 'liberty, equality and fraternity' further weakened the bonds that bound the heterogenous groups of the Ottoman Empire, both Muslim and Christian, to the Sultan-Caliph in Constantinople.

By the end of the Napoleonic period, it was clear that Russia, as one of the victorious allies, now posed a threat to both the western European powers and to the Ottomans. The prospect of the Russian army in Constantinople and the Russian navy controlling the Black Sea, the Bosporus and the eastern Mediterranean was both credible and also something the British, French or Habsburgs could not afford to contemplate. However, the Ottomans looked ill-prepared and ill-equipped to counter Russian ambitions on their own. A succession of reform efforts had led to further internal turmoil, with Janissary risings, the executions of viziers, and the deposition of sultans. In 1826, Sultan Mahmud II engineered a final confrontation with his rebellious, overpaid, parasitic and unpopular Janissaries. In yet another attempt to create a new army, relevant for the new era of modern warfare, the Sultan had ordered hundreds of men to be taken out of each Janissary unit and made into an elite corps based on new drills, tactics, uniforms and weapons. As expected, the Janissaries in Constantinople rose in revolt, but, inspired by the Sultan-Caliph's call for *jihad* and by the sight of the Prophet's banner raised at the Sultan Ahmed Mosque,[18] troops loyal to the Sultan, and armed men from across the city, slaughtered the Janissaries around the Hippodrome, while others were burnt to death in their barracks. The elite backbone of the Ottoman armies for five centuries was wiped out in less than an hour. Surviving Janissaries fled, while thousands of other Janissaries in provinces across the empire were hunted down and despatched. The entire corps, the military backbone of Ottoman imperial greatness, and the terror of Christian Europe for half a millennium, was abolished.

The European powers at the Congress of Vienna,[19] which had ended the Napoleonic Wars, had disregarded the Ottomans as equal partners, and under their encouragement Serbia and Greece had gained large degrees of autonomy, although the Greek War of Independence[20] had been marked by appalling atrocities on both sides. The process had been accelerated by further turmoil within the Ottoman army, and by the destruction of the Ottoman fleet at Navarino in 1827. Around the same time, the French had occupied Algeria, while Mehmet Ali,[21] the ruler of Egypt and nominal vassal of the Sultan-Caliph in Constantinople, chose to extend his own power into the Ottoman lands of Palestine and Syria. Here his armies – descendants of the Mamluks, under his son, Ibrahim Pasha – swiftly defeated the newly mustered 'modern' Ottoman army sent to counter his advance. After diplomacy had failed, Ibrahim Pasha led his forces into Anatolia and, having defeated another army at Konya, stood poised to advance on the Ottoman capital and seize it. At this stage Sultan Mahmud appealed to Britain and France for assistance, but when they turned him down, he had no option but to seek the support of his former enemy, Russia. Tsar Nicholas I, who was soon to coin the phrase that the Ottoman Empire was, 'the sick man of Europe', was commendably quick to respond, and Mehmet Ali halted his son's advance. Britain and France sent ships to the Dardanelles and, in the 1833 Treaty of Unkiar Skelessi, the Russians agreed to withdraw from Ottoman territory, while Mehmet Ali was granted control of Egypt, Syria, Tripoli and Crete.

The whole episode had made the British and French deeply worried that the Ottomans were, to all intents and purposes, vassals of the Russians, and it brought home to them the fragility of the Ottoman

Empire, and the possible consequences should it collapse. British policy was now that 'the Ottoman Empire was to be preserved, supported, reformed and strengthened'. Lord Palmerston, the British Foreign Secretary, declared, 'All that we hear about the decay of the Turkish Empire, and its being a dead body or a sapless trunk, is pure nonsense. Given ten years of peace under European protection, coupled with internal reform, there seems no reason why it should not again become a respectable power.' On this basis, the 1840 Convention of London committed a broader European coalition to 'maintaining Ottoman integrity'. They got their ten years, but not much more. Unfortunately, the ambitions of the European powers continued to diverge, and British and French military support to the Turks against the Russians, in the Crimean War of 1853 to 1856, starkly demonstrated the realpolitik of a vastly changed world.

The 1856 Peace of Paris had removed the Russian naval threat in the Black Sea and gave the Ottomans another 20 years of relative stability, in which they initiated another round of internal political, social and economic reforms. In contrast, Europe found itself dealing with the fallout of the 1848 revolutions, and the collapse of the 1814 'Concert of Europe', so painstakingly, and successfully established at the Congress of Vienna.

There was a revival of great power competition, between a new French Empire, under Napoleon III, an increasingly bellicose Prussia, and a declining Habsburg Empire. Britian was becoming an increasingly powerful maritime force, but its complacency had been shaken by the Indian Mutiny, while a resentful Russia was looking for new opportunities to resume its imperial march to the south and to the east.

In 1859, the French had thrown the Habsburgs out of northern Italy, while Cavour and Garibaldi had taken advantage of this to unify the Italian peninsula, from the Alps to Sicily, including the Papal States. 'We have made Italy. We must now make Italians,' declared the Piedmontese statesman Massimo d'Azeglio. In 1866, the Prussians had defeated the Austro-Hungarian army at Sadowa, and in 1871 they, and their German allies, had inflicted a catastrophic defeat on Emperor Napoleon III at

Sedan, which had led to the collapse of the French Third Empire, and the rise of the Second German Reich.

In 1875, the Ottomans experienced new disasters, when they suffered bankruptcy, with all the attendant problems, on top of a series of droughts, flooding and famines. Large-scale creditors, notably Britain and France, withdrew their support,[22] inflation wiped out a nascent middle class, and rising taxes provoked social unrest and nationalist rebellions in the Balkan provinces and in Armenian eastern Anatolia. A new cycle of Muslim and Christian atrocity and counter-atrocity led to a parliamentary and public outcry in Britain, much of it orchestrated by the great Liberal Party leader William Gladstone. In Constantinople, Sultan Abdulaziz I was deposed and committed suicide, while his replacement, Murad, was rapidly perceived to be mentally unstable and he too was also swiftly defenestrated. Murad's brother now became Sultan Abdulhamid II, who initiated his reign with his 1876 constitution – a bold, albeit divisive and unsettling, programme of political, religious and economic reform. In a sustained period of peace, such a programme may, possibly, have stabilized the Ottoman Empire, but the Russians, watching this power-play in Constantinople, sensed an opportunity to undo the verdict of the Crimean War and the Peace of Paris, without fear of British intervention. Therefore, in 1877, after the Ottomans had rejected their demands for Bulgarian autonomy, the Russians launched the eighth war in their long confrontation with the Ottomans.

The Russian plan was to advance through the southern Caucasus and eastern Anatolia in order to take the great fortress of Kars, while in the Balkans they intended to establish an independent Bulgaria, recover the territories lost in the Peace of Paris, and re-establish themselves on the Black Sea. They were successful in the east, taking Kars, while their bloody campaign in Bulgaria forced a mass exodus of hundreds of thousands of Muslims from south-east Europe, who made their sad, tired way to Anatolia. After a gruelling seven-month siege, the Russians finally took the fortress and town of Plevna, marched through Thrace, occupied the old Ottoman capital of Edirne, and, by March 1878, they had reached San Stefano, only 8 miles from Constantinople. Nothing now seemed to stand between the Russians and the destruction of the Ottoman Empire, and the incredible but possible prospect of the re-establishment of an Orthodox empire in its place.

Instead, worried about the reaction of other European powers to their maximalist agenda, the Russians signed the Treaty of San Stefano, which gave Serbia, Romania and Montenegro independence, provided autonomy to Bosnia and Herzegovina, and created a large, Russian-occupied Bulgaria which stretched from the Black Sea to the Aegean. In July 1878, only three months after San Stefano, Britain and Austria-Hungary compelled the Russians to accept the Treaty of Berlin, and the return of half of their newly created Bulgaria back to the Ottomans, along with Edirne. Britain gained Cyprus. Within a year of his accession, Sultan Abdulhamid II had lost nearly one-third of the remaining Ottoman territory and, in 1882, the British would establish a de facto Protectorate over Egypt, securing, with it, their control of the newly opened Suez Canal.[23] In the face of these defeats and losses, Abdulhamid II turned his back on reform and, instead, approached the problems of his empire through the familiar mechanisms of authoritarianism and repression.

The war with Russia exacerbated every tension within Ottoman society, as they struggled to discern a path forward in the face of decline and defeat. The empire's weakness in the Balkans, the Caucasus, the Middle East and North Africa gave the European empires ample opportunity for imperial expansion and, with it, further great power confrontation. Reformers clashed with conservatives, Ottomans with nationalists, and secularists and liberals with the religious establishment. The Sultan sought to thread a path between being more Ottoman, thereby reaching out to all subjects of the empire regardless of religion or ethnicity; more Islamic, in order to bolster his authority as Caliph and the nominal leader of all Muslims; and, at the same time, more Turkish, that core element of Ottoman history and power. This gravity-defying act may have been possible under a strong sultan, with the Ottomans on the front foot, but after a century of turmoil and failure it was a doomed project.

Abdulhamid II's response to opposition was now a crackdown on dissent, and a reversal of much of his own constitutional reform agenda, and that of his predecessors. He had his supporters, as all dictators do. The military craved a reassertion of Ottoman power, the religious class supported his Islamization programme, and many just sought revenge for the betrayal by so many former Ottoman subjects. Casting around for friends, the Sultan secured a close association with the new, expansionist German Empire, and with its ambitious head of state, Kaiser Wilhelm II. Protestant Christian Germany would train the Muslim Ottoman army, and German industry and engineering would power Turkish economic renewal. At the heart of this would be a new and exciting project: the Berlin–Baghdad railway, linking Constantinople to western Europe, to the great centres of Islamic classical history, and to the Holy Cities of Mecca and Medina. It was in this context that Kaiser Wilhelm had had a passage blasted in the walls of the Old City of Jerusalem, in order to accommodate the gilded Prussian eagle on the top of his impressive Teutonic helmet.

However, more legion than Abdulhamid II's external friends were his internal enemies and opponents, who opposed his closing of parliament, his suspension of the constitution, his religious obscurantism and his authoritarianism. In 1908, as their old enemy, Russia, was still recoiling from the revolution that had followed its shock defeat against Japan in the Far East, and while the French and the British, fearful of an increasingly aggressive Kaiser, were secretly honing their own joint military plans to confront Germany, the Turkish Committee for Union and Progress (CUP) staged a constitutional revolution of their own within the Ottoman Empire. The CUP was a long-standing, broad and eclectic coalition of Ottoman optimists and pessimists, inspired by the past, fearful of the present, and with a diverse set of plans and hopes for the future.[24] The coup of 1908 was hardly on a par with the storming of the Bastille, but it did force Abdulhamid II to reinstate his 1876 constitution and, in the elections later that year, CUP candidates took 287 out of 288 seats. A counter-revolution in the following year led by conservative members of the religious classes was met with violence by the military adherents of the CUP, including an officer from Salonika, Mustapha Kemal.[25] Abdulhamid II was deposed and went into exile.

His successor, Sultan Mehmet V, would preside over the final decade of the Ottoman Empire.

———

After the 1908 revolution, the Austro-Hungarians had annexed Bosnia and Herzegovina, Bulgaria had declared full independence, and Crete had proclaimed a formal union with Greece. The French had occupied Algeria in 1830, and in 1848 they had made it an integral part of 'Metropolitan' France. They took Tunisia in 1881, while the British had put Egypt 'under protection' in 1882. In 1911, taking advantage of the turmoil in Constantinople, Italy had occupied the two Ottoman provinces of Tripolitania and Cyrenaica in North Africa, forming the new political entity of Libya. They had also seized the Dodecanese Islands off south-west Anatolia, including Rhodes, taken for the Ottomans by Suleiman the Magnificent in 1522. The 1912 Treaty of Fez had made Morocco a protectorate of France, leading to a major diplomatic incident with the Germans, while Spain continued to retain its holdings on the Moroccan coast. The glory days of massed fleets of Ottoman and Barbary Coast galleys sweeping down on Christian towns, forts and harbours were long over, and the whole North African coastline was now under one form of Christian jurisdiction or another.

Worst of all for the Ottomans were the two Balkan Wars. In October 1912, an alliance of former Ottoman provinces – now the independent states of Bulgaria, Greece, Montenegro and Serbia – declared war on the empire in order to seize Macedonia and the great port city of Salonika. These were all peoples who had marched or sailed with the Ottoman armies and navies in the great days of Ottoman conquest in the east and the west, and in the Mediterranean Sea. Now, attacking on multiple fronts, they overwhelmed the unprepared Ottoman armies, who withdrew to positions about 30 miles from Constantinople, leaving Edirne under siege. Salonika, captured by the Ottomans in 1430, fell to the Greeks in November, and in armistice talks, the Ottoman government agreed to the ceding of Edirne – the Ottoman capital from 1369 to 1453, and second city of the empire for over 400 years. This was too much for the CUP leadership. Talaat Pasha and Enver Pasha[26] stormed a cabinet meeting, killing the Grand Vizier's guard and the Minister for War and, putting a gun to the Grand Vizier's head, forcing his resignation. It was a fruitless operation, as Edirne fell to the Bulgarians in March 1913. However, the Balkan powers now rounded on each other and started to attack the Bulgarians. Sensing an opportunity, Enver Pasha retook Edirne. It was both an important and a symbolic victory, but this success could not disguise the fact that the Ottomans had lost almost all of their vast territories in Europe, including some of the oldest provinces taken in the 14th century.

The wars were not 'religious wars', as such, but they were conducted by 'peoples of religion' who put a high premium on their religious identity, and the bloodshed reflected a deep atavistic loathing on both sides. Every party seized on both history and religion to construct myths and legends that relied on the selective employment of historical inspiration, historical grievance and historical entitlement. The Balkan Wars reignited and exacerbated anti-Christian feeling among Ottoman Muslims, as a further several hundred thousand refugees streamed into Constantinople, and across the Bosporus into Anatolia. In retaliation, Mehmet Talat ordered the expulsion of 150,000 Greeks, long-term Ottoman subjects. Ottoman and Muslim tolerance – a hallmark of their huge, multi-ethnic and multi-cultural empire for so long – was now in increasingly short supply.

When Serbian militants assassinated Archduke Franz Ferdinand and his wife in Sarajevo on 28 June 1914, the Ottomans at first sought an anti-Serb alliance with Britain and France, which was rebuffed. They turned then to the Germans, with whom relations had been growing since the Treaty of Berlin in 1878. By August, as the Austro-Hungarians were about to attack Serbia, and thereby initiate a cataclysmic global conflict, a secret agreement had been signed between Berlin and Constantinople, aimed at their mutual enemy, the Russian Empire. By joining the Central Powers, the Ottomans found themselves fighting alongside the Habsburg heirs to centuries of Christian–Muslim conflict in the lands between Belgrade and Vienna, and also in concert with their recent Christian Bulgarian foes. They were staggeringly ill-equipped for the demands of modern industrial mass warfare but, like governments and populations in many other countries, the Ottomans saw war as offering a cathartic experience that might somehow bond the empire back together and might provide some almost mystical panacea for the political and societal traumas of the previous decades. Enver Pasha captured a prevalent mood in Constantinople when he contemplated war with Russia: 'Our hatred is intensifying; revenge, revenge, revenge, there is nothing else.'

Winston Churchill,[27] the British 'First Lord of the Admiralty', had inflamed Turkish and Ottoman sensitivities when, in August 1914, on the outbreak of war with Germany, he had arbitrarily 'requisitioned' two Turkish warships being built in British shipyards, which had been paid for by vast 'public subscription'. Seizing on this opportunity, the Germans had managed to evade the Royal Navy in the Mediterranean and bring two of their own cruisers into Constantinople, which they then, very publicly and ostentatiously, 'gifted' to the Ottomans, while the German crews paraded on the deck wearing Turkish fezzes. Enver Pasha then sent the cruisers into the Black Sea, sporting Ottoman flags, where, to the perplexity of the Russians, they bombarded the port of Odessa. By November 1914, the Ottoman Empire was at war with Russia and with Russia's allies, Great Britain and France. It was to be a disaster for all involved, leading to the collapse of both the Russian and Ottoman empires, and involving the Allied Powers in a series of campaigns that engaged millions of soldiers, cost hundreds of thousands of casualties, and catalysed the massacre of the Armenian population of the Ottoman Empire. Ottoman entry into the war undoubtedly extended the Allies' conflict with Germany and Austro-Hungary by a number of hugely costly years.

In December 1914, Enver Pasha, gambling on a quick Russian collapse, had driven his 100,000-strong Turkish Third Army into the Caucasus, hoping to reverse the losses of the war of 1877–78, and to recover the eastern provinces of Anatolia, and the great frontier fortress of Kars. Logistic lines of communication for the 500 miles east beyond Ankara were appalling, as was the weather and, by the end of the battle of Sarikamis in late December, the Turks had already lost nearly 90,000 troops.

An attack on the Suez Canal in early 1915 was equally unsuccessful, as was a call for *jihad* by the Sultan-Caliph, designed to test the loyalty of the Muslim soldiers of the British and French empires. However, in spring 1915, the Ottoman Empire made, once again, one of their extraordinary recoveries, when they held the Gallipoli Peninsula in the Dardanelles against a bold Allied amphibious operation. Characterized by overconfidence, romanticism, poor planning, inefficiency and uninspiring leadership, the Anglo-French ambitions were broken on the back of German staff professionalism; the brave, stoical defence of the Turkish infantry; and the heroic command example of Mustapha Kemal. In spring 1916 there was a further Turkish victory, at Kut-al-Amara south of Baghdad, where a British-Indian division was besieged and forced to surrender. The British and Indian prisoners had a miserable captivity, with the Muslims treated far more harshly than their Christian fellow soldiers, although their commander, General Charlie Townsend, spent the rest of the war in relative comfort on the island of Buyukada, some miles off Constantinople in the Sea of Marmara.

The Allied threats, and some early Russian successes in the east, had inspired the Patriarch in Russian Armenia to call for a general Armenian rising against the Turks, which had considerably more success than the competing call by the Caliph for *jihad*. This call, and the Armenian response, provoked the government in Constantinople into deadly countermeasures. Whether the horrible fate of many Armenians in the Ottoman Empire was designed or planned as deliberate 'genocide', or whether the deaths were the result of bureaucratic indifference, appalling administrative inefficiency, banditry and a desire for revenge in the midst of the chaos of an existential struggle, is still heatedly debated. Whatever the mixture of causes, around 1.5 million Armenians died, and their deaths remain a source of trauma and remembrance in that widely dispersed community, to this day.

By 1917, the military effort was causing vast hardship, with inflation, desertions, disease, famine and starvation. The empire was only saved from complete collapse by the inertia of the Allied armies in Salonika, where they had concentrated after the failures in the Dardanelles, and the onset of the Russian Revolution, in which the Tsar was deposed in March, and the Bolsheviks seized power in October. The Germans took advantage of the Russian collapse to seize vast swathes of land in the east, signing the Treaty of Brest-Litovsk with the new Soviet government in March 1918. A parallel treaty between Soviet Russia and the Ottomans was signed in the German headquarters in the same month.

Not anticipating this Russian collapse, which in reality had become increasingly likely after the failure to open supply routes to the Black Sea, the Allies had incrementally explored other ideas to bring about Ottoman collapse. One of these was to exploit the nationalist ambitions of the Arabic leadership and the Arab population of the Ottoman Empire. This option became even more attractive in the wake of the failure of the Turkish attacks on the Suez Canal, and especially after the disappointments of the Gallipoli campaign.

Hussein Hashemi was the Sharif of Mecca, and a direct descendant of the Prophet Muhammad. He was *ashraf*, 'honoured', because of his ancestry, a man with legitimacy and moral authority among Muslims. He was also an opponent of the CUP's centralizing instincts and measures, and he had refused to back the Caliph's call for *jihad* against the British and French. The much-publicized mass execution of Arab nationalist leaders in Damascus by Djemel Pasha hardened his position. Encouraged, in correspondence, by the British High Commissioner in Egypt, Lieutenant Colonel Sir Henry McMahon, Sharif Hussein decided to take advantage of the opportunities presented to the Arabs by the world war, and rebel. He was rapidly supported by the British, who sent him guns, explosives, money and Captain Thomas Edward Lawrence.

In January 1916, when still an intelligence officer in Cairo, Lawrence had written of the prospect of an Arab revolt. It would be beneficial to Great Britain, he wrote, 'because it marches with our immediate aims, the break-up of the Islamic bloc and the defeat and disruption of the Ottoman Empire, and because the states that Sharif Hussein would set up to succeed the Turks would be harmless to ourselves, as the Arabs are even less stable than the Turks'. In June 1916, the Arab Revolt began in the Hejaz region of western Arabia. They took the Holy City of Mecca on 9 July 1916, when shells from the nearby Ottoman garrison hit the Great Mosque, setting fire to the canopy of the Kaaba and destroying the name of Caliph Uthman on the mosque's façade. This damage turned out to be a potent propaganda weapon for the Hashemites, who portrayed the Ottomans as having desecrated Islam's most holy site, and the Arab defenders took it as an omen that the Ottoman dynasty would fall, as the Turkish equivalent of Uthman is Osman.

Lawrence progressively galvanized the Arab Revolt, identifying Prince Feisal as the most promising of Sharif Hussein's sons, developing a strategy for the most effective use of the irregular Bedouin 'cavalry', harassing the Turkish lines of communication, especially the Hejaz railway between Damascus and the Holy Cities, and making the case for ever-greater British support for the Arabs. In the meantime, the British imperial armies were advancing, in strength, against the Turkish positions in the Sinai and the Levant. In June 1917, General Edmund Allenby had arrived in Cairo to assume command of the Egyptian Expeditionary Force from General Archibald Murray, who had had some successes in 1916, but who had suffered defeats at the first and second battles of Gaza in March and April 1917. At the same time, General Stanley Maude in Iraq had recovered from the reverses of Kut-al-Amara the previous year and had taken the former Abbasid capital of Baghdad.

Soon after his arrival in Cairo, Allenby had received the news of Lawrence's success in taking the port of Aqaba on 9 July and, shortly after that, the news of his own son's death. Conscious that the battles of Ypres and Passchendaele were beginning to unfold on the Western Front, and that he could expect no reinforcements, Allenby had reorganized his army, including establishing more formal arrangements with the forces of the Arab Revolt. In late October 1917 he won the third battle of Gaza, after a brilliant deception plan and an inspiring attack on Beersheba, which had outflanked the heavily defended Ottoman positions. It was as a result of this success that Allenby had marched through the Jaffa Gate on 11 December 1917 to receive the great key of Jerusalem from Mayor Hussein al Husseini.

In spring 1918, the German army, massively reinforced from the Eastern Front after the collapse of Russia, had launched a series of spectacular, large-scale offensives on the Western Front. However, by July, they had failed to achieve their objectives. Now, under Marshal Foch, the

Allied Supreme Commander, the Allies, including the Americans and other contingents, had launched their own set of highly successful, sophisticated, combined-arms operations that had driven the Germans back to the borders of their own country. Here they sued for peace, culminating in an armistice which came into effect at 11 o'clock in the morning of 11 November 1918. By this stage Allenby had also renewed his offensive in the Middle East, having received more troops from the empire and the dominions, and in September he had broken the Ottoman lines at the battle of Megiddo,[28] aided by Lawrence's bloody victory at Tafas,[29] and he continued to advance rapidly north. Damascus, the great classical city of Syria and capital of the Umayyad caliphate, fell on 30 September, and Prince Faisal and Lawrence entered it the next day, the Bedouin of the Arab Revolt sharing an awkward occupation with the Australian Light Horse. Aleppo was captured by Prince Feisal's Sharifian cavalry on 25 October.

In late September, that ally and former enemy of the Ottomans, Bulgaria, surrendered. The Turks were now cut off from Germany, and the CUP government collapsed and its members fled the capital. Sultan Mehmet V had died in his palace on 3 July, so he did not live to see the extinction of the empire, and he was succeeded by his brother, Mehmet VI, who became the 36th Ottoman sultan, and the 115th Islamic caliph. On 30 October, the Armistice of Mudros had been signed on board the British warship HMS *Agamemnon*, anchored in Mudros harbour in the Greek island of Lemnos. It ended hostilities in the Middle East theatre of operations between the Ottoman Empire and the Allies. Among its provisions, it granted the right of the Allies to occupy the forts controlling the Straits of the Dardanelles, which had so fatally compromised the Gallipoli campaign, and also those on the Bosporus. The Ottoman army was demobilized, and the victors were meant to divide up the empire, in recognition of the sacrifices they had made in sustaining it through the 19th century, and now fighting against it in the 20th. The Italians would take the south-west mainland areas, near their island possessions in the Dodecanese; the British would get Iraq, Palestine and the Constantinople region; the French aspired to Greater Syria, including Lebanon, and south-east Anatolia, with its large Kurdish population; the Armenians dreamed of a new, Greater Armenia, stretching from the Black Sea to the Mediterranean; the Greeks, whose nationalist dreams were fuelled by the history and mythology of classical times, were encouraged to occupy Smyrna, and to assert control over western Anatolia.

The Allied Powers had already signed the Treaty of Versailles with Germany on 28 June 1919, exactly five years to the day since Gavrilo Princip had assassinated Archduke Franz Ferdinand and his wife, Sophie, in Sarajevo. Now, on 10 August 1920, the Ottomans faced a similarly humiliating experience, as they signed the Treaty of Sèvres in France. Its harsh terms stirred up hostility and Turkish nationalism, catalysing a nationalist rebellion in the Anatolian mainland, against the rump-Ottoman government in Constantinople. Mustapha Kemal Pasha, the great Turkish and Ottoman hero of the Dardanelles, and now the founding leader of the Turkish National Movement, stripped the Ottoman signatories of the Treaty of Sèvres of their citizenship, and he ignited the Turkish War of Independence. In a series of bloody engagements with the Greeks, where history, religion and ethnicity added to the violence and brutality of the fighting, inspiring atrocity and counter-atrocity among military and civilians alike, the Turks prevailed. Defeating the Greeks at the 21-day battle of the Sakarya, in August–September 1921, 30 miles from his capital of Ankara, Mustapha Kemal and his soldiers halted the Greek advance and, with that, thwarted the ambitions of most of the Allied Powers. The Turkish writer Ismail Sevuk later described the importance of this battle with the words, 'The retreat that started in Vienna on 13th September 1683, was stopped after 238 years.'

A year later, Mustapha Kemal Pasha defeated a further Greek army, and his troops marched into Smyrna on 9 September 1922, ending three years of Greek occupation. The initial occupation was largely peaceful, but a few days later a great fire broke out, possibly started deliberately, and thousands died as the Turks took advantage of this catastrophe to finally extinguish the centuries-long presence of the Christian Greek and Armenian communities in the city. Mustapha Kemal Pasha then advanced on Constantinople, in order to challenge the other provisions of the Treaty of Sèvres, and a potential conflict between the Turks and the Allied forces, at Chanak on the Dardanelles, was only narrowly averted. In a world where the Bolshevik threat from the Soviet Union was rising, and the Allied Powers were war-weary, there was little enthusiasm for a new war with the Turks. During the ensuing armistice, one of the largest forcible population movements in history took place, with 1,250,000 Greek Orthodox being moved from Asia Minor, eastern Thrace, the Black Sea region and the Caucasus, to Greece and other Christian states in the Balkans. In return, nearly 400,000 Muslims were evacuated from Greece, to move to Constantinople or Anatolia.

———

On 24 July 1923, the Turkish government, at last, signed the Treaty of Lausanne, at the end of a peace conference which had opened on 20 November 1922. It supplanted the Treaty of Sèvres and broadly set the boundaries and borders of the new state of Turkey (see map on p. 17). It also contained a 'Declaration of Amnesty', granting immunity for crimes committed between 1914 and 1922. Lloyd George, who was a great Hellenophile, declared the treaty 'an abject, cowardly and infamous surrender', while historian Ronald Suny stated that the treaty 'essentially confirmed the effectiveness of deportations, or even murderous ethnic cleansing, as a potential solution to population problems'. The Republic of Turkey was officially declared on 29 October 1923, with Mustapha Kemal Pasha as its first president. In 1934, Mustapha Kemal would be granted the title, and surname, of Ataturk, Father of the Turks, in very public recognition of the role he had played in building the modern Turkish Republic. He would die in 1938. Sultan-Caliph Mehmet VI had hoped to live out his days as some form of spiritual leader for the world's Muslims, in a role akin to the Agha Khan of the Shia Ismaili sect. It was not to be. On 1 November 1922, in one of its first political acts, the Grand National Assembly of Turkey government, in its new capital city of Ankara, in the centre of Anatolia, had voted to abolish the Ottoman sultanate, lowering a curtain on 600 years of imperial history, and Mehmet VI was declared *persona non grata* and expelled from Constantinople. On 17 November 1922, fearing for his safety, the last Ottoman sultan, an Anglophile, had been taken by launch to the British warship HMS *Malaya*. He had departed for exile in Malta, and subsequently the Italian Riviera, accompanied by his first chamberlain, the bandmaster, his doctor, two confidential secretaries, a valet, a barber and two eunuchs.

On 19 November, Mehmet VI's first cousin and heir, Abdul Mecid Efendi, was elected as Caliph. He was to be the 116th Islamic caliph, and the last. When Abdul Mecid was declared Caliph, Mustapha Kemal refused to allow the traditional Ottoman ceremony to take place, bluntly declaring, 'The Caliph has no power or position except as a nominal figurehead.' In response to Abdul Mecid's request for an increase in his allowance, Mustapha Kemal wrote, 'Your office, the Caliphate, is nothing more than an historic relic. It has no justification for its existence, and it is a piece of impertinence that you should dare write to any of my secretaries.' Shockingly for much of the Islamic world, but perhaps unsurprisingly, given Mustapha Kemal's clear antipathy to the institution, on 3 March 1924, less than 18 months after the abolition of the Ottoman sultanate, the caliphate was abolished. The Turkish Republic would not allow the bodies of either Mehmet VI or Abdul Mecid to be buried in Turkey.

Epilogue

It is arguable that the concept of Christendom finally 'died' on the battlefields of World War I, where Muslims fought alongside Christians in both alliances, and where slaughter, economic exhaustion and defeat had led to the collapse of the three main Christian European empires – those of Russia, Germany and Austria. These Christian European empires were now replaced by secular, even anti-clerical republics, who actively sought to keep the church out of politics. Indeed, the new Union of Soviet Socialist Republics had atheism at the core of its ideology and imposed it with murderous brutality, while the German Third Reich would conduct its wars and its social policy with complete contempt for nearly 2,000 years of Christian teaching.

Christendom, as a concept, had encompassed the idea of 'those lands where Christianity is dominant', and where rulers, however inadequately, upheld the teachings, customs, ethos and practice of Christianity. The Christian church had become the defining institution of the Roman Empire and, although this had been diluted when the Western Empire had disintegrated, western Europe had soon coalesced again around a revived Latin church and a resurgent imperial tradition. As the caliphate was the 'organizing principle' for Muslims so, for many centuries, was Christendom for the Christians, and throughout most of its history the notions of 'Europe' and the 'western world' had been intimately connected to the concepts of 'Christianity' and 'Christendom'.

However, there had always been deep political divisions within Christendom, as there had been within the caliphate. Catholics and

Orthodox Christians disdained each other, and Christian unity had been fatally compromised by the tragedy of the Fourth Crusade; Catholic and Orthodox soldiers had routinely served in the ranks of the Ottomans, while the Janissaries were all forcibly converted Christians; the Italian city-states had a highly self-centred trading relationship with Muslim states and rulers; competition between France and England had been intense and long-lasting; while that between France and the Holy Roman Empire had led to the spectacle of contending popes, and even a formal alliance between the Valois and Bourbon monarchs and the Ottoman sultan-caliphs. The behaviour of many of the popes themselves also helped to catalyse the Reformation and to contribute to the rise of Protestantism. The Knights of St John may have been fighting for the Pope and Christendom on the battlements of Rhodes and Malta, but they did so against a backdrop of Christian schism and division. Despite all this, the concept of Christendom had retained a strong resonance among Christian peoples, especially in the period between the ninth and the 17th centuries, when the caliphate continued to present such 'a clear and present danger' on both land and sea.

The European 'Wars of Religion' are usually taken to have ended with the Treaty of Westphalia in 1648. From this time, and particularly from the period after the Ottomans had fallen back from the gates of Vienna, the focus of European rulers discernibly began a long shift away from religious conflicts, either between Christian factions or against the external threats from Islam. The 18th century, encompassing the 'Age of Enlightenment',[1] the formation of the great colonial empires, and the continuing decline of the Ottoman Empire, began to mark the end of the geo-political 'history of Christendom'. From here on in, the broad focus of European history shifted to the development of the 'nation-state', accompanied by increasing liberalism and secularism, culminating in the French Revolution and the Napoleonic Wars at the turn of the 19th century. These splits within Christendom, and the decline of the idea of Christendom itself, meant that the Ottoman Empire came to be perceived as just another imperial 'player', whose strength or weakness had consequences for other imperial rivals in the great 'balance-of-power' struggles. The Islamic religion, beliefs and teaching of the caliphate no longer had the appeal that they had had when Islam was in the ascendancy, nor inspired the same fear as when

Arab and Ottoman armies had marched to war, or their navies had contested the seas.

———

The formal abolition of the caliphate by the Republic of Turkey in 1924 was by no means the end of the story. However, while many Muslims looked to find a 'worthy successor' to the last Ottoman caliph, there was no one in the Islamic world who had the unquestioned moral authority to adopt the title, thereby assuming the mantle of, at least, spiritual leader of the Muslim world.[2] The slow decline of the Ottomans from 1683 had meant that, well before World War I had precipitated the final collapse of the empire, Christian powers had already been able to take back territories held by the Muslims for centuries, or now exercised control over them. By 1914, the Mediterranean was already a British 'lake'. All the Ottoman lands in the Balkans, less a toehold in Thrace, were gone, as was North Africa, including the great powerhouse of Egypt. Under the 1920 Treaty of Sèvres, the lands formerly conquered by the Arab Rashideen, the Umayyad and the Abbasid caliphates were also lost to the Ottomans and, in turn, largely divided among the European victors of World War I, France and Great Britain. Therefore, in the wake of the abolition of the caliphate, the only country in the reformed Middle East, from the Atlantic to the borders of Afghanistan, that could lay a claim to be independent was the new and weak Republic of Turkey (see map on p.17).

In this political context, the Turks had already abrogated any claim to the caliphate, the Egyptians would not accept it, and the Persians were Shia 'heretics' who had rejected the whole idea of the Sunni caliphate since the deaths of Ali, Hassan and Hussein in the seventh century. The Hashemite Sharif of Mecca was usurped by the Wahhabi fundamentalists of the House of Al Saud in 1925 but, like Godfrey of Bouillon rejecting the title 'King of Jerusalem', the kings of Saudi Arabia stopped short of claiming the title 'Caliph', and instead took the appellation 'Custodian of the Two Holy Places'.

Despite the dissipation of the idea of 'Christendom', the French had based their claim to Lebanon and Syria, in no small part, on their leadership of the crusades, and their championing of Catholics and other Christians during the long period of Muslim domination of the region following the fall of Acre in the 13th century. Although the Hashemites had taken Damascus in 1918, and Prince Feisal had had himself crowned as King of Syria, the French had defeated his small force at the battle of Maysalun. Feisal had withdrawn to join his brother Abdullah in the new British mandate territory of Trans-Jordan. From there, he had gone to be King of Iraq, another British mandate territory. On Feisal's departure, the French commander, General Gouraud, had gone to the tomb of Saladin in the great Umayyad mosque in Damascus, and is supposed to have kicked it, saying, 'Awake, Saladin. We have returned. My presence here consecrates the victory of the Cross over the Crescent.' It was nearly three-quarters of a millennium since the battle of Hattin.

The British, also with a touch of early 20th-century Romanticism, established themselves in the Holy Land, exercising League of Nations 'mandates' in Palestine and in the new 'Kingdom of Trans-Jordan'. Within Palestine, the British controlled the 'Heavenly City' of Jerusalem, as well as the biblical towns of Bethlehem and Nazareth and, once again, the great crusader ports of Ascalon, Jaffa and Acre. The combined Franco-British areas corresponded very closely to the original crusader states of the 11th and 12th centuries, a fact not lost on Muslims, and this new reality was further exacerbated by the British commitment to establish a 'homeland' in Palestine for the Jewish people. The fact that the Balfour Declaration contained the sub-sentence, 'nothing shall be done which may prejudice the civil and religious rights of existing non-Jewish communities in Palestine', did little or nothing to assuage the anger of the indigenous Arab population, and Muslims in general. There was opposition to the British mandate in Palestine from the outset, and rising levels of violence that would culminate in British withdrawal in 1948.

The British also took modern Iraq, including the great capital of the Abbasid caliphate, Baghdad. Here, however, their interests were more strategic and commercial, giving the British de facto control of the Persian Gulf, given the weakness of Persia, and also giving them access to many of the increasingly important oil fields of the region. However, here too, the British faced early problems as they were confronted with violent challenges from the Sunni tribes, the Shia inhabitants of the holy cities of Najaf and Karbala, and the Kurds of the north, whose hopes of an independent state had been dashed by Mustapha Kemal.

Although the French and British empires had reached their greatest territorial extent in the 1920s, these two powers had been comprehensively weakened by the exertions and losses of World War I. The grandiose claims for 'self-determination' that had been made in the Treaty of Versailles had been aimed at the peoples of the European Christian empires, but they were also read and listened to by the subject peoples of overseas colonial possessions. These now included the newly 'mandated' territories of the former great Islamic dynasties and empires. The Sultan-Caliph's call for *jihad* against the Christians of the Allied Powers may broadly have fallen on deaf ears, but it had not gone altogether unheeded.[3] The caliphate may have gone, and with it an organizing principle for the *umma*, but it left a void that the Christian powers could not necessarily fill with their talk of 'nations' and 'states', 'citizens' and 'passports', 'borders' and 'national identity'. Turks, Arabs, Persians, Berbers and Egyptians all felt infused with a feeling of lost 'greatness', and with it they also developed a profound sense of historical entitlement, historical grievance and historical inspiration.

This manifested itself in increasing resistance to the western powers throughout the 1920s and 1930s, encouraged by the revolutionary liberation message of the Soviet Union. Resistance, not least to the attempts to establish a Jewish 'homeland' in Palestine, was also encouraged by Nazi Germany, seeking to weaken and undermine the British and French positions in the region. In World War II, the attitude and actions of the Muslim Middle East could have been decisive in the outcome of that global conflict. However, Egypt failed to revolt against the British, and an uprising in Iraq was swiftly put down. Turkey remained neutral, Vichy French territories in the region were quickly taken, and Muslim soldiers in the British imperial forces, and in the Free French, largely stood firm in their loyalty, volunteering in large numbers to serve the Allies.

However, in victory the Allied Powers found themselves divided, and the high-water mark of this new Christian western influence across the region soon passed. The Americans had not entered the war to support Great Britain and France in sustaining or re-establishing their empires, and the Soviet Union was actively in the vanguard of 'resistance' and 'independence' movements across the world, not least among the new majority-Muslim countries. The French had retreated from the Levant in 1946, and Great Britain had ceded independence to the countries of India and Pakistan in 1947. In May 1948, David Ben-Gurion had proclaimed the establishment of the State of Israel, after the British mandate had lapsed, and set in train four wars between the new Jewish state and its Arab Muslim neighbours over the next 25 years. Egypt and Iraq had achieved nominal independence from Britain in the 1930s, and the Suez Crisis of 1956 ended British influence in the former, while the murder of the Hashemite rulers in Baghdad in 1958 ended it in the latter. The French pulled out of Morocco and Tunisia in 1956, and their long and bloody war in Algeria ended in independence for the Algerians in 1962. When Great Britain completed its 'withdrawal from East of Suez' in 1971, ending nearly a century and a half of acting as 'protector' of the Arab tribes of the Persian Gulf, Colonel Gaddafi also threw them out of Libya.

Despite all the countries of the Middle East regaining, or establishing, their independence by the early 1970s, and despite a shared geography, history, and language, written or spoken, there seemed to be no real appetite to re-institute any form of the caliphate. Egyptian President Gamal Abdul Nasser's 'pan-Arabism' seemed to be the closest model for some form of renewed regional unity, and that ambition had foundered in the wake of the 1967 war with Israel. In 1973, the surge in oil prices, and the wealth that went with it, allowed the new monarchical Gulf states to make themselves increasingly independent of, and detached from, the historical centres of Arab Muslim greatness in Damascus, Baghdad and Cairo. The Muslim Brotherhood, a pan-Islamic religious and social movement, which gained modern prominence after the failures of Arab nationalism, always remained ambivalent about its support for a caliphate. Turkey, meanwhile, had already been a member of the US-led North Atlantic Treaty Organization (NATO) since 1952, and increasingly looked to Europe for its economic and social models.

In 1979, Egypt made peace with Israel, which led to it being expelled from the Arab League for the next two decades. In the same year, the Shah of Iran fell, ushering in the Islamic Revolution of Ayatollah Khomeini. Persia was now not merely a Middle Eastern power, competing with the Arab states for regional dominance as it had done for centuries, but it also sought to be a Muslim revolutionary force across the region. In addition, it became an increasingly active champion of Shia communities, whether majority or minority, in Iraq, Syria, Lebanon, Yemen and in the Gulf states. The seizure of the Great Mosque in Mecca, by *takfiri* ideologues, ended in significant bloodshed and forced the rulers of Saudi Arabia to take any idea of a social reform agenda off the table for the next three and a half decades.[4] On 24 December 1979, the Soviet Union sent its armies into Afghanistan and, for the next decade, money and Islamic ideological fervour, from across the Muslim world, was diverted to Central Asia in the struggle against the 'atheist invaders'. In 1989, in a move that would contribute to the fall of the USSR two years later, the Soviets withdrew from Afghanistan, having been held to a bloody stalemate by the Afghan *mujahideen*, their Sunni Muslim Arab fellow-fighters, and American weapon supplies. Victory was seen as a triumph for Islam across the Muslim world, and thousands of radicalized young men returned to their countries inspired by their successes. One of these was Osama bin Laden, of the influential Yemeni bin Laden family, who had helped oversee the establishment of the Al-Qaeda terrorist group, whose political philosophy was directly descended from that of the original Kharijites of the seventh century. Osama bin Laden saw in this Afghan military triumph the potential catalyst for a rebirth of the caliphate, a return to those Muslim values that had inspired the successes of the Arab and Ottoman caliphates, the expulsion of all western presence and influence from across the Muslim world, and the destruction of the State of Israel.

In 1990, President Saddam Hussein of Iraq, fresh from a punishing, decade-long conflict with the Shia of the new Islamic Republic of Iran, sought to cover his considerable financial losses by invading Kuwait and threatening to take the war into the oil-rich Kingdom of Saudi Arabia. Osama bin Laden saw his opportunity, and he went to see King Fahd to offer the services of his battle-hardened fighters from Afghanistan, against this threat from Iraq. However, to his horror and disgust, and that of many social conservatives across the Muslim world, King Fahd agreed to host nearly half a million American and other western troops in the 'Land of the Two Holy Cities'. Saddam Hussein was evicted from Kuwait in 1991, but this presence of 'infidels' in Saudi Arabia, and the continuing existence of the State of Israel, was Osama bin Laden's *casus belli* against the House of Saud, and the catalyst for his fatwas of 1996 and 1998 against the 'Zionists and Crusaders'.

A series of large-scale terrorist incidents in the late 20th century culminated in the attack on the Twin Towers in New York City on 11 September 2001, precipitating the US-led invasions of Afghanistan and Iraq. High among the objectives of Al-Qaeda's new phase of *jihad* was the restoration of the caliphate and, with it, the former glory of the

Muslim *umma*. Al-Qaeda was largely destroyed in Afghanistan, and Osama bin Laden was killed in Pakistan in 2011, but his organization, and the inspiration behind it, lived on in Iraq and Syria, in Yemen, where Al-Qaeda in the Arabian Peninsula (AQAP) became one of its most dangerous and sophisticated branches, and in the Horn and the Sahel region of Africa.

In 2012, as a result of the continuing insurgency in Iraq, the fallout from the 'Arab Spring', and the start of the civil war in Syria, the shockingly violent *jihadi* group of Islamic State in Iraq and Syria (ISIS) grew and prospered. In due course, ISIS eventually challenged Al-Qaeda for leadership in the fight against the infidel, heretic and apostate enemies of Islam. In 2014, ISIS 'invaded' Iraq, and on 29 June, in the Great Mosque of Mosul, their leader, Abu Bakr al Baghdadi,[5] declared himself to be Caliph Ibrahim, and the 'Islamic State' to be the new world-wide caliphate. The Islamic State map of their new 'caliphate' demonstrated the scale of their ambition, encompassing as it did every land controlled by Muslims under all manifestations of the caliphate, including Spain, south-east and central Europe, up to the gates of Vienna and, in some versions, all of India, in recognition of the Muslim Mughal Empire and dynasty, and much of sub-Saharan Africa. Abu Bakr al Baghdadi and Islamic State demanded the religious, political and military obedience of all Muslims, although his claim to be 'Caliph' was almost universally rejected by the Muslim community. It would take a lengthy, bloody, multi-national, multi-faith counter-insurgency campaign to eliminate the territorial hold of Islamic State in the Levant and Mesopotamia, but the core appeal of the Islamic State message remains strong in many parts of the world, not least among the growing Muslim communities in the former lands of Christendom. 'Caliph' Ibrahim himself died detonating a suicide vest in a hideout in north-west Syria in October 2019. Only history will tell if the idea of a caliphate died with him.

Notes

INTRODUCTION

1 A fatwa is a ruling on a point of Islamic law, given by a recognized authority. Osama bin Laden was not a 'recognized authority'.
2 General Eisenhower's wartime memoirs were called *Crusade in Europe*.
3 In historical terms the word 'crusade' refers to a specific series of military expeditions made by Europeans to the Holy Land between the 11th and 13th centuries.

CHAPTER 1: RISE OF THE CALIPHATE: YARMOUK AND AL-QADISIYYAH 637

1 The Seleucids (312–63 BC) were one of the successor dynasties to Alexander the Great's empire.
2 Shah Shapur I was the first Persian monarch to use the title 'King of Kings', *Shahanshah*.
3 The Ghassanids occupied areas in the Levant and were originally from South Arabia. They had converted to Christianity and mostly remained Christians, even after the expansion of Islam.
4 The Lakhmids migrated from Yemen and occupied lands in the east of the Arabian Peninsula.
5 Trajan was Roman Emperor from 98 to 117, and led the Roman Empire to its greatest territorial extent. He was given the title *Optimus*, 'the best', by the Senate.
6 St Paul the Apostle was not one of Christ's original 'Twelve Apostles', and he did not know Jesus. He was converted to Christianity as a result of a vision on the road to Damascus. His influence on Christian thought and practice was immense, and has been characterized by Paul Johnson, in his book *A History of Christianity*, as being 'profound as it is pervasive'.
7 Constantine was born in modern Serbia. His mother, Helena, is credited with his eventual conversion to Christianity. Ancient tradition claims she was the first to discover the True Cross *c.* 327, and Constantine built the Church of the Holy Sepulchre on the site of its discovery.
8 The tetrarchy was a system instituted by Emperor Diocletian in 293 to govern the vast Roman Empire by dividing it between two emperors, and two designated successors, caesars. While sensible in theory, it proved to be divisive and fragile, and was largely discarded when Constantine became sole ruler of the Roman Empire in 324.
9 I have used the name Constantinople throughout the book, including after its capture by the Ottomans of Sultan Mehmet II in 1453. The name of the city was only officially

changed to Istanbul in 1930, sometime after the establishment of the Republic of Turkey, and after the capital of the new republic had been moved to Ankara.

10 Nicomedia was capital of Bithynia, and the centre of Emperor Diocletian's persecution of the Christians in 303. Constantine had used the town as his interim capital, while the city of Constantinople was being built.

11 Adrianople would be renamed Edirne when it was taken by the Ottomans in the 14th century, and would be the Ottoman capital until Constantinople fell to Sultan Mehmet II in 1453.

12 Canadian theologian Douglas Hall stated that, 'Christendom means literally the dominion or sovereignty of the Christian religion.' It was largely a medieval concept that evolved from the fall of the Western Roman Empire in the fifth century AD and the rise of Charlemagne in the eighth century AD. Christian journalist Malcolm Muggeridge claimed that Christ founded Christianity, but Constantine founded Christendom. Christendom became intimately associated with Christianity and the western world, and it undoubtedly contributed to the idea of a unified European identity.

13 Al-Hashem is the family name of the Hashemite monarchy of the Kingdom of Jordan, direct descendants of the Prophet Muhammad.

14 The Al-Quraysh were a tribal grouping of Arab clans that inhabited and controlled the city of Mecca. As affluent merchants, they dominated commerce between the Indian Ocean and East Africa. After Muhammad's rise in the early seventh century AD, leadership of the Muslim community traditionally passed to a member of the Al-Quraysh, as was the case with the Rashideen, Umayyad and Abbasid caliphates, and possibly the Shia Fatamids.

15 Gabriel means 'man of God' in Hebrew. Revered in all the Abrahamic faiths, Gabriel is an archangel with the power to announce God's will to mankind.

16 While the Koran is a 'divine text', the *hadith* are a collection of accounts of Muhammad's actions, advice and sayings that Muslim jurists agree 'have provenance'. In this the *hadith* is more like the Christian Bible.

17 Buraq has been described as 'a white animal, half mule, half donkey, with wings on its sides'. In some traditions, Buraq became a steed with the head of a woman and the tail of a peacock. The 'flight' on Buraq was a way of explaining how Muhammad could have gone from Mecca to Jerusalem and back in a single night.

18 The present-day Al-Aqsa Mosque was built by the early Umayyad caliphs, Abd al-Malik and Al-Walid I, in the late seventh and early eighth centuries.

19 The Dome of the Rock is an Islamic shrine at the centre of the Al-Aqsa Mosque.

20 Avars and Khazars were militant Turkic tribes from the Caucasus and central Asia.

21 *Ridda* is Arabic for 'apostasy'.

22 Sir Muhammad Iqbal (1877–1938) was a distinguished South Asian Muslim philosopher, poet and politician.

23 Now joined to the more modern Iraqi city of Najaf, and a major pilgrimage site.

24 *Takfiri* is the Arabic and Islamic term for 'excommunicational', denoting a Muslim who 'excommunicates' a co-religionist for apostasy or heresy, for which the *sharia* punishment is the death penalty.

25 Despite a Muslim ban on the depiction of the human form, the Shia have a tradition of flying flags, etc., with the images of Ali, Hassan and Hussein upon them. This was particularly prevalent among the Shia members of the Iraqi Security Forces, and the Shia militias in Iraq after the fall of Saddam in 2003. It was a source of great provocation to Sunnis.

26 *Al-Kahina* is the Arabic term for 'priestess soothsayer', given to Dihya, the Berber queen of an area in Algeria, because of her alleged ability to foresee the future. She died at the battle of Tabarka in around 703, at the age of 127 (sic), and her head was sent back to Damascus as proof of her death. She is still considered as one of the most famous figures in the history of Berber resistance to the Arab conquests of the seventh century.

27 The name 'Gibraltar' comes from Arabic name 'Jabal Ṭariq' or 'Mount of Ṭariq'.

28 'Assassin' is now a generic word for those who carry out politically motivated killings. The original Assassins were a Nizari Isma'ili order (a sub-set of the Shia) that existed from 1090, just prior to the crusading period of the 11th to 13th centuries, and who were extinguished by the Mongols in 1275. Marco Polo understood the word to be derived from their use of the drug hashish. In the course of 200 years they killed hundreds of people, including one king of Jerusalem (they also made an attempt on the life of King Edward I of England), three caliphs (they almost killed Saladin as well), and dozens of other Muslim and Christian leaders.

29 For much of the Abbasid era, Baghdad would be the largest city in the world, with a population around 1 million people. Constructed in the form of two semi-circles, it was known as 'the Round City' and had many parks, gardens and promenades. There were extensive city walls, and the Sultan-Caliph's Golden Gate Palace was in the heart of the city.

30 This inclusion of western professional armoured knights among the Byzantine forces was what would give Emperor Alexius I Comnenus the idea that help from the west would be most useful.

31 Clovis was the first king of the Franks, a grouping of western European tribes. During the crusader period of the 11th to 13th centuries, 'Franks' became a generic name among the Muslims for any western European, whether French, Norman, German, English or Italian.

32 On 16 July 1054, in a breaking point in long-standing tensions between the Catholic Church based in Rome and the Orthodox Church based in Constantinople, Pope Leo III excommunicated the Patriarch of Constantinople, Michael Cerularius, and the entire eastern church. In retaliation the eastern church excommunicated Leo III and the Roman church with him. The churches have never reunited, although there were several attempts at formal reconciliation over the centuries, particularly during times of crisis for the Byzantine Empire. The mutual excommunication of 1054 was only 'lifted' by Pope Paul VI and Patriarch Athenagoras in 1965.

CHAPTER 2: VICTORY IN THE EAST: JERUSALEM 1099

1 The 1095 Council of Clermont was where Pope Urban II had put out his call to arms to 'liberate the Holy City of Jerusalem', and thereby initiated the huge military pilgrimage that would be known to history as the 'First Crusade'.

2 Crusade is an anachronistic term, derived from the French word *croisade*, 'an expedition of people bearing the sign of the cross'. It did not come into popular use in English until the 18th century. The contemporary term was 'military pilgrimage', but I have largely used 'crusade' throughout.

3 Sultan Suleiman's walls are those of present-day Jerusalem.

4 The Nubians were a Nilotic people from the Upper Nile region, between Aswan and the confluence of the White and Blue Niles. At this time many of them were still Christian, but they often provided soldiers for the rulers of Egypt.

5 These would be the County of Edessa (1097), the Principality of Antioch (1098), the Kingdom of Jerusalem (1099), and the County of Tripoli (1109). Kerbogha had besieged Baldwin in Edessa for three weeks while on his way to relieve the siege of Antioch. He had failed, and his delay contributed to the crusader success against his army.

6 Lothringia was a successor kingdom of the Carolingian Empire, broadly covering present-day Luxembourg, the Netherlands and eastern Belgium. It was named after King Lothair II. Lorraine was the area where Godfrey's castle of Bouillon was situated.

7 Bishop Adhemar was in his forties at the time of the First Crusade. He had already made a pilgrimage to Jerusalem in 1086, and his brother, William Hugh of Monteil,

was also on the crusade. A 'combat cleric', Adhemar had taken an active part in the fighting at Nicaea, Dorylaeum and Antioch. He died of typhus.

8   Having crossed into Anatolia, after their meeting with Emperor Alexius I Comnenus in Constantinople, the crusaders and their Byzantine allies had taken the city of Nicaea. To reduce the logistic burden, the crusader leaders then divided their forces in two, for the march to Antioch. At Dorylaeum, the Seljuk commander, Kilij Arslan, had ambushed Bohemond's force, and only swift action by the other commanders, including Raymond, had saved the Christian army.

9   Baldwin's brother, Eustace of Boulogne, had returned to France after the First Crusade. He was approached to succeed as King of Jerusalem, and got as far as Italy before he heard that Baldwin of Bourcq had already been crowned.

CHAPTER 3: DISASTER AT THE HORNS: HATTIN 1187

1   The Kingdom of Jerusalem, sometimes known as the Latin Kingdom, was one of four Christian states formed during or after the First Crusade. The others were the County of Edessa, the Principality of Antioch and the County of Tripoli. The latter were nominally independent states, but they were all closely tied to the Kingdom of Jerusalem and acknowledged a nominal precedence to the King.

2   As the western crusaders were generically known as 'Franks' to the Muslims, so the Muslims of this period were generically known to Christian Europeans as 'Saracens', whether they came from Arabia, Iraq, Syria or Egypt. The term remained in general usage until the 18th century, although from the 14th century the Christian powers were increasingly confronted by the forces of the newly ascendant Turkic Ottoman Empire.

3   Guy of Lusignan arrived in the Holy Land sometime in the 1170s, to join his brother, Aimery. He was from Poitou, part of the Duchy of Aquitaine, and therefore owed allegiance to Queen Eleanor of Aquitaine, King Henry II of England, and subsequently to King Richard the Lionheart.

4   See Chapter 1, endnote 28.

5   There were rumours that Melisande was illegitimate. She never married and had died, young, in a convent.

6   Raymond had been captured at the battle of Harim in 1164 by Nur ed Din, when an expedition into Egypt by King Amalric I of Jerusalem had left the crusader states vulnerable to attack from the east.

7   Reginald's humiliation had been compounded by his act of contrition being witnessed by local Muslim and Christian leaders. When Emperor Manuel departed, Reginald had to hold the bridle of his horse.

8   *Outremer* is the French word for 'overseas' and was a generic term for the four crusader states.

9   Turcopoles (from the Greek, and literally meaning 'sons of Turks') were locally recruited mounted archers and light cavalry employed by the Byzantine Empire and the crusader states. Some were the product of mixed marriages, some were *poulains* who were trained and equipped as light cavalry. Both military orders eventually established the post of Grand Turcopolier.

10 At the height of their power, the Knights Templar had a network of nearly 1,000 commanderies across Europe and the Holy Land, and an overall strength of between 15,000 and 20,000, of whom about 1,500 were knights, and maybe a further 10,000 were sergeants, who were non-noble but fought alongside them.

11 The original seventh-century hospital had been enlarged by Emperor Charlemagne. In due course it could accommodate up to 2,000 patients. The Hospitallers also wore a black mantle with a white cross on ceremonial occasions.

12 The Hospitaller 'Maltese cross' purportedly represented the four cardinal virtues of Prudence, Temperance, Fortitude and Justice, and the eight beatitudes of the biblical story.

13 Baldwin II had no sons, so had looked for a suitable husband for his daughter, Melisande. Fulk of Anjou was rich, experienced in war, had already been a pilgrim to the Holy Land, and had close connections with the Knights Templar.

14 Zengi was a Seljuk Turk. His father had been beheaded for treason, and Zengi had been brought up in Mosul by Kerbogha.

15 Voltaire famously declared that the Holy Roman Empire was 'in no way holy, nor Roman, nor an Empire'. It existed as a theoretical entity from the time of Charlemagne, and was given more structure and institutional reality from the middle of the 12th century under Frederick Barbarossa, and the form 'Holy Roman Empire' was used from 1254 onwards. Constituting a huge, rambling organization, of many forms of lordship, the pretensions of the Emperor often brought him into confrontation and conflict with the Pope.

16 Frederick Barbarossa (Red Beard) is considered one of the greatest of the medieval emperors, combining longevity, ambition, organizational skill, battlefield acumen and political perspicacity. Joining the Third Crusade, he would die crossing the River Saleph in Turkey in 1190.

17 Louis VII was notoriously pious. He had two daughters by the fabulously wealthy Eleanor of Acquitaine, but no son. She described her relationship with Louis VII as 'more like being married to a monk than a king'. She and Louis divorced in 1152, and she married Henry of Normandy and Anjou, later King Henry II of England, the same year. They had five sons, including King Richard the Lionheart and 'Bad' King John, and three daughters.

18 At this siege, the Grand Master of the Templars and 40 of his knights were cut off in the breach, captured and beheaded.

19 Tikrit was also the birthplace of Saddam Hussein.

20 Shirkuh is a Persian-Kurdish name for 'lion of the mountain'. Short, fat and from humble origins, Shirkuh was also generous, brave and much loved by his soldiers.

21 King Amalric I was the second son of King Fulk and Queen Melisande, and he had succeeded his elder brother, Baldwin III, in 1163. King until 1174, he had launched a number of expeditions into Egypt. His chidren were Sybilla, who married Guy of Lusignan, Baldwin IV, the 'Leper King', and Isabella, who would be married off four times as a pawn in the succession plans of the Kingdom of Jerusalem.

22 Despite the Fatimid caliphate being Shia, the bulk of the Egyptian population had remained Sunni.

23 The Ayyubid dynasty would last as a significant 'player' in the region until the 1260s, when the decades-long power-play between the Ayyubids, the crusaders, the Mamluks of Egypt and the Mongols reduced them to relative impotence.

24 Count Raymond of Tripoli ruled the kingdom in King Baldwin's name until he reached his majority in 1176. Baldwin IV proved to be a remarkable ruler, given his tragic afflictions, demonstrating impressive judgement and physical courage.

25 Emperor Manuel I Comnenus reigned from 1143 to 1180, leading a renaissance in Byzantine military and economic power, and in cultural influence. His defeat at Myriokephalon in 1176 was a huge strategic reverse for the Byzantines, and marked their final effort to recover the interior of Anatolia from the Seljuks.

26 The Kaaba is a stone building at the centre of the holiest mosque in Mecca. Its literal meaning in Arabic is 'cube'. It is the direction for prayer for Muslims around the world, although early Muslims had faced in the general direction of Jerusalem. It is reputed to have been built by Abraham and Ishmael, the son by his wife Hagar, and therefore predates Islam.

27 Saphadin was the Frankish form of Saif ad Din, the 'Sword of Faith'. He was an outstanding military administrator and would do much to manage the family struggle that followed Saladin's death in 1193. During the Third Crusade King Richard the Lionheart offered both his younger sister, Joan, and his niece, Eleanor, in marriage to Saphadin. Saphadin became Sultan of Egypt, and died at 72, in 1218, during the Fifth Crusade.

28 In 1183 Saladin besieged Kerak during the marriage of Humphrey of Toron and Isabella of Jerusalem, the younger sister of Baldwin IV and Sybilla. Informed of the situation, Saladin agreed not to target the tower in which the newly married couple's chamber was located.

29 The Patriarch of Jerusalem, Heraclius, to whom the honour of carrying the True Cross would normally have fallen, was ill at the time and remained in Jerusalem, along with Queen Sybilla.

30 In 1190, Gerard of Ridefort was, once again, captured by Saladin. This time he was swiftly executed.

31 Tyre was an almost impregnable crusader fortress port, around 160 miles from Jerusalem. After Hattin it was one of the last safe Christian strongholds, until Acre was retaken from the Muslims in 1191.

32 Conrad was the younger brother of William Longsword of Montferrat, who had been married to Queen Sybilla.

33 The Third Crusade (1189–92) was an attempt by three European monarchs of Christendom – King Richard I of England, King Philip II Augustus of France and Frederick I Barbarossa, Holy Roman Emperor – to reconquer the Holy Land after the disaster of Hattin and the capture of Jerusalem by Saladin in 1187.

34 Count Raymond of Tripoli died in late 1187 overcome by shame and sorrow, and his wife, Eschiva, died around the same time. Baldwin of Ibelin, who had refused to serve alongside King Guy, died in the same year, while Balian helped thwart Guy's attempt to retain the crown of Jerusalem by marrying his step-daughter, Isabella, sister of Queen Sybilla, to Conrad of Montferrat, who was crowned King. King Conrad died two days after his coronation, at the hands of the Assassins. Eight days later, Isabella was married to Conrad's successor, Henry of Champagne, who died, falling from a balcony, five years later. In due course Isabella married Guy of Lusignan's older brother, Aimery, who was King of Cyprus, and who now also became King of Jerusalem, by marriage. Balian of Ibelin died in 1193.

CHAPTER 4: EXPULSION FROM EDEN: ACRE 1291

1 The Teutonic Knights were founded as a further military order of 'warrior monks', after the retaking of Acre in 1190. Their full title is 'The Order of the Brothers of the German House of Saint Mary in Jerusalem'. After the fall of Acre, and the final loss of the Holy Land, they would concentrate their crusading efforts in the Baltic area, creating an independent State of the Teutonic Order. Knights from all over Europe would serve with them, including the future King Henry IV of England. They were decisively beaten by a Polish–Lithuanian army at the battle of the Grunwald in 1410, but survived as an order until their dissolution by Napoleon in 1809.

2 Otto of Grandison and John of Grailly were very distinguished soldiers. John had been with Edward I when he came to Palestine in 1272 and had stayed as seneschal. They would both survive the fall of Acre.

3 Al-Ashraf had succeeded his father very recently, and had inherited the plans for the assault on Acre. He had survived an assassination attempt on the day of his enthronement.

4 The Fourth Crusade had divided up the Byzantine Empire between the new Latin Empire and the Republic of Venice. From its foundation in 1204, the Latin Empire

was immediately challenged by the Byzantine 'rump states' of Nicaea, Trebizond and Thessaloniki, and most of its territories had been lost by 1261, when the last Latin emperor, Baldwin II, fled his poor and depopulated capital of Constantinople. The revived Greek Empire was a shadow of its former self, and a poor counterweight to the rising threats from Mongols and Mamluks.

5 Prester John was a legendary Christian patriarch and king, sometimes supposed to be a descendent of one of the three magi of the Christmas story. Assumed to be based somewhere in India or central Asia, the crusaders had early reports of the Mongol successes against the Muslims, and had nurtured a hope that this was Prester John coming to their aid.

6 King Louis IX was widely acknowledged as a saint in his own lifetime. Dying at Tunis, his body was subjected to a process known as *mos Teutonicus*, 'the German Way', by which his bones, flesh and entrails were separated and 'hygienically' returned to France.

7 Edward stayed in the Holy Land for nearly four years, until 1274, even though his father, King Henry III, died in 1272.

8 The uprising in 1282 was known as the Sicilian Vespers, because the Vespers bell was the signal to kill the garrison. It gave rise to one of the few known medieval jokes. In 1494, King Charles VIII of France told an envoy from Florence that he was going to invade Italy, and that he would be moving so swiftly that he intended to be in Milan for breakfast, and in Rome for lunch. 'In that case Your Majesty,' said the envoy, 'you may well be in Sicily in time for Vespers.'

9 From 1257 to 1260, the Genoese and Venetians, perennial rivals for commercial advantage across the eastern Mediterranean and in the Levant, fought the 'War of St Sabas', named after a church in Acre, a conflict that may have cost up to 20,000 lives, at a time when the crusader kingdom already was under Mamluk threat.

10 Pope Nicholas IV was the first Franciscan to be elected to the papacy.

11 The Tower of Flies was a formidable defensive structure, which was attached to a giant chain that could be strung across the harbour. The first crusaders to come to Acre believed they had arrived at the biblical city of Ekron, where one of the major Philistine deities was Ba'al-zabub, Beelzebub, the Lord of the Flies. A tower already existed, so it was named the Tower of Flies.

12 St Sabas had been the focus of the Genoese and Venetian conflict of 1257–60.

13 Modern-day Izmir, on the Aegean coast of Turkey.

CHAPTER 5: THE WALLS FAIL: CONSTANTINOPLE 1453

1 Hagia Sophia was built by the Byzantine Emperor Justinian I. It was the world's largest interior space, and remained the largest cathedral in the world until Seville Cathedral was completed in 1520. It was converted to a mosque in 1453, and was the principal mosque in Constantinople until the construction of the Sultan Ahmed Mosque in 1616. President Mustapha Kemal Ataturk opened the building as a museum in 1935, and President Erdogan reclassified it as a mosque in 2020.

2 The Morea was the Greek name for the Peloponnese peninsula in southern Greece during the Middle Ages.

3 After the battle of Varna, the Christian commander, John Hunyadi, managed successfully to defend Belgrade, keeping Hungary safe for another 70 years, until the Hungarian defeat by Sultan Suleiman at Mohacs in 1526.

4 The Hexamilion ('six-mile') was a defensive wall constructed across the Isthmus of Corinth during the reign of Emperor Theodosius II. After Murad II's artillery assault had destroyed it, it was largely abandoned.

5 The Bucoleon Palace, overlooking the Sea of Marama, is assumed to have been built in the reign of Emperor Theodosius II. It remained the main palace for the Byzantine court until the 11th century.

6 The Blachernae Palace, at the northern end of the Theodosian Walls, existed from the sixth century, but only became the main residence of the emperors under Alexius I Comnenus. After the Fourth Crusade, the Latin emperors used the Bucoleon Palace again, until their fall in 1261.

7 Giustiniani Longo was from the powerful Genoese family of Doria, who also provided many distinguished admirals. He was probably a native of Chios, which the Genoese held from 1304 to 1566, and learnt his profession as a mercenary.

8 Chios was famous for mastic, a word derived from the Greek for 'to gnash the teeth'. It is a resin, and the gum beads were known as 'the tears of Chios'. The Ottomans made death the penalty for stealing mastic.

9 A *ghazi* is an individual who participates in military expeditions and raiding. The term was applied to the early expeditions of the Prophet Muhammad, and later taken up by Turkic military leaders to describe their wars of conquest. In later years the honorific title of 'Ghazi' was given to those Ottoman rulers who showed particular success in extending the domains of Islam. The title conferred great political legitimacy. In the 20th century the term 'Ghazi' would be bestowed on Mustapha Kemal Pasha, founder of the modern Republic of Turkey.

10 Janissary is derived from *Yeni Ceri*, 'new soldier'. Probably established under Sultan Orhan in 1326, they were the first modern standing army. They may have been the first infantry force to be equipped with firearms, under Sultan Murad I. They grew in establishment from a few thousand, to maybe 10,000 by the time of the siege of Constantinople, 15,000 in the 16th century, and possibly nearly 40,000 by the 1683 siege of Vienna.

11 The 'narcissism of small differences' is the idea that the more a relationship or community share commonalities, the more likely the people in it are to engage in interpersonal feuds and mutual ridicule because of hypersensitivity to minor differences perceived in each other. In Jonathan Swift's book *Gulliver's Travels* he writes of two groups entering a long and vicious war over which was the best end to break an egg.

12 For nearly three centuries after this event, all ambassadors and envoys to the Sultan had their arms bound in his presence.

13 Nicopolis, often referred to as the Crusade of Nicopolis, was one of the last large-scale crusades of the Middle Ages. Largely a Burgundian–Hungarian enterprise, although there were several smaller contingents, including from the Knights Hospitaller, it was a disaster, largely brought about by the impetuosity and arrogance of the Burgundian knights. Most of the crusader army was destroyed or captured, and Sultan Bayezid I had around 3,000 prisoners executed in front of him, until his commanders begged him to stop.

14 In their desire not to appear to be slacking, the Mongols took to killing the prisoners taken in earlier campaigns and even, according to some historians, beheading their own wives.

15 After the defeat at Smyrna, Mehmet I gave the Knights Hospitaller permission to build the castle of St Peter on the site of ancient Halicarnassus, on the Aegean coast. The castle and its town became known as Petronium, from which came the modern name Bodrum.

16 The Hungarians had taken up the historical mantle of 'defenders of Christendom' from the Orthodox Christian Serbs who had, by the mid-15th century, been vassals of the Ottomans for several decades.

17 John Hunyadi, born in Wallachia in 1406, assumed responsibility for the defence of the southern borders of Transylvania in 1441. Although defeated at Varna in 1444, and in the Second Battle of Kosovo in 1448, his defence of Belgrade in 1456, against Mehmet II, shortly after the fall of Constantinople in 1453, was crucial to stopping the Ottoman advance for another 70 years. John Hunyadi died the same year.

18 Vlad Dracula and his brother, Radu, were the sons of Vlad Dracul (the Dragon), who became ruler of Wallachia in 1436. They were held as hostages by the Ottomans and

grew up alongside the future Sultan Mehmet II. In 1462, Mehmet II sent envoys to demand tribute and Vlad had them impaled. One of the victims was Hamza Bey, a close friend of the Sultan. These actions provoked a bloody war with Mehmet II. In one episode, Vlad, as part of his campaign of terror, had created a 'forest of the impaled' with up to 20,000 victims. Eventually, Vlad, looking for support from Matthias Corvnus, King of Hungary and the son of John Hunyadi, was imprisoned for 13 years. He was killed in 1477, fighting the Ottomans.

19 *Sipahis* were originally professional cavalrymen deployed by the Seljuks, and were adopted by the Ottomans. *Sipahi* units were mostly made up of land-grant holders. They formed their own distinctive social class and were rivals to the Janissaries. There was a recognizable feudal element to the *sipahis*, who held land, and were entitled to all the income off that land, in return for military service. It was vital for the Ottoman Empire to keep expanding, to be able to create more *sipahis* and to reward service.

20 An *orta* was the main military division of the corps of Janissaries, and was the equivalent to a Roman century, or a modern infantry company.

21 *Pera* means 'beyond' in Greek, and it referred to an area surrounding the ancient coastal town of Galata, which faces Constantinople across the Golden Horn. From 1273 to 1453, it was a colony of the Republic of Genoa, gifted to the Genoese after their support for the Byzantines against the Latin Empire. In 1348, the Genoese built the prominent Galata Tower. After the Genoese backed the Byzantines during the siege of Constantinople, Mehmet II dispossessed them in favour of the Venetians, despite the 'love-hate, on-off' relationship the Venetians and Ottomans had over several centuries.

22 Links from the great chain that guarded the entrance to the Golden Horn can be seen in museums in modern Istanbul.

23 'Pasha' was a high rank in the Ottoman political and military system, typically granted to governors, generals and dignitaries. Pashas ranked above *beys* and *aghas* (the head of the Janissaries was an agha), but below viziers. All viziers were pashas, not all pashas were viziers. *Beylerbey* was a commander-in-chief, a title occasionally given to the sons of sultans, and to governors of major Ottoman territories.

24 Hamza Bey, sent as an envoy to Vlad Dracula, would be imprisoned and impaled, while Baltoghlu Pasha would die fighting Vlad the 'Impaler' in the forests of Wallachia.

25 In the Ottoman Empire, a *millet* was an independent court of law under which a confessional community (Orthodox, Catholic, Armenian or Jewish) was allowed to rule itself. It was a rather random system, linked to the payment of the *jiyza* tax, and possibly instituted by Mehmet II to bind these groups to the empire, but it worked well in practice. It is worth recalling that Muslims only became a majority in the Ottoman Empire after Selim the Grim's overthrow of the Mamluks in 1517.

CHAPTER 6: THE KNIGHTS AT BAY: RHODES 1522

1 The Bay of Kallithea is about 5 miles south of the city of Rhodes, on the eastern side of the island of Rhodes.

2 Vizier is most likely derived from the Arabic word *wazara*, 'to bear a burden'. A vizier was a hugely empowered individual, who stood between the sovereign and his subjects. The Grand Vizier was chief of the Imperial Council under the Ottomans, and could often be the delegated commander of large-scale military campaigns. Sometimes governors of important provinces could be called 'viziers'.

3 The Spanish began their colonization of the New World in 1493, one year after the first voyage of Christopher Columbus. Their empire would expand across the Caribbean Islands, half of South America, almost all of Central America, and much of North America. Maybe 2 million Spanish emigrated to the New World, while the indigenous population collapsed by up to 80 per cent. Spain and Portugal formalized a division of the whole world between them in the 1494, papally endorsed, Treaty

of Tordesillas. Hernan Cortes overthrew the Aztec Empire in 1521, while Francisco
Pizzaro began the Spanish conquest of the Inca Kingdom of Peru in 1532. Thereafter,
vast quantities of silver crossed the Atlantic to fuel the Spanish war machine.

4   A *tercio*, Spanish for 'a third', was a military unit of the Spanish army during the
Habsburg period. They often fought at sea, as at Lepanto in 1571. Well equipped,
disciplined and trained, they were comparable to the Roman legions. With their mix
of pikes and firearms, they dominated the battlefield of Europe throughout much of
the 16th and 17th centuries.

5   The *Reconquista* was a series of military campaigns waged by Spanish Christian
kingdoms against the Muslim kingdoms, beginning in the eighth century and
culminating with the defeat of the Nasrid Kingdom of Granada, by the 'Catholic
Monarchs', Ferdinand of Aragon and Isabella of Castile, in 1492. Spain was to be
the only territory taken by Arab Muslims to be lost to the Christians, and it has a
particular place in Muslim iconography. In 2004, Al-Qaeda detonated a bomb in
Madrid station, after the Spanish Prime Minister had committed Spain to join the
2003 US invasion of Iraq.

6   After the final defeat of the Muslims in Spain in 1492, the 'Catholic Monarchs' issued
the Alhambra Decree, aimed at the Jewish population. Around 200,000 Jews converted
to Catholicism, while up to 100,000 were expelled from Spain. Many went to North
Africa, while others looked for sanctuary in the Ottoman Empire, and many settled
very successfully in Thessalonica. Suleiman the Magnificent later referred to King
Ferdinand, saying, 'You call him King who impoverishes his states to enrich mine.'

7   The Safavid dynasty ruled Persia from 1501 to 1736, establishing the Twelver
denomination of Shi'ism as the official religion of the Persian Empire. Throughout
much of their long reign, the Safavids were in conflict with the Ottomans, in the same
areas where the Romans and Byzantines had fought the Sasanians.

8   In 2016, President Erdogan of the Republic of Turkey opened the third bridge across
the Bosporus. It was named after Sultan Selim.

9   Abu Bakr al Baghdadi, whose real name was Ibrahim Awad Ibrahim al Badri, was
leader of the Islamic State of Iraq and the Levant, ISIS, and self-styled Caliph. He took
his *nom de guerre* from the name of the first Rashideen caliph, Abu Bakr, and the great
capital city of the Abbasid caliphate, Baghdad. Both continued to have great modern
resonance. He was killed in 2019, detonating a suicide vest, during a US-led Special
Forces raid.

10 For his courage and gallantry in defending Rhodes in 1480, the Pope had elevated
d'Aubusson to be a cardinal.

11 A *tenaille* is an advanced defensive work, in front of the main defences of a fortress.
It was a free-standing structure, with access to the main walls, from where it could be
reinforced. It was designed to channel attackers into 'killing zones'.

12 As a monastic Order, the Knights of St John embraced the custom of anonymity.
Hence, with the exception of the Grand Master, and a small number of other Knights
whose deeds commanded attention, we know little of the 700 Knights Hospitaller who
fought and died during the epic siege of Rhodes, and in both earlier and later battles.
Knights dedicated their whole lives to the service of God, and therefore exalting the
individual within a shared endeavour was seen as akin to blasphemy, so their names
were never 'officially' remembered.

13 For Martin Luther, the last straw appears to have been when the papacy had delegated,
or sub-contracted, the right to sell plenary indulgences to the rich Fugger banking
family of Augsburg.

14 The Cretans were also, at that time, part of a Franco–Venetian alliance that was in
conflict with the Habsburgs.

15 Lindos is a fort and harbour, halfway down the eastern side of Rhodes. It is dominated
by an acropolis and the remains of the vast Temple of Athena. When they finished the

conquest of the island of Rhodes in 1310, the Knights Hospitaller built a large fortress on the acropolis, as part of their defences against the Ottomans.

16　St Euphemia was martyred under the Christian persecutions of the Emperor Diocletian. Why she became important to the Knights of St John is unknown.

CHAPTER 7: THEY SHALL NOT PASS: MALTA 1565

1　Mdina, the Arabic for 'city', served as the Maltese capital city from antiquity to the Middle Ages. It is contiguous with the town of Rabat, the Arabic word for 'suburb'. Its walls were sufficient to withstand sieges before the advent of gunpowder, but were never upgraded and were deemed vulnerable by the mid-16th century.

2　This is the origin of the 'Maltese Falcon', immortalized in the 1941 film of the same name.

3　The Valois family provided the kings of France from 1328 to 1589. The early Valois kings were mostly preoccupied with fighting the English in the Hundred Years War. England lost their last holdings in France, less the port of Calais, at the battle of Castillon in 1453. This was the same year that Constantinople fell to the Ottomans. The last phase of Valois was marked by the French Wars of Religion, which would culminate in the St Bartholomew Day massacre. Henry II was killed in a freak jousting accident in 1559, leaving four sons: Francis II, married to Mary, Queen of Scots, died young; Louis died as an infant; Charles IX, largely controlled by his mother, Catherine de Medici, died of tuberculosis in 1574; and his brother, Henry III, was assassinated in 1589.

4　The corsairs of the Barbary Coast, alone and in conjunction with the Ottoman fleet, constituted a huge and long-term military and economic threat to the European Christian powers. Whole stretches of the European coast were devoid of settlements, and between 1530 and 1780, it is estimated that around a million people were enslaved. Although the majority of corsair activity was in the western Mediterranean, Barbary pirates sailed into the Atlantic, and as far as England and Iceland. The threat was only finally subdued when the French conquered Algeria in 1830.

5　The Treaty of Madrid forced the French king to renounce his claims in Italy, to surrender Burgundy to Emperor Charles V, and abandon sovereignty over Flanders and Artois.

6　Upon encountering King Louis's sodden, lifeless body, Suleiman is said to have, magnanimously, lamented, 'I came indeed in arms against him; but it was not my wish that he should thus be cut off before he had scarcely tasted the sweets of life and royalty.'

7　The helmet-crown consisted of four crowns set inside an Austrian-style helmet and topped with 'a plumed aigrette with a crescent-shaped mount'. The crown was made of gold and studded with 'enormous 12-carat pearls, a head-band with pointed diamonds, 47 rubies, 27 emeralds, 49 pearls, and a large turquiose'. Grand Vizier Ibrahim Pasha had had it commissioned from Venetian goldsmiths, although why he did this is uncertain. Suleiman had it paraded through the streets of Belgrade and Nis, and reports of its opulence were partly responsible for Suleiman's title of 'Magnificent'. The helmet-crown was probably eventually melted down, while the helmet itself, the lowest level of this ornament, may have been presented as a gift to Emperor Ferdinand I Habsburg, in the next century.

8　In 1537, Barbarossa had captured a number of islands in the Aegean and Ionian Seas. Pope Paul III had assembled a Holy League fleet to confront the great corsair, commanded by the Genoese admiral, Andrea Doria. In 1538, in a maritime clash off Preveza, the Ottoman fleet prevailed, and Doria was widely accused of lacking drive and aggression in the fight. Part of Doria's cautious approach may have been an unwillingness to risk his own ships (he personally owned many of them), and partly because of a visceral hatred for his Venetian allies in the coalition.

9　Andrea Doria was from an important Genoese family, and one of the most renowned admirals of the age. He fought for the French against the Holy Roman Empire and defeated a Spanish fleet in 1528. At the end of his contract with the French, he entered the service of Emperor Charles V and commanded several expeditions against the Ottomans. His defeat at Preveza in 1538 had led to Ottoman dominance of the eastern Mediterranean until the battle of Lepanto in 1571. His nephew and heir, Giannettino Doria, was killed in a coup, while his great-nephew Gian'Andrea Doria would command the right-hand division of the Holy League fleet at the battle of Lepanto in 1571. Andrea Doria died in 1560 at the age of 93.

10 While Birgu was the original Maltese name, Senglea was named for Grand Master Claude de la Sengle.

11 The Peace of Cateau-Cambrésis marked the end of the 65-year struggle between France and Spain for control of Italy, leaving Habsburg Spain as the dominant power there for the next 150 years.

12 Giannettino Doria was killed during the Freschi conspiracy in Genoa in 1547.

13 A Gascon, Romegas had served in the Hospitaller galleys for years. He had even, at the Pope's request, led a naval expedition against Protestant Huguenots in France. In 1555, his vessel had capsized in Malta's Grand Harbour during a violent storm. When the storm had passed, knocking was heard from inside the upturned hull, and when a hole had been punched through the timbers, Romegas emerged, with his pet monkey, after having stood for hours in an air bubble under the keel. Courageous in battle, Romegas suffered as a result of the incident; his nervous system was affected, for he could hardly drink a glass of water without spilling its contents.

14 Szigetvar is a town in southern Hungary. The name means 'island fort'. By the 1550s, the Ottomans had captured all the lands and castles in the region, except Szigetvar. Sultan Suleiman besieged the fort on 6 August 1566, but he died on 6 or 7 September. The castle fell the next day, marked by a final, valiant suicidal charge by Nikola Zrinski, the garrison commander, and many of his men who preferred death to capture.

15 Sultan Selim II was the son of Roxelana and was known as 'the Blond' or 'the Sot'. He completed the conquest of Cyprus early in his reign, but his fleet was destroyed at the battle of Lepanto in 1571. He was a generous patron of poetry, the arts and architecture. He died in 1574, at the age of 50, slipping on a marble floor while inebriated.

16 The knights dispersed, with many of them going to the court of the Russian tsars. The legacy of the Knights Hospitaller still lives on in the modern Order of the Knights of St John and their commitment to charity and to first aid.

CHAPTER 8: 'THERE WAS A MAN CALLED JOHN': LEPANTO 1571

1   Galleasses were specially designed and equipped floating fortresses. They were a new addition to maritime warfare, and no one was certain how well they would perform.

2   *Real*, 'Royal', was the Spanish Habsburg flagship at Lepanto. It was built in the Barcelona shipyards and was the largest galley of its time. It was 200 feet long and 20 feet wide. It had nine guns, was propelled by 290 oarsmen, and carried some 400 sailors and soldiers. It was luxuriously ornamented, and it was painted in the red and gold colours of Spain, while its poop was elaborately carved with and painted with religious images. A replica, built to mark the 400th anniversary of Lepanto, is in the maritime museum of Barcelona.

3   Don Juan of Austria was the 24-year-old half-brother of King Philip II of Spain. His extraordinary story is told later in the chapter.

4   The ships of the Barbarigo's left flank galleys flew yellow flags, those of Gian'Andrea Doria's right flank flew green, and Santa Cruz's reserve force sported white.

5   Barbarossa had died peacefully in Constantinople in 1546, having finished his five-volume memoirs. His death was greeted with huge relief by Christian Europe. In 1540, Emperor Charles V, in recognition of the scale of the threat that Barbarossa represented, had contacted him and offered him the appointment of Admiral-in-Chief

of the Habsburg Empire, including being ruler of Spain's North African territories. Barbarossa turned down the offer. Barbarossa was buried in a tall mausoleum near the modern ferry port of Besiktas and the Istanbul Naval Museum. In the many years following his death, no ship would clear the Serai Point without firing a salute, a practice revived by the Turkish navy in 2019.

6 *Sultana* had been gifted to Mustapha Pasha in 1565, to be the flagship for the invasion of Malta. It was painted red, and reported to be slightly smaller that Don Juan's *Real*. After the battle, the great Islamic banner on *Sultana* would be taken back to be hung in the Escorial, where it would be destroyed by fire almost exactly a century later.

7 Related to, but not to be confused with, the great corsair Dragut, who died at the siege of Malta in 1565.

8 The Society of Jesus, the Jesuits, was founded in 1540 by Ignatius Loyola, a Spanish nobleman with a military background, and six companions, with the approval of Pope Paul III. Their foundation and activities were part of a strenuous Counter-Reformation effort by the papacy, to address the dire need of the Catholic Church to reform itself, in the face of the growth of Protestantism.

9 The Capuchins, named after the hoods they wore (*cappucio*), were formed by Franciscan friars in 1528 in an attempt to take the Franciscan Order back to the founding principles and example of their founder, St Francis of Assisi.

10 The Moriscos, the Spanish word for 'Moorish', were former Muslims and their descendants, whom the Catholic Church and Spanish crown had commanded to convert to Christianity or face compulsory expulsion. Muslims had never been a majority in Spain, and, by the time of the fall of Granada in 1492, they were around 500,000 out of a population of 7 or 8 million. They were always distrusted, particularly at times of open warfare with the Ottomans, and in the context of threats from Barbary corsairs. This fear grew at the time of the siege of Malta in 1565, and in 1567 King Philip II of Spain's decree regarding the Moriscos had led to open revolt.

11 Pius V was Pope from 1566 to 1572. He was notable for his role in the Counter-Reformation and had a justified reputation as a fearless defender of Catholic doctrine and enemy of 'lax' practices. He excommunicated Queen Elizabeth I and the English Protestants. His role in negotiating the formation of the Holy League in 1571 was absolutely pivotal, given the participants and personalities involved. He also helped subsidize the construction of the new Maltese capital of Valetta.

12 Miguel de Cervantes enlisted in a Spanish Navy infantry regiment in 1570, and was badly wounded at Lepanto, losing the use of his left arm and hand. He served as a naval soldier until 1575, when he was captured by Barbary pirates and held captive for five years, until ransomed. He wrote and published the two parts of his great literary masterpiece, *Don Quixote*, in 1605 and 1615. He died in Madrid in 1616.

13 The Marquess of Santa Cruz had taken part in the relief of Malta in 1565 and had been instrumental in supressing the Morisco revolt of 1569. His death in early 1588 meant that the Spanish Armada was entrusted to the leadership of Alonso Guzman, 7th Duke of Medina Sidonia, who was totally unsuited for the role, having no military experience on either land or sea. Conscious of the deficiencies of the Spanish Armada, he was quoted as saying that the fleet set sail, 'in the confident hope of a miracle'. It was not forthcoming.

CHAPTER 9: 'LIKE A FLOOD OF BLACK PITCH': VIENNA 1683

1 Charles, Duke of Lorraine, was born in 1643 in exile in Vienna, as his family territories were occupied by the French. He had been destined for the church but switched to a military career when his elder brother died. He married the widow of a king of Poland, and twice stood for election to be King of Poland. With an excellent record of military service, he had been appointed Commander of the Imperial Army in 1683. He died of a pulmonary embolism in 1690.

2 Marco d'Aviano already had a reputation for 'miracle healing', and Emperor Leopold I sought his help when his wife seemed unable to conceive a male heir. He rapidly became the Emperor's adviser on almost all issues. As war with the Ottomans approached, Pope Pius V had appointed him to be Papal Envoy to the Habsburgs. He continued to serve with the imperial armies after Vienna, and often intervened for mercy to be shown to Muslim captives. He died of cancer in 1699, aged 67, and is buried in the same Capuchin church vault as the Habsburg emperors.

3 There is little doubt that J. R. R. Tolkien took the epic siege of Vienna in 1683 as the inspiration for much of his masterpiece, *The Lord of the Rings*. Vienna is Minas Tirith, the Holy Roman Empire is Gondor, the forces of Mordor are the Ottomans, however unfairly, and John III Sobieski and his Polish cavalry can be seen as the Riders of Rohan.

4 The Topkapi Palace, from the Turkish for 'cannon gate', served as the administrative centre of the Ottoman Empire, and main residence of the Ottoman sultans, from its completion in the 1460s under Sultan Mehmet II, until the completion of the Dolmabache Palace in 1856. It was originally called the Imperial New Palace and is situated on Seraglio Point, overlooking the Golden Horn. It was significantly expanded under Sultan Suleiman the Magnificent. In 1924, after the end of the Ottoman Empire, the Topkapi Palace was converted into a museum.

5 This 20-year truce had followed the imperial defeat of the Ottoman armies at St Gotthard Pass in 1664.

6 The Bektashi were originally one of many Sufi orders within Sunni Islam, practising a mystic form of the religion. However, by the 16th century the order had adopted some tenets of Shia Islam, including a veneration of Ali the son-in-law of Muhammad, and were therefore viewed with suspicion by the orthodox religious establishment. The Bektashi had acquired significant political importance in the 15th century, when the order dominated the Janissaries, but this significance declined when the Janissaries were suppressed in 1826.

7 *Seraskier* was the title given by an Ottoman sultan to a vizier who commanded an army. A *seraskier* had almost unlimited power of life and death over his subordinates.

8 Sultan Suleiman invited John Zapolya, his one-year-old son, and all the Hungarian commanders of Buda for dinner and, a new experience for most Europeans of the time, coffee. While entertaining them, his Janissaries, disguised as 'tourists', seized the fortress and disarmed its Hungarian defenders. Zapolya and his heirs were 'gifted' Transylvania as compensation .

9 The unfortunate physician who had pronounced the Sultan to be dead was quickly killed.

10 Despite his commitment to Catholicism, Emperor Charles V Habsburg had felt compelled to sign the Peace of Passau after pressure from both Catholic France and the Protestants in his empire had led to him being driven out of Germany.

11 The papal Counter-Reformation programme had eventually been codified at the Council of Trent, which held 25 sessions between 1545 and 1563, in an attempt to confront the abuses within the Catholic Church that Martin Luther had highlighted, and to confirm which Protestant practices constituted 'heresy'.

12 The English Civil War, between King Charles I Stuart and the forces of Parliament, was being fought at the same time, with many of the same religious and political factors at play, and conducted with similar levels of bloodshed and violence.

13 The Leslies of Balquhain and Fetternear were reputed to be the most successful Scottish mercenaries of the 17th century. They had served the Habsburgs loyally through the Thirty Years War, and Walter Leslie had ended up as an imperial count. His nephews, Andrew and James, both fought in defence of the city in 1683. They were among many 'soldiers of fortune', including the Irish and Scottish Catholics of the 'Wild Geese', who sold their services for money, or out of religious conviction, to the competing dynasties of Europe.

14 Many of Vienna's citizen undertook missions to deliver messages to and from the Duke of Lorraine and the imperial army. It was an extremely dangerous undertaking. One of the best known of these messengers was a merchant called Georg Franz Kolschitsky, whose exploits in carrying information through the Turkish lines had made him a hero of the siege. An unsubstantiated story has it that, at the conclusion of the siege, a great amount of coffee had been found in the Ottoman camp. Kolschitsky, who knew Ottoman culture well and who recognized the potential of coffee, had secured, as a reward for his efforts, the rights to establish the first coffee shop in Vienna. Some have claimed that the croissant also had its origins in the siege of Vienna, although others put its origin as far back as Charles Martel's victory over the Muslims at Tours in 732. Whatever the truth, Islamic State attempted to ban croissants during the Syrian civil war.

15 Eugene of Savoy was born in France but, rejected by Louis XIV for military service, he had transferred his loyalty to the Habsburgs. He was nineteen at the siege of Vienna, and his military career would span six decades. He went on to win Europe-wide renown for his achievements against the Ottomans, and against the French, particularly in partnership with the Duke of Marlborough. He died in Vienna in 1736.

16 At the conclusion of the siege, John III Sobieski believed, incorrectly, that he had found another of the precious banners of the Prophet Muhammad in Kara Mustapha's camp, and he had this sent to Rome.

CHAPTER 10: HE STOOPS TO CONQUER: JERUSALEM 1917

1 Born in 1861, Allenby was educated at Haileybury College. He failed entry into the Indian Civil Service and was commissioned into a cavalry regiment, the 6th (Inniskilling) Dragoon Guards. He fought in South Africa and was a classmate of Douglas Haig at Staff College. He served on the Western Front from 1914 to 1917, and ended up as commander of the Third Army, before falling out with Haig. Promoted to General, he was surprised to have been sent to the Middle East.

2 Thomas Edward Lawrence was a British archaeologist, writer, academic, diplomat and army officer. A noted Arabist, he volunteered for the British Army and was posted to the Arab Bureau intelligence unit in Cairo. In early 1916, he was despatched to Mesopotamia to see if he could help extricate the British forces besieged at Kut-al-Amara. Later that year he went to the Hejaz, in order to make an assessment of the Arab Revolt that had broken out in June 1916. The rest really *is* history.

3 Field Marshal von Falkenhayn had been Chief of the German General Staff from September 1914 to August 1916, when he was removed after German failures at the battle of Verdun. He went to Romania and, in September 1917, he became supreme commander of two Ottoman armies in Palestine. His failure to halt Allenby led to his removal, but his decision to make Jerusalem an 'open city', and his role in stopping the removal of the Jewish population from Palestine, stand in his favour.

4 Along with Enver Pasha and Mehmet Talaat Pasha, Djemal Pasha was one of the 'Three Pashas' that took the Ottomans into World War I on the side of the Central Powers, and who ruled the Ottoman Empire during the war. He fought in the two Balkan Wars and became Governor of Syria in 1915. His attacks on the Suez Canal failed. He was known by the Arabs as 'the Butcher'. His role in the Armenian Genocide was ambiguous. Put on trial after the war, he went to Georgia to negotiate with the new Soviet Russian government, and was assassinated by an Armenian.

5 Franz von Papen became Chancellor of the German Weimar Republic in 1932. He was instrumental in the rise of Hitler, but, although tried at Nuremberg after World War II, he was acquitted.

6 St Stephens' Gate is on the eastern wall of Jerusalem. Most of the city walls and their gates were rebuilt by Suleiman the Magnificent, after the defeat of the Mamluks by the Ottomans in 1517. It is the traditional start point of the Christian *Via Dolorosa*.

7   David Lloyd George was Prime Minister of the United Kingdom from 1916 to 1922. Despite the concentration on the Western Front, he wanted to make the destruction of the Ottoman Empire a major war aim. He played a critical role in support of the Balfour Declaration of 1917, and was a major player in the Paris Peace Conference of 1919.

8   The Second German Reich (Empire), was formed during the Franco-Prussian War of 1870–71, when the majority of South German States, less Austria, joined with the North German Confederation. The Prussian king, Wilhelm I, became Emperor, the Prussian Minister President, Otto von Bismarck, became Chancellor, and the Prussian city of Berlin became the new imperial capital. When Wilhelm II had become Emperor in 1888, he had dismissed Bismarck, and the German Empire had thereafter embarked on a much more aggressive and activist set of foreign policies, not least in the Middle East.

9   At a commemorative service in 2017, a century later, the proclamation was also read out in Armenian, in acknowledgement of that important community of the Old City.

10   The Balfour Declaration also stated that the British government would only support the establishment of a Jewish homeland in Palestine, '… it being clearly understood that nothing shall be done which may prejudice the civil and religious rights of existing non-Jewish communities in Palestine'.

11   The Sykes-Picot Agreement was a secret treaty between the United Kingdom and France, assented to by Russia and Italy, to define mutually agreed 'spheres of influence and control' in an eventual partition of the Ottoman Empire. It was signed in January 1916. Britain was to get what is Palestine, Jordan, south Iraq and an enclave containing the ports of Haifa and Acre, while France got control of south-east Turkey, the Kurdistan region, Syria and Lebanon. Russia would have received Constantinople and the Straits, while Italy got southern Anatolia. From the British-Arab perspective it reneged on British promises regarding a national Arab homeland in the area of Greater Syria. The agreement was made public by the Bolsheviks in November 1917, and led to an outcry among the Arabs.

12   The 'correspondence' was ten letters exchanged from mid-1915 to early-1916 between Britain's governor in Egypt, and the Sharif of Mecca. In them the British Government agreed to recognize Arab sovereignty and independence in a large region in exchange for the sharif launching the Arab Revolt against the Ottoman Empire. Given the moral authority of the latter, another key reason for seeking an arrangement was to counter the Ottoman declaration of *jihad*, and to maintain the support of the 70 million Muslims in British India.

13   Operation *Michel*.

14   The Bay of Mudros is on the Greek island of Lemnos.

15   General John Churchill, Duke of Marlborough, was a remarkable soldier and statesman. He is acknowledged as one of Great Britain's greatest military commanders. His successes at a series of battles helped the Habsburgs maintain the balance of power with the French Bourbon kings, while continuing to confront the Ottomans in the east.

16   Prince Eugene of Savoy had already been at the siege of Vienna, both sieges of Buda, the second battle of Mohacs, and the battle of Zenta. His relationship with Marlborough was a critical factor in their joint success against the French.

17   The Seven Years War was a global conflict, although fought mostly in Europe and the Americas, involving most of the European powers. The opposing alliances were Britain, primarily backed by Prussia; and France, backed by Spain, Sweden and Russia.

18   The Sultan Ahmed Mosque, also known as the Blue Mosque for its magnificent interior, was built between 1609 and 1617.

19   The Congress of Vienna was a series of international diplomatic meetings to discuss and agree a new layout of the European political order following the defeat and abdication of Emperor Napoleon Bonaparte, after nearly 23 years of continuous war on the continent. The Congress had opened in September 1814 and, remarkably,

it continued uninterrupted, despite Napoleon's subsequent escape from Elba. The Congress's agreement was actually signed nine days before the battle of Waterloo.

20   The Greek War of Independence lasted from 1821 to 1829.

21   Mehmet Ali was an Albanian Ottoman military commander, who first rose to prominence when he was sent to help recover Egypt from Napoleon's occupation of 1798. He was made pasha in 1805, and purged Egypt of its last Mamluk power bases. He had failed to suppress the Greek rebellion.

22   A great weakness of the Ottoman Empire by the 19th century was that, over the centuries, in return for political support from a variety of European powers, they had made a series of highly generous commercial and taxation concessions known as 'capitulations'. These were highly unpopular and left the Empire vulnerable to diplomatic and economic pressures, and heavily exposed to problems in the financial systems of other countries. They were eventually formally abolished in the Treaty of Lausanne in 1923.

23   The 193-mile-long Suez Canal was officially opened on 17 November 1869, cutting the journey distance from the Arabian Sea to London by approximately 5,500 miles. It was vital for its connections to India and its imperial possessions in the east, and the British government succeeded in obtaining a controlling interest in the canal in 1875, seven years before they established a 'Protectorate' over all Egypt.

24   The Committee for Union and Progress was often known as the 'Young Turk' Movement.

25   Mustapha Kemal was born in Salonika in 1881. He enrolled in the Ottoman Military Academy in 1899 and graduated in 1905. He had joined the CUP in 1907 and played a role in the 'Young Turk' Revolution of 1908. He served in Libya, fighting against Italian occupation, and was also in both Balkan Wars, helping liberate Edirne. He commanded the 19th Division of the Fifth Army at Gallipoli.

26   Along with Djemal Pasha, Talaat Pasha and Enver Pasha constituted the 'Three Pashas' who largely controlled the Ottoman Empire for the duration of World War I. All relatively young, their leadership was a disaster for the empire and extended the duration of the war. They were complicit in the 'Armenian Genocide'. Talaat would be assassinated in Berlin, Djemal assassinated in Tblisi in Georgia, and Enver would be killed in a cavalry charge in central Asia.

27   Winston Churchill was a prime mover behind the plan for an attack on the Dardanelles, which might knock the Ottomans out of the war and open supply lines, through the Black Sea, to the faltering Russian Empire. The failure of the campaign, for a while, dimmed his political career, and he took a military command on the Western Front. He would continue to have a keen interest in the Middle East after the collapse of the Ottoman Empire.

28   The Greek name for Megiddo was Armageddon, and the site guarded the western branch of the most important trade route linking Egypt with Mesopotamia. Because of its strategic location, it was the site of many battles over many centuries. Allenby was fighting nearby in late 1918 but probably chose to name his action after Megiddo because of its biblical and historical resonance. Fighting was still in progress when the Armistice of Mudros was being signed on 30 October 1918.

29   In the autumn of 1918, a retreating Ottoman army column, under the high command of Djemal Pasha, had entered the Arab village of Tafas, where the commander had ordered his soldiers to massacre all the inhabitants. Lawrence and the Bedouin of his Sharifian cavalry entered the village shortly afterwards, and Lawrence gave orders to attack the Turks and to 'take no prisoners'. Around 250 German and Austrian troops who had been captured earlier in the day were now summarily executed. Lawrence wrote about the massacre and its aftermath in shockingly vivid detail in *Seven Pillars of Wisdom*.

EPILOGUE

1   The Age of Enlightenment (also the Age of Reason) was an intellectual and philosophical movement that occurred in Europe in the 17th and 18th centuries. It featured a range of social ideas centred on the value of knowledge learned by way of rationalism and empiricism. It also championed political ideals such as natural law, liberty, progress, toleration, fraternity, constitutional government, and the formal separation of church and state. As such, its adherents rejected both the claims of the Koran to be the divinely inspired, final word of God, and the Catholic Church's doctrine of papal infallibility.

2   Mustapha Kemal Pasha had offered the title of Caliph to Ahmed Sharif as-Senussi of Libya, on the condition that he reside outside Turkey, but Ahmed declined, confirming his support for Adbul Mecid.

3   From the time of the Crimean War and the Indian Mutiny, the British had supported the Ottoman Empire against the expansionist ambitions of Tsarist Russia, and they had propagated the view, among India's Muslims, that the Ottomans were caliphs of Islam. Meanwhile, the Ottoman sultans, from Mahmud II to Abdulmejid I, helped the British by issuing pronouncements to the Muslims of India, telling them to support British rule.

4   Under King Abdullah, hundreds of thousands of young Saudis, men and women, were sent out of the kingdom to be educated. Seemingly designed as a 'Trojan Horse' to outflank the religious conservatives, this programme created a critical mass of people receptive to the reform agenda of Muhammad bin Salman, who initiated his Vision 2030 when his father, King Salman, came to the throne in 2015. Muhammad bin Salman has always said that his reforms were a continuation of a process that had been interrupted in 1979.

5   Abu Bakr al Baghdadi's real name was Ibrahim Awad Ibrahim Ali al Badri. He took his *nom de guerre* from the name of the first caliph, and the capital of the Abbasid caliphate. An equally discredited successor chose to call himself Abu Ibrahim al Hashimi al Quraishi, taking the tribal and family names of the Prophet Muhammad.

Bibliography

Asbridge, Thomas, *The Crusades, The War for the Holy Land*, Simon & Schuster, London (2020)

Atwan, Abdul Bari, *The Secret History of Al Qa'eda*, Abacus, London (2006)

Baer, Marc David, *The Ottomans, Khans, Caesars and Caliphs*, Basic Books, London (2022)

Bicheno, Hugh, *Crescent and Cross*, Cassel, London (2003)

Bradford, Ernle, *The Great Siege*, Hodder and Stoughton, London (1961)

Bradford, Ernle, *The Great Betrayal, Constantinople 1204*, Hodder and Stoughton, London (1967)

Brockman, Eric, *The Two Sieges of Rhodes 1480–1522*, John Murray, London (1969)

Busbecq, Ghiselin, *The Turkish Letters*, Eland Publishing, London (2005)

Caponni, Niccolo, *Victory of the West*, Macmillan, London (2006)

Crowley, Roger, *Empires of the Sea, The Final Battle for the Mediterranean 1521–1580*, Faber and Faber, London (2008)

Crowley, Roger, *City of Fortune, How Venice Won and Lost a Naval Empire*, Faber and Faber, London (2011)

France, John, *Victory in the East, A Military History of the First Crusade*, Cambridge University Press, Cambridge (1994)

Frankopan, Peter, *The First Crusade, The Call from the East*, The Bodley Head, London (2012)

Freely, John, *Istanbul, The Imperial City*, Viking, London (1996)

Goodwin, Jason, *Lords of the Horizon, A History of the Ottoman Empire*, Chatto and Windus, London (1998)

Howarth, Stephen, *The Knights Templar*, William Collins and Son Co, London (1982)

Humphreys, C. C., *A Place Called Armageddon, The Epic Battle of Constantinople 1453*, Orion, London (2011)

Keegan, John, *The Face of Battle*, Penguin Books, London (1983)

Kennedy, Hugh, *Caliphate, The History of an Idea*, Basic Books, New York (2016)

Mansel, Philip, *Constantinople, City of Worlds 1453–1924*, John Murray, London (1995)

Marozzi, Justin, *Baghdad, City of Peace, City of Blood*, Allen Lane, London (2014)

Mather, James, *Pashas, Traders and Travellers in the Islamic World*, Yale University Press, London (2009)

Mayall, Simon, *Soldier in the Sand, A Personal History of the Modern Middle East*, Pen and Sword, Barnsley (2020)

Prawer, Joshua, *The Latin Kingdom of Jerusalem, European Colonialism in the Middle Ages*, Weidenfeld and Nicholson, London (1972)

Riley-Smith, Jonathan, *The Knights of the Hospital of St John in Jerusalem and Cyprus 1050–1310*, Macmillan and Co, London (1967)

Rogan, Eugene, *The Arabs, A History*, Allen Lane, London (2009)
Rogan, Eugene, *The Fall of the Ottomans: The Great War in the Middle East 1914–1920*, Allen Lane, London (2015)
Rogerson, Barnaby, *The Last Crusaders, East, West and the Battle for the Centre of the World*, Abacus, London (2010)
Runciman, Stephen, *The Fall of Constantinople 1453*, Cambridge University Press, Cambridge (1965)
Runciman, Stephen, *The Crusades* (3 vols), Folio Society, London (2002)
Shiono, Nanani, *The Siege of Rhodes*, Vertical, New York (2006)
Shiono, Nanani, *The Battle of Lepanto*, Vertical, New York (2007)
Stone, Norman, *Turkey, A Short History*, Thames and Hudson, London (2010)
Tuchman, Barbara W., *A Distant Mirror, The Calamitous 14th Century*, Macmillan, London (1978)
Tyerman, Christopher, *Fighting for Christendom, Holy War and the Crusades*, Oxford University Press, Oxford (2004)
Warner, Philip, *Sieges of the Middle Ages*, Bell and Sons Ltd, London (1968)
Wheatcroft, Andrew, *The Enemy at the Gate: Habsburgs, Ottomans and the Battle for Europe*, The Bodley Head, London (2008)
Willocks, Tim, *The Religion*, Arrow, London (2007)
de Wohl, Louis, *The Last Crusader*, Lippincott, Philadelphia (1956)

Index